Charles Gilman Currier

Outlines of practical Hygiene

Charles Gilman Currier

Outlines of practical Hygiene

ISBN/EAN: 9783743334434

Manufactured in Europe, USA, Canada, Australia, Japa

Cover: Foto ©ninafisch / pixelio.de

Manufactured and distributed by brebook publishing software (www.brebook.com)

Charles Gilman Currier

Outlines of practical Hygiene

OUTLINES

OF

PRACTICAL HYGIENE

BY

C. GILMAN CURRIER, M.D.

ASSOCIATE OF THE AMERICAN SOCIETY OF CIVIL ENGINEERS; FELLOW OF THE NEW YORK
ACADEMY OF MEDICINE; MEMBER OF THE NEW YORK PATHOLOGICAL SOCIETY;
FORMERLY VISITING PHYSICIAN TO THE NEW YORK CITY HOSPITALS;
MEMBER OF THE AMERICAN PUBLIC HEALTH ASSOCIATION, ETC.

THIRD EDITION, REVISED AND ENLARGED

NEW YORK
E. B. TREAT & CO.
242-244 WEST TWENTY-THIRD ST.
1898

A sound Mind in a sound Body, is a short but full Description of a happy State in this World. He that hath these two, hath but little more to wish for; and he that wants either of them, will be but little the better for anything else. Men's Happiness or Misery is most part of their own Making.

JOHN LOCKE, 1692

COPYRIGHT, 1893, 1898, BY
C. GILMAN CURRIER

PUBLISHER'S NOTE TO THIRD EDITION.

This revised and enlarged edition is believed to incorporate all of essential progress in sanitary science and practical hygiene that has been established up to the present date. The work has been in use as a text-book in some of our leading Universities and independent schools. The previous editions have been completely exhausted ; and a new issue is called for to meet present demands. The opportunity has been used, for the author to revise, correct and enlarge the work, although this has necessitated some delay.

April, 1898.

PREFACE

THE preparation of this book was undertaken at the instance of busy practitioners and students who emphasized the lack of a compendious work upon *practical* hygiene embodying the most modern truths and which, at the same time, was adapted especially to American conditions. While the subject-matter has been shaped in conformity to these requirements, the most recent work of foreign investigators and practical men has been fully considered, and their results have been incorporated in the following pages wherever suitable.

Besides having at his command all modern treatises of importance that bear any relation to the subjects touched upon, the author has zealously and regularly consulted the current periodical literature that has appeared up to the date of publication of this book.

Some of the monographs used have been indicated in the text. In view of the existence of the *Index* published by the *Board of Managers of the Association of Engineering Societies*, and also of the *Index Medicus* and of other accessible catalogues of new and old literature, it seems out of place to attempt in a single, small book of this character to give a bibliography. The best books of this kind rarely attempt it. Those which essay it produce only unsatisfactory and necessarily incomplete results. Even a partially complete list of the works consulted would seriously increase the size of the volume.

In addition to using his own and the principal special libraries, the author has striven to control his statements by verbal criticisms from intelligent workers who are not prone to publish their views, yet whose opinions are of extreme value.

The dominating principle throughout the entire text has been to maintain a judicial attitude in every detail, allowing no scope to vagaries. Accepted truths alone are embodied in the teachings of these chapters. Very positive opinions advanced upon any subject are rarely given unless they are those of the majority of leading thinkers. In the few cases where very limited authority exists for an opinion, attention is especially called to that fact. In speaking of influenza, no mention of Pfeiffer's bacilli is made, since they are neither generally accepted nor practically important.

Even the views regarding "sewer-gas" are not those of any one person, although they were most forcibly impressed upon the author while he listened to the lectures of Professor Robert Koch, of Berlin, some years ago. So, too, in the pages upon Climate, the principles enounced embody the condensed opinions of *many* who have studied the question for years. Wherever errors have been alluded to, it has been because of their prevalence, and they have been estimated as fairly as possible.

Being devoted strictly to the *prevention* of disease, the book does not discuss therapeutic measures except in so far forth as they belong legitimately within the domain of hygiene.

Since the purpose throughout has been to make important truths as clear as possible, simple expressions and the most intelligible terms have been employed. Greek and other foreign synonyms have not been unnecessarily introduced. The book is designed to elucidate the truths of science, and not to mask them: accordingly, all jargon has been excluded as fully as possible.

While most of the illustrations have been prepared especially for this work, some are from outside sources not expressly acknowledged in the body of the book. Fig. 15 is from the Chauncy Hall School in Boston. Fig. 37 is from Prausnitz. Figs. 12 and 13 are from the Barstow Co. Figs. 30, 36 and 36a are after designs by the Sturtevant Co. Figs. 49 and 51, from the Dubois Co. Mr. Mackay, of the National Boiler Co., provided the original of Fig. 24. Gillis and Geogheghan supplied drawings from which Figs. 21 and 23 were prepared.

To Dr. S. T. Armstrong, Mr. L. De C. Berg, Prof. Charles Carpmael, Sergeant F. B. Dunn, General A. W. Greely, Mr. L. D. Hosford, Dr. C. H. Knight, Dr. William B. Wood, thanks are due.

Of the very many others to whom he is indebted, the author feels bound especially to thank the officials and workers of the Canadian Inland Revenue Department, of the United States Geological Survey and of the Department of Agriculture (including the Weather Bureau). The results of researches by special experimenters and laboratories have been used as freely as the limited size of the book would permit.

CONTENTS

	PAGE
SOIL AND CLIMATE	1
CLOTHING AND PROTECTION OF THE BODY	42
BATHING AND PERSONAL HYGIENE	56
PHYSICAL EXERCISE	70
SCHOOLS, AND THEIR INFLUENCE ON HEALTH	88
OCCUPATION	110
LIGHTING	124
BUILDINGS AND STREETS	140
HEATING	160
VENTILATION	194
FOODS	214
FOOD PREPARATION AND ADAPTATION	250
DIET	267
WATER AND WATER SUPPLIES	285
DISPOSAL OF FLUID WASTE. SEWERS	315
HOUSE DRAINAGE. PLUMBING	333
OTHER DISPOSAL OF HUMAN EXCRETA	359
DISPOSAL OF GARBAGE AND OTHER SOLID REFUSE	368
DISPOSAL OF THE DEAD	372
BACTERIA AND DISEASE	378
INFECTIOUS DISEASES	397
DISINFECTION. RESTRICTION OF COMMUNICABLE DISEASES	430
VITAL STATISTICS, LONGEVITY. DEGENERACY	457
INDEX	471

OUTLINES OF PRACTICAL HYGIENE

SOIL AND CLIMATE

CLIMATE is dependent chiefly on the heat that the surface of the earth receives from the sun, and on the way in which great, continuous oceanic and atmospheric currents move to distribute this warmth. The high heat of the interior of the globe has no effect upon our climate.

The crust of the globe, upon which we live, is of rock-formations having each a varying number of mineral components. By the mechanical action of past or present glacial ice in motion, and by the influence of water and weather, as well as of minor factors, these rocks have been much worn away. Thus diluvial and alluvial matter, and also loose rock-masses of various sizes, have been produced, and transported perhaps to a considerable distance. In this way most of our soil is formed. When these broken-up mineral substances are suitable, and when climatic and other conditions favor, vegetation arises, and from the resulting products much soil is further added.

With animal life (and the burrowing of worms), by the results of human influence and the products of civilization, there come still further additions and changes. These latter factors may be very important. Schliemann, in excavating at the site of ancient Troy, had to remove more than fifty feet of "dirt." Then, beneath the Grecian city Ilion were six different town locations, each of which was built upon the dirt-covered ruins of its predecessor.

Artificial soils, in the course of time, resemble those formed wholly by purely natural processes, and may become hygienically fit for the location of residences. Yet organic waste, in an incompletely transformed state, is an element of danger and should be guarded against.

In choosing a location for a dwelling, it is well in general to avoid very flat ground. A gentle slope is much better. Especially undesirable are the bottoms of depressions having no drainage outlet for the excessive subsoil moisture (or ground-water), as malaria and other diseases are to be feared in such localities.

A bald, treeless and grassless plain is undesirable as giving too great temperature changes. A deep, narrow valley is objectionable in that it has insufficient circulation of air. Neither an open summit nor a flat surface at the foot of a hill is as satisfactory from a hygienic point of view as the intervening slope. The upper half of a declivity furnishes usually the most desirable site. If there be a well-drained break above in the continuity of the slope, it is of value as intercepting the ground-water and lessening any possible dampness of the site. Evergreen trees, growing on the uphill side of the residence, temper the severity of cold night air. Trees on the northern side of a site serve as a valuable wind-break in winter. The location should be such as to afford an abundance of sunlight.

Sandy and gravelly soils, allowing the underground water to drain out freely, are dry and therefore desirable. Unless the sand is in very fine grains, these soils furnish a very durable foundation. If stony or clay depressions underlie a soil, and thereby cause it to retain water permanently, such stagnant water under the surface causes a sandy, loamy, or other soil to be unhealthful. With clay soils, great importance attaches to careful drainage so adapted that no water stands in the ground. Rocky foundations should likewise always have the water that comes to them drained off. Even the firmest rocks will (when dry) take up and retain a varying percentage of moisture. Ordinary soils can hold a very large amount of water by means of their innumerable particles. When drainage is defective, this ground-water (or "soil-water") is not freshened, and an excess of water is present which becomes *stagnant* and unhealthful. If such ground be so situated that it is occasionally kept moist for a long time and then drained naturally, it is less healthful than a porous soil that is always well drained.

When the ground is frozen, the amount of water present is increased by one-tenth. The ground has then lost its permeability to water, and it also lacks the usual permeability to air. At such times, whatever falls upon the surface is not liable to enter the frozen ground. In its ordinary condition, very many bacteria enter the soil with the filth, waste fluids, and water that are poured upon it. Their numbers decrease very rapidly from the surface downward; so that it is not common to find them very deep down. Often we find that they do not exist more than six feet beneath the surface. Hence deep ground-water may be considered as organically one of the purest natural waters.

The bacteria of the soil feed upon organic matter that may be present, especially when that is in the form of filth thrown upon the ground and allowed to sink into it. These minute forms of organized life thereby produce important and healthful chemical changes in the matters that they feed upon. The oxidative processes are most prevalent, if oxygen is abundantly supplied to these bacteria. In the absence of oxygen, the reductive processes of beneficial chemical change are there predominant. Both bacterial processes can go on at the same time. The results of their activity differ according to the chemical nature of the organic substances present, according to the varieties of bacteria occurring, and somewhat also with the degree of warmth and the moisture of the ground. The complex organic compounds which we class as filth and waste thus become converted into water, carbonic acid gas, ammonia, nitric acid, and salts by the decomposition which bacteria induce, and to the accomplishment of which these minute micro-organisms are essential (although the fatty waste matters apparently become converted into glycerine and fat-acids without the intervention of bacteria).

These low forms of microscopic life are usually, therefore, not only harmless, but are even very valuable aids to health. In view of what has just been indicated, they may justly be regarded as natural scavengers. Unfortunately, however, some disease-producing micro-organisms—although in general less hardy than the ordinary soil bacteria, and despite the more or less effective "antagonism" of these latter—can thrive in the soil and in filth for a varying length of time, and still be the active cause of disease among human beings or animals.

Furthermore, an excess of filth deposited upon the ground may soak down to a depth below the levels at which bacteria or plants thrive. Thereby, the ground may remain permanently polluted, unless the filth is removed by the ground-water or other means. Cases have recently occurred where, by soaking down far off into limestone rock used for water supply, bacteria in refuse water have apparently caused cases of typhoid fever. All of these things are important in connection with sewage-disposal problems. Indiscriminate throwing of household filth or other waste upon the ground is a menace to health. The cleaner the ground is kept, the more healthful is the site. The organic destructive processes, above indicated, cause the percentage of oxygen, in the air that is present in the pores of the ground, to be less than in the free atmosphere outside. The amount of carbonic acid increases proportionately with the amount of organic decomposition that is taking place.

The heat of the summer sun of dry, barren regions destroys many of the harmful bacteria that may chance to be on the surface of the ground. Light and pure air also exert, to a variable extent, a beneficent influence in this direction. As will be found indicated in the chapter that treats of Disinfection, bacteria differ greatly in their sensitiveness. Of the harmful and other bacteria that are alive in the soil, some rise to the surface with the moisture that is drawn up by capillary attraction and by evaporation from the upper layers. Such bacteria as happen to be on the surface, may (*when dry*) be carried far through the air with particles of dust.

Dust is composed of finely-divided clay and almost everything else. Not only does it consist of mineral substances, powdered vegetable matter, animal tissues, and so on, but very harmful substances may enter as well. Chemicals of an irritant or poisonous nature may thus be diffused about. The waste products of disease, if carelessly thrown upon the ground, or if proper cleanliness be not observed, may, by drying and pulverizing, become dust that carries with it the causes of disease and death. Few if any intelligent physicians doubt that tuberculous "consumption" is disseminated in such a way. The infectious germs of the disease are very numerously abundant in most of the matters coughed out of the lungs of those in whom the tuberculous disease is present. These matters, drying and becoming powdered, may, as rather coarse dust, scattered far and near, infect very susceptible people into whose lungs many such germs of disease are inhaled with the dust of places frequented by diseased people. Other diseases can probably arise by similar disregard of extreme cleanliness.

The dangers of dust in streets are lessened when these are well provided with smooth, impervious pavements that are constantly kept clean. When moistened, dust becomes mud. In this moist condition neither it nor the bacteria that are in it or on it can be carried by the wind. Filthy mud is much carried about by shoes and in other ways. When dry, this becomes dust. The finest dust particles remain suspended in the air. They do not contain bacteria as often as coarser dust does. Their presence is evident when a narrow ray of sunlight is allowed to enter a darkened room. The light, then reflected from their surfaces, makes them visible. Fine dust and smoke in a rainless season make the air hazy, as seen in our "Indian summer." Smoke not only makes the air less clear, but adds dust and impurities other than that.

To examine the dust of the air microscopically, a small drop of glycerine put in the middle of a glass slide may be left lying or be moved for a given time against the air. Then a cover-glass is laid upon this, and it is ready to be examined. Solidified flat surfaces of nutrient agar, gelatine, or other bacterial culture medium, exposed to the air for a given time, then covered and set aside for development of bacteria and moulds that may have fallen, give a fair idea of the varieties, and a rough comparative idea of the numbers. An air pump is required for the more elaborate methods, which, however, are not wholly satisfactory.

The temperature of the surface of the ground tends to vary with that of the air immediately above it. Sandy soils, and those that are light or "limy," absorb more of the sun's heat than clay or fine loam. The drier, darker, and coarser the soil, the more does it heat up under the sun's rays. When ground is moist, the evaporation of the moisture causes the ground to become less heated than would be the case with the same ground when dry. Those soils which absorb heat most rapidly tend also in general to radiate out their heat with proportionate rapidity, and thus they cool off very fast when the sun has ceased shining upon them.

At a distance of a foot or more below the surface of the ground very little change of temperature is caused by the sun shining upon the soil. Between thirty and one hundred feet down the yearly range of temperature is hardly more than two degrees. At one hundred feet and a little beyond, the temperature tends to remain unvaryingly constant.

When mining shafts and other deep works penetrate much beyond one hundred feet, the temperature gradually rises. In deep mines the heat, increasing steadily with the depth, proves an obstacle to very deep working.

Forests exert a great influence upon climate. Fluctuations of temperature are lessened by woods. In them and in their vicinity the air is somewhat cooler during the daytime and warmer at night. In winter, these differences are not notable except in evergreen forests. At all times, trees give protection against winds. In and near forests more rain falls and the climate is more temperate than in similar unwooded regions. All foliage and thickets, as well as the deadwood and leaves strewed over the ground, allow the water of the upper layers of the soil to remain longer than when the open ground is exposed to the sun's rays. The snow melts there more slowly in spring. Forests accordingly lessen the tendency to freshets which is present when great open surfaces of snow melt rapidly in thawing weather. They furthermore equalize the flow throughout the year by yielding up their moisture only gradually, and thus they have water to feed the sources of rivers during the drier and hotter months of the year. The air of forests is comparatively free from dust.

Grass-covered land does not become so warm from the sun as does land devoid of vegetation. On the former the sun's rays are intercepted by the grass and so do not reach the ground, while the radiation from the grass causes considerable coolness during the day-time. The same free radiation causes a rather rapid cooling at night. Thus, the evenings are cooler amid grassland than on barren ground. Greater moisture of the air in grassy regions is brought about by this radiation, which likewise explains the greater frequency of dews, mists, and frost seen in such localities. In a region of swamps, the moisture of the air is still more marked than over grassland. The moisture given off into the air over a region of forests and meadows increases the amount of clouds, and thus shields the region somewhat from the fierce rays of the summer sun.

The nearer a place is to the equator, the warmer, as a rule, is that place. Yet this fundamental principle is modified by various factors :

(1) The higher we rise above the sea, the cooler is the climate. Thus, Mexico City is in summer cooler than New York.

(2) The country about it affects the temperature of a given district. Hot deserts aggravate the heat of summer, and cold mountains generally lower the temperature. Mountains may make a place much warmer and drier by cutting off cold winds and moisture.

(3) The prevailing winds greatly affect the climate. This we see everywhere. The " chinook " is a notable instance of a benign influence of this kind in winter. It is a warm, dry wind on the eastern slopes of the great mountains in the northwestern part of the United States. Like some similar winds elsewhere, it occurs when some influence draws or drives a current of air over a high mountain range.

(4) Cultivation of the soil, the influence of civilized life and industries, as well as local and other factors have a slight effect on climate.

(5) Regions near the ocean and great bodies of water have the air moister than on uplands. This causes more rain and clouds and less dust there. The heat is less intense, the fluctuations of temperature are not so great, and regular winds are more prevalent. The neighboring great bodies of water take up a portion of the heat and consume it in evaporating moisture during the day, while at night they yield up this heat. Thus the temperature fluctuations

of the day and of the year are restricted in an ocean climate.

(6) Inland regions have a larger yearly range of temperature, the days being much warmer than the nights. There is less cloudiness and moisture in the air than is the case with the coast regions. The sun's heat, therefore, prevails with more fierceness, and the ground becomes very hot; while for the same reasons it cools off rapidly at night.

High altitudes have the air less dense and less moist than in places nearer the sea-level. The radiation of heat through the air is great. So the air is relatively cool, yet under the long and warm sunshine the ground gets comparatively very warm. At night the free radiation causes both air and ground to cool off very rapidly. This has much influence on vegetation, and both the variety and abundance of trees are under natural conditions more limited on high mountains and table-lands than on less elevated ground. The pressure upon the blood-vessels being much less in the rarefied air of high altitudes, it must be borne in mind that in most people this aggravates a liability to hemorrhages as well as a tendency of the blood to escape from the smaller blood-vessels more readily than occurs when in lowlands. The more practical and precise importance of this fact in connection with the climatic treatment of disease and its effect upon people having heart disease and other ailments will be given a little further on. At great heights, respiration is stimulated, partly because, perhaps, of the lessened percentage of oxygen in the air. At an altitude of seven thousand feet, the rarefaction of the air causes it to have only three-fourths as much oxygen in a given volume as is found at the sea-level. Therefore mountaineers develop large chests. It is important to notice, also, that they are, in general, very vigorous people.

When the air is dry, summer heat is much less unhealthful than when moist. In tropical lowlands, rains usually prevail when the summer is at its height, and are often very copious. The nearer such regions are to the equator, and the nearer they are to the coast, the more does the moisture of the air increase. For a portion of the year, winds are apt to prevail there with considerable steadiness, and in some places with great force. The climate of each place differs somewhat, of course, with its situation. The heat of the tropics is usually very oppressive. Elevated tropical regions can afford very delightful climates.

Owing to the abundant moisture and warmth of hot lowlands, decomposition and various oxidative processes are there exceedingly active, and vegetation is very luxuriant. Insect life, and the microscopic forms of plant life which are regarded as the cause of malaria, are more abundant and virulent there than in cooler climates. Various diseases, such as cholera and yellow fever, are peculiar to or originate in the tropics, and yearly cause many deaths. Typhoid fever is in such places very prevalent; while digestive and diarrhœal disorders in general are there especially to be dreaded by a northern race like our own, which cannot so well maintain perfect nutrition as can the native races of such tropical regions. Hence we tend to deteriorate in every way under the enervation and direct effects of tropical heat.

Acclimatization, therefore, in very hot climates, is for the average natives of our country very difficult or even impossible. Such energetic labor as is here healthful becomes dangerous there, owing to the difficulty of getting rid of the excess of body heat produced by all physical effort. If of pure race, the offspring of such immigrants is usually inferior in vitality, and the stock is unprolific. Restraints in diet and living, although important, are not sufficient to obviate the influence of the natural obstacles to health. The average immigrant succumbs to tropical influences, or weakens and degenerates under them, unless the place of residence be at an altitude of at least 2,500 feet above the sea-level. The general uncleanliness and bad sanitation of tropical places are detrimental to the health of all residing there. People of southern stock are best able to withstand tropical influences. Those who are lean and sinewy, with dry skins, and who also have sound constitutions, are best fitted for residence in hot climates.

By taking proper care, the great majority of human beings can thrive, for a while at least, in climates quite outside the extremes of those occurring in our temperate regions. A "polar" climate is one where the average yearly temperature is below the freezing point. On the other hand, in the "tropical" climate the average yearly temperature is above our comfort limit of 77° F. The world's regions of excessive heat are interior deserts, where the absolute maximum of (officially authentic) recorded temperatures (in the shade) is published as being from 118° F. to 122 F. This highest temperature is reached in the month of June (in the northern hemisphere), and the desert regions of the southwestern portion of our country are shown to have a summer heat about as high as any in the world.

Air and Its Impurities

The air, which we incessantly need for breathing, and which is indispensable for the combustion of fuel and for nearly all organic processes, has a rather uniform proportion of the essential vital element, oxygen. The percentage of oxygen in air is about 20.9. Even in manufacturing cities the percentage does not sink more than one-half of one per cent. lower than that. This is due to the fact that the impurities and diminished oxygen of the air resulting from our various vital and manufacturing processes are rapidly provided for by the constant movements of the atmosphere. Into the enormous volume of the atmosphere, vitiated air is mingled and diffused, rendering the air about us pure enough for breathing purposes so far as the oxygen is concerned.

The air breathed out from the lungs contains over five

per cent. less oxygen than that breathed in. The amount of oxygen in the atmosphere may be considerably less than twenty per cent., as in the rarefied atmosphere of an elevated region, and yet be eminently healthful. Under various natural and artificial conditions people can maintain health and yet live and work where the proportion of oxygen is far removed from the normal as above given. It can therefore safely be asserted that it is not owing to any deficiency of oxygen in the air that our cities are less healthful than the country.

Ozone is an actively oxidizing form of oxygen. Besides being produced artificially in various ways, it appears to be formed in extensive oxidative processes and in active evaporation of water. This latter process would seem to explain its presence in sea air. Peroxide of hydrogen is formed at the same time. The usual test for ozone is to expose to the air, steadily drawn through a simple box by means of an aspirator, strips of paper which have dried upon them a mixture of one part of iodide of potash to ten parts of potato starch. The exposure to the air should be in the shade and for a definite time, in order that comparisons may be made with an approach to accuracy. The depth of the blue color, resulting from the action of the iodine on the starch and induced by any ozone present, varies with the proportion of the ozone. This method is not exact. The same may be said of all other methods. The absolute importance of ozone seems, in the light of recent investigations, to have been overestimated. Examinations of the air when epidemics were prevailing in the vicinity have shown that the air then contained about as much ozone as during times of greatest health. The presence of ozone appears to be of value chiefly as indicating an absence of easily oxidizable substances in the air.

Nitrogen makes nearly four-fifths (79 per cent.) of the volume of the air. It is an inert, gaseous element, moderating the activity of the oxygen associated with it in the atmosphere. It does not influence animal life.

Carbonic acid gas, called also carbonic dioxide (CO_2), is present in pure, free air to the extent of less than one-thirtieth of one per cent. of the volume of the air tested. Dr. C. T. Williams and others state that desert air contains none of this gas. Whenever the proportion of this gas reaches one-tenth of one per cent., the air is regarded as excessively contaminated and unfit for breathing. This is not because such a proportion, or even several times that, is necessarily harmful in itself if breathed for a brief time. It is rather because other more harmful and less easily demonstrable excretory products are given off into the air at the same time that the carbonic acid gas is exhaled. Where the air has more than 3.5 or, perhaps, 4 parts of this carbonic acid gas in 10,000 parts of air, it is considered as below the standard of purity. Yet, as will be told later, very many public and private buildings are allowed to have more than three times as much as this percentage of the gas in the air of their ill-ventilated rooms. Whenever the proportion of carbonic acid gas exceeds 1 part in 1,000 volumes of air, the air may be considered as unquestionably needing purification.

This ever-present constituent of the ordinary air comes not only from the lungs of all breathing creatures, but it results from all combustions and decompositions as well. As already indicated, a varying amount is present in the soil and is increased by the action of oxidative bacteria there. Growing plants consume some carbonic acid gas during the day time; at night they exhale this. An average adult gives off into the air between 1,050 and 1,350 cubic inches (or, say, three-fourths of a cubic foot) of this gas in an hour. Parkes set the amount at six-tenths of a cubic foot. The proportion varies according to the individual and the state of health, of activity, and of nutrition. It increases very much with exercise. The total yearly amount coming from all the human beings on the earth is estimated as being less than half as much as results from the total combustion of fuels and of light-producing substances and in various processes. Yet the entire enormous quantity becomes so diffused off by air currents, that the normal proportion, above given, of this gas in the atmosphere is maintained.

Since this is adopted as a standard by which to measure impurities of the air, and with which, in its fluctuations, other more or less subtle impurities also fluctuate, their proportions increasing with the increase in the amount of carbonic acid gas, the percentage of this present in the air frequently has to be determined with accuracy. For this purpose, Pettenkofer's method is probably the best. To describe all the necessary details in full would require a number of pages, for it is a long and complex process that calls for the skill and facilities of a trained chemist.

> This test is based on the fact that when, with a given amount of air in a bottle, we shake up a solution of barium hydrate, the carbonic acid gas of the air unites with a portion of this barium hydrate and forms water and the insoluble carbonate of barium. The difference between the amount of barium hydrate present in the solution beforehand, and that which remains after agitating well and long with the air to be tested, indicates the amount of carbonic acid gas present in the volume of air taken. A standard solution of oxalic acid is employed for determining the amount of the barium hydrate used. The indications of the barometer and the thermometer must be considered in the calculation and are to be recorded at the time that the air is collected for the test.
>
> A bottle that is clean and dry and of exactly known size (*e.g.*, one holding between two and five quarts) is used for receiving the air. This may be introduced into the bottle by means of a clean air-drawing appliance, such as a bellows or a double rubber bulb, connected with a tube drawing out the air from the bottom of the bottle and thus completely displacing the original air in the bottle by the room air which is to be tested. When the bottle has probably had the air in it changed several times, it is covered with a clean rubber cap. Then it is transported to a laboratory for the addition of the barium hydrate solution.

Of the various less accurate but easier processes used for determining the amount of carbonic acid gas present in a given air, one of *Wolpert's* deserves notice. It employs a solution of carbonate of soda, to which is added a very small amount of *phenolphtalein*, a substance very sensitive to the presence of alkalies. These cause this phenolphtalein in solution to become red. When the air is shaken up with the solution, part of the carbonate of soda becomes bicarbonate of soda owing to the presence of the carbonic acid gas. The thereby lessened alkalinity causes the red color to disappear. By reading the scale and following the directions that go with the apparatus, an approximate idea can be obtained of the amount of carbonic acid gas present in the volume of air required to convert the soda salt. The author is informed by R. R. Wade, chief of the Massachusetts District Police, that this Wolpert test may at times err to the extent of 3.4 parts in 10,000. This test calls for a certain degree of skill. Its convenience recommends it. It is accurate enough for the detection of a great excess of carbonic acid gas in the air.

Water, as will be explained below, is present (as vapor) in the atmospheric air. Analysis shows also traces of ammonia, sulphurous acid, and sulphuric acid. The latter is quite constantly found in the smoky air of manufacturing cities that are situated in valleys, and which consume coal that contains more than one per cent. of sulphur.

Various metallic poisons may occur in the air near certain industries. When numerous smelters, ore roasters, and reducing works are in active operation, the air is not only irritant by reason of sulphurous and other unhealthful gases, but chemists can then detect arsenic, antimony, and other most undesirable substances in the air. The immediate neighborhood of such places cannot be considered healthful.

Sewer-gas is probably not, as a rule, so dangerous to the health as it has been represented. Occasional leakages of illuminating gas into sewers constitute a serious danger, and this, as also sewer-gas, will be further spoken of in other chapters. The gases present in sewers are chiefly important as indicating that bacteria are present, causing decomposition processes. Such a condition calls for more careful attention to cleanliness. Harmful bacteria—such as, for instance, those that cause diphtheria—may be present in sewers. These, if not held down and washed away, or otherwise destroyed, are much more to be dreaded than any odorous gas that is properly called sewer-gas. The odorous fat-acids and various organic gases, which are so unpleasant in localities given over to "rendering establishments" and some other industries, are much more evident to the sense of smell than in themselves demonstrably harmful. The æsthetic sense is, however, offended by these, and should be respected. Since bad odors commonly indicate that organic matter is decomposing, their source should always be carefully investigated. If it prove a probable nursery for harmful microörganisms, it should be removed.

The air exhaled from the lungs may contain organic poisons. The latest statements of Brown-Sequard relative to this important question have, at the most, received only partial confirmation. Some contradict him. At any rate, it is wise to shun as harmful all filth from diseased persons, especially if it be in the form of dried dust and dried matters coughed up from the lungs. Careful experimenters have recently shown that bacteria like those that cause the disease can, in typhoid fever cases, be exhaled in very small numbers with the breath from the parched mouths of patients. This has not been generally accepted as proven. At the worst it seems only a minor danger. The point to be taught is that extreme personal cleanliness is in general an important safeguard, and that the unclean, whether diseased or apparently well, are not to be regarded as desirable neighbors.

Moisture in atmospheric air.—A considerable proportion of the water precipitated upon the earth's surface as rain evaporates very speedily and is diffused throughout the air. Much more moisture is taken up into the air from the surface of the ocean, and from the top of the apparently dry ground, to which moisture rises from the wet layers of the soil beneath. The amount of moisture held by the air varies greatly according to time, season, and place. A certain degree of warmth is necessary to the taking up of moisture by the air. The colder the air, the less watery vapor can it hold. The air outside our windows on a cold day is much drier than the warmed air within, provided that the latter has found moisture to take up, as will be explained in the chapter on Heating.

The moisture of the air being one of the most important elements of a climate, it is important to explain the meaning of a few indispensable terms used to indicate the amount. When no more moisture can be absorbed by the air, the air is said to be *saturated*. The air is never completely saturated. The *absolute humidity* is the amount of vaporized moisture (in grains) present in a given volume (cubic feet) of air. Some observers measure this by the number of grammes of water-vapor present in a cubic metre of air. The percentage of *relative humidity* indicates the proportion of watery vapor which the air actually contains at a given temperature, as compared with the highest possible amount that it could contain at the same temperature. By the *dew-point* of air containing a given amount of watery vapor is meant the exact (lower) temperature at which that air cannot hold any more moisture in the form of vapor, but must deposit it as dew, cloud, rain, etc.

The most absolutely accurate method of ascertaining the amount of moisture in the air is a careful chemical test. There are other means that are accurate enough. By observing the temperature at which dew is deposited, we can, by the use of proper tables, determine the amount of moisture in the air and the relative humidity. The easiest but least accurate way of reaching the same result directly is to use a *hair hygrometer*. This consists of an open brass framework and dial, over which an indicator is moved by reason of its being attached to a pulley around which is a long hair (cleaned by long soaking in ether). At its upper end the hair is attached to the brass framework. This hair is kept straight by a small weight (ten grains or so) suspended from it. The hair shortens and lengthens according to the amount of moisture in the air. Thereby the attached indicator is moved over the graduated arc of the dial. Hair hygrometers, although somewhat inaccurate and variable, are regarded by many as being fairly reliable if carefully tested and compared at least twice a year with a good *psychrometer*.

Psychrometers are generally used to ascertain the amount of moisture in the air. This most accurate and simple instrument consists of two sensitive thermometers fastened side by side an inch or more apart, the bulbs being freely exposed to the air. These two should be identical in every respect, except that a single thickness of clean washed muslin is on the bulb of one of these thermometers, and is kept moistened with distilled or other very clean water during the test. The evaporation of the water from this muslin cover cools the bulb slightly and causes this thermometer to register a somewhat lower temperature than is indicated on the one with the dry bulb.

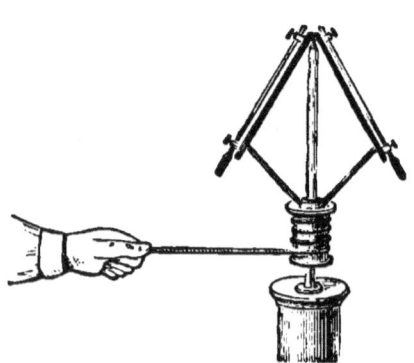

FIG. 1.

The drier the air around it, the lower does the mercury in the wet-bulb thermometer sink beyond that of the dry thermometer. The best way is, when in the shade and facing the wind, to sling this around at a uniform rate by means of a cord or other arrangement. The knack of using this is easily acquired. Fig. 1 shows a more elaborate arrangement for having the wet- and dry-bulb thermometers exposed evenly to the air.

The usual psychrometer, having two parallel thermometers on a piece of wood, answers equally well.

To interpret the results, a long series of tables is employed, and can be obtained of most instrument-makers. They can also be found on pages 81 to 91 of the "Instructions for Voluntary Observers," issued by the United States Weather Bureau in 1892, which book also gives more elaborate instructions in regard to meteorological instruments and their use. Tables also for determining the temperature of the dew-point are there given.

A climate having a very high relative humidity is not in general desirable for either well people or invalids. The average "relative humidity" of our Atlantic States is from sixty to seventy-two per cent. Where the amount of moisture in motionless air is very great, a moderately warm temperature may be very oppressive if the relative humidity be much above seventy per cent. This is because the amount of water that is vaporized from our bodies, and which serves to diminish our body heat by its evaporation, is very much lessened when the moisture in the air becomes considerable. When the air is warm besides being very moist, the important cooling processes of radiation and convection from the skin are much restricted. The heat produced by the vital processes within the body becomes at times a source of danger to health in the summer weather of our Atlantic coast cities; and in "muggy" summer weather, the relative humidity then being greater than seventy-five per cent., exercise is far from healthful. The moisture rather than the heat of our summers in the eastern half of the United States explains the much greater prevalence of sunstroke there.

A relative humidity ranging from thirty-five to sixty-five per cent., while the temperature is about 70° F., is quite comfortable. If considerably below this, as in our driest upland regions, dryness of the throat and air passages may be experienced. Very moist weather is apt to favor the development of various diseases.

Precipitation of Moisture

When currents of air containing considerable moisture (because of their relatively greater warmth) encounter cool bodies of air, usually at higher levels, or go against cool mountain sides (especially when those are clad with forests), the moisture of this warmer air is precipitated. Yet a precipitation of rain or snow thus occurring does not always descend to the level plains, nor even to the lower parts of mountains. This is because the air of lower levels is warmer than that high up, and so can vaporize and thus take up moisture precipitated into it. By reason of the cold air of high mountains, they receive much precipitated moisture. The windward sides of mountain ranges receive much more rain than falls upon the side that is away from the prevailing winds.

Since the great ocean currents of moist air flow to the eastward, we find that the districts on the western (or southern) coasts of our continents receive, as a rule, more rain than falls elsewhere. Thus, the western parts of the British Isles and Scandinavia receive more than twice as much rain as falls in the eastern parts of those countries. Studying a rainmap of the western part of our continent, we see that the warm eastward currents of the Pacific Ocean are deflected to the northward, and cause much more rain on the northern portion of our Pacific coast than on the southern part.

In San Diego, at a latitude not far south of the thirty-third northern degree, and very near the coast of the Mexican possessions, the annual rainfall is about ten inches in an average year. As we go northward along the coast the amount of yearly rainfall almost constantly increases. At San Francisco the rainfall is about twenty-four inches. At the boundary line between California and Oregon, on the coast, more than seventy-one inches of rain fall each year. At the mouth of the Columbia River the amount is eighty-three inches; and at the entrance to Puget Sound (Cape

Flattery), ninety-four inches. At Neah Bay, in the State of Washington, more than one hundred inches fall in a year. Along the coast of Alaska, the rainfall is so excessive that the climate there resembles that of the wettest (western) portions of the British Isles and Norway. Yet the southern coasts of British India and adjoining districts have a much greater rainfall.

Contrary to what occurs on our Pacific coast, the rainfall in the Atlantic States increases usually as one goes southward, the heaviest recorded rains for the eastern coast having been in the Carolinas and further south, especially in Louisiana. As will be repeated in speaking of water supply, the annual amount of rainfall decreases in general as one goes from our coasts toward the interior. Yet local conditions greatly influence the rainfall of certain places. Notably do the high mountain ridges in the western part of the United States cut off the greater part of the moisture brought to our Pacific coast. Accordingly, the regions for a thousand miles to the eastward of the one hundred and twentieth meridian (of longitude west of Greenwich) have usually less than twenty inches of rainfall in a year. Parts of Montana, and a few other fortunate localities, especially the region in the southern half of Utah, directly south of the Great Salt Lake, may have even more than thirty-five inches of rainfall in a year.

From the northern part of the Great Salt Lake, let a line be drawn, on a map, toward the west—or, better, south of west—until the one hundred and twentieth meridian is reached, and then let the pencil be drawn to the head of the Gulf of California, but with the line curving slightly westward, so as to include half of that part of California that is south of the latitude of San Francisco. Another line drawn southward along the one hundred and thirteenth meridian, from the lake to the Gulf of California, produces a triangular sort of figure, which includes the most desert parts of our country. There are occasional oases in this arid region; but in many portions less than two inches of rainfall occur in a year, and in some parts the records show no rainfall whatsoever. This region remains a desert, however, chiefly because of the absence of water. Fine yields of alfalfa, the cereals, and various other crops can be raised with profit on such soils by the aid of irrigation. Even "alkali lands" can be made to yield abundant harvests by this means, if at the same time underdrainage be employed.

While places in southern California are much drier than those on the exposed coast of our Northern Pacific States, it must not be forgotten that local conditions, as before remarked, greatly influence the rainfall and other climatic conditions of any given locality there. The mountains, rising to the height of several thousand feet above Puget Sound, and which lie between it and the ocean, intercept much of the moisture brought to the coast by the warm, moist Japanese current. Hence the cities upon Puget Sound get less rain than falls upon the sea-coast.

Yearly Fall of Rain (and Snow)

(Measured in inches. Ten inches of snow = one inch of rain)

Average of Many Years

	Jan.	Feb.	Mar.	April.	May.	June.	July.	Aug.	Sept.	Oct.	Nov.	Dec.	Yearly Total.
Halifax....	5.63	4.94	5.48	4.16	4.75	2.66	4.07	4.20	3.60	5.40	5.50	5.37	55.76
Montreal...	3.71	3.08	3.46	2.27	2.87	3.35	4.13	3.30	3.19	3.38	3.72	3.73	40.19
Boston.....	4.30	3.60	4.30	3.70	3.40	3.40	3.50	4.30	3.00	4.30	4.60	3.50	46.10
N. Y. City..	4.00	3.90	4.10	3.40	3.00	3.30	4.50	4.80	3.80	3.50	3.60	3.30	45.20
Chicago....	2.20	2.30	2.50	3.10	3.60	3.60	3.70	3.50	2.80	3.20	2.70	2.20	35.00
Jacksonville, Fla.	3.10	2.40	3.50	2.90	4.20	6.10	6.10	6.60	8.10	5.70	2.60	3.00	55.30
Galveston..	4.10	3.00	3.10	3.00	4.10	4.90	3.00	5.40	7.10	4.80	4.70	4.40	51.00
San Antonio	1.61	2.42	2.14	2.67	3.02	3.23	2.37	3.40	4.06	2.01	2.55	1.97	31.45
Denver....	0.70	0.50	1.00	2.10	2.70	1.40	1.50	1.50	0.90	0.80	0.80	0.70	14.50
Victoria, B. C.	6.12	5.11	3.64	1.61	1.13	0.91	0.88	0.75	1.40	3.35	3.85	5.56	34.31
Olympia, Wash.	8.30	7.10	5.00	3.40	2.30	1.60	0.70	0.70	2.80	4.50	6.50	9.50	51.40
San Francisco.	4.50	3.80	3.10	2.10	0.60	0.20	.....	.....	0.20	1.20	2.50	5.00	23.60
Los Angeles.	4.08	3.74	2.27	1.29	0.31	0.09	0.02	0.10	0.04	0.82	1.71	3.84	18.31
San Diego..	1.60	2.10	1.00	1.00	0.30	0.10	0.10	0.10	0.10	0.30	1.00	2.10	9.80
City of Mexico.	0.19	0.25	0.44	0.66	2.13	4.70	4.32	5.20	4.31	1.83	0.52	0.18	24.23

The figures of the above table show the marked rainfall differences between various parts of our continent. On the Pacific coast little or no rain falls during midsummer, while the winter and early spring are there very rainy. In the eastern half of the continent much rain falls during the warmer months. The season of greatest rainfall varies there with the region. Compared with the rest of the world, our country shows a very high average of fine climatic conditions, and this is especially marked as regards the equable and abundant distribution of rain over the eastern half.

The rainfall is measured by being received into a funnel sunk two inches in a cylinder that is two feet deep, and that has a diameter (at the top, at least, if the bottom be a narrower cylinder) of exactly eight inches on the inside. The funnel allows the rain to enter through a small opening (to prevent evaporation) into a cylindrical receiver which is exactly twenty inches deep, and 2.53 inches in diameter.

Thereby the water received has one-tenth the area of the funnel-top, and this facilitates exact measurement. Outside of this cylinder is an overflow attachment which can be used for melting and measuring snow. Snow also can be measured by selecting a level, open space, without drifts, and noting the depth by passing a stick in several different places through the freshly fallen snow. It is usual to count ten inches of such snow as the equivalent of one inch of rain.

An excellent sunshine recorder is made by Mr. J. P. Friez, 107 East German Street, Baltimore, and costs twenty-five dollars. "Light recorders" are not to be recommended.

High relative humidity (exceeding seventy per cent.) adds to the discomfort and unhealthfulness of rainy weather. Other forms of moisture than rain can lessen the desirability of a locality. Rain followed by bright, clear weather is very agreeable. Thus, one of the attractions of the City of Mexico in summer is the late afternoon rainfall preceded and followed by clear weather. The unhealthful dust, so objectionable in some of the places in the western United States selected as invalid resorts, is thus laid or washed away by this rain.

Fogs are a more unhealthful form of moisture than rain. They are very prevalent along the northern parts of the Pacific coast in winter. On our Atlantic coast, the tendency to fog increases as one goes from New Jersey to Newfoundland.

Cloudiness Expressed in Percentages

Average from Records of Many Years

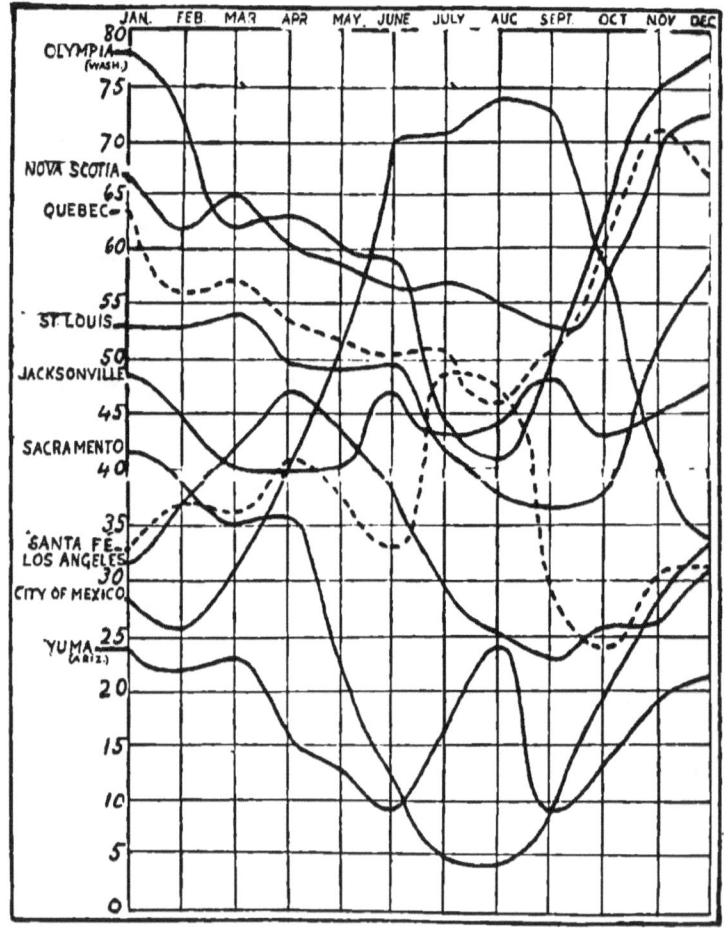

Fig. 2.

Extreme cloudiness makes a locality undesirable, especially for the residence of invalids. The eastern half of the United States has less of cloud percentage (55 per cent.) than is set down as the average for the remainder of the earth. The western half of this country averages considerably less cloud than the eastern half. From the above chart (Fig. 2) an idea can be got of the much greater prevalence of cloudiness in some places than in others, and of the average fluctuation from month to month. As indicated there, the northwestern portions of our country are the cloudiest. From Oregon to Oonalaska the percentage gradually increases, and at the latter place an entire month may pass without much more than two per cent. of clear sky being seen. August with us usually has less cloudiness than other months. Of the regions in the eastern half of the United States, the places on the southern shore of Lake Ontario have the largest percentages of cloudiness.

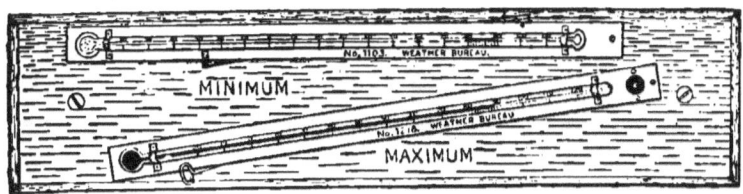

FIG. 3.

Temperatures are measured by means of thermometers. Those having mercury in the bulb and capillary tube are best; for mercury expands evenly at all temperatures that we usually encounter. As this substance congeals at 39° below zero, spirit-thermometers are used for measuring extreme cold. A thermometer can be tested by putting it with a standard one, and reading the register while both are exposed together to the same temperatures, away from currents of air. For testing at the freezing temperature, crushed ice in a funnel is used. Thermometers should also at least be compared in boiling water and steam (at sea-level, or with corrections therefor). Several intermediate temperatures of water in a vessel should be tried. "Maximal and minimal" thermometers are useful for registering the highest and lowest temperatures reached. The accurate position of these is shown by Fig. 3.

Automatic recording thermographs serve to register the temperature fluctuations by means of a pen which traces a continuous line on a chart that is moved by clockwork. Such instruments, made after Dr. Draper's pattern, can be had for from fifteen to thirty dollars. For out-of-doors use, thermometers should preferably be on the north side of a building, and placed more than a foot away from any wall. They should be at least twelve feet above the ground, besides being shielded from the wind. The intensity of the sun's heat is measured by exposing to the sun a thermometer that has the bulb coated with soot, to lessen reflection and loss of heat from the usual shining surface. "Solar radiation thermometers" are neither reliable nor important.

The mean daily temperature is got by adding the highest temperature of the day to the lowest temperature of the same day, and dividing this product by two. On the average, this gives a temperature nearly a degree too high. Adding the daily averages for a given time (month, year, etc.), and dividing by the numbers of days that we have taken, we get the average for the time in question.

Mean Daily Range of Temperature (Fahr.)

Average of many years

	Jan.	Feb.	Mar.	April.	May.	June.	July.	Aug.	Sept.	Oct.	Nov.	Dec.
Toronto................	15.2	16.0	14.4	17.1	18.5	19.7	19.4	18.6	17.9	15.4	12.7	12.9
Boston..	18.0	17.8	16.0	16.6	17.9	19.0	17.8	17.6	16.9	17.1	16.1	16.0
Albany................	16.9	16.8	15.0	17.4	18.8	18.5	18.0	17.8	17.2	16.6	13.8	13.7
New York City.........	14.0	14.8	14.8	16.5	16.6	16.5	16.0	16.2	15.2	15.6	13.9	13.1
Jacksonville..........	16.8	16.6	17.4	17.1	16.4	15.6	15.8	14.9	13.7	13.8	17.1	17.1
Augusta, Ga...........	18.4	19.7	22.0	21.8	21.3	19.7	19.4	18.4	17.9	19.8	20.9	19.4
San Antonio...........	21.0	21.8	21.2	21.5	20.4	19.9	21.6	21.4	21.6	21.1	21.2	21.2
El Paso, Texas.........	25.5	27.2	29.2	33.1	33.0	31.9	29.0	27.0	26.5	27.7	26.2	24.8
Chicago...............	16.1	15.5	13.9	15.4	15.2	14.9	14.7	13.3	14.1	14.0	13.9	13.5
Denver................	25.9	24.2	26.1	24.5	25.9	27.4	27.3	26.3	28.2	26.8	25.2	24.3
San Francisco.........	9.1	10.4	11.2	10.9	12.2	12.2	11.5	11.3	12.8	11.8	10.2	8.8
Tatoosh Isl'd, Wash....	6.7	6.9	8.2	8.7	9.2	9.6	10.6	10.7	8.5	8.1	6.8	7.0
City of Mexico.........	24.0	26.0	27.0	26.0	24.0	21.0	21.0	19.0	17.0	19.0	21.0	23.0

The mean daily range of temperature is the difference between the highest day temperature and the lowest night temperature of the twenty-four hours. This is a very important climatic factor. (See table, where these are averaged by months.) If the highest point that the thermometer ever reaches in a given locality be compared with the lowest ever reached there, the difference between the two gives the *absolute range* of temperature. It is not the rule that these two extreme temperatures are reached in one year.

In this country the absolute range of temperature is very great, notably so in the regions north of the Missouri River, or more particularly in northern Dakota and Montana. The smallest absolute range in the United States is at San Francisco. Other places on the immediate Pacific coast have only a slightly greater range. There the freezing point is never reached, and the variability of the temperature from day to day in winter is much less than is the case in places further to the eastward. This equability is a valuable feature of the climate that recommends the California coast for many invalids and semi-invalids. In this respect, however, Nice (like some other places on the Mediterranean Sea) surpasses all of our best climates. As regards the absence of high winds (mistral), snow and ice, our Pacific coast, although humid, is superior to Nice and the other Franco-Italian resorts.

As for the probability of rain, presumably less rain occurs in the region between southern California and San Antonio, Texas, during the winter months, than falls in Nice at the same time, and certainly there is more wind in the latter place. Florida and the regions near it have more rain at that season, but the cold there rarely reaches the freezing point. The same is recorded of Delaware. The greatest ranges of temperature throughout the year are in this country observed along the Missouri River, and from Lake Superior westward to the Missouri.

Density of the Air

Fig. 4.

Barometers are used to measure the pressure or density of the atmosphere. At the sea-level, this pressure of the air is about 14.67 pounds upon every square inch of surface. This corresponds to the pressure of a column of water nearly thirty-four feet high, or of mercury thirty inches high. So, to measure variations in this pressure, a straight tube of glass, about thirty-eight inches long, closed at the upper end, and having an inside diameter of at least one-fourth inch (and preferably more), is skilfully filled with mercury so that a vacuum exists at the top. This is hung exactly upright, with the lower (open) end resting in a small vessel of mercury free to receive the pressure of the air. Around the greater part of the tube is a casing of brass. (See Fig. 4.) There is an arrangement at the bottom for adjustment in all good instruments. At the upper part is fixed a more or less delicately marked scale, and perhaps other aid to reading the variation visible at any time in the exact level of the convex summit of the mercury column. It is well to have barometers standardized by hanging near accurate ones and adjusting the level of the mercury so that both correspond. In giving readings of the scale, the temperature should also be given from a thermometer which is on the *middle* part of the casing. Then the reading may, by means of easy tables, be figured as though made at 32° F. The reading is also reduced to sea-level, the standard by which all are compared.

DENSITY OF THE ATMOSPHERE 29

Aneroid barometers are less accurate but more convenient. They can be made as small as a watch, but are usually five inches across. Their interior mechanism is delicate. (See Fig. 4a.) The essential part is the large, flat, air-tight box (*A*) in the bottom. It is made of corrugated, thin German silver, and the air must have been exhausted from it. It is attached beneath and is held up by a strong spring (*B*) above. As the box *A* expands or contracts, the mechanism causes the indicator (*H*) to move over the dial. The dial is arranged so that the indications compare with the height of the mercury in a mercurial barometer. The words "rain," "fair," "very dry," etc., must not be taken as an accurate guide to the probable weather. Aneroids are of value to mariners, because of portability and early sensitiveness. Mercurial barometers are less liable to get out of order and are more accurate. Aneroids usually err in registering too high. For determining high altitudes, these are apt to err greatly, as Mr. Whymper has recently shown anew. The large self-registering aneroid barometers made by Richard, in Paris, are very good for constant records.

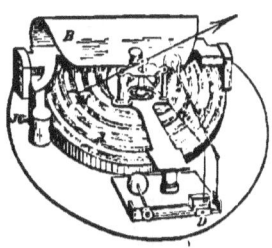

FIG. 4a.

As we rise further and further above the sea-level, the density of the air lessens, and the column of mercury falls in a geometrical ratio as the altitude becomes greater. At a little under 11,500 feet, we find that the pressure is only two-thirds of that at the sea-level. At a height of a little more than 16,400 feet, the mercury in the barometer has fallen to fifteen inches. The importance of this to some invalids will shortly be mentioned. The top of Pike's Peak, in Colorado, has a barometric pressure of about 17.8 inches and an altitude of 14,134 feet.

The pressure of the air around one is at times slightly increased beyond that usually occurring at the sea-level. In diving-bells and other devices used for working under water, it may be several times as great as the ordinary atmospheric pressure. The air there is impure, although it may contain more than the ordinary amount of oxygen. Those who work in such air should be sound and picked men, and should not come abruptly to the lessened pressure of the ordinary air. Otherwise considerable danger is incurred. The great pressure of the air in such places drives blood to the inner organs of the body, and the drum of the ear is forced in if entire, and if at the same time the natural communication between the middle ear and the nose be obstructed.

Weather Probabilities

The barometer is high when the upper layers of air are settling down toward the place of observation, and also when dry or cold air is acting upon it. A "low" level of the mercury in the barometer can come when the air about it is moist, and especially when great bodies of air around it are rising by reason of their being warm, and thus more expanded and lighter. As warm air rises into cooler air, its moisture becomes condensed. When air is warmed, and therefore rises, this produces a slight lessening of pressure. The air rushes in to equalize this pressure. In this way, winds are caused to blow, and, other conditions favoring, storms then develop.

Various local factors complicate the prediction of weather. Mountains can intercept much bad weather. The St. Lawrence Valley, for instance, lacking such protection, has very many storms. Furthermore, most of the storms in this country tend to move toward the northeast part.

In studying barometers, we should consider fluctuations as of more importance than the mere level of the mercury. The tendency is to overestimate the importance of the observation of single barometers. The value of their use on land lies chiefly in comparing many different observations taken at the same time over a large area. Then, on a map, lines are drawn through the places where the barometer readings (corrected to sea-level, for uniformity) show the same height of mercury. Such lines are called *isobars*, and for every tenth of an inch in the recorded level of the barometer, a separate line is drawn. The thermometer readings are recorded at the same time ; and, on the map, places recording the same temperatures at the same given moment, have dotted lines drawn through them. These lines are called *isotherms*. On the United States daily weather charts, the space between two of these dotted lines indicates a difference of ten degrees in temperature.

All storms are accompanied by clouds. Whether with or without rain, storms progress at the rate of from five to forty-five miles an hour along tracks which are easy of definite recognition. When (as is usually the case) they are accompanied by low barometer, we call them "cyclonic," because the air nearest the region of the earth where they are moves spirally inward to rise at the centre and to spread out above. Toward the centre of these the barometer is low, and the storm centre is always where the pressure is lowest. The word "cyclone" does not necessarily indicate a severe storm. The advance of "high" areas of pressure is very certain to bring cooler weather, and often "cold waves" and brisk to high northwest winds, but not usually rain.

The above explanations, taken in connection with the following six paragraphs, embodying the results of many years' Weather Bureau observations, aid one to interpret the weather map published daily and posted in conspicuous places throughout the country:

"The general movement of storms in the United States is from west to east, and we may liken them to a series of rather rounded atmospheric waves of which the crests are marked 'High,' and oval troughs or depressions between are marked and called 'Low.' These alternating Highs and Lows, several hundred miles apart, have an average easterly movement of about six hundred miles per day.

"High winds and rain, or snow (if it be cold enough), usually precede the low area, often extending to a distance of six hundred miles; in advance of the low centre, the winds are generally southerly, and consequently bring high temperature. When the centre of the Low passes to the east of a place, the wind at once shifts to the north. This brings lower temperature and clearing skies, and in winter cold waves or northers. The temperature on a given parallel west of the Low may be reasonably looked for on the same parallel to the east when the Low has passed; and frost will occur along and north of an isotherm of about 40° if the night is clear and there be but little wind. Following the Low comes an area of High, bringing sunshiny weather, which in its turn is followed by another Low.

"By bearing in mind a few general rules as to the direction and rate of movement of the Low and High, with the blowing of the wind from the High toward the Low, coming weather changes may be foreseen by a glance at the map. The centres of Low do not move across isotherms, but follow their general direction.

"The cloud and rain area in front of a Low is about the size of the latter and oval, with the west side touching the centre of the Low in advance of which it progresses.

"When the isotherms run nearly east and west, no decided change in temperature will occur. If the isotherms directly west of a place incline from northwest to southeast, the weather will be warmer; if from northeast to southwest, it will be colder. Southerly winds prevail west of a nearly north and south line cutting the middle of a High; also east of a like line cutting the middle of a Low. Northerly winds occur west of a nearly north and south line passing through the middle of a Low, and also east of a similar one through the middle of a High.

"An absence of decided waves of High or troughs of Low pressure indicates a continuance of existing weather which will last till later maps show a change, usually first appearing in the west."

Winds

On the Pacific coast, as also in the Gulf States, the winds are usually from the water toward the land. This is also somewhat the case in the Atlantic States during the summer. In general, however, because of the earth's rotation on its axis, our winds come from the westward rather than from the eastward. In the western half of the United States, east of the Rocky Mountains, north and south winds are more common. In southern California, winds may come from the east at times. Like all those coming over deserts, such winds are there very dry and hot. In the eastern half of the continent, the most wind occurs in early spring; in the western half, winds usually blow hardest later in the season. In San Francisco the maximum is in July. Elsewhere, the summer winds are, as a rule, much gentler than those of winter.

A wind-vane is more sensitive when the tail-piece is split so as to form a slight angle, as seen in Fig. 5. It should be at least ten feet above all buildings, trees, etc., that could obstruct or change the wind in any way. When noting the direction of the wind, the *true north* should always be considered, and not the uncorrected direction in which the magnetic needle points. The arrows on the United States weather charts point in the direction toward which the wind is blowing.

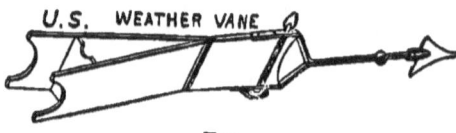

Fig. 5.

For determining the velocity of air currents, wind-gauges called *anemometers* are used. Like weather-vanes, they must be well above roofs, etc. By means of rotating aluminum cups (Fig. 6), and an electrical or other mechanism beneath, a velocity even as slight as half a mile an hour can be recorded. These cups measure four inches across, and the distance from the centre of the axis, on which the four cups rotate, to the centre of each cup is 6.72 inches, according to the United States standard. To have caused five hundred rotations of the apparatus, the wind must then have travelled a mile. This arrangement is apt to indicate more miles than the wind actually travels in a given time.

Fig. 6.

The force depends on the velocity and is proportional to the sinus of the angle at which the wind strikes a surface opposed to it.

To determine the pressure on each square foot of a flat surface exactly facing the wind, we find the square of the actual number of miles which the wind would travel in an hour. This, multiplied by 0.004, gives the result in pounds of pressure on each square foot. When there is only a very slight movement of the air, our unaided senses fail to detect it, and even smoke rises straight upward. When the wind has a velocity of thirteen miles an hour it is called a light breeze. This only serves to move the leaves and small branchlets of trees. It is called a strong breeze if moving thirty-four miles an hour, and this is able to move the large branches of trees. At forty-eight miles per hour it can render walking in the open air somewhat difficult, and it is then called a fresh gale. A hurricane moves ninety miles an hour.

Choosing a Climate

In the choice of a suitable climate for invalids, the chief disease that we consider is tuberculous consumption of the lungs. As in other parts of the world, so here in America we see very great relief and even permanent cure result from a careful change of climate and occupation before the lung changes have advanced very far. Willpower and a resolution to fight the disease are of value. Whatever climate be chosen, much sunshine and a dry location are most important. With mild warmth, a low relative and absolute humidity are always desirable, although Iceland and the western Hebrides and Shetlands are moist and yet have not much of this disease.

Some places in Georgia are not desirable, despite their other merits, for the reason that the soil there is moist. The absolute humidity at Los Angeles, although the town is inland, is considerably greater than either in Boston or New York, for instance, and this is somewhat against the pretensions of the place and similarly of some others. The coast places of southern California, though at times of value, are in general not the most desirable places of resort for such cases. Experienced physicians find that, contrary to theory, the tendency to hemorrhages is there greater than at considerably higher places having less equable climate. Practical experience shows that the presence of malaria in southern California is a positive detriment to most places there. The sumptuous hotels and crowded, tawdry resorts of that region are not the most favorable places for patients.

Sunny sea climates, such as the better parts of Florida, are excellent. It is the comparative equability that recommends that region, and not its latitude; for New Orleans and other cities in the South show about as large a percentage of deaths from "consumption" as is recorded in Boston and other northern cities. Florida is, in certain portions, too moist for some cases. The more one remains in the open air, and the more simply one lives, the better as regards freedom from this disease. Overcrowding in cities, and the indoor life necessitated by severe climates, are unhealthful. The reasons for this are given in the chapter on infectious diseases.

Sea climates are to be chosen only when *dry* as well as sunny, and in this respect some places are obviously much better than others. Orotava, on the island of Teneriffe, justly enjoys, like some of the islands of Polynesia, a high reputation as a climate resort. Long ocean voyages, where the patient can be comfortable, and especially where the ship does not enter the hottest tropics, are very valuable and may be the means of inducing a complete cure even where the case has advanced to the stage of cavity-formation. The interesting and varied sea-trip to California, by way of the Isthmus of Panama, is much better than the all-rail route for those going from one side of North America to the other, provided that time is not of value.

A climate recommended for the cure of tuberculous consumption must not be a moist one, and the soil must certainly not be damp. In a very high, dry, and sunny region the disease is of very rare occurrence among the natives; yet such people are quite liable to perish from consumption if they be removed to close quarters in less favored regions. North Africa offers places—such as, for example, Biskra and Thebes (but not Cairo)—where the most healthful conditions of desert climate can be found. Not only lung disorders, but also chronic rheumatic troubles improve in dry lowland deserts. Our desert regions do not offer the facilities for diversion and comfort that are to be had in northern Africa. Yet a carefully selected locality in America will furnish the desirable combination of a very interesting occupation and a dry, healthful climate.

In certain desert regions, especially along valleys, it appears that rheumatism is, like malaria, much more prevalent than elsewhere. Both these diseases must be guarded against. Where dry alkali plains are used for grazing great herds, it is common to have irritation of the mucous membranes of the eye and breathing organs result from the unpleasant dust.

In the interior of the United States, great altitude has, as elsewhere over the world, a notable influence on climate. This has been explained in the previous pages. In the great high plains of the western half of our country, the long distance from the ocean causes a dryness that mere altitude does not produce. Thus, New Mexico and the regions lying north and northwest of it are dryer than the higher districts of Switzerland. This dryness, the clear sky, and pure air give a valuable remedial quality to most of the habitable regions lying for a thousand miles east of the Rocky Mountains, although the fluctuations of the temperature incident to the altitude (usually of a mile or more above sea-level) are very evident. A residence in the elevated regions of the western half of the United States seems in general very desirable for people who have slight tuberculous disease, or seem liable to develop it.

Long practical observation proves the value of highlands in general for the climatic treatment of consumption. The table-land of Mexico must be included among the regions having a favored climate. Patients that are in the *early stages* of the disease, *without fever*, and *in whom the progress of the lung degeneration is not active*, are usually *most fitted for high mountain and upland residence.*

Such tonic climates are beneficial in cases also of "fibroid phthisis" that are not very far advanced, and in such diseases as pleurisy and pneumonia, that were originally acute, yet which linger along without the usual recovery. They improve on removal from the lowlands to an elevated climate, if the inflammatory condition has already sufficiently subsided. Ocean climates are for these cases less satisfactory.

Cases with considerable fever and wasting, and those that do not respond to other treatment, should not be promised a cure, or even relief, through removal to a higher altitude. Nor should cases needing sedative treatment be sent to mountains. These, like the more rapid cases of "scrofulous pneumonia," are better off in an ocean climate if they are to leave their homes at all. An ocean voyage is more suitable for them than removal to the mountains if, on the fullest consideration and consultation, any change seems advisable. The privations of the voyage and the discomforts of stormy weather are trying to most cases; and, although valuable for some invalids, an ocean voyage may for others hasten the fatal ending.

Where the **throat** or **bowels** are **ulcerated**, a consumptive case should remain at home. The same may be said of active and steadily advancing softening of the lungs. While chronic bronchial catarrhs are best off in sea climates, a copious bronchial catarrh, considered as such, is most satisfactorily treated in a dry and elevated region. Such diseases as emphysema or bronchiectasis should not be treated by sending them to high altitudes.

The climate of southern California does not appear to be suitable in general for bronchial disorders with free expectoration, although cases of dry, hacking cough appear to do well there. San Antonio, Texas, at an altitude of 675 feet above sea-level, is a favorably located place for cases that should avoid high altitudes. Yet its hotel accommodations are hardly equal to those of New Mexico, Colorado, and Pacific coast resorts.

High altitudes do not necessarily provoke hemorrhage from the lungs. The rarefied air is there apt to cause the blood to seek the capillaries of the skin and other body surfaces rather than those of the lungs. This is proven by common observation. The author has known cases of beginning consumption, that had hemorrhages while in northern Minnesota, at an altitude of about 1,200 feet, yet showed a decided improvement on changing the residence to the City of Mexico, 7,432 feet above sea-level.

The rarefied, dry air of high inland regions seems very destructive to the vitality of the bacillus of tuberculosis. Even in the most crowded and squalid populations of Mexican uplands and the elevated tropical Andean cities, the absence of the various tuberculous and " scrofulous " disorders impresses a foreigner who visits the hospitals of those places. Not only is this a most valuable feature of elevated regions, but also the rarefied air stimulates the lungs to increased movement. The chest is thus afforded a sort of special gymnastics, as it were, and this action is deemed of considerable curative value. This is very beneficial for persons whose lungs and chests are imperfectly developed, and for those having spasmodic asthma, not accompanied with much emphysema.

All the cases for which high altitudes are suited should at least be capable of gentle exercise out-of-doors, and should have some constant occupation that involves a considerable amount of open-air exercise. Hotel life is generally very undesirable, and those invalids are best off who can adapt themselves to simple living. The sleeping-rooms should face the south, there should be facilities for warming, and at night fresh air should not be excluded.

Heart-disease patients having an organic defect or feeble circulation are *not to be sent to high altitudes.* The same may be said of all feeble and aged persons having a lung trouble of any sort. They should not seek an upland residence. Any nervous disease or neurosis is usually better away from high altitudes. This is meant to include irritable, excitable, sleepless cases. An oceanic climate is generally preferable for them.

All general diseases that are at all advanced, and especially diseases of the liver and kidneys, render a resort to a region of high altitude undesirable. The same may be said of rheumatism and gout. While catarrhal troubles associated with tuberculosis are not to be directed to elevated regions, an ordinary gastro-intestinal catarrh with chronic diarrhœa may become greatly improved or even cured after a brief residence in a cool and dry mountain region.

Altitudes of Western Routes

As it is at times important to know how high levels our railways reach in crossing the continent, it seems well to give a few figures. Thereby a case of fatty heart and great debility, or any other case for which a high altitude appears very undesirable or dangerous, can be directed to seek the best route. The all-rail route to the City of Mexico is amid highlands after New Mexico or southwestern Texas is entered. In summer these are the only healthful routes to be taken. Of the railways, the Mexican Central is the best, and does not have to go as high as some others. The route by way of the Isthmus of Panama from the Atlantic to the Pacific oceans is, in cold weather, a very pleasant one. In winter, one can safely reach Mexico by water. In South America, much higher levels are reached by railways than in North America.

The Canadian Pacific, like all but two of the transcontinental railways in the United States, crosses the great mountain ridges of the West at an altitude of over a mile above sea-level. The Colorado roads are highest of all, reaching a level of nearly 10,000 feet. The Union Pacific, in thirty-three miles, rises (or descends) more than 2,200 feet. Its highest altitude is 8,247 feet. The Atchison road summit is at a level of 7,622 feet. The Great Northern and the Southern Pacific roads reach an altitude of nearly a mile above sea-level. The latter is 5,082 feet high at a place in Texas 208 miles east of El Paso. Westward from the Rio Grande its highest level is 4,614 feet. It also descends in one place to a distance of 263 feet below sea-level. This route, then (with or without the Texas Pacific), has slightly lower altitudes than the northern routes. The latter are, however, much more agreeable in summer.

Winter Pleasure Travel

For the luxurious who seek to avoid the severity of the northern winter, the southern hemisphere, the lands south of the Mediterranean, and regions near the Red Sea and Indian Ocean, offer very attractive climates as well as the pleasures (and inconveniences) of travel. The islands of the Pacific and Atlantic oceans are very accessible nowadays, and Cuba is very pleasant at a time when the Atlantic coast to the northward is very bleak.

Absolute humidity is an important climatic factor to be considered in choosing a winter residence. Moist places are not usually desirable. Mexico, Arizona, New Mexico, and Texas offer pleasanter winter climates than the regions to the northward. In speaking of temperatures, mention was made of the equability of the climate at Nice.

With it, San Remo should be included as a pleasanter resort. Northern Africa has a still more delightful climate. Florida affords a desirable winter resort; so also various dry places in Georgia and the Carolinas, although inferior to the Mediterranean coast (especially the African). As will be seen by reference to the table on page 22, considerable rain falls in Florida, but more in summer than in winter. Mexico and Egypt are very dusty in the winter, yet the pure air and abundant sunlight there make the organic matter of dust less harmful than in the northern cities. It is not generally realized that Mexico City is most delightful in summer, because of the rain which then lays the dust. Winter resorts often lack facilities for providing sufficient artificial heat in case of unusually severe weather.

Vacations and Camping Out

For those who wish to utilize a brief vacation so as to derive the fullest advantage from a health-restoring and re-creative point of view, it is hardly necessary to intimate that the freer of conventionalities the life is, and the less one is fettered by the dictates of fashionable society, the better. Flannels and serviceable light clothes are desirable.

If camping out, the site should be dry and not have water near the surface. A location away from industries or residences is best, and the use of many fine wild sites can be had for the asking. A rather barren soil is in general preferable. Moist river bottoms and valleys are not to be chosen for camping grounds. It is safer to be in a boat upon the water of a stream or lake than on damp, low ground near it, or near which marshes lie.

The northern and inland regions are dryer than those further to the south and on the coast. The air of the coast districts south of the Hudson River has much more moisture than is found in Maine, and hence Maine is preferable to the regions south of it, and especially to those further south than New England. The prevailing winds should be considered in selecting a summer resting place. These winds being usually from the south and west, a place on our Atlantic coast is best located when it lies to the northeast of a large sheet of water. The hot winds are thereby tempered.

North of Cape Cod the ocean, even in summer, is too cool for comfortable sea-bathing, especially if the stay in the water be prolonged. New Jersey and the regions south and southwest of it are apt to be very warm in summer. There, as also further to the north and east, sandy districts, such as Long Island, may be much hotter in summer than places where vegetation is growing.

The lower St. Lawrence Valley is much cooler than that part of Canada near the great lakes. The regions near Lake Superior are much cooler than those upon the other great lakes, and the shores of Lake Erie may be very uncomfortable from the heat. The mountains of the great Appalachian chain furnish cool and beautiful summer resorts. The Green Mountains of Vermont, and the White Mountains of New Hampshire are agreeable and healthful at an altitude of even less than 1,500 feet. As one goes further to the southwest, a higher altitude must be sought for comfort. In the Blue Ridge, south of Pennsylvania, places at an altitude of 2,000 feet may be very hot if in valleys. There, and further south, a summer resort should be at least 2,500 feet above the sea-level, and not shut in by ridges or peaks. Wherever one goes, it is important to see that the *water supply* is very free from chances of contamination. If the vacation must be limited to a few days, the later in the summer one takes it the better.

CLOTHING AND PROTECTION OF THE BODY

By the perfection of its intricate mechanism, the human body is in health kept at very nearly the average temperature of 98.6° F. The body-heat is always increased by muscular activity. An excess of food tends also to raise somewhat the temperature of the body. Furthermore, the amount of actual heat produced is increased directly and indirectly under the influence of cold about us. On the other hand, the heat-production is lessened under the influence of surrounding warmth and when by means of clothing the body is kept warm.

Less than one-fiftieth part of the heat produced within the human system is required for warming the food and drink after they enter the mouth. Nearly ten times as much more is used up for warming the air that we take into our lungs and for the work of vaporizing moisture from the large surface of the lung tissue,—which moisture goes out of the lungs with the air exhaled. The skin, however, affords the chief means of relieving the system of its surplus heat. More than five-sixths of the heat produced by the body is given off from its skin surfaces.

This heat is given off from the skin by (1) radiation, (2) conduction, (3) evaporation of moisture. All of these processes may be operative at the same time. Variations in their activity are largely affected by the temperature and density of the air, by its degree of moisture and its amount of movement. The clothing exerts also a great influence upon the quantity of heat that escapes through the skin.

With the evaporation of a quart of water from the skin the body loses more than one-fourth of the average surplus heat that it has to give off in a day. When the air is rarefied and also when it is warm, dry and in motion, the daily evaporation of moisture from the skin is considerably more than a quart in amount. The quantity of heat that is given off in the process of vaporizing this moisture may be very great. Yet in cold weather the evaporation of water from the skin does not count for much. When the air is warm, still and very moist, not very much heat is lost by this process. The water that then comes out of the sweat-glands remains condensed upon the skin as "sweat."

Radiation is proportionately greater from a small body than from a large one, and this process acts by warming cold objects with which we are in contact. Much heat is thereby lost when we are near cold walls or are in contact with cold furniture, cold beds, chilly bed-clothing, etc. When the air is very moist, and evaporation is ineffective, radiation becomes correspondingly active and aids the process of conduction to relieve the body of much heat. Conduction is operative when the air is actively in motion and when it is either hotter or colder than the skin. In strong, cold winds and by the use of fans, etc., conduction causes much heat to be lost from the unprotected skin. Both conduction and the less important factor, radiation, are usually most active in proportion to the coldness of the air; although the air is not directly warmed to any extent by radiant heat.

In the most favored mild climates, these natural regulative processes render it possible for human beings to exist without any clothing. In cold weather, however, clothing is indispensable. Otherwise a great amount of heat is lost. Loose clothing also serves somewhat to protect us from the sun's heat. The light-rays of the sun tend to be absorbed and given off as heat rays, thus augmenting the discomfort of the body in warm weather. It is well always to remember that black cloth, whatever the material, absorbs more than twice as much heat as cloth that is white or of a pale yellow. In summer, these latter as well as the grays and other lighter shades of clothing material are, for these reasons, to be preferred to blue or black fabrics.

Screens of various kinds that intercept, or ward off from the body, the direct and reflected heat of the sun are of evident utility in hot weather. Hats worn at such times should be light in both weight and color and so arranged as to allow circulation of air over the head. It may here incidentally be stated that the hard and close-fitting rims of the ordinary hats that men wear are not so healthful for the scalp as are the looser ones and those which do not to any extent compress the skin and the vessels and nerves beneath.

For clothing material, leather (and rubber), wool, silk, linen and cotton tissues are most commonly employed. As regards the conduction of heat through dry clothes, it in reality makes comparatively little difference (except for the reason to be given in the next paragraph) whether woollen or any other of the usual fabrics be chosen. When it is desired to prevent loss of warmth, the main consideration is the thickness of the clothing and the amount of air that a given weight of clothing contains between its fibres and layers. The more loosely a given weight of material is woven and arranged and the more air present in the tissues, the better does the fabric serve the purpose of preventing escape of warmth from the body. Motionless air is a poor conductor of heat. Hence extra layers of clothing (by adding just so many layers of air) cause more warmth to be saved to the body. So, too, bed-clothing that is light and "downy" is warmer than when the same amount of material is woven into a covering (of the same size) that is comparatively dense and thin.

Woollen tissues have, usually, a certain advantage over cotton and linen goods in these above-indicated qualities. The great elasticity of wool causes cloth that is made of it to possess much lightness and porosity, and to maintain this even when moistened. Yet worn-out and unclean garments, of any material, are hygienically inferior to fresher and cleaner apparel; for they have lost their original elasticity, have their air-spaces considerably filled up, and any uncleanliness that they may have is in itself objectionable.

Woollen underwear that has been washed a number of times (especially if the washing have been thorough and in very hot water) shrinks and "felts up" with splitting of the wool fibres. Ordinary flannel is made of the shorter and more curly wools. The protruding fibres of such rough flannel and other woollen underclothing that has been changed by washing may be so irritant to certain skins as to prevent some people from wearing any woollen fabrics next to the skin. "Merino" or "part-woollen" underwear then usually suffices. Many persons find such goods preferable to woollen garments. These articles made partly of cotton and partly of wool can take up nearly nine-tenths as much water as the various kinds of proprietary "natural wool" underwear are capable of absorbing, and are much less costly. "Shoddy" goods are undesirable. Processes of rendering cotton fabrics more like flannel are employed in Germany with very good results ; but they do not appear to have become known here to any extent.

Clothes that fit very tightly are defective because they diminish the air-spaces that are present with rather loose clothing and which—being valuable non-conductors —serve to guard the body against cold. Yet, on the other hand, the winter clothing should not be exceedingly loose ; for such a condition favors a rapid loss of warmth by promoting the very free circulation of air within, as well as the entrance of the chilling blasts of air from outside. When the air in contact with the skin or between and in layers of clothes is warmed, it tends to rise and can be driven out completely by cold air entering inside of loose garments. Very long dresses and trousers are objectionable, as they catch and retain much unclean dirt. Thereby disease germs and other filth may be carried into clean houses and cause disease to be increased.

The outside surface of the outer garment (if worn chiefly for warmth) should be closely woven and firm (as it is when made of long and firm wool), however "fluffy" and lightly woven the inner and lining layers may be. This is apart from any consideration of the greater cleanliness of very smooth surfaces. The lamb's-skin coats of various pastoral races, who wear the fleece inside and the smooth inner-skin surface on the outside, are very sensible winter garments. Fur garments are hygienically best when made thus, with the fur toward the body. The leathern or hard cloth "pea-jacket" worn by people exposed to fiercely cold winds cannot easily be improved upon. Lined with some light woollen stuff, such as flannel (which is remarkably permeable to the wind), the outside (of smooth leather) offers nearly one hundred times as much resistance to the wind as this flannel does.

An excess of clothing is to be avoided, as it promotes perspiration by developing a warm layer of air next to the skin. Any dry underclothing can, by reason of its hygroscopic property, absorb a small amount of perspiration. New, clean, light and dry wool tissue, such as flannel, can take up considerably more than its own weight of water into the air-spaces of the fabric. Cotton, linen and silk are inferior in this respect. This fact renders woollen undergarments preferable to those made of the other substances, provided that the wearer's skin is not irritated by wool. Wool has the further advantage that it does not tend to cool the skin so much as silk, linen or cotton, all of which become inelastic on moistening, and also give off their absorbed water more rapidly than wool does. Thus linen, and to a less degree cotton or silk, can cause at times an unhealthful and uncomfortable cooling of the skin. In weather that is uniformly very hot, cotton cloth is to be preferred, as being a thinner fabric than woollen goods, and also because cotton is a better conductor of heat and vaporizes water more rapidly.

When the wearer is exposed to rain or moist air, so that the clothing is liable to become wet and to remain so, woollen clothing wards off the danger of "catching cold" better than garments made of cotton, linen or silk fabrics. Yet all moist clothing (which of course includes foot-wear) should be removed and dry garments substituted as promptly as possible. Moist clothes are chilling when the air is cooler than the body, because, in the first place, they conduct off heat from the body much faster than when they are dry. Secondly, the evaporation of the water contained in wet clothes produces cold. In these respects, woollen garments when wetted are the least dangerous to the health.

To keep rain and excessive moisture of the air from penetrating into our clothes, **waterproof** outer garments are much used. If wholly impervious to moisture and air, such waterproof articles not only keep out moisture and cold, but they also prevent any of the perspiration of the body from passing out as it does through all loose and permeable cloths. So this body-moisture tends to condense as water on the inside of the waterproof overgarments. Rubber cloth (which includes "Mackintosh" fabric) is less satisfactory than oil-cloth or paraffined cloth. Better than these are the various processes that allow air to circulate through cloth, yet make the texture waterproof. These processes rely upon impregnation of the cloth with alum combined with soda-soaps, both added separately. Others treat woollen goods, for instance, with alum, lead acetate, and gelatine.

When rubber boots are worn, loose porous slippers or soles should be inside. These, as well as the socks, should be removed as promptly as possible after the necessary use. The inevitable softening of the feet (in the "vapor-bath" produced in the rubber boot by the perspiration) can be lessened somewhat by the use of a drying-powder dusted upon the feet before drawing on the boots. A powder made of one part of zinc oxide or talc to two or three parts of starch, or one such as is indicated on page 50, may be of value here. Despite their obvious defects, india-rubber overshoes prevent many a "cold." "Arctic" overshoes are an indispensable aid to health during our winter weather. Whenever leather is made absolutely waterproof it has similar defects to rubber in so far as the weakening effect upon **the skin of the feet is** concerned. Enamelled leather has lost much of its permeability to air, and is therefore not as healthful as ordinary unvarnished leather. Russet leather and canvas are good for shoes, as they permit considerable air to pass through their substance.

Persons suffering from cold feet and chilblains in winter find some relief from using cloth shoes, and by changing any shoes several times during the day. The foot-wear should also be allowed to lie in dry air and lose the moisture derived from the feet. Shoes should be cleaned on the inside at times as well as on the outside. The dirt of our streets is liable to contain many harmful bacteria. Hence shoes ought to be carefully wiped before the wearer, coming from the street, enters a house. Long-legged boots impair the ventilation of the feet. Better are laced boots and brogans (fashionably termed "Bluchers"). Very low shoes are better still. In dry, moderate winter weather, these are sufficient, at least for men; but cloth overgaiters can be added for warmth if desired. The practical value of existing devices for ventilating the foot and shoe, through holes in the bottom of the sole and in the back of the heel, has not yet been demonstrated.

Shoe-heels should be broad and low. The front edge of the heel may reach a little further forward on the outside than on the inside; but in no case should it be placed so far forward as to cause pressure upon the arch of the healthy foot. The toes of shoes, and of stockings also, should be broad. Neither children nor others should wear shoes, or even moccasins, that are not "rights and lefts." This is because the inside of the foot is very differently shaped from the outside. Useful and healthful shoes should conform to the actual anatomy of the foot. A disproportionately small foot is not beautiful.

If an outline tracing of a wholly natural human foot be made by having the naked foot upon a sheet of paper and then drawing a pencil around the outside of the foot, it will be seen that the toes are not cramped and pressed in together as when one has always worn ill-fitting and narrow-toed shoes. The second toe may be as long as the great toe or even longer. The leading anatomical authorities and great artists of all times have usually represented it so. The great toe ought to point straight forward, and no very marked inward projection should exist on the inside edge of the foot at the joint of the great toe. If a line be drawn from the middle of the heel through the centre of the great toe (Meyer's line, the dotted line in Fig. 7), this line is nearly parallel with the inside and front part of the healthy, natural foot. Most practically important is the fact that this line corresponds with the highest part of the instep and arch of the foot (*c*, Fig. 8).

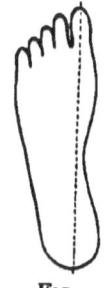

FIG. 7.

The highest portion of the upper-leather of a shoe, at the part where it covers the instep, should therefore be toward the inside of the instep and well inside of the middle line of the foot. The propriety of this is seen by considering Fig. 8, which represents a cross-section of a normal foot at the region of the instep. (This section is made through the cuboid and the three cuneiform bones. It is on a much larger scale than Figs. 7, 9 and 10.) Thus it is clear that the foot is high on the inside and much lower and thinner on the outside. The lasts upon which shoes are made, should conform to all of these anatomical features.

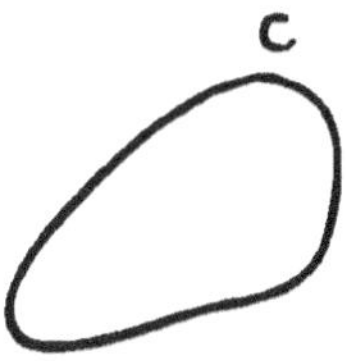

FIG. 8.

Walking-shoes should have broad toes. Fig. 9 represents the sole of a shoe which is a compromise between the ungainly square-toed shapes and the unhealthful, pointed styles. It proves a serviceable shape for constant use. If made straighter on the inside and broader at the toes and

FIG. 9.

also at the outside of the instep, that would be a little better. In any case, the inside should be quite straight. A projection on the side to accommodate a slight bunion is undesirable as tending to aggravate the evil. The shoe should be longer than the foot by at least half the breadth of the great toe. If a pointed shoe be desired to meet the often-recurring demands of fashion, the shoe must be longer and the point should (for a normal foot) be to the inside of the middle line of the foot. The inside is therefore rather straight, however curved the outside. (See Fig. 10.)

Fig. 10.

The upper and outer part of the shoe leather should not press upon the little toe with any force. Otherwise corns are produced. This tendency is lessened and the shoe otherwise improved when the last is made fairly thick in front and raised somewhat at the end so that the last, in its forward part, touches the ground only at the portion corresponding to the ball of the foot. At the region of the ball of the foot, the sole of the last should not curve very much from side to side, although—as just said—the sole ought to curve from front to rear. At the arch of the foot, it may curve a great deal; yet the outside must there be low. Walking-shoes should have thick soles as well as low heels. Children ought to have their shoes shaped on the above-indicated principles. Improper foot-wear is very bad for their feet.

To prevent foot-sweat and bad odors (from decomposing substances on the skin of the feet and on the stockings and shoes), the feet ought to be frequently washed and not over-warmly clothed. The stockings need to be changed very often, as they rapidly take up much decomposable matter. For lessening foot-sweat, one may dust on freely a powder made of one part of salicylic acid, thirty parts of alum (or zinc oxide) and seventy parts of talc powder. For softening corns and calluses, alkaline solutions (such as one part of caustic potash to twenty of water) are to be used.

Clothing should not be tight in any part. Hard, tight hat-bands, tight collars, belts or corsets and constricting garters not only restrict the circulation of air next to the skin, but also more or less seriously interfere with free local circulation of blood. A tight collar is conspicuously bad in this respect; for it tends to impede the flow of the venous blood. Various eye and brain troubles are considered by experts to be caused and aggravated by tight neck-bands. Tight garments are mentioned on page 45.

Corsets restrict the natural respiration and impair the tone of the abdominal muscles, which then inevitably become weakened. Thereby the tendency of this part of the body to lay on fat is favored. By weakening the abdominal wall and driving some organs downward (as well as compressing and forcing others upward) corsets cause a protruding and unsightly deformity of the parts of the body below the waist and destroy the fine outlines of the hips. The earlier in life that corsets are adopted and the tighter they are worn, the more do they prove harmful and disfiguring. Corsets destroy the suppleness and grace of the body, besides impairing the health. Where a support for the abdomen is needed, as for weakly and diseased women, one of the various bandages, that hold the parts up instead of pressing them downward, is preferable to a corset. In case of unduly large breasts, corsets (when suitably made) can give some support by resting on the hips.

Poisonous colors are at times used in cloth as in other fabrics. Chrome yellow and other forms of lead sometimes cause clothing to be poisonous. Arsenic is the most commonly present of the harmful substances that cause underwear to be irritant. Skin inflammations may thus result from the use of red and other shades of colored stockings and other improperly dyed clothing that is worn next to the skin. The colors may be called aniline dyes; but arsenic is, in most of the harmful cases, used (in the form of arsenious acid as a reducing agent) in their preparation, or arsenic enters as an ingredient of the "mordant" employed to "fix" these aniline colors into vegetable fabrics. Arsenic occurs in many colored prints and ginghams.

Light muslin and other goods can be made so fireproof that they will not flame up on contact with gas or other flame to endanger the life of the wearer. The process need not be poisonous, although it may lessen the durability of the goods. The light, easily-burning cloth is washed, then soaked in a solution of alum, ammoniac chloride, borax or other salts. Some particularly recommend for this purpose a solution of tungstate-of-soda (one part to five or more parts of water).

Low-necked dresses are not healthful, for the upper part of the chest needs to be covered. Children require clothing that is warm and protects every part. The knees ought especially to be covered at all times. If they be left bare in cool weather, such exposure is very harmful. The nose and the ears need protection against the cold of our northern winter.

Outer clothing should frequently be shaken and beaten in the open air and away from windows, kitchens and living rooms. This method of cleaning is better than the use of whisk-brooms and brushes; for brushes drive some of the dirt (and possible accompanying bacteria of disease) into the fabric. Uniform and consistent cleanliness is a most valuable aid to the highest health. This is explained in the chapter on Infectious Diseases. Here it is to be said that all articles of clothing ought to be kept scrupulously clean. The cast-off cell secretions and excretions of the skin tend to decompose, give off odors and produce irritant substances. On the delicate skin of babes any unclean clothing is very irritant.

The clothes, therefore, should not only be washed, but also all chemicals used, even if pure soda and soap, should be rinsed out with pure water. Greasy secretions from the skin are readily absorbed by underwear; and, for their cleansing, alkalies are used such as soap, ammonia and washing soda. Water that is boiling, or even very hot, shrinks wool; yet such hot water or steam is the best reliance for disinfecting all clothing that has been exposed to infection. The clothing of those suffering from typhoid fever, cholera, tuberculosis, scarlet-fever or any " catching " diseases must be disinfected. See chapters on Infectious Diseases and Disinfection. White underclothing and washable garments are best for nurses and invalids in such diseases.

Bedsteads are best when without curtains or drapery. They ought to be simply made. Those of brass or iron are preferable to wooden ones. The cumbersome and uncleanly bedroom furniture of a few years ago is properly yielding place to simpler and more useful patterns that are smoother and afford fewer places for harmful dirt (or vermin) to remain in, hidden from the reach of the average cleansing. The space under bedsteads should be clear, and nothing should be there to obstruct thorough cleansing and the free circulation of air. Folding beds are defective in not corresponding to these requirements, and because they rarely have the bed-clothes sufficiently well aired.

Mattresses and pillows are best and most elastic when made of steamed and curled hair, which should be freshened and cleansed from time to time. If economy be necessary, they may be thin with some one of the best recent patterns of spring-beds or woven-wire mattresses beneath. Wool is better for mattresses than vegetable substances. For convenience in airing and changing it about, the mattress may be made in two or three equal-sized and interchangeable parts by means of cross-divisions. Dr.

Hills, of Harvard, finds that a certain red-striped ticking, extensively used for mattress-covering, contains much arsenic. The most recent improvements in air mattresses make them serviceable for invalids and delicate people when travelling amid unusual discomforts. They are not as good for general use as clean hair mattresses. They have the merit of being easily disinfected.

If feather beds be used for infants, the feeble and aged, or for others in our extremest winter weather, these beds should be aired well for more than an hour every day, and this in the sunlight if possible. Feather beds allow less waste of heat by radiation and by the evaporation of moisture. Hence they are comfortable in the extremest cold. Yet, in the end they weaken the skin by keeping it too warm.

Feather pillows are much less self-ventilating and elastic than hair pillows. Pillows should not be thin, nor very high. In the ordinary sleeping position of lying upon the side, the pillow should not be higher than suffices to keep the spine perfectly straight. If one lies on the breast with the arm thrown behind the body, no pillow is needed.

All beds and bed-clothing should be well aired before the beds are made up after using. Damp bedding is unhealthful. In cold weather the chill of the bed-clothes in a cold room should be lessened for an invalid or delicate person by the use of such things as jugs or rubber bottles filled with warm water. If beds have been used by invalids having infectious diseases, disinfection should be compulsory. Steam, if practicable, is the best means to employ for disinfection. Sprinkling the bed and bedding with patent or proprietary disinfectants is, like all other means, inferior to steaming.

Bed-clothing should be of light weight. As explained on page 44, a given weight of wool protects the body better against cold if made into two lightly woven thin blankets rather than one heavy one. It is in all cases well that the outer surface of the bed-clothing be smooth. Besides allowing less dirt to sift in, this lessens loss of warmth from the conducting away of air in cold weather. If eider-down coverlets be used, they should be of unusually good quality, and side-fastenings or other means should be attached for so keeping them in place that restless sleepers cannot toss these coverings off and thus chill the body. Some people, who in waking hours wear by choice rather scanty clothing, are apt to suffer if the bed-clothing be insufficient.

BATHING AND PERSONAL HYGIENE

Our clothes, and especially the customary close foot-wear, are a restraint upon the healthy processes of the naked skin, and obstruct the natural casting off and removal of the dead outer layers together with what passes out of the pores. Thereby these decomposable excretory products are kept longer upon and near the skin than would be the case under proper natural conditions. This is particularly so with the feet. The stocking, being between the skin and the shoe, absorbs and rubs off a portion of the secretions and waste such as is given off constantly from all skin surfaces. If the stockings or socks be not changed very often, part of the organic and other "dirt" enters into and remains upon the material of the shoes. More, however, lingers upon the skin. Hence the skin, especially of the feet, should be often washed ; for the unclean excretory products upon it can harbor and favor the development of bacteria of various sorts. When the skin is cleansed, clean underwear should at once be put on, for that recently worn has skin dirt upon it.

The skin can be cleansed to a certain extent by rubbing and scraping it with cloths or other appliances, whether dry or moistened (with water, alcohol, ammonia-water, etc.). If it be very greasy, gently rubbing it with benzine (on cotton) cleanses it very thoroughly, yet such means are not to be recommended for general use. Scales are softened by oil, and can then be more readily removed.

Baths of clean water are the most efficient means of cleaning the skin. Tub-baths of warm water are the most effective for this purpose, as the agreeable temperature of the water allows one to remain in the bath for some time. Thus the outer cells of the skin are loosened and gently removed. As the skin is usually greasy, the water is enabled to take off this outer waste skin with the other " dirt " better when an alkali is used. So we can add a little sal-soda or other alkali to the water, especially if that be "hard." It is customary to wash the skin with the use of alkalies combined with fat so as to make soap. In hard soap, soda is the alkali ; for soft soaps, potash is used.

Soaps almost invariably contain an excess of alkali. For ordinary skins in health, this is very proper. When the skin is inflamed or very sensitive, this excess of alkali is a defect. At such times we prefer a soap that is neutral ; that is, one in which the fat is in such abundance as to take up all of the alkali. Only a few makers supply these. The statement of the manufacturer is not often a reliable guide as to the purity of a soap. To test for alkalinity we take a weak solution of the soap or soaps, as well as one of a standard soap of good quality. The same weight of each is taken and dissolved in the same amount of water. Testtubes holding these different soap-solutions are arranged side by side in a rack. Then, of a *phenolphtalein* solution (one part in three hundred parts of alcohol) one or two drops are added to each of the solutions. If a little free alkali be present, a rose tinge arises at once. If the alkali be more abundant, a deeper red results. In pure water, or in a neutral or acid solution, this phenolphtalein remains colorless. Litmus paper is inferior to this.

Soaps that are colored are not usually desirable. Perfumed soaps are not necessarily any better than those that are odorless, and may be irritant. Soaps made of lighter fats, such as, for instance, cotton-seed oil, float upon the water of the bath. Soaps which are popular in a region are fairly good for use there. A much-advertised kind is not necessarily better than others. Conspicuous " puffing " has made certain imported soaps sell very widely, although in the land whence these come they have only an ordinary standing among competent specialists. Soft soap of good quality may be used when a tough skin is very dirty, or when scales are to be removed from portions of the body where there is no inflammation. Where the skin is irritated and inflamed, as, for example, in eczema, soap and water must be used very cautiously if at all. Very rough towels are not needed for drying the skin. The delicate skin of babes must not be washed too often or rubbed at all vigorously. All soap should be rinsed from the skin by the use of pure water. Those who have very dry skins do not need the soaps and the abundant washings that are proper for greasy skins. When the skin is very dry and brash after a bath, a gentle rubbing with oil may be useful. All bath water should be clean and pure.

While the use of soap and a warm tub-bath or swimming in comfortably warm water is the best means for cleansing the skin, shower baths with separate rooms for each individual are easier and more economical to use in public baths. For the philanthropic, who wish to aid the cause of good health and cleanliness, an excellent work is the introduction of such baths among the most unclean of the tenement-house population of cities. Of late the idea has been adopted from Germany by various charities, and among others by the New York Society for Improving the Condition of the Poor. This society has built an attractive bath-house at No. 9 Centre Market Place, New York City. Five cents is the charge to each individual using the bath for twenty minutes. The results are very satisfactory. The amount of water used there for each shower bath is forty gallons, which is ten gallons more than is considered a suitable amount for an ordinary tub-bath. It is not necessary to use chemical disinfectants for the towels, since steam is present in such places, and, as will be found explained later in this book, steam or very hot water constitutes the best of all disinfectants. Such baths can be arranged more economically than the one just cited and yet be very effective. It is important that such charities be open for cleansing filthy vagrants, and that a steam-jacket kettle or other appliance be at hand for disinfecting their clothing. Such people need cleansing, and the health of our populations requires that "the great unwashed," their clothes, and the places where they lodge be cleaned at times.

EFFECTS OF VARIOUS BATHS

Baths that have a temperature anywhere from 92° F. to 99° F. are spoken of as *warm*. Above that, they are classed as *hot*. When the temperature of the water is below 68° F., the bath is called *cold*. Many physicians, especially English ones, regard that a warm tub-bath makes one liable to take cold unless such bath be immediately followed by a cold douche. The Japanese and some people among us use very hot baths with extreme satisfaction and apparent good results. Excessive warm bathing weakens the skin.

Cold bathing, especially when indiscriminately advised, often does more harm than good. The robust can stand it, although occasionally it causes skin disease among them. The torpid are seemingly invigorated by its momentary stimulus, at least for the time being. For the feeble, however, cold bathing may be very harmful. In heart disease of any consequence it is not to be permitted. For such cases the temperature of the water used should be near that of the body and not above 98.5° F. A bluish appearance of the skin after cold baths indicates that these should be discontinued. The very young or very old, the weakly, and people with organic disease of any kind must use cold baths very cautiously if at all. Such baths are not suited for menstruating or pregnant women, and should not be taken when the stomach is full.

A cold bath, taken rapidly by a person in good average health, causes at first a chilly sensation. This is speedily followed by a brief warmth and glow of the skin, because the small blood-vessels of the skin are dilated from relaxation after the original stimulus of the cold. More blood, too, than usual is sent through these dilated blood-vessels because the heart is stimulated to unusual activity. At the same time, there is an increased production of heat within the body. This comes chiefly from the muscles, and is greater when the cold bath introduces at the same time the healthful exercise of swimming.

If one remain in cold water for a long time, the cold causes the blood-vessels of the skin to remain contracted (causing the skin to appear purplish), and blood is thereby driven to the inner organs and congestion of varying seriousness results. Of course, the body loses heat in cold water. The amount of this may be more than four times as much as would be lost under ordinary circumstances without the bath. In midsummer, this loss of body heat is often a healthful relief. Many also contend that cold baths are a valuable means of treating fevers. That will not be discussed here. It may be stated that cold baths are not suited for all cases.

Turkish baths are hygienically preferable to *steam baths* (called also Russian baths). In the latter, moist air is used. In the Turkish bath, the air is warm and *dry*, having a temperature of $115°$ F. and upward. In the Orient, a very much greater heat is sometimes used. This dry and hot air causes much water to pass out through the pores of the skin. After this, attendants usually knead and wash the skin. Then a cold spray or a plunge into cold water, with gentle drying of the skin, completes the essential part of the bath. Various accessories and luxurious appointments go with most public baths of this type. Certain features may be introduced that can hardly be commended as healthful.

Turkish baths cause the skin to be washed very thoroughly, both by its own copious sweat and the soap and water used. Most persons feel brighter and perhaps stronger for a while after such baths. These cause the urine to become more acid and concentrated. They also lessen the body-weight by more than a pound, since they take off water through the skin. Where the kidneys work defectively such means are of value ; but for such cases the public baths do not afford the best means of employing this hot-air treatment. A little portable apparatus, familiar in hospitals and sick-rooms, answers for invalids in kidney diseases. When organic disease of the heart or great bloodvessels exists, Turkish baths are dangerous. Some consider them valuable in cases of neuralgic and rheumatic disorders, slight bronchitis and beginning " colds." People and races that use such baths very often are apt to appear inferior to the average in " stamina " and general vitality. How much the weakness has to do with the baths, it is not easy to say.

Baths of various sorts are uselessly multiplied in variety and complexity. The "mud baths," "electric baths," and ever so many other kinds seem to be, as Dr. W. Hale White, of London. expresses it, " immensely overrated by all sorts of impudent quacks, who issue pretentious advertisements designed to attract persons to particular bathing establishments in which these quacks have a pecuniary interest."

Bath-rooms should be heated. Furnace-heat or fires are there useful for drying off the steam. Bath-rooms must be well ventilated ; and care must be taken that no gas empoison the air. This applies especially to the primitive ways of heating water by peculiar set stoves seen in some places. The walls and ceiling should be very smooth. Linoleum covering is good for the floor. If tiled, sheets of cork may be over the tiling wherever the bather is to step out of the bath. Porcelain bath-tubs are cleanly and usually durable. The largest weigh between eight hundred and one thousand pounds. Hence they are very cumbersome. They are also exceedingly expensive. Recently bath-tubs made of compressed wood-fibre have been introduced, which resemble porcelain tubs in appearance and cost much less. They have the advantage of not being cold to the touch, and weigh much less than one hundred pounds each. If only they prove durable after long trial, they are bound to become deservedly very popular.

Cosmetics produce neither health nor beauty. If used at all, they must never contain harmful substances. Lead is apt to occur in preparations for the hair, and mercury is usually present in the complexion washes so extensively advertised. These various articles often cause disease, and people should be warned against their use. Complexion depends upon pigment particles deeper in the skin than nostrums can reach. The various preparations for removing superfluous hairs are unreliable and harmful. Even the employment of the electric needle, for such purposes, in very skilful hands is not particularly satisfactory. Visible scars result from its use. Glycerine with at least one-sixth part of water added is better for the skin than when used pure. Equal parts of glycerine and yolk of egg make a soothing application.

Powder applied to the face ought to be regarded as so much dirt. In some cases it visibly injures the complexion.

By clogging the pores and drying up the skin, it can do harm. If used, the simplest—such as finely powdered starch—is the best. To keep this from injuring the skin, it is well that beforehand a slight amount of oily matter of the blandest and freshest quality be applied and then wiped off. Lanoline, fresh almond oil, sweet oil or vaseline may be used. These lessen the liability of face powder or other dirt to obstruct the openings of the sweat-ducts or fat-ducts upon the surface of the skin.

Shaving causes the hair to grow stiffer, and so is not to be advised for those who wish a fine, silky beard. Irritation from shaving comes with the use of a dull razor. Razors should be rinsed, dried and strapped immediately after using. Barbers often cause irritation of the skin. If their instruments, soap, hands, etc., are not strictly clean, skin disease may result. Dangerous erysipelas of the face occurs at times from such a cause. The microörganisms, that cause this and other diseases of the face, are destroyed by dipping the razor or other utensils for a minute in boiling water, if this be practicable. The beard, like the hair, should be kept clean. The beard ought to be washed very often. The scalp usually needs washing no oftener than every ten or fourteen days. If "dandruff" scales be present, oil or vaseline may be used before washing. Mild soap or yolk of egg may be rubbed gently upon the scalp. Then this is to be well rinsed off. "Hair-restorers" are wholly useless.

The mouth needs to be rinsed out after every meal. Babies should have their mouths rinsed with water to which a very small amount of saleratus has been added. The nipples of a nursing woman correspondingly need cleaning off with similar solutions. Bathing the nipples occasionally with weak alcohol and water is beneficial.

Teeth are liable to decay when the hard enamel coating is lost from their outside. Then, various bacteria slowly eat away the inner (organic) substance of the teeth, and acids dissolve mineral matter that is not broken away. Thus the decay of the teeth results. Injury or other cause that cracks or breaks the enamel, favors decay by removing the enamel coating. Acids have the same harmful effect. Hence the importance of rinsing the mouth after eating, especially when acids or sour fruits have been used. As alkalies neutralize acidity, there is an obvious advantage in cleaning out the mouth with water to which saleratus or other alkali has been added in small amount. Benzoic acid in solution seems to be the most effective substance for washing out the mouth and destroying the bacteria that cause decay of the teeth. One part of this may be dissolved in four parts of alcohol with addition of a slight amount of flavoring such as peppermint-oil and thymol. Of this, a teaspoonful is used in somewhat less than a wineglassful of water to cleanse around the teeth after the food has been carefully removed by soft wooden or quill toothpicks.

In cleansing the teeth, the most important thing is this removal of all particles of food away from the teeth. Soft toothpicks and threads drawn between the teeth are most useful in this respect. After meals and before going to bed, the mouth needs brushing more than in the morning. Saleratus-water is then always desirable for rinsing the teeth. Brushes must not be stiff, and are less important than the other cleansing means spoken of in this paragraph. They should neither irritate nor push up the gums. For cleansing off yellowish and other growths on the surface, a wet cotton cloth having upon it a little " prepared chalk " is valuable. A tenth part of its bulk of magnesia and also a little orris-root may be added if a more elegant dentifrice be desired. Pumice-stone is not fit for such use.

Filling is necessary for decayed teeth even in early years. The process consists in removing all the decayed bone and leaving a cavity so shaped that it will hold the filling, of whatever material that may be. Gold filling causes too tedious and painful an operation to be tolerated by all children. Various other substances then answer the purpose. Amalgam fillings are very durable and efficient. Some dentists advise that the grinding-teeth, coming in the sixth year, be removed as soon as they appear to crowd the other incoming second teeth, as otherwise the liability to decay is increased by the crowded condition of the teeth. It is well, however, to wait some time and see if the jaw do not enlarge and accommodate itself. In any case it is better that these six-year grinding-teeth (first molars) be pulled out than that the teeth be filed apart when very crowded.

Infants cut their lower two front teeth when they are not far from half a year old. Before babies are ten months old, they usually have also cut their upper four front teeth. Then the teeth appear at intervals of a few months. Before children are thirty months old, all these "milk teeth" ought to have appeared. There are twenty in the entire set. These should be pulled out early enough to prevent the permanent teeth from being twisted or badly placed. Even if the permanent teeth are somewhat irregular, they can often be easily brought into place, by use of lips, tongue and other gentle pressure, if this be enjoined upon the child very early and attended to with patience.

The permanent teeth come gradually between the sixth and the twelfth year, except that the "wisdom teeth" come a number of years later. This is the most critical period for the teeth. They should then be examined at least once in six months. If young people indulge freely in sweet things, they especially ought to be careful to rinse the mouth and clean the teeth.

The ears should be kept clean by washing as far as the outer opening of the tube leading in to the middle ear. Hard or pointed instruments should never be put inside of the ears. With the youngest children it is important to be very careful that no water enters their ears during the process of bathing or washing. The brownish "ear-wax" tends to come out of the ear without any outside assistance. The movement of the jaw-bone aids this natural process. All use of water to wash out the deep parts of the ear canal, the use of hair-pins, "ear-spoons," matches, rolled-up edges of towels, and other things introduced into the ear, tend to roll up this wax in hard masses which cannot then always get out and may totally obstruct the ear passage.

Water entering the ears, as well as all other substances or fluids introduced there, can cause inflammation and trouble, even in adults. After surf-bathing or plunging in any water, the water should be got out of the ear by means of a sidewise throwing movement of the head. For those in whom the drum-membrane between the outer and middle ear is not perfect, but has a perforation, however small, all diving or bathing that causes water to enter the ear is objectionable and may produce serious trouble within the head. Unclean water is naturally worse than clean water in this respect; yet all water is undesirable in the ears. Nose catarrhs and "cold in the head" tend to travel from the interior and back of the nose up into the ear. It is not well to blow the nose hard at such times or when the nose is filled with water after bathing. Rash and bold operations upon the tissues of the inner nose are not usually satisfactory.

Cold blasts of wind, especially when moist, tend to cause ear troubles. Pledgets of cotton-wool, however, when introduced into the ear to protect it against such influences, tend to weaken the skin if such pledgets be worn in-doors. They are not in general advisable for use in warm places. The danger of blows upon the ears is great. Such things may cause lasting deafness or worse results. Stopping the ears with thick cotton lessens the harmful effects of very loud noises and concussions.

The eyes are best cared for by attending in every way to the general health. The water used for the eyes should be very clean. If any "eye-water" be used, nothing is to be recommended that is stronger than a two per cent. solution of boracic acid (or borax) in camphor-water, to which ten per cent. or less of alcohol may be added very cautiously if it be well borne. Open-air life where the eyes are guarded from glare is better for the eyesight of children than school-work. They should not attend school before they are seven years old, unless in forward and restless cases where the home influences are not favorable. At all times care should be taken that the light is strong enough, but not too strong. The eyes of the young must then not be used upon very small objects, nor upon those which have to be held near in order for clear vision. Children should not play in dark rooms with pictures or books that require them to strain the eyes. Other aspects of this question are treated in the chapters upon Schools and upon Lighting. The young babe must not be held near a bright flame nor where it faces any strong light.

The eyesight is injured, or at any rate impaired for a while, by various causes touched upon in this book. The impropriety of having very tight collars or neck-bands and their tendency to cause eye disorders is mentioned elsewhere. (See page 51.) In general, the eyes may be said to be affected by occupations where irritation and wounding are very liable to occur, and where constant minute work has to be done with poor light. It is very rare to find a calling in which a chance may not be afforded for some injury to the eyes. Considerable discrimination is required as regards every aspect of such questions. Thus, in the matter of typewriting machines, it is regarded that the keys that are white and angular (not round) are best for the health of the worker. Lenses, to magnify the work, are useful and hence advisable for people engaged upon minute work such as, for instance, engraving, lithographing, watchmaking, fine drawing, delicate sewing and embroidery. Those who have weak eyes, or who have lost one eye, should occupy themselves with other work than these above indicated. Bookkeeping may be considered a much more suitable and less dangerous occupation for the one-eyed than any work which causes them to come into the neighborhood of machinery.

Various drugs are clearly harmful to the eyes. Not to speak of those used or abused in cases of eye trouble, quinine may be mentioned as in all probability causative of disease of the eye, in case that excessive amounts are repeatedly given. The liability of people who use alcoholic liquors extensively, to have cataracts and affections of the nerves and retina, is insisted upon by specialists. Tobacco, too, like lead-poisoning, is causative of eye disorders. It may cause color-blindness. (See chapter on Occupations for remarks on color-blindness.)

The eyes at work, and when looking at near objects, should occasionally be rested by taking them off of the work and causing them to be directed upon more distant objects. This is especially so if in order to see well one has to hold the work less than thirteen inches away from the eyes. The light must be strong enough to enable one to see objects clearly; a shade is needed to shield the eyes from the glare of bright light. Ventilation of rooms ought to be sufficient to obviate the eye-irritation that is liable to come from dust and smoke. Those to whose eyes the inevitable dust or smoke of their occupation is very irritant ought to try some other calling. Some eyes, otherwise of the strongest, are very sensitive to such influences.

In machine-shops, the foreman may attempt at once, by means of a strong electro-magnet, to remove any iron sliver that may have entered the surface of the eye. Schubert recommends a very fine and clean wire loop as better for the purpose. Before use, it should be dipped for a moment in boiling water or passed through a flame and allowed to cool. "Eye-stones" are unfit for removing bits of dirt, sand, etc., from the eye.

Defects of vision need the careful adjustment of eyeglasses. People ought not to refrain from the use of spectacles through fear of seeming aged; for, although glasses do not render the eyes perfect nor even strengthen them, the neglect to use the glasses needed for advancing years strains the accommodation and weakens the eyesight still more than would be the case if glasses were used.

Concave glasses are used to relieve near-sightedness (or *myopia*). Convex glasses are needed to relieve the far-sightedness (or *presbyopia*) which is quite apt to have begun when one has got well along in middle life. These convex glasses (used accordingly to relieve aging eyesight) must be as strong as the wearer can use without discomfort. Yet at the same time they should enable one to distinguish perfectly well such near objects as would be indistinct but for the aid of glasses. These convex glasses become more powerful when the distance between them and the eye is increased by setting them further down over the bridge of the nose and toward its tip. Yet this is not a proper expedient to employ regularly, since such adjustment means that the glasses are not strong enough. Hence stronger ones should be chosen.

With near-sightedness, on the other hand, it is best that we recommend, in all ordinary cases, the weakest (concave) glasses with which one can see well. The tendency is for weaker and weaker glasses to be needed as the wearer grows older. Near-sighted children, who in studying or at other work can without the aid of spectacles see objects thirteen or fourteen inches away, should not use glasses for seeing near objects. It is well that children under ten years of age be not allowed glasses, because the eyes may be very seriously injured when the glasses are broken in playing. The near-sighted worker should have glasses no stronger than suffice to render the work clearly visible at about eighteen inches away. The working glasses must be from two to three "dioptrics" weaker than those used for seeing to a distance. The long-distance glasses should never be used for seeing near objects. The only exception to the rule given at the beginning of this paragraph is to be made when the near-sightedness is extreme. Then an error may be made in selecting glasses that are too weak. The employment of the ordinary test-glasses must then especially be supplemented by using the ophthalmoscope as well. Yet—as Bruecke has remarked—it is rarely necessary to subject children to any other than the usual test-glass trial of the eyes. Astigmatism is recognized by testing, and calls for special glasses.

After cataract operations, the strongest convex glasses are needed, and at least two pair of spectacles are required. One pair is for handwork and reading; the other for seeing objects at a distance.

When the work is finished, for which glasses are needed, these should be taken off. Experience does not recommend those complex glasses which are cut so that in one lens they seemingly combine the advantages of glasses for seeing to a distance and also for distinguishing near work (the former being in the upper, the latter in the lower part of the same frame).

For reading or for near work, spectacles are far better than the more elegant eye-glasses that are held on the nose by means of a spring. Spring eye-glasses can, however, if desired, be used for seeing to a distance. Spectacles are more reliable because they remain fixed in an approved and adjusted position, and thereby the eye sees through the middle of the glasses if they have been properly selected in the beginning. When the glasses are "strong," especial consideration must be given to framing the spectacles so that the plane of each lens is perpendicular to the axis of vision, or as nearly so as the maker can possibly arrange them. All competent opticians understand how to adjust the optical centre. The glasses should be just far enough away from the eye-ball to keep the glass from being touched by the lashes in the moving eye-lids. Hence the "bridge" of the spectacles has to be adjusted somewhat according as the bridge of the nose is prominent or depressed.

Adjusting spectacles ought to be a business in itself. Dealers in variety goods and other articles do not usually have the special experience that is desirable for determining just what glasses are best. Certainly, the cheap spectacles and eye-glasses sold by ignorant and irresponsible people are to be avoided. Yet very high-priced spectacles are not necessarily the best. Rock-crystal is not so valuable as is sometimes represented. Whether the lenses be made of soft (crown) glass or of hard (flint) glass is not nearly so important a matter as their proper selection and the correct adjustment of the framework that holds the glasses.

Dark glasses protect the eyes from glare. Blue glass has the merit of lessening the red and yellow rays of light. Mica used in spectacles, instead of glass, protects the eyes from heat. For people handling fireworks, etc., such eye-protectors in an asbestos mask (which may be part of an entire asbestos suit) are very valuable.

PHYSICAL EXERCISE

THE ideal of human perfection must always include enough of the animal to insure that, with the finest mental capacity, there be always a strong body in sound health. Whether we reason from the teachings of the anatomical table, the laboratory and the bedside, or scan the records of all peoples from the remotest antiquity to the account of yesterday's doings, we shall find that the races which are physically strongest are invariably among the foremost. This statement requires an explanation. It needs to be emphasized that big, strong muscles constitute only a portion of what is rightly called physical strength. The term should rather embrace the healthy complex harmony of the entire system. Although fine muscles are valuable, mere muscularity is for most people anything but desirable. Even in purely physical contests of entire fairness, the most muscular bully is not at all sure to be the winner.

It must be admitted that adequate strength and quality of nerve, together with a perfect balance between all the organs of the body, are necessary to the physical excellence upon which health and success depend. The developments of our prevalent civilization tend to weaken prosperous nations by promoting indolent and enervating luxury and luxuriousness among the affluent and those who imitate them. The extreme division of labor that accompanies our industrial and commercial progress, and the artificial conditions under which the struggle for existence is carried on, cause the vast majority of the people to be employed in more or less unhealthful toil. This includes most sedentary workers, whose occupation, like that of the others, calls for so much expenditure of vital force, that there is little energy remaining when the day's work is over.

Diversions of some kind are needed for all of the workers in a population. The opportunities for these differ greatly according to the facilities afforded by place and season. The work from which one has just ceased should influence the nature of a recreation. The manual laborer hardly needs any extra physical exercise ; while for the clerk, writer, or similar sedentary worker, any mild and agreeable muscular exertion is beneficial unless there exist some unusual and special reason against it. The diversions to be recommended as healthful are those which can truly be considered to be *recreations*. The more they serve to remove the disproportion that the habitual occupation creates between the over-used and the insufficiently used portions of the organism, the better they are. The hygienic importance of recreation for laborers is touched upon in the chapter on Occupations.

Muscular exercise is necessarily accompanied by the production of much more carbonic acid gas than the body produces in a state of rest. The muscular system is the part where this gas is developed by the actual consumption of carbon-containing articles of food. Most of this carbonic dioxide is cast off from the body through the lungs. Through the lungs also, oxygen (from the air breathed in) enters the system to combine with the carbon which muscular work causes to be used up.

This also develops heat ; for whether carbon be consumed in a fire, in a gas flame or in muscles, *heat in all cases results*. This heat may be very welcome or otherwise, according to the weather and other conditions.

Besides these products of exercise, there is a certain degree of waste of the nitrogenous substance of the muscles. When one is in fair health and when the muscles are habitually exercised in a given way, the amount of used-up muscle substance (which chiefly goes off by the kidneys) is less than in overwork or in irregular, spasmodic or excessive exercise. In the latter case, much tissue-waste is, in good health and under favoring conditions, thrown out of the body. If these conditions be less favorable, the nitrogenous waste is in a less perfectly oxidized form. If these products be retained in the body, stiffness of the muscles results. If serious kidney disease be present, more or less dangerous symptoms result from the accumulation of such excretory products within the system. While gentle exercise favors the removal of these poisonous substances, excessive exercise increases their amount and aggravates all their bad effects.

Muscular exercise has the beneficial effect of increasing oxygenation and of promoting assimilative processes. Not only is the removal of superfluous tissue thereby favored, but the nutrition of the entire body is improved as well. Under exercise that is suitable and in no way excessive, the perfect condition of all the organs of the body is best maintained. Hence, gentle exercise is in general healthful.

Moderate exercise not only improves the condition and appearance of the skin, but enables it also to become a more efficient aid to the casting off, in the sweat, of various waste matters. All muscular exertion causes the heart to increase the number of beats and at each beat to drive more blood through the entire system. Excessive exercise and "athleticism" tend to injure the heart and other organs, and are accordingly harmful. One of the greatest dangers, if not *the* greatest danger of injudicious exercise, is its tendency to induce more or less serious heart diseases. Muscular activity that is irregular and immoderate is most apt to produce these disorders. Exercise that goes beyond the limits of beginning fatigue is especially unhealthful when organic disease exists.

Carefully managed physical exercise can do much to develop the muscular system, and in a less degree it increases the quality and power of other organs. The lungs may be specified as illustrating this to a certain extent. Yet the heart, on the other hand, permits only a very limited increase in the amount of its regular work. If the strain put upon the heart be considerable, a diseased condition is quite certain to result, and other organs may be affected as well.

Unusual and excessive exercise, especially on the part of a person of sedentary habits, may cause acute dilatation of the heart, as Allbutt and others have demonstrated. Yet nature will usually relieve this, and the derangement may entirely disappear if the case be properly treated. This almost invariably means that we must allow complete rest for a time. If, however, such warning pass unheeded and excessive exercise be persisted in, that very often produces incurable heart troubles. Athleticism is frequently harmful because of the undesirable incitements to strain and overdo. Athletes are often of less well-balanced physical health than they appear to be. Professional athletes and prize-fighters may be no more given to alcoholic and other excesses than are the average of the class from which they come. Yet they are very often short-lived and apt to reveal a marked physical deterioration at a time of early middle life when others are in the fullest realization of their best health and vital energies.

Even among horses, and other animals that are bred with the utmost selective care to insure the highest possible excellence of organic adjustment, death from a giving way of the heart under strain is not exceedingly uncommon. Average human beings are not as a rule endowed with such perfect physical balance and condition of all the organs of the body that they can with impunity struggle for athletic prizes. Every one has limitations beyond which it is unsafe to go. In some, the limits of safety are reached much sooner than in others.

Heredity counts for very much in the matter of physical capabilities. The descendant of a strong race is in general fairly well qualified for severe exertion. If such a person develops great muscular strength, the nerves, heart and other organs are better adapted to work in perfect harmony with the powerful muscles. Despite all this, weaklings can, by judicious and unremitting application, develop superb muscles. The author has known a number of such cases. One of them was the physical marvel of his time, and—although of slight frame—was regarded by all as the strongest man in the world. His heart and blood-vessels failed him suddenly, and he died about thirty years earlier than he presumably would, had he not aimed at more than the moderate muscular development best adapted for the average person.

Proper and regular exercise of an organ causes increase in the size, quality and power of that portion of the body. Conversely, an organ is weakened by disuse. Yet very mild exercise serves to maintain the healthy nutrition of a part. A muscle that has been exercised until it is greatly hypertrophied, tends to degenerate when the exercise is no longer maintained. Just as it is in all cases desirable to be very slow in the gradual working up to a high degree of muscular development, so it is well not to lapse at once into sedentary or indolent disuse of the muscles. After a period of prolonged preparation for extreme muscular effort, it is wisest not to abandon absolutely the habit of exercising. Spasmodic and irregular exercise is inferior to that which is in every way uniform.

Dr. Morgan's well-known book on " University Oars " showed that the picked men, who had been selected from the best material in the two leading English universities for a number of years, appeared usually to have come out of the annual races without any serious injury. Yet such men would be very certain to have inherited strong constitutions and finely balanced systems capable of enduring strain without serious injury. Civilized life had not deprived them of the stronger qualities of the more primitive, physical type of mankind. Those who have organic defects of heart, nerves, or any other important part of the body, ought always to be debarred from attempting such competitive athletic exercises.

While all independent struggles and successful overcoming of hardships are most invaluable instruments in the formation of character, it is not to be admitted in a hygienic treatise that the most popular athletic contests are as a rule beneficial to the participants. To the spectators, the contest may have been of service in getting them out-of-doors and inducing them to breathe a little more fresh air (on their way to the arena) than would otherwise have been the case. The chill of a November day causes the prolonged attendance upon a foot-ball match game to involve some risk to the health of the onlookers. For those who are contesting in the game it can hardly be regarded as the most beneficial of exercises. The following lines are quoted (with omission of names) from one of the leading, non-sensational New York daily newspapers of last autumn. At that season several accounts of somewhat the same substance appeared every week and after nearly every game :

"The game was a good one. J. was ruled off for slugging, W. taking his place. Capt. D., of the —— team, had a bad scalp wound, and ten minutes were lost while it was sewed up, after which he pluckily continued the play. S. sprained his ankle severely and had to be helped from the field, C. succeeding him ; and B. was stunned in a wedge rush, and L. took his place. Such minor matters as bleeding noses and flesh cuts were not counted, and both teams were like Comanche Indians in their war paint when the game was over."
"There has not been a game played in this neighborhood within a year of any importance where there have not been from one to half a dozen men injured."

Physical exercise is a most valuable and almost indispensable means of preserving the health ; yet all excesses are harmful. Exercise should cause a moderate use of many muscles, in a proper attitude of the body and amid healthful surroundings. The thereby increased activity of the vital processes is most healthful when the exercise is as regular as is consistent with interest. That in the open air is best; and when it is enjoyable and involves a slight effort of the mind, the purpose of recreation is well fulfilled.

Manual work of all kinds, and especially out-of-door work, offers great opportunities for excellent exercise. It should not be excessive. Even if it become drudgery, the work that the muscles perform tends usually to improve the general health. The superb health of the more favored and temperate laborers shows the value of such exercise. For most children, instruction in such work as gardening is of great value. In the guise of play, the child is thereby taught wonderful secrets of nature, the faculties are trained, and there is besides the satisfaction of having achieved something. The muscular exercise of such play-work is of great importance. Especially should the young be taught a proper position of the body in all exercises. Labor with the most plebeian utensils is consistent with perfection of form and figure if only one be caused always to hold the body rightly.

Out-of-door life and activity not only furnish the best means of recreation for sedentary workers, but also are most healthful and desirable for all. Children particularly need such exercise, and it is indispensable as a means of renewing and improving the vitality of those who study much. Vigorous out-of-door play in childhood develops moral and intellectual qualities and is an all-important aid in fitting one for fighting later in that fierce struggle for life that nearly all have to face. The restless energy of youthful years needs such means for its exercise and discipline.

All proper sports are good for children. Even football does not endanger life and health among boys as do the match games of those who have reached the stature and years of manhood and are struggling in fierce rivalry. Yet a judicious supervision should be exercised. Competitive struggles are not to be favored when the exercise is thereby made an end rather than a mere means of maintaining health. Weakly children that have defective organs must not be allowed to be drawn into the severer exercises of their robust school-fellows. A run which is invigorating for one can be dangerous for another.

Young children, boys and girls alike, are to be encouraged in their play and taught how best to exercise; yet such guidance should never be made irksome to them. Skilful instructors can make this teaching interesting. In swimming, rowing, military drill (with very light guns), riding and in every other kind of play-exercise, there are both good and bad ways of doing such things. Most important is it that only proper methods be taught. Slouchy ways and lack of ease in gait and manner can be amended by training. The clothing should be suitable and loose about the neck, chest and elsewhere. This applies to women and girls as well as to males.

Games and sports are most beneficial when away from dusty rooms or streets. Places where crowds gather are less healthful than open country or parks having a well-drained soil. If contests take place in an enclosed space where many gather to look on as well as to exercise, street dirt, at times very unclean, is brought in more or less abundantly on shoes and clothing. Germs of disease that may chance to be present in such street-dirt are more dangerous than any bad air that may, under ordinary circumstances, be present.

This lack of extreme cleanliness constitutes one of the main objections that may be urged against gymnasiums. The increased respiratory action of the lungs, when the muscles are being exercised, causes such disease-germs as are present in the inhaled dust, to come into very extensive contact with the delicate lung surfaces. Hence all parts of a gymnasium should often be thoroughly cleaned, and the nature of the work done there of course requires free ventilation and abundant sunlight.

Gymnasiums are patronized quite extensively in our cities, where open-air exercise is not available because of the great size of a city and because of unfavorable weather. When the colder months of the year allow neither the sports and open-air recreations of winter nor those of warmer months, gymnastic facilities are of most value. Where only gentle exercise is taken, such as is adapted to the constitution and capabilities of the subject, much good results. A competent instructor is of extreme value in such cases. Classes for exercising are very good if care be taken that the powers of the weakest member be in no wise overtaxed. A careful medical examination should be made before one begins a systematic training or enters upon severe gymnastic work. Any restriction from the free drinking of water is not to be commended in methods of training.

The error in regarding excessive muscularity as equivalent to health has already been indicated. Exercises that are regular and do not strain are best. Many exercisers are led to believe that the development of big muscles is the result most to be desired. In this they are almost always influenced by the person in charge of the gymnasium. This is partly due to interested motives, but is largely because a limited specialist is not apt to have accurate views.

Elaborate apparatus exists in every complete gymnasium. By the use of these appliances, almost any muscles can be systematically developed. Heavy weights are rarely to be advised. The customary mattresses and also nets should be used to guard against danger from falling where any perilous feats are attempted. In general, multiplicity and complexity of apparatus is undesirable as far as the hygienic value of a gymnasium is concerned. The instructor is of more importance than the appliances.

Very simple apparatus answers every purpose of the gentle exercise conducive to high general health. Even if one desire to develop the body so as to surpass all others in muscular strength, the most crude and elementary appliances are quite sufficient. A household gymnasium room should have a few dumb-bells. *Hanging rings* are the most valuable single apparatus of all. Two rings, six inches or more in diameter, are held above the level of the eyes by two ropes not more than twenty inches apart. These ropes are securely fastened above into strong beams in the ceiling. Such rings afford healthful exercise for all, from the frailest, weak-chested child to the consummate athlete. The latter, however, by using them for extreme muscular exertions similar to those of the "parallel bar," is apt to develop the upper back muscles to excess and to produce the semblance of round-shoulderedness, as Lagrange has pointed out. Even in early childhood the head should never be allowed to hang downward. In middle life and later the effects of this are serious at times.

For exercising the abdominal muscles, so as to reduce corpulency or to prevent it, such hanging rings are of value, the body being suspended by grasping these rings. While the body is thus held up, the lower limbs are brought to a right angle with the trunk. Then they are allowed to drop to their former place. These movements are slowly repeated several times. Most surgeons recommend the use of such rings for those wishing to use natural means that shall prevent hernia. The belly muscles are certainly strengthened by such exercise. For women, children and the weakly, the strengthening and exercise of the chest and of **the** above indicated muscles, as well as of others that **these** hanging rings call into **activity, are very** valuable.

One need not swing with them nor make any but the slightest efforts to raise the body.

Walking is the most important and valuable of all exercises. It certainly is so when the term is understood to include brisk walking. Running is practically only a somewhat severer form of the same sort of exercise. Walking exercises the muscles of other parts than the legs. The loins, the back and even the chest and arms are somewhat exercised in walking. This is less the case than in special exercise adapted for the upper parts of the body; yet it amounts to more than most persons realize. That the action of the heart is thereby somewhat increased, and that the lungs are exercised much more actively, even in an easy walk, than when the body is at rest, are facts obvious to all.

In a brisk walk, the amount of air inspired and of the carbonic acid gas that is given off from the body may be three times as great as when one is at complete rest. In walking up a steep rise of ground, the exercise is still more severe. As is well known, this causes us to "lose our breath." That means that the muscles are producing more carbonic acid gas than the lungs can at the immediate moment remove from the blood that is in them. By resting from these too severe efforts, we "catch the breath," and, the exercise being moderated, the lungs are again enabled to work well. Under the influence of exercise, the lung-power tends to improve; and exercise of the lungs, by such gradually increasing but moderate muscular activity as is afforded by carefully regulated walking, forms an important part of the open-air treatment of lung disease.

Walking is the most valuable of all exercises, because it is usually not severe and yet is a fairly sufficient exercise for all persons of all ages. It moreover is less liable to involve excess than other exercise; and it has the great merit of being always available and so simple and of necessity so connected with our daily life that all must with some regularity employ this healthful muscular exertion to a certain extent, however indolent they be. Many, it must be admitted, somewhat successfully shirk even this exercise. Yet it is the one that involves so little loss of time in preparation, as compared with other kinds of physical activity, that the number of the enlightened who neglect it is very small indeed. This statement is not strictly correct as regards the inhabitants of the southern and western parts of our country. Where the influence of the Latin races has wholly or in part dominated the civilization of the warmer portions of our continent, it is not an easy matter to make the natives realize that walking does not necessarily mean either extreme poverty or a deranged brain.

Children ought to be taught to walk well. The gait should be graceful, and at the same time the effort must be as slight as possible. In all walking, an erect but easy carriage of the body is desirable. The shoulders need invariably to be held well back, even though the body be bent forward as is usual in mountain climbing. The step should be firm and even; at the same time it ought to be elastic and gliding. The toes should point forward or slightly outward. Extreme "toeing out" is, like "toeing in," to be avoided. The arms are not to be worked vigorously, and a graceful walk, to use the language of a ballet-master, "does not call for any movement on the part of the neck or of the waist." Indeed, the most graceful natural walk, that of the women of some portions of middle Italy, is possible with rigid neck while considerable burdens are carried upon the head. Some observers regard the carrying of burdens upon the head as a valuable means of rendering the walk more graceful and of improving the figure.

Such an easy walk is to be commended not only from an artistic point of view but from the utilitarian standpoint as well. With an easy gait one can cover more ground than with a clumsy one. This is said in full recognition of the fact that some professional pedestrians have not a graceful gait.

Walking, like running, can be overdone, and then, like all excessive exercise, can cause harm. Mountain climbing must not be undertaken without preliminary and gradual preparation. This applies especially to people of sedentary occupation. If such persons, wholly out of training, attempt to ascend high mountains they often suffer from the extreme and unusual effort.

Swimming in clear waters, that are not chilly, furnishes a splendid exercise. In summer it is an ideal recreation; for, besides affording a pleasurable and purifying bath, it exercises many muscles, and the increase of body-heat produced by this muscular activity is at the same time removed by the cool water. The chief danger to the health is that of remaining so long in the water as to become chilled. The possibility of drowning must of course be counted among the dangers of imprudent bathing. Those who cannot swim run great risks by bathing near deep waters. Seafaring men and others are frequently drowned within a few strokes of shore, solely because of having neglected to acquire the easy art of swimming.

The practical value of learning in childhood how to swim is obvious. While such knowledge may occasionally cause the foolhardy to risk their lives quite unnecessarily, the instances of that are very few indeed compared with the cases of advantage coming from an ability to move the body through the water or to keep afloat when overboard. Swimming is not only a most manly exercise, but should be learned by girls as well as by boys. It exercises the shoulder muscles considerably. This is important for women who desire handsome arms and shoulders. However plump a woman may be, the outlines of the body are always better when the muscles beneath are fairly well developed.

Rowing is a very valuable and agreeable exercise. Besides having the advantage of being a fresh-air recreation like all forms of boating, rowing in fair style (with shoulders and head well back and arms and back straight) involves the exercise of many muscles. Where one person uses two oars, one in either hand (the oars in that case being called "sculls" by the English and by some Americans), rowing is a very healthful and symmetrical exercise. If a boat is suitably shaped, it is extremely safe. Even on the ocean and in storms that shatter and wreck great ships, a properly built small boat rowed by a skilled man is quite safe as far as danger from the waves is concerned. Whenever a rowboat by any chance becomes capsized, a slight knowledge of swimming will enable one to get back to the boat, which of course cannot sink if built of wood and not weighted with metal or stone.

Canoeing is inferior to rowing as an exercise, although it has the advantage of allowing one to face forward while propelling the little craft. The ordinary canoe is very frail and "cranky" when sailed, and gives an inferior muscular exercise because of the comparatively limited hygienic value of the use of the double-bladed paddle. Birch canoes and their imitations afford a very good means of exercise for the upper part of the body, although not advisable for the weakly. The shoulders should be held well back. The single paddle is to be used for a time on one side of the canoe and then for a while on the other side. The knack of twisting the paddle is, like the skill of the gondolier, not easily to be understood by a description in a few words. It is readily acquired, however, by observing a paddler and by practice. Yet, for all but the expert, a canoe is an unsafe craft.

Skating is an exhilarating and fascinating exercise for cold weather. It involves vigorous use of many muscles and promotes activity of the lungs. It is especially healthful because of the abundance of pure air and absence of dust that accompany its practice outside of rinks. The dangers (and discomforts) that belong to skating (and roller-skating) need not be spoken of here in detail. As people often break through the ice, it is proper to mention here that a long rope, stretched so that the middle is over the hole in the ice while each end is held at a safe distance from the place of danger, affords a means of rescuing the unlucky skater who is in the icy water. Planks may also be run out over the ice. Since, however, lives are at times lost because the victim of such an accident is held under ice-surfaces, the very simple apparatus shown in Fig. 11 is recommended. It does not seem to be known in this country. Its use was illustrated to the author some years ago by Baron Esmarch, then in charge of the Hygienic Museum in Berlin. The essential part is a wooden sphere, like a medium-sized nine-pin ball, made of maple or more buoyant wood. A long (manila) rope is attached to this by an iron semicircle from which two pins enter the wooden sphere. One pin being in either end of the axis of this ball, it rotates freely. By its weight, the ball serves to break ice upon which it is thrown from a distance. Floating on the water, it enables the victim of the accident to catch the light, strong rope, and thereby to be rescued.

Fig. 11.

Tennis is a deservedly popular game. Women, however, should be careful to avoid too great indulgence in this beautiful pastime. Like all one-handed games, it is most useful as an exercise when the left hand is at times used instead of the right. This alternate exercise, however clumsy, is best. Sprains, fractures and internal displacements result from too active devotion to the exercise, especially when one is out of training. On wet ground (especially turf) tennis may be dangerous.

Jumping rope ("skipping rope") is a fairly good exercise for girls. Used in moderation, it is not so harmful for healthy people as it is sometimes said to be.

Baseball is a less perfect exercise than football or various other games. **Cricket** is somewhat preferable. **Football**, as already said, is a fine exercise if not carried too far. Then it may be perilous.

Fencing, like sword-play in general, tends to cause lateral curvature of the spine, especially in the immature, as Lagrange has shown. This great defect is due to the necessarily one-armed nature of the exercise. It is however a useful occasional exercise of eye, nerve, muscles and other organs. Sabre practice seems more valuable as an exercise than fencing.

Boxing serves to exercise the muscles and other organs, but is hedged about by such drawbacks that one cannot recommend it. Even though this is claimed to be a "manly art of self-defence," it is quite the usage for the assertive but not very beneficially productive classes, that are most conversant with this exercise, to resort to "self-cocking revolvers" and other technically unfair means of settling their frequent altercations.

Riding spirited horses, although in nearly every respect hygienically inferior to proper walking as an exercise, induces about the same extent of muscular action, and causes the lungs to throw off nearly as much carbonic acid gas as comes from them when one is walking. Even under the artificial conditions in which it is used in cities, riding affords a commendable exercise, especially for the capricious, the indolent and the gluttonous. It requires more preparation than most exercise, and so, many of those who take it up are liable to use it only irregularly and to abandon it before very long. It is not so desirable for weak girls or boys as for men and women who are passing middle life. The usual (one-sided) side-saddle position is not hygienically the best. The distinguished London surgeon, Mr.

Treves, in mentioning some of the physical defects that riding causes besides round shoulders in "weedy" children, says that "lateral curvature of the spine is certainly often induced and fostered by riding." Various English and other anatomists and physicians have called attention to the troubles of the lower part of the body due to riding and have stated that parturition may be more difficult among women who ride much.

Bicycling is in general more valuable, yet tamer and much less dangerous than horseback exercise. Mishaps may occur with it at times, and involve local or general injury. The fascination of the easy and swift machines, which hopelessly distance all horses in combined speed and endurance, is great. Yet this causes over-exercising and strain, especially if one has to ride far against a strong wind. Only "safety" machines should be used. One can learn their use in four or five half-hour lessons; yet at least a dozen rides are required before sufficient facility is acquired.

Hills are very severe obstacles for the beginner. One should not hesitate to walk up steep places and push the bicycle. In a long tour, this is very desirable as a change from the monotonous movements. The "gearing" of the machine must be adjusted to the individual and according to the character of the country to be traversed. The ball of the foot touching the treadle (or "pedal"), when at its lowest in working the machine, should be slightly lower than the heel, although professionals do not all indorse this recommendation. Light leather shoes are best. The clothing should be light but elastic. Woollen materials best answer the purpose. A light jacket should be carried for preventing chill if the rider is to rest on the way. The danger of "catching cold" or acquiring rheumatic or other ailment is considerable if, after exercising, one neglect to remove at once the clothes that are wet with perspiration.

Bicycling exercises many muscles besides those of the lower limbs. The most improved machines cause much less trouble from *vibration* than was the case with the older bicycles. Yet even the best pneumatic tires do not entirely obviate this defect. Therein lies one of the drawbacks of the useful exercise. The main danger is in the tendency to overdo. Competitive strain is here, as in other exercise, apt to prove pernicious. " Record-breaking " is a dangerous incentive. For those who have hernia or any other disease than mild forms of rheumatism, bicycling seems unsuited. Although presumably irritative of the perineal organs, especially when one bends forward in the usual unsightly and unhealthful manner, it may be said that bicycling is regarded by physicians as relieving rather than aggravating hemorrhoidal troubles.

The general opinion among practitioners of medicine and the leading medical journals appears to be that bicycling is not an exercise that one should recommend to women. The tricycle is preferable. Both these exercising machines are an artificial constraint in that they require one to keep on quite level, smooth and usually dusty roads. They are not so easy to transport as they seem, and they do not allow that intimate contact with nature that comes from tramping in rugged and wild country. Their use is limited by season, wind and weather. The majority of those who follow bicycling with great enthusiasm at first tend gradually to lose their interest in the exercise. So, after this and all other artificial exercises are discarded, *walking remains as the one necessary exercise that is also the most healthful of all.*

SCHOOLS, AND THEIR INFLUENCE ON HEALTH

THE prosperity of the commonwealth demands not only the best training for all children, but requires that every possible precaution be employed to prevent any impairment of health among scholars or teachers. The ideal of instruction methods is that school influences be such as will contribute in every way to improve the pupil, whether progress be measured from the mental, moral, or physical standpoint.

We cannot fail to recognize that diseases inevitably arise among children whether they attend school or not. At the same time, it is very probable that several important diseases would at any rate be less abundant, and perhaps wholly absent, if schools and their hygienic management were of the best. In view of the hundreds of millions of dollars expended yearly in this country to further the education and training of those who will become future citizens and parents of citizens, it is most important to consider the chief features of school hygiene.

The diseases which most deserve to attract attention because of their connection with schools are : (1) Those due to infection ; (2) those due to defects in the appliances, the building and its furnishings, and in the methods of school-work.

To prevent infectious diseases, it is necessarily of importance to disinfect all objects that have become infected and are liable to keep alive or convey the germs of disease. Sometimes an entire school-house has to be closed for a period and completely disinfected throughout. If the

IMPORTANCE OF CLEANLINESS

building be faulty in construction, and "honeycombed" with places where the germs of disease can lodge and flourish, the usual superficial disinfection may be quite inadequate.

All children should have been *vaccinated*. The harmlessness and value of vaccination are explained in the latter part of this book. In the same portion will be found a consideration of disinfection processes and those diseases spoken of as infectious. Children that have communicable diseases should be excluded from schools. This includes even such mild (and usually disregarded) disorders as *ringworm* (and similar troubles), and also some cases of sore eyes, especially granular eyelids (*trachoma*). The most enlightened physicians recognize clearly that such diseases are distinctly contagious and sometimes freely spread from child to child by contact. Many a "sore throat" is a mild case of diphtheria that is unrecognized unless very carefully observed. It is wisest for teachers to be alert in such matters. School inspectors or, at any rate, supervisors should have medical training made a necessary qualification for their office, and their decisions should be accurate and early when infectious dangers are suspected.

Systematic teaching of the principles of strict cleanliness, and of the reasons why neatness is desirable and why it should be effected in certain ways, must be viewed as of extreme value to school children. This is especially so when they come from the lowest classes, where intelligent training in the essentials of such things is impossible to them at home. By properly teaching them true cleanliness, they are made to acquire ideas which will cause them later to be more valuable citizens than if such practical health education be neglected. If more attention were given to hygienic instruction in schools, it would be better for all, even though such instruction restricted the time to be allowed for the more superfluous, though showy, learning. School baths, too, are a valuable auxiliary to health, and the developing tendency to introduce extensive shower baths into public schools and institutions is a healthful one. Disregard for personal cleanliness, if persistent, is a menace to the welfare of others, and should be a barrier against the entrance of a child into a school.

When a case of the very infectious diseases is present in a home, all children living in the same family should be excluded from school. It is well also to keep out all others who play with these children or come into contact with them. The latest edition of the "Manual of the Board of Education" of New York City wisely provides that "if a contagious disease of any description exists on more than one floor of a tenement-house, or if the disease existing on only one floor be small-pox or typhus fever, all children living in the house must be promptly excluded from school." In case of scarlet fever, they are then to be kept out until three weeks after the beginning of the last case. For measles, one week less is required. To restrict diphtheria, such children living in infected houses are not to be allowed to return to school till "one week after the termination of the last case on the floor or in the house." It would be better if longer exclusion were enforced. In case of other diseases, it is best that children be excluded who do not get medical certificates of freedom from the possible infection. Evidence, also, that disinfection has been properly carried out is very desirable. All new pupils should likewise have such satisfactory health certificates.

A child that has had *scarlatina* is not to return to school until after the skin has entirely ceased scaling off, and after all sore throat and all other signs have disappeared. This requires the greater part of two months. *Small-pox* requires about the same length of time. So also does *whooping-cough*. *Measles* requires at least a month of exclusion, and *erysipelas* nearly the same time. In all cases, any scaling must have ceased. All the other eruptive diseases, and also *mumps*, make it necessary that the child shall remain away for at least two weeks. In *chicken-pox*, the period of exclusion is best fixed at from three to four weeks. However mild a case of *diphtheria*, or a sore throat resembling that disease, a child that has just had it should not return to school until three weeks after the beginning of the attack. A severe case should have entirely recovered before beginning school-work or any other tasks. The same may be said regarding *typhoid fever*. A more complete consideration of these diseases will be found in the chapter on Infectious Diseases.

Tuberculosis is one of the last of the diseases that are to be apprehended from school attendance, if any kind of supervision be maintained and if care be taken to disinfect all expectorations. All scholars and teachers should spit only into suitable spittoons, arranged so that they can be easily and certainly disinfected. The pupils should be required to use these spittoons invariably, instead of handkerchiefs, to spit into. A handkerchief, on which are dried discharges from a "cold in the head" or other catarrhal conditions, should not be moved about much in the air. Wherever feasible, it is to be advised in such cases that cheap Japanese napkins be used and forthwith thrown into a suitable receptacle. These paper napkins can then be burnt, or otherwise speedily destroyed.

School buildings should as a rule be located as nearly as practicable in the centre of the district that they serve. Liquor-shops, offensive businesses and all other demoralizing or unhealthful nuisances should if possible be driven away from the vicinity of a school. Where statutes exist providing for this, they should be rigorously enforced. The construction and equipment of school buildings are of extreme importance. In our more crowded cities, too little recognition is given to the hygienic value of sufficient space in and around the school-house. In any case it should be separated from all others about it by a considerable distance.

The building ought not to be high, and should be spacious within. In the overcrowded sections of our largest cities these ideals are too often wholly disregarded. If in such situations the building be necessarily high, owing to surrounding structures, the lower floor is hygienically of little use for any school-purposes. Play-rooms need to be well aired and light. It is in general not well that children have to climb many stairs. The staircases should be easy of ascent, and the children not influenced to go up these rapidly. The older children should have the upper stories for their rooms, although this should not be at the expense of the younger scholars as regards sufficient daylight.

Northern light is always the most desirable, and school-windows that look toward the east or northeast are also good, because the direct glare of the sun will have moved sufficiently away before the time for the beginning of school. Yet in winter these sides of a school-building may be too cold unless the heating and ventilation be of the best. Western exposures are undesirable for such schools as hold session late in the afternoon. A southern exposure is in general best for living rooms, because of the healthful influence of the sun. Yet with school-children we have always particularly to avoid anything that will impair the eyesight. The glare of the sun shining upon the page or work of a scholar or other worker is bad for the eyes. If, however, curtains or blinds be used so as to accommodate the child near the window, those pupils who are in the further and darker parts of the room receive insufficient light. A few authorities recommend a southern or western exposure as being, all things considered, the best. The majority prefer northern light.

Whatever way the rooms face, the light should not be materially obstructed by reason of the nearness of buildings, trees or other things that regularly or irregularly come between the work and the sky. Some school-buildings are made long from east to west, and narrow from north to south, so as to have them only wide enough to allow one row of several school-rooms on each floor. These may then be situated upon the northern side, while the southern side is taken up with large, sun-lighted corridors. For warm climates, the plan is certainly practicable. Whatever the construction, the corridors should at least have windows at both ends.

Windows should reach as high as possible up toward the ceiling; for the light from the upper part of the window is the most valuable and reaches farthest into the room. This light from the top of the window should not be wasted by inserting there any rounding ornamental wood-work or other obstruction to the free entrance of light. The sashes should not be heavy or broad. Double windows in winter are best for the colder portions of the United States. They serve to keep the room warmer, and prevent the light from being obstructed by condensation of moisture out of the air in the room, as is so common in the form .of "frosting" upon windows of single thicknesses of glass. Such frosting acts like ground-glass to obstruct the light. The combined area of all the window surfaces should be equal to at least one-fifth of the floor area. The walls, at the edges of the windows, should be splayed or bevelled outward and inward, so as to allow the greatest possible entrance of light without weakening the construction of the walls. The use of "bull-nosed" bricks aids this purpose somewhat. The lowest parts of the windows should be at least as much as forty inches above the floor, and some recommend that they be as high as the tops of the heads of the pupils. Where the windows are low, as on the staircases, iron bars are useful to prevent venturesome children from falling out.

Window-shades of strong, light gray cloth, such as is called "Hollands," are of great value for those windows through which the sun shines. They should be upon spring rollers. Where window-ventilation is relied upon, and the familiar upward- and inward-slanting board be desired at the top, in order to throw air into the room, the wood of this may be substituted by a glass pane in a sash, flush on the upper surface. If kept clean, it obstructs the light less than wood, and serves to divert the incoming currents of air away from the heads of pupils.

Light from above and slightly in front of the worker is best, but is not commonly to be had. Usually, the windows have to be relied upon. Then the light should come from the left. Thus it does not dazzle or reflect, as when from the front, and is not apt to throw shadows, from the arms and body, upon the work. For artificial light, whenever needed in school-rooms, incandescent electric lights are best, and several small lights are preferable to single large ones, as throwing less shadow.

The height of school-rooms should not be less than eleven feet. Fifteen feet is usually regarded as the greatest height that they should have, and some object to having the height of school-rooms more than fourteen feet, since they are apt to develop an undesirable resonance if much higher than that. The higher the walls and windows, the better the light. An oblong shape is usually preferred. The width ought not to exceed twenty-three feet, and the length should not be greater than thirty feet. It is desirable that for each pupil in a school-room there be allowed twenty square feet of floor area. Thus, a room twenty-seven feet long and nearly 22.5 feet wide would be suited for thirty-five pupils. Often, however, less than half this floor area is allowed, as in places where careful attention is not paid to the health of the pupils, and where they are crowded together because of niggardly appropriations. This crowding is especially liable to occur where the teachers are paid according to the number of pupils that they have in charge. For each average scholar two hundred and fifty cubic feet of air space should be allowed. More than this is desirable. If less than two hundred cubic feet be allowed, satisfactory ventilation is not, as a rule, easily effected.

Floors should be of firm hard-wood (or Georgia pine), very well matched, and the seams, joints, and all crevices filled with asphalt or other wood cement. They should be oiled two or three times a year, as explained at length in the chapter on Building. Hard-wood laid in asphalt is recommended by European builders. Where a cold cellar is beneath, the under side of the floor beams should be sheathed. Otherwise the floor is dangerously cold. It is best not to have the cellar cold; and, indeed, one of the first essentials for properly warming a small school-house or a church is to have the cellar warm in the beginning; but, of course, only with clean air. The walls of a school-room to above the height of the head should be wainscoted on the colder sides of the room with wood that is not very soft. It should be very smooth, and afford no place for the lodgment of dirt. No projecting mouldings or other ornamental additions that could catch or hold dirt should be permitted.

No blackboards should be between the windows. Where there are blackboards on the wall, the wood-work should reach up to the lower part of these. The walls in general above the wooden wainscoting should be as smooth as possible, and of a light grayish oil-painted surface, thus being easy to keep perfectly clean. White is preferred for the ceiling, as reflecting better and increasing the light upon the work of the pupils. Smooth oil-paint is cleaner, and a better reflector of light, than " sand-finished " paint on ceilings; yet builders prefer to use the latter, and claim that it lasts better.

Temperatures between 65° F. and 68° F. are usually considered best for school-rooms. With stoves it is difficult to keep the heat uniform, especially when no ventilating flues exist. If stoves be used, and the size and location of the room require much heat, two stoves of medium size, and on opposite sides of a room, are better than one very large one. The stoves ought to have fresh-air inlets provided. (See Fig. 12.) Stoves should also be "jacketed"

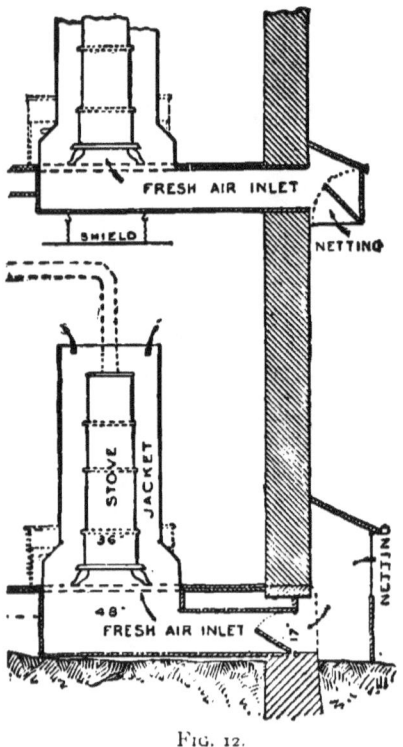

Fig. 12.

with a casing or mantle (as shown in the figure), to allow the warm air to circulate throughout the room, cooler air entering from beneath to replace that which has risen by being warmed. This principle can also be employed with suitably constructed wood-burning stoves, as shown in Fig. 13. The air should not be kept uncomfortably dry. If a stove-pipe enter into a chimney on the wall of a school-room, a ventilating flue opening should be introduced at the lower part of the chimney. This will draw bad air out of the room at the lower part, because the heat coming from the stove-pipe causes an upward movement of air in the chimney. (See chapter on Ventilation.)

A well-managed hot-air furnace gives very satisfactory heat. Direct steam-heating—that is, by means of radiators in the rooms—cannot be commended for school-houses. Indirect steam heat, as shown in Fig. 23, where fresh air passes between coils of steam-pipe, is equally good and more apt to be well attended to. This is perhaps because it costs more, and because a higher class of labor is required to manage it than is considered sufficient for a furnace. Mechanical means of insuring ventilation, as well as the use of special chimneys for the purpose, are spoken of in the chapter on Ventilation. It is most healthful and not much more expen-

Fig. 13.

sive to have an abundant inflow of air, warmed to a moderate temperature (say, not much above 100° F. where it leaves the furnace), supplied to a large school-room on a cold day, rather than half as much warm air coming in heated to a much higher temperature.

The fresh air, whether warmed much or little, should enter on the upper part of the wall and leave at the lower part. For each child in a school-room there should be allowed a fresh-air supply of no less than thirty cubic feet per minute. To supply this, large conducting pipes are necessary; for the average velocity of air flowing through such pipes, as they are usually managed, is considerably less than three hundred and sixty feet a minute, and perhaps only half that amount. Hence a pipe, or the pipes, conveying warm air at the rate of three hundred feet a minute to a school-room with fifty pupils, must at the least have a sectional area of five square feet. Ventilating through windows exposes the children to draughts, and is the least healthful way of admitting air to school-rooms. It is also the most uneconomical way in winter.

Cleanliness of the school-room and school-house in all its parts should be enforced. Mats and shoe-scrapers should be used before entering, and overcoats and street clothing ought not to be brought into the school-room. Children should not have their feet remain wet after coming into the school-room. Just as it should be an offence for a child to spit on the floor when proper spittoons are provided, so no paper, particles of food, or other dirt should be allowed to be thrown upon the floor. All portions of the floor, walls, and furniture being as smooth as possible, much of the inevitable dust can be removed by mops that are slightly moist. Feather dusters ought to be prohibited here as elsewhere. If the floor be swept, the dust may be allowed to settle before the windows are opened. After school-hours and during recesses, the rooms should be well aired through the opened windows, if no risk of chilling the children be thereby incurred.

The cellar should be kept clean. *No privy should be within the walls of the school-building,* nor should it be where it may chance to contaminate a well. "*Dry closets*" in connection with hot-air heating are, at times, apparently a means of propagating disease and diffusing bad odors. This seems certainly the case when an intricate and involved system of exhaust-air flues under floors is connected with the dry closets. It has been found that therein the currents of air can occasionally become reversed, and are then a means of carrying germs of disease and foul odors from the cellar and the vault, back to the rooms and between the floors. Furthermore, it is observed that "dry closets" are more draughty than they should be. The strong inflowing current of air is apt to chill those who use such places. Water-closets, or earth-closets, or even well-kept privies, are preferable to such devices, and less liable to work harmfully whenever a janitor neglects to attend properly to his duties and allows the necessary fires to go out.

There are other deviations from health, besides the contagious and infectious diseases, that are brought about through failure to attend scrupulously to the welfare of the scholar. At the most critical years of childhood, disease tendencies are very apt to manifest themselves, and then nature must be aided in every way to fight impending or beginning disease. Bad air in schools is one of the constant perils to the child, and liberal ventilation is necessary in order to the prevention of disease among those who have to spend hours every day in the school-room. Massachusetts is the only State that compels by law an abundance of fresh air in school-rooms. The welfare of the future citizens of America demands that other States follow the lead of Massachusetts.

Physicians cannot too strongly urge the importance of having teachers instructed in the essential principles of ventilation. The trained medical judgment must always recognize the very great value of abundant fresh air, especially to delicate children. Headaches, so common among school-children, especially when overworked, are very often due solely to impure air. They may also be due to eye-defects. If the feet of children are allowed to be cold, good health and progress cannot be expected.

It is important that teachers receive hygienic instruction in the elements of health culture and disease prevention. Such a minor ailment as nose-bleeding, in ordinary cases, is often due to a constriction of the blood-vessels of the neck ; and then it is relieved by loosening collars and keeping children in fairly correct attitudes. Children tend too often to slouchiness of gait and posture. They should not be allowed to contract the chest by rounding the back and stooping while at work. They must not remain long in one-sided positions. Play or work that calls for the exercise of only one side of the body is deforming. Permanent curvatures of the spine may result when the seat is too far back from the desk or bench used by the weakly scholar. Any tasks causing an attitude that is constrained or wearying, deserve the attention of medical supervisors, and should be restricted or abolished, if possible.

Recesses must not be very far apart. Every schoolhouse needs ample play-grounds. The younger and more delicate the children, the more do they need frequent relaxation from the constraint of routine work. An hour of constant application is too much for them. Merely sitting still is too irksome for a very young child. The unsympathetic and unintelligent adult cannot always be made to realize this. Play should follow tasks when the children are very young. The movements of the light school gymnastics, adopted long ago from the German methods, afford a relief and at the same time a healthful exercise for children. These exercises are best in fresh air. During recesses, the rooms should be aired by opening the windows, if that be practicable without any risk from cold. It must not be forgotten that the young need to eat often. The suggestions of intelligent teachers as to what their pupils shall not eat may be of extreme value, especially when the parents are ill-qualified to guide their children aright.

Eye troubles are perhaps the most important of the injuries which may result to children when insufficient recognition is given to their needs and weaknesses. The various external catarrhal eye disorders are more or less contagious, or in any case it is safest to act as though they were. If the eyes be sore or weak, attendance at school is usually undesirable. Most important of all school dangers is the tendency to the development of near-sightedness (or " myopia "). The extensive and prolonged studies of Herman Cohn and others have established the certainty that children, entering school with normal eyes, often become near-sighted after a time. The further along the pupils are in progress, after years of diligent study, the more marked is the near-sightedness liable to be. This is not the only eye-defect that study may induce, yet it is by all odds the most conspicuous. It is a disease of indoor life. To lessen the tendency, careful and constant attention must be given to insuring suitably strong light. Over-use of the eyes must be guarded against.

Close concentration on fine work at home of necessity aggravates this tendency, and the light supplied children in their homes is often much worse than that which they are furnished in school. The amount of out-of-school study work imposed upon the young scholars should be limited. Whatever they do at home, they should not, when at school, be made to bend over fine type and badly printed maps, or other fine work and delicate shading that keeps the eyes at a constant strain. The light must be adequate in the darkest portion of the school-room. The strain of regarding near objects for any length of time is injurious to the eyes, and must be avoided as much as possible. Better is it to have the well-lighted walls decorated with maps, illustrative designs, and other things that can be so brought into the plan of desirable instruction. In this manner the eyes are given their proper physiological rest by being taken away from near objects and having to look a considerable number of feet away.

Writing must always be carefully taught, and scholars should not at any age be made to take notes so rapidly as to develop a bad handwriting. Text-books are so easily to be had of any scope that they make note-taking quite needless when this is done at the expense of the penmanship. During early education, a practical, easy handwriting must be taught, and careful formation of the letters insisted upon till the habit of good writing is permanently formed. Rapid writing should be acquired only gradually, and not striven for at first. Fine handwriting and feats of penmanship are undesirable. A straight up-and-down hand is hygienically better in the long run than a style that slants much. The upright handwriting is more legible and does not require the scholar to twist and bend the body into curves that may result in permanent deformity. The adaptation of the desk and seat to the pupil are important in preventing distortion of the body, as will shortly be indicated.

Book paper ought to be so thick and strong as not to show an impression of ordinary printing on the opposite side of a page. It is best for the eye when somewhat dull and smooth on the surface. A dead-white paper is not usually considered so desirable for the eye as a very slightly yellowish or creamy tint. A decided yellow tinge is objectionable. So are all strong colors. The width of a printed column ought, in no case, to exceed four inches. The width of this page is slightly less than three and a half inches. If made much wider, that renders it more difficult for the eye to run from line to line in continuous reading.

Printed matter should be in type that is sufficiently large. This book is chiefly printed with type of the size termed *long primer*. That is large enough for all ordinary purposes. It should be distinct, of good quality, and not broken or worn.

Sufficient "leading" should be allowed between the lines of type. When type is—like the preceding paragraph—set "solid," the print is rendered less fit for the reader's eye, and therefore less satisfactory than in this line and the four lines preceding, as well as in the following five lines, where the "leading" between lines is unusually wide. The letters of each word should also be well separated, as here and in the remainder of this paragraph, where—as in all the above lines—the type is of the same uniform size. By thus having the words well "spaced," still greater distinctness is produced.

For all readers, pearl type, such as in these ten words, or of this size, agate, is altogether too small. The same may be said of nonpareil, which, unfortunately, is used in periodical and other reading matter extensively circulated among children and others. Minion is larger, yet must be considered bad for the eyes; for it is much too small. Even the next larger size, brevier, is not large enough, although very commonly employed. Bourgeois type comes next in the scale; but for prolonged reading, as in encyclopædias and numerous other much-used books, as well as periodicals and newspapers, it is inferior to long primer, which is a standard size for most well-printed books. A still larger size, such as small pica, is better for young children. For the very young, pica, as seen in these two lines, is none too large. Great primer type should be employed in the first books that are put before the eyes of the youngest children.

School desks should have the seats slightly under them. Thus a perpendicular line dropped from the inner edge of the desk (*E*, in Fig. 14) ought to reach the seat at a point at least one inch inside (that is, to the rear) of the edge (*K*). This "*minus distance,*" as it is technically termed, by which the desk overhangs the seat, ought not to exceed two inches, for the reason that the pupil may be impeded in freedom of movement if the edge of the seat reaches very far under the desk. Such an objection should rule when both desk-lid and seat are rigidly fixed, as it then is not sufficiently easy for a scholar to sit down or rise to a standing position. When the edge of the seat is to the rear of a perpendicular line dropped from the edge of the desk, the condition is technically termed a "*plus distance,*" and is hygienically objectionable; for then the pupil has to bend the spinal column too much, and is apt to acquire therefrom a permanent slouchy, stooping attitude. This also causes a throwing of the shoulders habitually forward.

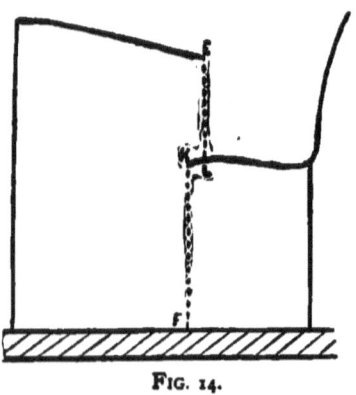

FIG. 14.

A desk, except in the narrow horizontal portion furthest away, ought to be slanted slightly toward the pupil. For resting the book in reading, an angle of not much more than forty-five degrees is desirable. This can be secured by an adjustable lid such as is shown in Fig. 15. When that lid is not thus turned back, the top of the desk has a smooth surface with an angle of about fifteen degrees, as indicated in Fig. 14. Such an adjustable arrangement may cause the light to be obstructed. Hence it is not suitable for all places.

Seats ought to be single and not connected with the desk behind them. It is often desirable that there be a hinge movement (as in Fig. 15) that allows the lower part to be turned backward. Thus entrance and exit are easy, and the child can readily rise in place to the standing position. Desks are usually too high above seats. The rear edge of the desk (*E*, Fig. 14) should not be much higher than the level of the elbow. Otherwise the shoulder is too much raised when the forearm is upon the desk, as in writing.

Desks that are too high tend to cause lateral curvature of the spine, the spinal column becoming convex toward the side of the arm (usually the right) that is habitually employed for writing.

FIG. 15.

The vertical line (*EL*, Fig. 14), technically called the *difference*, should in an average case equal about fifteen per cent. of the child's height. This interval ought to be adjusted to the child and not rigorously set by tabulated rules. If this distance be made too short, the child is caused to bow the body forward too much. The length of the leg from the knee downward regulates the distance (*KF*, Fig. 14) from the seat to the floor. It may arbitrarily be set at about two-sevenths (or a little less than thirty per cent.) of the child's height. In all cases, the sole and heel of the child's foot should rest lightly upon the floor.

The seat ought to be curved to make sitting comfortable. Figs. 14 and 15 indicate the nature of these curves. At the point *K* the edge must be well rounded off. The back of the seat ought to slant a little to the rear and curve backward. It also may slightly protrude above the slight depression for the hips, so as to rest the forward curve of the small of the back. There ought to be no marked concavity from side to side. There appears to be a growing tendency to adopt the single backward curve (shown in Fig. 15). Yet that style ought always to slant somewhat backward as well as curve backward in its upper part. Schulthess has shown anew that, unless carefully corrected and supplied with proper seats, children tend to acquire a backward curvature of the spine (*kyphosis*).

Adjustable seats are excellent, especially where the attendance is not large, and where the scholars at the same time are liable to be of quite different sizes. Some cities, like New York, have in the public schools ten different set sizes of school furniture. Even that is less satisfactory than the use of desks and seats which can be fixed to accommodate the stature of the scholar, instead of the scholar being constrained to be fitted to the unchangeable seat. There are various good patterns of these adjustable desks and seats. The smoother all parts of the school furniture are, the better for the health; for dust lingers least where there are fewest irregularities of surface. Some of the cheap but showy castings used for school furniture are very faulty in this respect, and are probably never dusted out clean. The smooth, simple iron-work shown in Fig. 15 is very good.

Too much work in and out of school is imposed upon many very young children, and almost inevitably results in injuring them in a more or less recognizable manner. This is particularly the case with the "nervous" and organically weak, who ought to be guarded most tenderly. If otherwise treated there, they are to be advised not to attend school. That is certainly so if they are there ruled by austere and narrow-minded teachers, or by those to whom teaching appears merely an unsatisfactory means of getting a livelihood instead of being one of the highest of noble callings.

Where obvious mental, moral or physical defects or diseases are present (and the skilled observer detects more of these deficient children than are usually recognized), it seems best that such pupils be taught quite apart from others. Thereby they can have the benefit of expert instructors, and especial consideration is given to their particular weaknesses. Their associations, too, are thus more fit for insuring improvement instead of deterioration. Even the condition of "nervousness" is less often due entirely to inherited conditions than is commonly supposed. Bad influences and imitation explain many of these cases.

Learning is not in itself the equivalent of either power or wealth. It usually tends rather to divert one from the paths of what is commonly deemed success in life. *Education* (or a bringing-out of the faculties of the plastic mind) is vastly more important than cramming the little head full of vain knowledge. That is, a child is better off if it be taught *how* to learn (while at the same time exercise of judgment and independent thinking are favored) than if it know lots of the customary useless things hammered into the shrinking or passive scholar by severe disciplinarians. The more sensitive children are fearfully cramped in their individuality by the usual methods, especially if at the same time they are "slow." This is conspicuously the case where teachers and school supervisors are chosen and kept in places purely through corrupt political "pull," however incompetent or inhuman they may be.

Impatient or austere instructors need often to have it impressed upon them that occasionally very stupid children develop into the greatest intellectual leaders of their century. Many a "slow" or backward child has become a genius or an immortal conqueror who, by sheer ability and force of character, has risen superior to restrictive influences and has in part shaped the world's history for all time. If dunces were as deficient in power as the average teacher regards them, history and literature would have fewer distinguished names; for many of the world's great have—like Swift, Sheridan, Scott, and Wellington—in early years been reputed "blockheads" by their instructors.

Very many ordinary children become physically inferior as well as mentally dwarfed, and have their better possibilities suppressed under the harmful influence of harsh and unsympathetic teachers. Weakly children should never be punished by being deprived of play or out-of-door exercise. Those teachers who punish average children by keeping them from meals or shutting them up in terrifying and dark rooms deserve in most cases to be regarded as dangerous to the community. Fear of punishment affects young scholars much more than older ones. It produces dangerous and indeed fatal results. Statistics even show that a number of cases of child-suicide can be definitely traced to this cause.

School attendance should not be required of average children before the age of seven, and that is very often too early. If they attend regularly at an earlier age, the hours should not exceed three per day, the recesses and intermissions in study ought to be frequent, and it is wiser to teach them to play than to make them perform tasks. The "kindergarten" methods are not to be systematically employed with a child younger than four years. Even then, these methods must be of the gentlest, wholly without restraint, very gradual and avoiding all stimulus or the enforcement of tasks. Only the most devoted of intelligent women are fit to conduct such schools.

Kindergarten schools afford a valuable but incomplete substitute for the care of a true mother. They are most useful for children at either social extreme where a mother neglects her offspring whether by force of want and depravity or owing to heartlessness and a persistent devotion to empty and ephemeral pleasures. The children of such mothers, even though amid great affluence, are in their earlier years better off in well-conducted institutions and away from the wholly harmful influences of immoral, vicious and disease-carrying foreign nurses.

It is proper here to mention that recent thorough experiments have added to the accumulated evidence that much arsenic is present in many of the colors used upon various articles that go to make up the kindergarten outfit. Objectionable amounts of this poison may be present in some of the glazed papers commonly used for the little learners to "play" with.

Dr. Thorne, in his valuable monograph on diphtheria, emphasizes repeatedly the fact, well known to experts, that unrecognized diphtheria may prevail very extensively and be considered as only "sore throat." He further shows very clearly that, as is generally recognized among us, diphtheria is especially liable to occur among children in elementary schools, and that, as with various other diseases, so in diphtheria "by far the largest mortality in any age-group is that which takes place in the first five years of life."

Since, then, various diseases of the most serious nature, as well as milder ones, are unquestionably caused by intimate contact in these elementary "play-schools," it is well to keep children away if any teacher or pupil who attends such a school have any ailment or be known to come into contact in whatsoever way with any person having an infectious disease, or even be suspected of having been exposed to infection.

OCCUPATION

NUMEROUS diseases are conveyed from one worker to another through careless contact or by means of insufficiently cleaned utensils or other articles. The various disorders that may arise in that way are spoken of at sufficient length in the chapter on Infectious Diseases. Tuberculosis is the most conspicuous and dreadful of all of these. It is constantly disseminated from the unclean dirt of ill-ventilated rooms. All such infection is absent from properly cleaned places where there are no cases of the infectious diseases and to which places neither the diseases nor their products are brought. Hence the presence of consumption or any other infectious disorder should induce caution and a disposition to insist upon cleanliness and the removal of the *cause* of any filth. Workrooms when swept out at the end of the day (as is proper) ought to have moist sawdust then used for catching the dust. Yet this sawdust must be clean. Otherwise it is not fit to strew over the floor. Steam-heat insures the destruction of harmful germs.

Water-supplies, used for drinking purposes by working people, need especial consideration. In some localities, among mines and in various kinds of work, metallic poisons may regularly be present in the water. Distilled water for drinking is to be substituted for the natural water in such cases, and is usually easy to procure. Even if crudely produced and having a slight oily taste, it deserves to be commended as a healthful water. Great care should be taken by employers to see that no contamination exists or can occur in the water-supply (or *ice*) consumed by those working for them. Otherwise typhoid fever, cholera and other diseases may arise.

Very serious diseases occasionally attack those who handle wool, hides or rags that happen to be infected. The sanitary value of disinfecting all of these would seem unquestionable, although the watchword *cleanliness* must not unnecessarily be made an obstacle to any industry. Such things as are known to have been infected ought never to be used without adequate disinfection. It is best, and in the end most economical, that all clothing, from persons who have had small-pox or other dangerous infective diseases, be invariably burned and never sold as rags. Otherwise cases of disease are especially liable to occur among those who sort rags for paper mills. Proper disinfection is sufficient to render such articles harmless; yet disinfection is too often ignorantly or carelessly carried out.

Those who are liable to come into contact with infected objects should attend carefully to the condition of their hands, as slight injuries of the skin may afford an entranceway for disease germs to get into the system. In order to remove any bacteria or poisons that have just been carried into the skin (or deeper) with a knife or whatever else has accidentally caused a wound, this wound should (*immediately* upon being made) be rinsed clean. Boiled water is best for the purpose. If the cut skin bleeds freely for a minute, that outflow of blood is desirable, since it washes out the wound from within. A layer of collodion or other protective should be applied before using the hands after a cut or scratch.

Harmful gases have especially to be guarded against in various industries. Such chemical products may seem indispensable for certain kinds of work; yet they offer constant and serious hygienic dangers. Chlorine and sulphurous acid occur in some bleaching occupations and in certain **chemical processes.** Nitrous acid fumes are encountered in connection with "etching" and "pickling" various metals, as well as in aniline-color manufacturing and in acid works. Hydrochloric acid gas occurs chiefly in connection with soda manufacture. Among the harmful products of gas works, ammonia may be mentioned. It occurs also with the use of ice-making machines. All of these produce at first an excitation of the respiration, together with irritation of the breathing surfaces and of the outer eye. Further effects are catarrhal irritations, which may be very severe if the irritant gas be allowed to continue its action. When very strong, these gases can soon cause death. People differ greatly in their sensitiveness to these irritating gases.

Chemical safeguards can occasionally be employed to neutralize these dangers. Against chlorine gas, for instance, it is important to use inhalers holding cotton moistened with alcohol. With all these and with sulphuretted hydrogen and other extensively used chemical agents, the essential hygienic measure is to adapt the construction and arrange the details of the processes so that all possible precautions are invariably taken to lessen and control the risks and to guard the workers. "Sewer gas" is spoken of on page 15 and in later chapters. The general importance of ventilating against ordinary contaminations of the air is considered in the chapter on Ventilation. The necessity of removing gaseous and other products from the air is very important in certain occupations.

Many of the substances that form dust are harmful. That dust which most injures the lung tissue does not often carry the germs of tuberculosis. The high rate of mortality from tuberculous consumption among such workers as grinders of steel is because the fine, sharp particles of steel dust cut minute wounds in the lung surface. If, then, numerous tubercle bacilli be present in the dust of the close workrooms, these microörganisms can enter into the lung tissue more readily than if the delicate surfaces were not already wounded. Various other mineral dusts are injurious in somewhat the same way. All of these tend in any case to cause chronic catarrhs of the lung tissues.

Vegetable dusts likewise affect the lungs as a rule ; but they usually cause less serious symptoms than are produced by mineral dust. Occasionally, skin symptoms are observed from the action of such dust. Tobacco dust has the effect of weakening the system exposed to its influence and thereby rendering it more susceptible to various diseases. Flour dust (like fine coal dust) explodes at times very violently when in contact with gaslight or other flames. It is stated that black walnut sawdust is exceeding bad for catarrhal cases. In workrooms where dust abounds, exhaust blowers or suction fans (see Fig. 29) should be used.

Poisonous dust from lead, arsenic, and other metals, as also from various other substances used in the industrial arts, may act upon and through the digestive tract as well as by being inhaled. Lead is unhealthfully present in many articles of daily use. Even silk threads may be so loaded with it as to cause poisoning in some sewing-people who frequently moisten such thread with the lips. Typesetters, painters, crystal-glass grinders, and indeed any class of people coming into contact with lead, are more or less liable to take the poison into the system. The chief occupations involving danger from lead dust as such are working in white-lead manufactories, smelting, and allied lead-purifying work. *Chronic lead-poisoning* is recognized by the blue lead line on the edges of the gums. Colic and constipation are the most marked symptoms. Later, paralysis of the extensor muscles results.

The most important preventive measure is *cleanliness* on the part of the workman, as regards the person. Especial care is also called for to avoid getting lead into food or drink. The danger of lead coming into the system by the use of lead pipes and improperly made cooking vessels is spoken of in the chapters on Food and Water. Workers in occupations that involve lead danger ought carefully to wash the hands before touching the mouth or any food. Besides cleansing the person, it is well also for people working with lead to change the outer clothing before eating meals. Nothing should be eaten by them within the workroom. A drop or two of sulphuric acid may with advantage be added to the water to be drunk while at such work. Milk is found to be a useful drink in white-lead mills; yet of course it must not be left exposed in the workrooms.

Workers in "silvering" mirrors and in amalgamating processes, hat-makers, gilders and others who have to do with **mercury** are liable to poisoning by that mineral. Its effects are shown, in an early stage, by excessive flow of saliva and by soreness of the mouth. Later come nervous symptoms and trembling. As in poisoning from any other work, it is here necessary to remove the patient at once from further contact with the harmful substance. Careless use of corrosive sublimate as a disinfectant is dangerous. Hence such solutions ought to be slightly colored to prevent mistake. Careful labelling is always necessary.

Arsenic is especially liable to be dangerous to makers of artificial flowers. This poison causes irritant symptoms of eyes, throat and stomach. Removal from the cause is imperative whenever these symptoms appear. Extreme cleanliness is the main safeguard in all of the occupations involving danger of metallic poisoning from any source.

Some industries may be injurious or annoying to neighboring residents. A stench, however, is not of itself a direct cause of ill health. Whether the odor come from "rendering" establishments, glue manufactories, brick kilns or other works, a business of such an unpleasant sort which an individual finds offensive cannot always be driven off by legal processes, although at times such means may be of avail. Things that are positively nuisances are usually remediable, and apt to be bettered if existing enactments be enforced.

Inflammable liquids introduce an element of great danger. Naphtha and benzine, as used for "dry cleansing" of gloves and clothes, may be instanced in this connection. In no case should such explosive things be brought near a fire. In printing establishments, turpentine ought to be used instead of benzine or naphtha for cleansing the rolls. Very dangerous businesses should be removed to places remote from habitations if danger of explosion be involved.

Soundness of boilers ought invariably to be insisted upon. Reliable and competent inspectors are necessary. Ordinary engines are now so made that they do not require as great care as is necessary for boilers; and yet laws require any one to have passed an examination in order to receive a permit to run an engine in certain places. In the same places, however, the boiler can be in the charge of a very stupid and ignorant person. This is a menacing inconsistency, and means an increased liability to boiler explosions by mismanagement of the steam. Much greater steam pressures are now employed than were usual a few years ago. Steam-fittings must correspondingly be made of heavy iron having great tensile strength and malleability.

To the humanitarian, it seems particularly deplorable that, with the great improvements made in the construction of engines and boilers, no practical device for automatic stoking on steamships has ever been produced. Much injury comes, both directly and indirectly, to the men who have to do the stoking. Many deaths occur every month from the effects of such work. To sailors, the dangers of the sea are constantly lessening with the increase in improved steamships. Yet the quantity of dangerous sailing vessels that cupidity still keeps afloat is large, and is apt to continue so as long as underwriters will insure the cargoes.

Numerous thousands of workers are injured every year by imperfect machinery and labor-saving devices of various sorts. Such people reveal by their painful examples the importance of having legislative dictation insist that necessary safeguards be employed. Circular saws, belting and all machinery in motion should be more carefully guarded than is usual. Then we may expect that heedless and nervous persons will be less liable to injury than is now the case. Workmen are not always disposed to wear spectacles, masks, and the numerous other contrivances found of service in warding off injury such as comes with certain occupations.

The safety of the people demands that more thorough investigations be made of each of the numerous accidents upon our railways. In those parts of this country where due attention is paid to supervision and discipline, accidents are fewer, if we judge by the reports of the Interstate Commerce Commission. The speed of the trains is not the cause of the very many accidents reported regularly in the *Railroad Gazette* and other journals. Overwork and carelessness explain many of these casualties. More searching efforts to fix responsibility in every case, with the infliction of a suitable and salutary punishment, whether the guilty one rank high or low, would greatly lessen our railway accidents and their notable fatalities and mutilations. Automatic couplers have gradually been introduced even without legislation and have already proved of extreme benefit. Passenger cars should no longer have any kind of stoves in them. Steam from the locomotive is much safer as a means of warming.

Color-blindness is present in a varying percentage of people, especially among civilized races. It is an incurable defect. Of practical, every-day importance is the fact that railway employees and pilots are occasionally deficient in this sense, and cannot tell a red light or flag from one that is green. As these are the most common colors for signalling and are constantly used, it is important that applicants for positions requiring acuteness of this sense be examined by a suitable test. For this purpose, fifty or more small skeins of worsteds of various colors are thrown together. The pile thus formed should contain several shades of green, gray, yellow, pink, red, brown. Violet, purple and blue skeins are also to be included. Three larger skeins are always needed to be referred to as "sample colors." Following Holmgren, we select, for these three colors, a bright red (rather yellowish), a purple pink (magenta, medium light), and a light apple-green.

To test a person, the large *green* sample skein is placed on a white cloth or paper laid over a table. At a little distance from it, the other skeins are laid in a loose pile. The person being tested is asked to pick out from this pile, without naming the colors, any skeins that seem to be of the same color as this sample skein, whether darker or lighter. To instruct a man who seems embarrassed, the examiner may select a few skeins properly and then return them to different parts of the pile with the request that they be again picked out in the same way.

If thereupon only the greenish shades are taken out by the person being tested, and are readily placed with the larger green skein, the eyesight may be pronounced satisfactory as regards color perception. If grays or browns and others are also thrown in, a further test is made.

For this, the large purple (or magenta) skein is set apart from the pile of worsteds. Then the man is asked to put with it the small skeins of a similar color. If he then select only greens, grays, blues or violets, he is color-blind as regards either green or red. He is also color-blind if he adds light green and light brown or dark green and dark brown. Such an applicant for a place involving the recognition of signals should be rejected or referred to a specially skilled expert. For engravers and etchers, color-blindness is said to prove rather an advantage than otherwise.

General Considerations

Cheapness of industrial products is very often got at too dear a price. This is inevitably the case if the cheapness, so incessantly striven for in most occupations, has caused the standard of manhood to be lowered, or if women are employed without respect for their sex and their weaknesses, or whenever children are forced or even allowed to do work fit only for older people. The immediate gain to unscrupulous employers and the capitalists and authorities that sanction or aid them is as nothing compared with the harm resulting to the nation from lowering its quality of virtue, morality and health. Children should never be permitted to work steadily in industries or in mercantile establishments before the fifteenth year. Even then, their hours of work ought to be only half as many as those of adults. They should also be required to attend schools, both general and technical.

Where women work in factories, they should be compelled to rest for at least a month after child-birth. Properly conducted day nurseries for the care of the babes of workingwomen are of great value to the community. With these, there should be kindergarten or other schools provided for the young children of such mothers as have to work away from their homes during the day-time. Private beneficence has inaugurated numbers of these. The charge to the mothers is there very small, and the hygienic care of the children is usually very efficient. These places need to be under the best medical supervision. Extreme precaution must be employed against the entrance of infection or any possible diffusion of disease. It is, for instance, dangerous to have a consumptive in charge of the babies in such places, and the nurses or the children admitted should not have been near a case of scarlet fever, measles, diphtheria, or other communicable disease.

Hygienists and economists, as well as others capable of

impartial thinking, echo the cry of the laborer for **fewer hours of work.** The last half century in Europe and in the better parts of America has witnessed a notable rise in the wages of workers. Yet, during that time, the hours of work have been lowered in number from ninety to less than fifty-seven per week. The Lancashire cotton-spinner, in his efforts to supply, with his products, the demand of the entire world, dreads the competition of his rival in Massachusetts and wherever else the hours of labor are shortest. He is not concerned about what is produced by India, Russia, or other lands where the laborer toils many hours for a pittance. Rivalry need not generally be feared from people who are overworked and underpaid.

Legislation to improve the condition of the worker has almost invariably resulted in enhanced material prosperity and in higher moral and physical health of both the individual and the community. Experience has demonstrated that self-helpfulness among laborers is not lessened by legislative action directed toward improving their condition. Steam has so vulgarized labor that independence and individuality are rendered possible only in so far as the worker escapes from the trammels of prolonged and monotonous toil.

Short shifts should be the rule in the various industries where excessive effort is called for, and the number of hours there required of a worker should be small. Occasional intervals should be allowed, as for rest and food. Those engaged in occupations involving danger of poisoning, by inhaling or otherwise receiving harmful substances into the system, should not remain exposed in the dangerous atmosphere for more than a very brief time.

Brain-workers need to beware of undermining their health by incessant application. Excessive and unintermitting outlay of nervous energy and persistent concentration of the faculties for prolonged, exacting work wear out the human machine, and induce distressing nervous disorders to blot out early a painful life. Occupation of some sort is necessary to contentment and affords the best safeguard of happiness. Work is eminently beneficial to all. Yet continuous and unvaried exercise of the same energies means exhaustion if not deterioration. Variety is necessary to human perfection. Overwork in any line of mental activity does not give the most satisfactory results. Mr. Gladstone—whose active yet varied life is a constant object-lesson to the student of how to enjoy health in old age and yet work vigorously—illustrated this recently, in explaining his strength, by saying: " There was once a road leading out of London on which more horses died than on any other, and inquiry revealed the fact that it was perfectly level. Consequently the animals, in travelling over it, used only one set of muscles."

Diversity is beneficial for all human beings. Improving recreation, as Bishop H. C. Potter has recently said, is desirable for the weekly day of rest as well as for holidays. Picture galleries, museums and libraries should be open at the times when they can most serve the great body of the public. The freer these educational and recreative institutions are made, the better.

Workshops and workrooms should not only have the most effective appliances, but the health of the employed ought to be considered in every way. The rooms should be suitably warmed in cold weather. Many workrooms are kept too hot. Steam-heat, so generally used in new structures for manufacturing purposes, does not of itself insure sufficient moisture or change of air. Extra facilities for ventilation are needed in most cases. Manufacturers who properly ventilate their mills and other establishments find that the employed can do at least ten per cent. more work than when the air is bad. Much illness in offices is, in part at least, to be ascribed to imperfect ventilation. Some of the greatest corporations are strangely neglectful of their own interests by failing to provide better breathing air for the clerks in their offices. Physicians appreciate this better than architects appear to. These defective provisions for health seem in too many cases the result of dense ignorance rather than due to niggardliness. The light is very often badly arranged in such places.

For artificial illumination, incandescent electric lights seem ordinarily the most suitable. In mills and large establishments in general it is best that the electric supply come through several independent and well-insulated main wires. If there be only *one* wire, an accident can involve instant darkening with possible consequent panic under some conditions. Comfortable arrangements for providing meals are of advantage to all. The water-supply of manufactories ought to be very pure. In any case, measures should be adopted at time of epidemic or other infection to sterilize the drinking water. Cleanliness should be inculcated and facilitated in every way. Water-closets or their substitutes ought to be arranged with thorough regard for health and convenience. Toilet rooms for women must be entirely separate from those for men.

Tenements and other dwellings controlled by manufacturing concerns need to be more hygienically constructed than is usually the case. This is extremely important, since much of the life of the workingman's family is spent in the dwelling. In the more crowded parts of our largest cities, the tenement-houses are sadly unsuited for the rearing of healthy families. Germs of infectious disorders abound in such places, and disease therefore spreads freely. Uncleanliness is there alarmingly prevalent in streets, rooms and clothing. Systematic efforts to diffuse instruction in the ways of cleanliness and health do much to improve the condition of the occupants of these unhealthful abodes.

Most valuable is such teaching when directed intelligently to the plastic minds of the young. Even a wholly degraded family is apt to show clearly in various ways the healthful influences of such valuable training bestowed upon one of its younger members. Yet the usual misdirected "charity" tends to lower people. It needs to be restricted and organized; for otherwise this word, like the term "trades union," too often means a great wrong and covers a multitude of sins against the American poor.

If a portion of his wages be allowed to accumulate instead of being paid for rent of an undesirable tenement in a crowded city, the workman can acquire in time a healthful home in a country district, provided that he be willing to forego the tawdry allurements of a city. The family is under much more healthful influences in the properly selected country home than in a big city. Of course, it is understood that in such cases suitable sanitary precautions are observed, and that the site is well chosen. When dwellings are erected by a corporation for the occupancy of its work-people, self-interest and a desire to aid those who are directly connected with the prosperity of the industry ought to cause the work of construction and the sanitary equipment to be well done. If speculative outsiders or individual workmen attempt to construct such habitations, the result is often less satisfactory.

Unmarried workers in manufacturing communities should have special separate quarters provided for each sex. Hospital facilities ought to be made so agreeable and generally satisfactory to the population that they will voluntarily seek such superior accommodation whenever ill. Infectious diseases are always best treated in hospitals especially arranged for isolating such cases.

Mutual accident insurance, life insurance, health insurance and also a system of pensioning are very important for the welfare of workingmen and their families. Most workers, especially if skilled, receive considerably more wage money than they absolutely need, and this surplus is too often expended in a way that causes injury rather than benefit. Hence it is no hardship, but rather a most just and wise provision against want, that workingmen have a certain portion regularly deducted from the earnings due them. This portion should be at once transferred to trustees approved entirely by the employed and of extreme financial soundness and integrity. Funds of this sort afford a most important provision against destitution, disease and injury.

Coöperative associations for savings and loans induce frugality among people of small but steady earnings. They advance the cause of good citizenship, and hence improve the health of the community. In Philadelphia, these associations are very abundant, and a higher proportion of wage-earners own their homes there than in any other city in America. Perhaps it is as a consequence of this that extremists in the doctrines of socialism or anarchy are comparatively rare in that city. The coöperative savings and loan associations of New York State are founded upon a method and system which seem the best of any in America.

LIGHTING

Daylight is indispensable to health, and, like pure air, it should be abundantly supplied to all living-rooms. Some adults appear to maintain a fair degree of health while following occupations that allow them very little light besides that which is artificially produced. Yet the vital processes of the human body are more perfectly carried on when there is an abundance of daylight. Especially do children languish and fade when, because of extreme northern latitude and the winter season or otherwise, they are deprived of daylight. Like plants, all higher animals need sunlight or at least diffused daylight.

In darkness not only do harmful germs thrive best, but disease processes become more serious, and fatal outcome of illness or greater resultant weaknesses follow in consequence of restricted natural light. Electric light has been shown to have a certain value in forcing the growth of some garden vegetables and flowers. Such products appear inferior in quality. Inflamed eyes are of course to be guarded carefully from any bright light.

Bright diffused daylight is best for the eyesight. Such light is had in its perfection when one is near a large window that is on the unshaded north side of a building. Uniform, thin white clouds are agreeable modifiers of such light. Glare is very bad for the eyes, whether it be direct, as from the sun (or from electric or other light), or reflected from water, sand or white surfaces. It can be kept from the eyes somewhat by the use of comfortable, mild "smoked-glass" spectacles (or eye-glasses). Grayish or buff-gray Holland window shades on spring rollers are best for excluding an excess of sunlight from rooms. It is best that curtains be away from the upper portion of the window as much as possible; for the upper part of a window throws much more light into the room than does the lower part.

In school-rooms, studies, workshops, etc., the light should be such that any person of healthy, normal eyesight can read, write or examine the usual work continuously without any effort of accommodation of the eye and without experiencing any fatigue. When the light is insufficient and the eyes have therefore to be nearer than usual to the work in order to see well, this produces strain and fatigue which in the end are harmful to the eyesight. Bright light is therefore best for work; yet the light must not be dazzling when it reaches the eye.

To test whether the daylight in the darker portions of a school-room or workshop, for instance, is suitably strong on an average day, the standard test-type, as furnished by all opticians, can be employed with normal eyes at the proper distances as specified on the tables or on accompanying directions. Preliminary or corrective tests should be made with the same test-type and by the same eyes in places where the light is ample. Practically this is a very useful means of fixing a standard, and such a simple test is readily understood and appreciated by those in whose power and province it lies to remedy the deficiency.

A more precise and mathematical demonstration of the exact amount and quality of the light that reaches any given part of a room is afforded by the use of the Weber *photometer*. This, like other apparatus for measuring the angle of the light and the amount of visible sky, is excellent. But very few people are likely to possess these instruments of precision; and the much simpler means (that is, of using test-type as above indicated) will be found sufficient.

Technically speaking, the light in any part of a workshop or of a room in which one reads should, even on cloudy days, according to Cohn, have at least an illuminating power equal to that given by ten standard-candles that are from thirty-nine to forty inches away (*ten meter-candles*).

Daylight should be as little as possible obscured by trees, buildings or other things moving or standing between the sky and the window through which the light enters. Nothing should intervene between the source of light and the page read or the piece of work upon which one is engaged. For one who is writing, the light ought to come somewhat sidewise, as from the left and slightly from the front, so that the arm or hand does not shade the paper by obstructing the light. The desks in business offices could often be greatly improved in this respect. If directly facing a bright light, some sort of shade should be used to prevent all glare from entering directly into the eyes. For reading, the light may come from the side or over the shoulder.

The illuminating power of the daylight that reaches any object in an ordinary room is almost inversely proportional to the square of the distance of that object from the window. Thus on a page one yard away from an ordinary window, the light is four times as strong as on a page two yards away, and sixteen times as strong as when the page is four yards away. Hence the nearer the student's or clerk's desk or the workman's bench and work are to a window where glare is absent or guarded against, the better for the eyesight. As mentioned in speaking of school-rooms, windows should reach as high up toward the ceiling as possible when the further (dark) side of a room is used for work requiring light.

The higher the window through which light from the sky falls into a room, the better the light. Hence it follows naturally that we ought not to darken any living-rooms by draperies, hangings, lambrequins or anything else that obstructs the light coming in at the upper part of the window. If, in spite of this and other health considerations, heavy curtains are put up in libraries or other working-rooms, they are preferably to be so hung that they can readily be pushed away back to either side when light is needed. Where curtains are used to insure greater privacy, these should be limited to the lower part of the window as much as possible. A roller can be so arranged as to allow a shade to pull from below upward. Thereby it effects its purpose and yet allows the light to come in through the upper part of the window. There are curtain devices which cover, as desired, any particular part of a window; but they are found to be of limited popularity.

Open daylight from a surface of sky direct into a room is best. Yet this is, in narrow city streets and courts, not always to be had, and lower rooms may there be very dark. So, mirrors are at times used outside of windows to throw light into a room, and surfaces are whitened to increase the amount of light reflected. These means are a help, but of necessity an incomplete one. Reflected light (glaring or not) from a whitened wall is inferior to direct light from the sky, even if that be clouded. In "ells" and in upper rooms that are surrounded by higher and light-obstructing buildings, an excellent means of improving and increasing the light is to have a large glass window in the ceiling.

Light reflected from the walls of a room, if they are not of a dark color, is an aid to the brightness of the apartment. If this light be unpleasantly strong and glaring, it is to be modified. Dark surfaces reflect light poorly, whether they be on walls or in the shape of cloth or other substance upon which one is working. Therefore blackboards on the walls of school-rooms are by many considered as not so desirable for the eyesight as "whiteboards" on which the writing is done in black. Thus far, however, very little of practical value has been effected in this respect.

Artificial Light

Artificial light is always inferior to good daylight, even apart from any consideration of the more or less unhealthful products given off in large quantities by all artificial lights excepting the various electric lamps. All are much yellower than is desirable, and all involve a certain amount of danger from their use. A good light has as few of these defects as possible, is steady, brilliant and must usually be inexpensive.

Candles are the most costly and defective of the usual means employed. These primitive and picturesque lights are not much used where better can be had. Their portability and certain other qualities recommend them for a large number of mines, especially in the western mountains. As with various oils, the substance of candles forms combustible gas (hydrogen) by the heat of the flame. Carbon is also present. Its particles glow in the flame owing to the heat of the hydrogen burning in the oxygen of the air. This glow of the carbon gives the brilliancy. If not enough air be furnished for the amount of carbon and hydrogen (that the candle material supplies) to burn up in, or if too great an amount of carbon be present, the candle "smokes." The same lack of air or excess of carbon is found also to be the cause when lamps (or other lights) smoke.

In such cases, the carbon fails to be consumed by combustion, and hence the familiar sooty particles (lampblack) are given off into the air. Accordingly, glass chimneys are desirable, even with candles, since they not only prevent unsteadiness, but also concentrate more oxygen-containing air upon the carbon, hydrogen and other elements of the glowing flame. The wick should also be small, if soft fats are used for candles, as they then smoke less. Hard fats, wax, and spermaceti are best. The wick ought to have been dipped in boric acid or some other substance that causes it to burn to ashes.

ARTIFICIAL LIGHT

Like other light-producing materials, candles give off heat, water and carbonic acid gas. The standard "candle," by which the strength of a light is measured, varies. One accepted standard-candle is made of spermaceti so that 120 grains are burned in one hour.

Animal oils (such as whale oil and lard oil) are nowadays used much less than formerly for lighting. They are much safer than the various volatile fractional-distillation products of the petroleum-refining process, such as benzine, rhigolene, naphtha, etc. These are dangerously explosive, and their use ought to be very limited. Gasoline is considerably used in some places such as isolated hotels, and in cities it is used by a few large establishments because it is cheaper than gas. It is, however, dangerous, and is liable to give off very disagreeable and unhealthful gases into the air.

Kerosene oil (refined petroleum) of the best quality is superior to all of these for domestic or other general lighting. Kerosene has a much higher boiling point than the more inflammable petroleum products. In the process of manufacture it distils over at a temperature of from 300° to 480° F. Its specific gravity is a trifle more than four-fifths of that of water. With the immense use of refined petroleum, it is easy to procure it always of sufficient purity. Yet small retail dealers sell much oil that is below the required standard. Without constant inspection tests, low-grade oil is apt to be supplied. Legal restrictions upon the sale of dangerous illuminating oil should be rigorously enforced. If of inferior quality, kerosene is both dangerous and ill-smelling. Instead of using the more accurate and reliable test apparatus, and as a rough test, a rather flat watch-glass containing a few drops of kerosene may be held in the palm. As soon as it has become well warmed by the heat of the hand, a lighted match is touched to it; yet it does not then burn if pure and fit for lamps.

Kerosene lamps have either flat or round wicks. The

latter are hollow and fitted upon a short tube, into which air enters from below and then becomes warmed as it rises or is drawn up to the flame, where it produces perfect combustion. These round burners make a very perfect light. A familiar form of this is the "student's lamp." When used by people who are fairly careful, this, at its best, is preferable to a gas flame for the reason that it is not so hot as the argand burner, and because, although giving off much carbonic acid gas, good kerosene produces very much less of the various more harmful gaseous poisons that enter the air with the use of ordinary illuminating gas. It gives, besides, a steadier light, being independent of all changes in pressure to which gas is liable.

The more carbon we can cause to combine chemically with the oxygen of the air and the more hydrogen there is used up, the more complete is the combustion, and by consequence the hotter is the flame and the more brilliant is the light. So, in addition to employing the hollow round wick, we further introduce a contraction of the glass of the chimney near the burning oil above the top of the wick, in order to render the combustion more perfect. A Prussian commission, that recently investigated the question, determined that lamps which used round wicks were less liable to explode than the lamps where the wick was flat.

Lamps should ordinarily be made of metal, because of the danger of breakage in case that all is of glass. Yet carelessly constructed metal lamps are apt to heat the oil too much. A funnel-shaped lamp shade narrowed at the top and large and open at the bottom, made of glass or porcelain that is dark outside and white and polished within, is valuable for close work and shields the eyes, although of course cutting off very much light from the remainder of the room. A cloth shield interposed between the light and the head of one who is working near the lamp lessens the heat that is felt and also relieves the eyes from the glare.

The dangers of allowing the use of kerosene for quick kindling of fires are so well known that no further warning against such harmful practice should be needed here. It is best to lower the wick somewhat before blowing out a lamplight, and it is slightly safer to blow from *above*. The most serious cause of accidents with lamps is the custom of replenishing the oil without having first extinguished the light.

Illuminating gas consists essentially of carburetted hydrogen. It contains various gaseous compounds of the "marsh gas" and "olefiant gas" series. Even the best contains nearly ten per cent. of carbonic oxide (a very poisonous and odorless gas). Other gases may also be present. Ammonia, whenever present, is considered objectionable; for, by burning, it may produce the cyanide of ammonia, a poison. The peculiar odor of illuminating gas is due to the presence of naphthaline, sulphuretted hydrogen and bisulphide of carbon. This latter comes chiefly from the iron pyrites which is present in most of the gas-coal used by us. On combustion in our rooms, it forms sulphurous acid, which becomes sulphuric acid by mingling with the moist air. Nitrous acid, if present in gas, is a harmful element.

Gas can be made from anything that contains carbon and hydrogen. The U. S. Special Consular Reports for 1891 (on Gas in Foreign Countries) mention various cities of the world where crude petroleum, resin, wood and other substances are used. Oil gas is excellent for railway-car use, as it can be compressed more satisfactorily than ordinary gas. Bituminous coal is considered the best material.

Several different processes of dry distillation in iron retorts are employed. Of the details, it is particularly important that the washing and other purification be carefully carried out. It is to the interest of the gas companies that certain impurities be removed. Ammonia for instance is, like coke and the coal-tar products, a valuable article of sale. It furthermore attacks the mechanism of gas-meters, and causes them to be irregular and to register an actually smaller amount than the consumer receives.

The most dangerously poisonous constituent of illuminating gas is, as above indicated, carbonic oxide (carbonic monoxide, CO) gas. This is always abundantly present. It is several times as abundant in " water gas " as in ordinary gas. Such water gas furnishes the chief supply for New York City and other American communities, and is used because it costs less. It is made by passing water vapor over surfaces of burning coals. It is " enriched " by adding naphtha and other hydrocarbons rich in carbon. Naphthaline is added to produce the albocarbon light, which is white and brilliant, but is apt to smell very bad. The laws of some countries prohibit the manufacture of " water gas." Fortunately, the very harmful carbonic oxide gas, always present in the gas that we burn, is there associated with the strong-smelling gases above mentioned, and which usually betray its escape from gas-pipes.

Serious cases may occur, especially in winter, where gas leaks from a street main that is broken or otherwise defective. When, under such circumstances, the other gases are taken up by the soil, this odorless gas is drawn into warmed houses. Fatal cases have occurred in this way, even where the street had not an impermeable pavement. *Many of the vague ailments which have been ascribed to " sewer gas" are probably due to escaping or imperfectly burnt illuminating gas.* Therefrom occur headache, prostration and all too often the more serious symptoms such as an unconsciousness from which not even bleeding or any other known remedy will rescue the unfortunate victim.

That illuminating gas is a noteworthy cause of more or less serious illness is proven, in so far as the more obvious instances are concerned, by the frequency with which such cases are reported in the daily papers. Many of these accidents are explainable by a careless or stupid neglect of occupants of rooms to turn off the gas properly. A few others are due to a custom, which some hotels have, of shutting off the gas from their rooms during the night. In this way a light left burning low (and not recognized outside the room) is of course extinguished without being turned off in the room. Through the unstopped gas-cock, therefore, the gas enters the room early in the morning.

It is generally recognized that much gas escapes from gas-mains and pipes. It is stated that the amount of gas lost from London gas-works amounts to nearly one thousand million cubic feet a year. In New York, the loss is probably about the same. To detect leakage within a house or other building, one should examine the indicators of a gas-meter carefully. If any increase in the amount is recorded during a time when no gas is being burned (and not leaking through the burners) a thorough test must be made. To test house-pipes, they are stopped at the ends. Then air having a few drops of ether in it is pumped in. Wherever an odor leaks out of the pipe, the defective place is attended to before gas is allowed to enter the house.

Because of the serious dangers associated with its use, even for those who employ the utmost possible precautions, it is of extreme importance to the health of all that the gas supply be of excellent quality and purity, and that the pipes through which it is distributed be sound and jointed with the best mechanical skill. Subways, in which the pipes are kept dry and can be constantly inspected, are much preferable to the usual method of burying gas mains in the earth underneath streets.

Valves, gas-cocks and other means for shutting off gas must, like all gas-piping, be perfectly tight. Their mechanism should be perfect, and the simpler they are, the better. Electric and other convenient but complex gas-lighting appliances that work automatically are at times dangerous. After prolonged absence of a family from a house, the rooms need to be well aired even if the gas has, for a long time, been shut off at the street. At such times the explosive nature of the product of the mingling of gas with atmospheric air should always be borne in mind. When from 13 to 20 per cent. of illuminating gas is present in air, the compound is highly explosive. If the percentage of the gas mixed with the air be from 5 to 13, or from 20 to 30, the mixture is inflammable. Beyond these limits it is not so; yet the danger of poisoning is always present wherever the gas leaks.

When burners receive so little gas that their flames are low, they flicker, and also the combustion of the gas is then less perfect than when they burn with full force or nearly that. If there be an unduly great pressure of gas, this tends to make the gas flame "blow." Then the gas-cock has to be turned off a little so that the gas enters the burner under somewhat lessened pressure. *The burner should be so constructed as to burn up the gas completely and to prevent as much as possible the escape of any of the harmful components and products into the air of rooms.* Yet an excess of air must not be supplied; for that causes the carbon to be wholly burnt up, as in the Bunsen burner used in laboratories. There the carbon does not remain incandescent. If not enough air be supplied, the carbon goes off into the air as soot, and also a considerable amount of gas is then apt to escape.

For any work or reading requiring good, steady light, the usual "fishtail," "batwing" or other burner is inferior to an average kerosene-oil light if that be practicable. Even the little flat-wick oil lamp with a globe of water between the little chimney-protected flame and the work upon which it concentrates and increases the light, is steadier than the gas flame, and therefore better for the eyes of a workman if the light be broad enough. In summer it certainly is cooler. The various modifications of the ordinary gas-burners are numerous, but no one of all these is demonstrated to be notably superior to the others. Gas is more convenient than oil, and therefore certain to be used in rooms despite its dangers. The best burner, although it requires the most gas of all, is some one of the various modifications of the argand burner.

The *Welsbach* burner causes the gas to be completely burned up, and the light comes from the presence of an incandescent mantle which is heated by the burning gas. At its best, this burner gives a steady, white light. It has not proved quite as satisfactory as was hoped that it would. Those who recommended it highly at first do not all appear to indorse it unqualifiedly at present. Where "fuel gas" or water gas that is not enriched (as by the addition of naphtha) is used, this burner seems very economical. In any case it is better than most argand burners, until the incandescent mantle used with this peculiar burner burns out. The mantle can be renewed at a cost of fifty cents.

For large assembly rooms, theatres, etc., the Siemens' "regenerative" burner (see Fig. 16) may be recommended. It, like all large burners used under favorable conditions, gets a relatively large amount of light from a given outlay of gas. The gas becomes somewhat warmed before reaching the flame, and thereby the burner secures economy and better combustion. But, what is of extreme hygienic consequence, it also has a small flue-tube contrived so as to carry off the waste gas (if there be any) and the inevitable products of combustion. It also heats a room less than other burners. Such a principle can be applied to almost any burner, but this is too seldom done. With gas-stoves, there must invariably be some sort of perfectly tight flue-tube used to carry off the harmful products and prevent them from entering the air of the room in which the gas is burning (see Fig. 19).

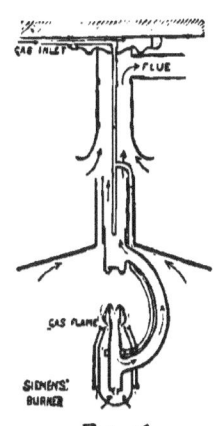

FIG. 16.

All artificial lights excepting electricity heat the air considerably and also contaminate it. A gas flame of only ten-candle brilliancy produces, in one hour, four times as much carbonic acid gas and five times as much heat as an adult human being does. A kerosene-oil flame develops only half as much heat as comes from a gas flame of equal brilliancy, although it produces even more of the undesirable carbonic acid gas. A kerosene-oil flame gives out into the air much less heat and carbonic acid gas than result from candles that make a light of the same brilliancy.

All of these accordingly contaminate the air of apartments in which they are burned; but ordinary gas, from the peculiarity of its manufacture, is certain to give off greater quantities of very harmful substances. Hence the less gas used in a house, and the fewer pipes and burners there, the better. Some ventilating arrangement by which the harmful products are carried off out of the room is necessary if the best health is to be maintained. For every cubic foot of gas burnt in a room in an hour, at least ten cubic feet of fresh air should be allowed every minute. So, every single burner consuming four feet of gas per hour needs at least forty or fifty cubic feet of air a minute. This will be further considered in the chapter on Ventilation.

Electric light, when at its best, is much safer and better than other artificial light. Although it has occasional dangers, these are limited to the effects of the conducting wire and so are more apt to be controlled than are those of gas. The *arc*-light is the cheaper of the two kinds used and gives the whiter light; but, owing to its very glaring and unsteady quality and its size, it is suited only for very large halls or out-door spaces. The other kind, the *incandescent*, is steadier and can be employed on a study-table instead of a "student's lamp" if there be a shade to keep the glare out of the eyes. It is then theoretically of better quality than the oil light. Practically this is not always the case. If the oil be of the best quality, and if from two to five minutes of time be given to prepare the lamp every day, the oil light, although of course quite inferior to good daylight, has an agreeable steadiness and uniformity which the electric lamps do not constantly possess in their present imperfect development.

Electric light is produced by causing an electric current to glow by passing through carbon. In the arc-light, the carbon is in the shape of two rods, each a few inches long (the positive above the negative) and separated by about one-eighth of an inch. A glass cup should be beneath the glowing light in order to catch the little bits of heated carbon that become detached, chiefly from the upper (hollowed-out) rod. In the incandescent electric light, the carbon is a filament within a pear-shaped glass bulb that is air-tight and has the air exhausted. These deteriorate and the light becomes poorer after they have been used a varying number of hours. It is claimed that they can be made to last for 1,200 hours or more. Practically, as they are supplied us in America, they usually do not last for even half that time. When a bulb is used up (as revealed by deterioration in the quality of the illumination), a new one is put on.

Dangerously strong electric currents are too often used for lighting (and other) purposes. We can assume that a constant current of 100 "volts" is not dangerous. Yet an alternate current of 160 "volts" can kill a human being. In view of the numerous fatal injuries that have occurred from using too strong a current, it is safest to limit the "voltage" to 120, as is the usage in some places. The wires should also be kept well insulated and not allowed to come into contact with telegraph wires or those used with telephones; for otherwise fires may be caused. Electric currents cause many fires, and the best management of the dangerous wires is at present very perplexing to insurance experts. Workmen attending to the maintenance of such wires should be required to wear rubber gloves and to use much caution.

The hygienic superiority of electricity over gas for illumination of houses or workshops lies chiefly in the fact that it produces none (or almost none) of the poisonous or other gases given off from gas-pipes and gas flames. Furthermore it gives less than a tenth as much heat as comes from the average gas-burners, the light in both cases being of the same candle-power, and no device being used to carry off the gas-heat as is so well done by the flue of the Siemens' burner. Even the hottest electric light is only one-sixth as hot as a hollow round kerosene flame, both being equally strong. The above comparisons are made from the observation of incandescent lamps. The arc-light is a much cooler lamp, yet its use, as already said, is limited.

The color quality of the incandescent light, such as we use in-doors, is hygienically slightly better than that of other artificial lights. Yet the electric light has unquestionably a yellowish quality, usually aggravated by the shades used. Ground-glass bulbs are not so much of an improvement over ordinary ones as is supposed by some. Bulbs or shades that are slightly blue are better, as they absorb some of the yellow light. Shades and dark eyeglasses, although wasteful of light or inconvenient, should be used to protect the eyes from the glare of the electric light, as this very bright glow can be harmful. The arc-light is most so; for it is more like the light of the sun in its quality.

Electric light may fairly be considered the best of our artificial lights, if we take everything into consideration. But it has not yet become sufficiently perfected to have displaced others. Indeed, it is always well to have oil or some other light to be employed whenever needed as a substitute or accessory. Halls, where panic or other danger might arise because of total darkness resulting from an accident to the electric apparatus or to the wires that conduct the current, need to be provided with a few oil lamps always in use. Of course this does not apply to places where inflammable or explosive substances are stored or manufactured. Theatres, hotels, etc., should however always have a few lamps, lighted by oil or candles, at stairways and in halls. Thereby at times many lives may be saved.

Owing to its unnecessarily great cost, electricity is more of a luxury than it ought to be. Batteries are a much more expensive means of supplying electric light than are dynamo-machines. A "dynamo" requires one nominal horse-power for every ten or twelve lights of 16 candle-power. In an establishment such as a hotel or manufactory, that works its own dynamo-machine to produce electricity, the electric light is cheaper than gas. It is exceedingly cheap to produce where water-power (even though not very near) is abundant and to be had by simply introducing a turbine wheel to utilize the power that otherwise would be wasted. One 1,000-candle-power arc-lamp suffices to illuminate 700 square yards of floor surface in a workshop, or ten times as much open space. For street lighting, twenty or thirty thousand square yards may be supplied by such a light. In rooms it is well to allow at least one 20-candle-power incandescent light for every thousand cubic feet of room space.

BUILDINGS AND STREETS

Building-sites should be clean and dry and ought also to allow abundant fresh air to all occupants of the structures erected there. Gravel and other porous soils with permeable subsoils are to be preferred. (See page 2.) In any case, the ground should be so well drained artificially, if not naturally, that the ground-water does not rise within several feet of the cellar or walls of the house. Wherever subsoil drains are laid, coarse gravel should be thrown in along the course of these drains; for gravel favors drainage, and the outflow is thereby in part at least provided for whenever any accident happens to the drain.

To prevent water from the soil rising into the lower part of the house, the cellar should have concrete floors and walls overlaid with asphalt or otherwise made water-tight. It is also desirable that this layer be tight enough to keep out gases that may chance to enter from leaky pipes. The foundation walls keep dryer when by the use of cement on the outside or by other means they are made impermeable to moisture. In loamy or moist soils a ditch-like depression, between the water-tight foundation wall and the ground beyond, serves to catch what moisture would ooze out of the ground and come against the wall. This ditch should have a drain at its lowest part, and it may need to be covered in, if water from the surface be liable to flow into it.

Bushes add to the moisture of the soil, and, when near the house-wall, they should be removed if the soil be only slightly permeable to water. Through thickets of bushes, any excess of ground-water does not evaporate so quickly as through uncovered turf. While a few high trees, suitably placed, serve to intercept the fiercest rays of a tropical sun, shade trees over and about a house in cooler climates are undesirable, from a hygienic point of view, since they lessen the healthful force of the sun and wind. As a wind-break for a house in an exposed or level situation, trees are desirable to the northward and northwestward or otherwise so disposed as to afford shelter against the bleakest winds in cold localities. It should be remembered that, like surfaces of water, trees appear to intercept "malarial" air currents. Thus it may not be well to remove a grove or thicket lying between habitations and a malarial swamp or "river bottom."

The only gases, coming from the ground, that require especial precautions to be taken are such as leak from gas-mains and gas-pipes and those due to the nearness of defective sewers and privies. These should constantly be guarded against. Solid and liquid uncleanliness of various sorts in and on the ground is much more to be apprehended than any gases other than illuminating gas. The ground must therefore be kept quite clean of all house waste.

Where building-sites are not expensive, it is the custom to build houses quite separate from neighboring ones. This plan renders rooms liable to be affected speedily by changes of the outside temperature. When buildings are together in a row, the loss of heat from the walls in winter is thereby lessened, and in summer, heat does not penetrate readily into the centre of a large structure. Yet the small, isolated homes of our country regions and villages are much more healthful than the crowded tenements or "apartments" of cities. The house standing by itself receives more sunlight and fresh air. It is for that reason, and because of its freedom from contact with others, less liable to have its inmates receive infection. It is also less apt to have the germs of disease enter it from infected bed-clothing, carpets, and other articles heedlessly shaken in the air by neighbors.

Yet all houses need to be freely ventilated or often aired out under the purifying influence of the sunlight. Otherwise the bacteria of disease thrive there whenever they enter.

In great cities, the crowding of buildings and especially the introduction of tall structures impairs the healthfulness of offices and habitations near by, because such lofty walls obstruct the natural circulation of air and impede the passage of daylight. When a building, as is the case in Chicago, has twenty stories and reaches 365 feet above the ground, or when, as occurs in other cities, buildings that are less than twenty-three feet broad extend for more than ten high stories into the air, these deserve to challenge attention as interesting architectural experiments, yet are very far from being hygienically proper. Especially is this so where the streets are very narrow.

By conflagration or severe storms, these lofty and frail structures are liable to become wrecked with great loss of life to all who may be in or near them. Furthermore, they favor overcrowding and are unhealthful—as already mentioned—because they lessen the necessary fresh air and light that people who are in adjoining buildings would enjoy but for the presence of the tall and dangerous buildings on the crowded streets of cities. Even in broad streets, such structures are undesirable.

Many very high buildings are quite deficient in the features necessary to strength and permanency. Owing to their defective construction, some of these have to be rebuilt in part at least before they have been standing long. They should have their floors and all their iron-work most carefully braced transversely or laterally so as to make trusses of these throughout the entire building. Careful bracing with wrought-iron or mild steel riveted in all parts does much to enable exceedingly high buildings to resist vibration effects and the results of heavy wind-pressure. Horizontal ties are needed for this.

Neither bolting nor the use of cast-iron is permissible in these structures. Columns made of cast-iron are very unreliable, being untrustworthy not only because of the inferior qualities of all such material but also because competition has caused much wholly bad cast-iron to be put upon the market. The defective nature of this building material may not be recognized before it is used.

The danger from accidents on passenger elevators used to convey people to the upper stories of such buildings is inconsiderable when all parts are well constructed, provided with safeguards, carefully and regularly inspected, and run very carefully by responsible persons.

Although houses in large cities may be placed close together side by side or even have no intervening lateral space whatsoever, a house should always be separated from the one opposite (either in front or to the rear) by at least the height of the taller of the two, the measurement being taken from the gutter upon the edge of the roof. Some degree of uniformity in height or, better, the establishing, by rigid building laws, of a height which no builder is allowed to exceed, is of hygienic value as favoring the unobstructed flow of air about all dwellings. *Trees* in limited number are desirable in park-like or wide streets, especially those frequented by the poor. The reason is that the shade afforded by suitable foliage allows the dwellers in close quarters to leave their rooms in summer and enjoy the healthful influence of fresh air without danger from the heat of the sun.

In laying out a city or its enlargement, restrictions as to the height and character of buildings ought carefully to be imposed. The city of Washington serves as a model as regards the liberal allotment of space. It is very difficult and costly to remedy existing overcrowded conditions. Wherever possible, numerous small parks should be scattered throughout a city. Usually it realizes too late that it has not enough of these and not enough long and broad avenues.

Building

Not only must the foundation and the lower part of a building be water-tight and thus guarded against the possible entrance of moisture, but the side walls as well ought to be constructed so as to keep out cold, heat, wind and moisture. All these results are secured when an air-space is introduced into the wall, for air is a poor conductor of heat and cold. It is also well to make the outside surfaces so close and dense as to allow neither rain nor wind to drive into the substance of the wall. In the ordinary wooden house, these qualities are found if there be tight and painted wood upon the outside and a tight sheathing or the usual papered plastering be properly fixed upon the inside of the customary air-space in the walls.

Wood is always better as a non-conductor than brick, stone or iron. Hence logs of wood, properly disposed, are preferable to stones as a material for the walls of a house, if no regard be had to the durability or other qualities than warmth. The æsthetic worshippers, who erect chapels of massive stone with no wood-work or other substance on the inside of the stone walls, have a hygienically undesirable building. Those of the congregation who are near the wall are more exposed to dampness and cold than those in the centre of the room. Less fuel would be required for warming, if such a structure were of wood. That material is in general more healthful than stone.

Wooden buildings are more liable to burn up than are those of brick or stone. If poorly constructed, they may be very noisy, because of transmitting sound very easily. Especially when old, they harbor vermin rather readily and are not so easy to keep clean and disinfect if once infected. This is particularly the case with log-houses, and notably so where, for various reasons, the bark is not removed from the tree-trunks.

Architecturally speaking, it may be said that the densest stone is probably the most durable and most satisfactory to the builder. Yet, for the hygienist, *porosity* of a building-stone is very desirable, since that insures the presence of a certain amount of air. This air makes the building material a poorer conductor of heat and cold. Hence brick, being porous, is hygienically preferable to stone for building walls and very much better than iron or other metal. Ordinary unglazed brick is permeable to air and moisture and can take up one-sixth of its bulk of water. Accordingly it is desirable that brick walls have oil-paint or some other waterproof coating on the outside surface so as to prevent the entrance of moisture. It is well that the outermost layer of bricks be dense and smooth, especially if not glazed or coated. Yet the inner layers ought to be porous.

An excellent non-conducting layer of air is created if we separate the walls by the distance of at least two inches and thus make **double walls**. The two layers of such a wall are rigidly held together by "bonding irons," glazed earthenware or other strong tie that shall keep the two separated layers in relative place and yet not carry moisture in to the inner wall layer. Such air-layers may be introduced into all of the four walls of a house, or perhaps only the most exposed wall is constructed in this way. This method serves to make the inner walls of a house dryer and of more equable temperature. Hence it is to be recommended as a very healthful mode of erecting brick or stone walls. It tends, however, to carry noise somewhat and adds a little to the cost. An uninterrupted vertical layer of asphalt between the outer and inner layers of a wall answers to a certain extent the same purpose. All of these devices must be continuous from the very lowest part of the wall upward; for water will pass through even a single, thin, horizontal course of brick or stone that is at all porous.

In cities where land is very costly and where a builder wishes to slight his work, or for other reasons does not care to add the extra bulk and expense involved in making a double or even a porous wall, it is not uncommon to find, even in very high-priced work, that plastering has been laid directly upon the stone or brick of the wall without leaving any space for lathing or for its substitute! The result is that painting and other ornamentation upon such walls is apt to crack and peel off and—what is a very unhealthful sign that should always be looked out for—darker, damp spots appear on the walls owing to the presence of moisture.

This dangerous defect can be prevented (at least to a certain extent) by using layers of hollow brick made of terra cotta, or porous terra cotta blocks are used against the brick.

Another way—but which is not quite so good—is to use hollowed, fire-proof, hard (vitrified) "furring." If the hollow brick blocks are used inside because of their air-spaces, care should be taken that the "bonding bricks," that are set transversely in order to hold the others together, do not go clear across or otherwise form a means of carrying moisture into the inner parts of the wall and thus defeat their healthful purpose. The ends of timbers that enter the wall need especially to be protected from moisture. Bricks used for partitions should be light and porous.

Roofs must, like the best walls, be water-tight and poor conductors of heat and cold. They ought furthermore to be as light in weight as is consistent with these two essential qualities and with strength and permanency as well. Metal roofs let in much heat in summer and much cold in winter. Wood is decidedly better; but for protection against fire, it ought to be covered with slate when slanting and with sheet metal when flat. If they are flat, city roofs offer very valuable recreative possibilities when judiciously utilized for roof-gardens. In Canada it is found that double roofing, an air-space being between the upper and lower layers, is a valuable aid to the maintenance of an even temperature. When the roof is double, the light snow is not melted into ice by the house heat, as it would be if the roof were only single. Hence the snow either blows off or, if remaining upon the roof, it makes an excellent non-conductor and thus protects the house against cold. Gutters ought to be an inch at least away from the wall or arranged so as not to pour water upon the walls in case of injury or stoppage of the pipes leading water down to the ground.

Building-stone should be derived from clean quarries and no filth be allowed to soil it. Bacteria can enter the porous substance and survive there much longer than they can in the open air. Thus, cases are reported from several places (at Pennsylvania State College and elsewhere) where sewage has unquestionably leaked into limestone with harmful results. Yet the lime-hydrate of fresh mortar and of plastering is destructive of any bacteria that may be drawn into or are already in the walls of new buildings, unless the lime has (after years) gradually become carbonate of lime. Where sandstone is used for building-fronts, it should be carefully prepared. If insufficient attention be given to a consideration of the strata, sandstone and limestones may be expected to flake or chip off, and are then also more liable to permit the entrance, and growth into the stone, of minute organisms. These are at best not very durable building materials considered from an architectural standpoint. Brick is hygienically preferable to sandstone or limestone.

Floors are improved by having light, non-combustible material put into the space under the flooring and over the ceiling of the room beneath. Such filling serves to lessen vibration and to deaden noises to a great extent. Light hollow brick made of terra cotta are excellent for the purpose, being fireproof and also poor conductors of heat and cold. They are used in the walls also of all the best iron fireproof buildings and greatly increase the hygienic value of such structures by making them cooler in summer and warmer in winter than if only iron were used. For ordinary, inexpensive floors, clean sand is an excellent filling, although heavy. Ashes are often used, but are not good, since some ashes take up moisture. Light earths of various kinds are good. Turf is especially desirable when it has been treated with quicklime so as to have become incombustible and to have acquired at the same time a disinfectant quality.

It is very important to recognize that danger to the health is involved when common earth from an infected soil is used for such filling under a floor. Frequent attacks of typhoid fever, pneumonia and other diseases have been attributed by scientific physicians to such unclean soil put under floors. Germs of infection may enter such material through defective floors, and much filth may be left there because of the filthy habits of the ordinary workman engaged upon the construction of a house. Very careful and reliable investigators have shown that when bad filling material is carelessly taken to put between floors, examination may reveal more bacteria present in such dirt than are ordinarily found in highly contaminated soils outside !

The uncleanliness between floors may tend to increase with time rather than to diminish; for in these dark and close spaces the natural processes of purification are not operative as they are in soils under the usual favorable out-of-door conditions. Therefore, floor-fillings of doubtful cleanliness should either be rejected or treated with fresh milk-of-lime, which furthermore may in certain cases be very valuable as a disinfectant for cleaning filthy floor spaces.

The boards used for floors should be tongued and grooved and also very carefully matched and joined. They ought to have been dried for months beforehand. Oak or other hard wood carefully selected is best. When yellow pine is used, the kind of boards called "comb-cut" are to be employed, the side of the grain being upward. The boards are then less liable to splinter and warp. Flooring boards, when laid double with tarred felt between the two layers, are much less resonant than when this protection against noise is omitted. Layers of tarred paper under flooring keep bacteria and moisture from going freely through defective boards. Above pipes, the boards should be especially arranged so as to permit ready removal whenever that becomes necessary. Between the boards no fissures or crevices should exist. Wood-cement should be used to fill up such unhealthful receptacles for dirt.

Floors may be treated with three coats of boiled linseed oil, and then waxed, or thin shellac varnish applied several times. This serves to make a good floor, impermeable to liquid and dry dirt. This is somewhat costly; the heated drying oil used may smell bad and is not of itself antiseptic. Dr. Scheffer's method is better and is so inexpensive that it can be used for almost any floor. The floor is of course to be as well laid as possible, the nails sunk and the boards planed and sand-papered smooth, if the cost of that be permissible. Any floor to be treated successfully in this way should first be scrubbed clean with soda, and after this it is to be made perfectly dry. Then, coal-tar is used to impregnate the fibres of the wood and to enter all fissures. If heated till of the consistency of oil, the coating will run in. Yet care is then needed that the heating be not done too near to the floor because of danger of fire. For this reason, it is generally preferable that the coal-tar be introduced in a cool state. This can be effected by incorporating into it one-fourth of its weight of heavy coal-oil. A thin layer of this mixture is applied in a cold state by means of a brush.

The floor should have been well cleaned, and a solution of corrosive sublimate in the strength of one part to one thousand of water (or a little more than one drachm to a gallon) may have been applied to the cleansed floor if necessary for antiseptic purposes. In any case, the floor must be dry before the tar mixture is applied. After the first coat has dried in for two full days, a second coat of the tar and oil is brushed well into all parts. A third and final coat is added two days after the application of the second coat. The odor disappears in a few days, and a smooth polished surface remains which is antiseptic, preventive of all parasites, and easily kept clean, needing only a slightly dampened mop or cloth to remove dust. A bunch of wool or a hair brush upon which a few drops of petroleum or linseed oil have been put may be rubbed over this floor surface to maintain or restore its polish. The same inexpensive coating can be used upon wall boards.

Cleanliness of the floor where it joins the wall is greatly aided by the use of a rounded, concave moulding for the junction of wall and floor. Crevices and irregular surfaces on walls and floors harbor dirt even in spite of the ordinary cleaning, and at times disease germs are in this dirt. Therefore water should <u>not</u> be used in excess for cleaning an ordinary floor, as it tends to go into and through the floor, and then dirt and bacteria are carried into the spaces underneath. Where a floor is water-tight, this objection does not exist. Hence linoleum or a similar covering is excellent for rooms into which much dirt, mud and water are brought. It can be cleaned off with a mop, and so no dust rises. Carpet-sweepers are hygienically better than brooms for carpeted floors, since brooms stir up much dust. Clean sawdust, tea-leaves or small bits of paper, that have been well soaked with clean water, and scattered over the dusty carpet or other floor, take up much dust at time of sweeping with brooms.

Carpets that are nailed down are not desirable in any room. Dirt gradually sifts through the fabric, and part remains on the floor or on the paper which may be between the carpet and the floor, while part of this dry dirt (which may contain germs of disease) makes its way down into and through the faulty flooring so common in our buildings. If used at all, carpets ought to be frequently cleaned. Carpet beaters ought to be very careful not to allow their dust to fly into the air so as to be carried toward any person or house. Machines for the purpose of beating carpets in cities ought always to have exhaust-fans to draw the dust into chambers where it is laid by means of sprays or other wet method. Carpets from sick-rooms require disinfection.

Concrete when of the best quality makes excellent non-combustible and water-tight floors. Asphalt has both of these qualities. It may be considered as having especial merit for the flooring on staircases and for public halls where many people enter who are not very clean and who bring much street dirt in with them. These floor materials, being water-tight, can readily be cleaned by water, and are better than marble in everything but appearance. The objection to them is that they are colder than wood. Cork-asphalt is a new material said to possess the advantages of both asphalt and vegetable substances. It is to be hoped that it prove upon long trial to have the merits claimed for it.

Old wood of houses may be in a decomposed state owing to various microörganic growths (moulds) in the substance of the wood. New wood, therefore, ought not to be brought, to any great extent, into contact with that which has long been used. The destructive parasitic process is also less liable to attack timber when it is very dry before oil or paint has been applied. Creosote, tar or similarly antiseptic preparations should be used freely upon wood wherever the ends of floor-beams come into contact with the wall or are elsewhere exposed to moisture. Architects say that our Oregon pine is never attacked by the destructive white ant of Australia.

Staircases ought to be plain and fireproof, well aired and open to daylight. They must be readily accessible from all the rooms that they are arranged to supply. In hotels and institutions, the stairs should be abundant and away from elevators or shafts which are liable to prove dangerous flues in case of fire. In such places, as also in theatres, the staircases ought invariably to be indicated by oil-lamps having uniform and distinctive colored chimneys and globes. It is also well that such special safety lights be always kept burning when the place is being used; for sad experiences have shown that gas or the electric current may, when fire has broken out, be completely shut off by accident or by misunderstanding due to the excitement of the occasion, and therefrom many lives have been lost.

Steps are not to be much more than a foot deep in any case and not above seven inches high. The presence of landings or short levels, at least as often as once in every eighteen steps, renders the stairs easier to climb, and ought to be introduced wherever women are to use the stairs. Spiral staircases are somewhat liable to induce accidents because of the narrowness of the inner edge of the wedge-shaped stair. Slippery surfaces are objectionable.

For fire-escapes, outside of buildings, upright ladders

are not safe for the average person to use. Ladders must slant somewhat and have flat treads. The best kinds are somewhat like ordinary stairs going down outside in a zig-zag manner from one balcony to another, these balconies being at each floor-level all the way from the roof downward. The various automatic fire-escapes offer an ingenious and apparently effective means of lowering a timid person by means of a rope. An endless chain is better as a permanent fixture. The most satisfactory reliance in time of fire is in good construction, laterally extending balconies and double exits front and back from every floor.

Windows ought to be high, for the light in the room is then better, as indicated in the pages on Lighting and on Schools. They ought to have a total surface equal to more than one-tenth of the floor area of the room that they light. Twice that amount of window-space is desirable. Some fire-commissions consider it dangerous to have the windows exceed thirty per cent. of the wall area, if another building be within forty feet of the wall and fronting it. In brick or stone houses, the window-sills ought not to be of wood.

Dining-rooms and kitchens are best situated when upon the north side of the house, if the location favor this. While it is often desirable that hotels have kitchens at the top of the building, nearly every practical reason is against that plan for private houses. A way of preventing all kitchen odors from invading a house is to have an exhaust-fan (see Fig. 29) to draw the air up the chimney and out of the kitchen, and it may be used also for drawing out vapor from a laundry. The cooking-room may be out in an extension; but no living- or working-rooms should be on the level of the cellar. Servants should not occupy basement rooms, although the inner and lower part of a house is much cooler in summer and warmer in winter. Such places have not enough light and fresh air as a rule, and servants are generally not very cleanly in their ways. The cellar should be especially clean and dry; for dirt from there goes up very often into the house. If the cellar and basement be dirty and moist, the house cannot be healthy. No cesspools should be tolerated there. Water-closets and other fixtures connecting with the house-drainage ought not to be very low down. In no case should they be below the level of the house-drainage soil-pipe that goes to the sewer.

Sleeping-rooms ought not to contain less than one thousand cubic feet of space for every occupant. It is desirable that such rooms be much larger than that. Alcoves and dark recesses are not healthful; for abundant fresh air and sunlight are needed in every bedroom. The rooms on the east, southeast or south sides are preferable for sleeping-rooms and nurseries. They get the winter sunshine, and do not suffer from the summer sun as much as those rooms that face the southwest and west.

Sleeping-room furniture and decorations ought to be of the simplest patterns. The harder the plaster of the walls and the smoother it is in finish, the better. Smooth, oil-painted surfaces are easiest to keep clean. All roughnesses and fissures upon the walls, or in the wainscoting or in whatever woodwork is present, are objectionable as being liable to hold harmful dirt.

Wall-papers often contain arsenic. Dr. Wm. B. Hills of Harvard found this poison in nearly a third of the 2,142 samples that he examined in 1889, 1890, and 1891, and it was present to the extent of more than one-tenth of a grain per square yard in nearly three per cent. of these samples. The following colors used on walls and ceilings appear to contain much arsenic: orange, chrome yellow, dark ochre, Venetian red, raw umber, sienna, brown umber. They are probably not harmful if used with oil; but may be injurious if used without oil, as in "distemper" or water-color painting upon ceilings. The improved Marsh test enables any competent chemist to determine from examination of a piece of paper, ten inches square, whether arsenic be present or not. The purity of the zinc and acid used for the test must be determined by a parallel test made without any paper or other suspicious substance being introduced.

Arsenic furthermore occurs in dangerous quantities in a considerable proportion of the colored and figured stuffs used for curtains and other house-furnishing goods. For this reason, draperies and hangings may be at times very unhealthful in sleeping-rooms. A much more constantly potent reason for limiting as much as possible the use of such things is that they hold dirt and shut out light. Cornices and raised plaster ornaments are open to the objection of catching dirt and making the wall less easy to clean than when they are absent. After it has been used for lodging a person with an infectious disease, a room should be disinfected as is explained in the chapter on Disinfection. The failure to follow out proper disinfection in hotel rooms has been clearly demonstrated to be the cause of many cases of infectious disease.

Dark rooms and halls where light and air do not freely enter are not healthful. The germs of disease find very favorable living places there. Hangings, draperies, soft carpets, fretted wood-work, if used at all in cloudy Northern lands, ought to be aired frequently and bright daylight should be allowed to come to them. The fashion of the day appears still to permit much more raised plaster ornamentation than is desirable. Lincrusta Walton seems the least objectionable of the uneven wall coverings. Smooth surfaces are most easily kept clean, and are therefore hygienically preferable to those which are rough or fissured.

Moisture is present in the walls of stone or brick houses for a long time after they are built, because several tons of water are used in the building of an ordinary city house. The main part of this is mechanically present and ought to be dried off before the house is used. Laying bricks or stone in an unprotected wall, even in frosty weather, causes the drying out of the wall to be slow. When bricks are laid in very cold weather, as is done in some of our most "rapid" cities, the moisture lingers long, and the masonry is not so durable as when the work is done in milder weather.

If it be necessary to occupy such buildings very soon after they are erected, they need to be well heated by burning gas, using furnaces and so on. Draughts of very warm air should be made to circulate and flow through the rooms. If in the warm season and if the weather be dry, sunlight and open air will do much to dry off the walls. With properly constructed double walls, the inner walls dry readily and remain dry. If in closed or other rooms the walls show wet spots, the rooms are not fit to be occupied and not yet ready for papering or painting. For demonstration, samples of mortar may be taken from various places in the wall, and then tested for moisture. If more than two per cent. of water be present, the wall is not to be considered dry enough for health.

Streets and Pavements

Streets ought to be well paved. Mud streets, so very common in prairie towns and in alluvial regions in general, are very destructive of wagons and wasteful of force. Moreover, they may harbor much filth. In cities, the (Telford-) Macadam pavement does not keep clean nor wear well.

Stone pavement, composed of granite blocks, wears best of all. It is excellent for heavy traffic and is adapted for slopes, because it offers a tolerable foothold for horses; yet it is objectionably noisy. Like all other pavements, it should have a good foundation, such as concrete. It is most hygienically laid when warm coal-tar mixtures are poured between the blocks. When the tar-cement sets, it is elastic and yet serves to keep filth from entering into and remaining in the spaces between blocks. The cost of the granite pavement in the form of " Belgian blocks " laid on the surface of Sixth Avenue in New York City is a little over $3.75 per square yard; for repairs, the cost is sixteen cents per year.

Wood pavement is often used where wood is cheap and where any relief from the prevalent mud is a great advantage. In none of our American cities is wood a durable pavement. Yet in Sydney, Australia, it is considered the ideal, because of their very durable wood. In Paris, creosoted wood blocks are much liked for paving. The usual cedar block does not last for more than from six to nine years. By that time it is rotted or worn too much to be good. In Chicago, it has been found that when much used by heavy trucks and wagons, cedar block pavements remained good for only three years.

The favorite form of these blocks is cylindrical. They vary from four to seven or eight inches in depth and have the grain running vertical to the surface of the street. They should not be of "sap-wood." The ground between the two lines of curbing ought to be carefully graded. The result is always much more satisfactory if a heavy steam roller be used to smooth the surface completely. Then this even surface is sanded over to a depth of three inches. Dry and well-seasoned planks, one inch or more in thickness, are used over this as a foundation for the blocks. Coal-tar and asphalt combined to make a cement are usually poured over the surface of the blocks to serve the preservative and hygienic purpose of filling up all fissures and spaces.

Fine gravel is then thrown over all, it being previously heated if tar-cement has been used as a coating. Carefully laid, this pavement is not inexpensive. It has the merit of being elastic enough to allow wheels to pass over it with very little noise. The hoofs of rapidly moving horses, however, make considerable noise on wood pavement. Hygienically, it is inferior to asphalt of good quality, since it offers in its substance more chance for the retention of disease germs and filth of various sorts.

There are other mineral and vegetable pavements which deserve consideration only in an exhaustive treatise on the special subject of paving. Iron, as used in Russia, is one of these. It is dirty and otherwise objectionable. Brick pavement ought to be mentioned, for it is used quite largely in certain regions where the geological formation makes this cheap, while other suitable material is expensive. Ohio cities offer the best chance to study this. It is claimed that satisfactory results are had there. Great lack of uniformity in quality is noticed in the usual brick pavement. Cork-pavement, or cork-asphalt, made by incorporating cork into asphalt blocks, is a novelty which is said to be adapted for the hardest wear and yet is not slippery. If wholly non-inflammable, as is claimed, it ought to make a good flooring for stairs and halls of fireproof buildings that are much used. "India-rubber" pavement (made of lime mixed with the waste from petroleum refineries) is used in London, but seems still in the experimental stage of its use.

Asphalt pavement, when it has a perfectly continuous, smooth surface, and when of the best quality, is the most healthful that we have. This needs to be kept very clean. To that end, it ought to be cleaned with rubber-edged scrapers whenever muddy. Frequent flushing with abundant water, as practised in Paris, is very important for securing real cleanliness. Some of our cities, like Washington, have large surfaces covered with this pavement. In Buffalo alone there is more asphalt pavement than in all the cities of Europe together.

The standard of the European pavement seems higher than ours. It may be very defective in some of our streets. Streets reveal unevennesses best when the asphalt surface is wet. The finest work is very good, even and durable, notably when of the Neufchatel or Sicilian asphalt. Yet that is very slippery at the beginning of rain, because of the manure and other organic matter present. The surface being so smooth and impervious to moisture, the manure and other dirt upon it dries rapidly, and from this comes much unpleasant dust wherever horses are used.

By reason, however, of the dryness as well as of the free exposure to fresh air and sunlight, and because of the ease with which it can be thoroughly cleaned, this is less liable than other pavements to have the dust upon it of a very harmful nature. Yet the necessity of cleaning is particularly evident with asphalt; and rainy weather affords the best time, from a sanitary point of view, for getting rid of the dirt. Asphalt surfaces take up much of the sun's heat and give it out only slowly. Heat softens asphalt. Hence such pavement is not fit for hot climates. It also does not keep well where steam-pipes are under or near it.

A solid foundation is indispensable. Otherwise the surface cracks and settles, thus losing its economic and hygienic quality of great smoothness. Over the very firm foundation, come six inches of hydraulic cement concrete. Then are added two or three inches of the compound of one part of bitumen with thirteen parts of asphalt and other ingredients, including sand and limestone, in varying proportions. Then heating, smoothing and rolling follow. The cost is about four dollars per square yard; a guaranty for fifteen years of careful maintenance being given. If car-rails run along streets having such pavement, it is well to have a row of granite blocks along the edge of the track. The flat-topped, grooved rail, laid flush with the pavement, imperils fewer lives of people driving on or over such tracks and disturbs their comfort less than ordinary rails.

Sidewalks should be smooth. The best artificial stone, made of powdered granite or other rock and Portland cement, seems preferable to natural stone. It is more durable than brick and also cleaner. Yet it should have a good foundation. Neither trolley-posts and wires nor elevated railways ought to be tolerated in thickly settled streets. Telegraph and telephone wires (always well insulated) ought to be in subways beneath the level of the street and not far from the junction of the street and the sidewalk. These subways should have sufficient space for the sewer at the bottom and the water-mains and gas-pipes on the sides. With man-holes for entering and ventilating these, trouble can readily be discovered and remedied; while all unhealthful, costly and obstructive tearing up of the streets is thereby obviated.

In dry weather, the streets ought to be sprinkled at least twice daily to lay troublesome dust and to cool the air in summer. Such wetting, to keep harmful bacteria from flying about, needs to be frequent ; but wetting the dust of the streets can interfere with the natural process of destruction of the bacteria that may be there. In that natural process the dry, pure air and abundant sunlight are very potent and healthful factors. Sea-water can be employed for sprinkling streets, although purer water is much better. In no case is it healthful to put water on the streets if it be contaminated with sewage or otherwise obviously impure.

Street-sweeping machines are from three to nine times as economical as hand labor for removing loose dirt from a given area. They cause much dust to rise into the air. Hand work is more satisfactory. The ground ought always to be sprinkled before sweeping is begun upon it. Despite occasional statements to the contrary, it may be considered that manure forms a large portion of our city street dust. This dust is considerably like dried sewage. In this there are at times numerous harmful bacteria which produce disease if inhaled. If they enter wounds, they can cause inflammation. The dangerous bacillus that causes tetanus (lockjaw) is found in manure.

Street-sweepings ought not to be used for filling vacant lots. It is best that such dirt be burned, as is done quite extensively in England. The question of the cremation of garbage will be found spoken of in a later chapter. There should be covers for the carts that remove street sweepings, ashes and garbage.

Removal of snow by melting it with hot water is too expensive. Carting off an excess proves the best way. If the Paris method (of melting the snow in part by the use of salt) be tried, the chilly slush that results ought to be carted away very promptly. For icy sidewalks, salt ought to be prohibited. To prevent slipping, sand should be sprinkled over the ice.

HEATING

In the colder months of the year, natural ventilation, by the entrance of cold air through ordinary walls and through the imperfect closures of windows and doors, acting with cold from other sources, produces in our living-rooms a temperature so low that it is neither healthful nor agreeable. Hence we not only construct our buildings carefully in order that the walls and other parts shall be as poor conductors of cold and currents of air as is economically possible, but at the same time we make careful provision so that artificial heat can be produced when needed.

The most approved temperature of the interiors of our buildings in winter varies according to the use for which the rooms are intended and somewhat also according to the individual preference. It is observed that persons of certain races, among the many foreigners peopling our great cities, are very uncomfortable unless the temperature of the rooms in which they live or work is kept much higher than that which others prefer. Owing somewhat to a difference in climate, Americans in general tend to heat their apartments more than the English consider proper.

In a workroom, where people are constantly in active motion, the thermometer should register less than 62° F. If used for sedentary work, the room should be several degrees warmer. With us, 70° F. is regarded by many as the proper temperature for a warm living-room or a schoolroom. This standard temperature is considered a little too high by some. Others wish to have rooms still hotter. A bath-room may properly be as warm even as 75° F. A sleeping-room during the night should not be warmed above 60° F. unless because of delicate and sensitive invalids. In theatres or places where people are sitting lightly clad, the temperature should be above 67° F. In well-constructed churches ten or fifteen degrees less heat is needed, since warmer clothing is worn there.

If thermometers be employed as indicators to aid in regulating the heat there should be more than one in a room, and these should be carefully placed at about the level of the head. It must be borne in mind that the outer wall of the room (especially if it receives no sunshine) is much colder in winter than the inner (partition) wall or the body of the air in the room. The walls, window-spaces (particularly when the windows are not double) and the floors (if a warm room be not beneath) are constantly losing heat that they receive from the warmer air of the room in cold weather.

In the best systems, where heating and ventilation are combined, this constant loss of heat by the cooling of the walls from outside is properly compensated for by having the fresh air that enters heated to a suitably higher temperature than that of the air in the room.

The bright rays of the sun, entering freely through the glass of the windows, contribute a little to the maintenance of a comfortable temperature in cold weather. Being absorbed by the floor, walls and various objects and furnishings in the room, these bright rays become converted into heat which cannot pass back through the glass, but remain within to warm the room somewhat. This, and the heat retained (by the walls and objects in the room) from previous heating, contribute a varying amount of warmth. Our main reliance in winter is upon more or less constant employment of artificial heat produced by the use of stoves, furnaces, coils of hot-water pipes, etc., which all derive their warmth from the combustion of some fuel.

Fuels (coal, wood, gas, etc.) contain carbon, hydrogen and other elements. In order that these shall burn, oxygen (as furnished by the air) is required; and this, uniting with the carbon and hydrogen of the fuel, gives off heat. One pound of average coal is considered to require about 160 cubic feet of air for its perfect combustion. Coke requires somewhat less, and charcoal a little less than coke. A pound of wood theoretically requires nearly 60 cubic feet of air in order to effect its perfect combustion. Peat requires nearly as much as wood. Practically, more than twice as much oxygen as these figures indicate should be allowed in order to insure perfect combustion. Yet it is wasteful to supply too much air; for this excess of air is heated before it goes up the chimney, and that requires the unprofitable use of some fuel.

We cannot, with hygienic propriety, allow the coal, wood or other fuel to burn openly in the middle of one of our rooms, as was the custom of our British ancestors of thirteen hundred years ago, and which crude method is used to-day somewhat, especially by savage races. With such fires, reliance is had upon a hole in the roof for the escape of the more or less harmful combustion gases and of the unused carbon (as soot and smoke). The results are very defective. Irritated eyes and lungs are not rare under such conditions; and, besides the unhealthful gases of combustion not being carried off properly, much unburnt carbon in the shape of soot is deposited about.

To prevent this waste of fuel and to secure its complete combustion, while at the same time all bad gases are carried off, the most perfect stoves and furnaces ought to be employed. These should secure the most economical results and be at the same time most healthful. By very completely using up the carbon and certain gases that escape and defile the air when defective heaters are used, the best furnaces, properly attended to, are of great hygienic importance.

All smoke obscures the air and thereby lessens the amount of sunshine. Without smoke or dust, water does not form fog or cloud. In those of our cities that burn soft coal, the question of smoke prevention has become a serious one. The Chicago "Society for the Prevention of Smoke" seems to have accomplished much toward repressing the smoke nuisance. The society had to institute suits in order to achieve their results; for it was found that few people would voluntarily take measures to lessen the defilement of the air that they were inflicting upon others.

Of the various devices advocated for lessening smoke from bituminous coal used in furnaces, automatic stokers are the best. Fire-brick arches and pre-heated air are also of value. Steam-jets do not seem so generally reliable. In furnaces, the ash-space should be less than half full of ashes, so that air can enter freely. The burning coal should be pushed to the rear part of grate-bars when more coal is added, and this fresh coal is to be put on the front part of the grate, and not thrown upon glowing coals. The coal should be fine. The doors should not often be opened, and any cooling off of the fire thereby is to be prevented. Thus the combustion is more perfect and less smoke is caused. The less fire there is, the less air is needed for it. To lessen a fire, it is better to shut off the entrance of air rather than to use dampers, etc. Pitchy wood, fats and coal oil cause smoke.

Anthracite coal is the best fuel that we have, although more expensive than softer coals. A pound of anthracite coal gives practically about one-and-a-half times as much heat as wood does. Peat is of a little more value than wood. Charcoal, coke, ordinary soft coal and illuminating gas are all between wood and coal in value, a given weight of one of these (or its equivalent of illuminating gas) giving considerably more heat than wood or peat, yet somewhat less than anthracite coal. Such soft coals as the George's Creek (semi-bituminous) varieties are decidedly better than many others as regards heat-power.

Coal should not be considered hygienically good if it have much sulphur. The sulphurous acid which is formed by burning sulphur-containing coal may contaminate the air to a serious extent. If, on analysis, a coal shows over one and one-half per cent. of sulphur, it is hygienically quite inferior. The economic value, cleanliness and great convenience of natural gas are unquestionable. The supply, however, is very limited. Gas-stoves are mentioned later.

Fuel, then, by burning gives off heat. If three-fourths of all the heat produced is utilized for warming, the result is to be regarded as very good. Stoves often get less than one-fourth of the heat that the most economical utilization of it would give. Open grates of the least scientific, ordinary patterns often have more than nineteen-twentieths of their heat go up the chimney without warming the room air at all. Most heat is realized when the combustion is perfect or as nearly so as is possible.

If the carbon of the fuel wholly goes up the chimney in the form of carbonic acid gas, by union with the oxygen of the air that feeds the flame, the most economical results are got. If some of the carbon goes off as soot and smoke, that is harmful waste. But worst of all is it when the combustion is so poorly managed that the carbon goes off as the poisonous carbonic oxide (carbonic *monoxide*) gas that is spoken of in the chapter on Lighting. Not only is forty per cent. of the heat thereby lost, but, by unintelligent management of a fire in a room or in a cellar where the gases can escape into the air of the house, a very dangerous and odorless poison is diffused.

In ordinary furnaces and stoves the combustion is most perfect when the layer of burning coals is thin on the gratebars and the air supply well adjusted. If air be carried through a thick bed of glowing coals or coke, the carbonic acid gas (of the combustion) tends to be carbonized back into the very poisonous carbonic oxide above spoken of, and the amount of this increases in proportion as the briskly burning coals are deep. If the actively burning layer of coals is very deep, exceedingly much of the carbonic oxide gas will be produced instead of the usual carbonic acid (carbonic dioxide) gas that is the proper product of all combustion. If the coals are only dimly glowing, the most economical and healthful use of fuel is secured. Carbonic oxide is also produced when red-hot iron surfaces are near a fire surface.

The lesson taught by all this is that stoves and furnaces ought to be large enough to insure sufficient warmth without keeping too great a fire. The iron-work must not be overheated at any time, and the air supply should be sufficient and controllable. In the (automatic) self-stoking furnaces, already alluded to, and in the best self-feeding stoves that are large enough not to need to be overheated in order to satisfy those who use them, satisfactory hygienic and economical results are obtained.

Dampers in furnace-pipes, stove-pipes, and in the smoke flues of heating arrangements in general, by being closed too soon after coal has been put on a fire, have caused many a poisoning with gas, and are always prejudicial to health. Much better is it to have tightly fitting doors upon the stove or furnace, so that by regulating the supply of air we can completely control the fire.

Smoke flues must invariably be non-combustible, and therefore they need to have eight inches, or nearly that much, of brick around them. Even in the costliest architecture, wood-work is at times, by culpable negligence, allowed to be so near to flues, fireplace backings and under hot hearths, that buildings are often set fire to or wholly burned up because of such defective construction. Joists or any other wood-work must never be built into chimney walls. No "furring" should be nailed to a chimney, and no woodwork should come within an inch of the outer walls of a chimney.

Chimney flues, when square, are to be lined with brick. Cylindrical earthen pipes (unjointed and unglazed) make an excellent round flue lining. As such pipe comes in lengths of about two feet, the cement-mortar, used to hold it, can be made very smooth within. This is very desirable as lessening friction. The diameter of such a flue should be from eight to twelve inches for an ordinary house fire. A furnace or fireplace requires a larger flue than a stove or range.

Each fire should preferably have a separate flue. Every flue should be as straight as possible, all curves ought to be very gradual, and in every portion of its entire length a flue should, as above said, have a very smooth inside surface. At the top is a chimney-pot or contraction of the outlet so as to make this somewhat smaller than the diameter of the flue. This chimney-cap should be of earthenware or metal. The draught is thereby made more steady.

The opening from the fire into the flue is also contracted whenever the flue is unnecessarily large, especially in fireplaces. There, this contraction may be by a sliding valve over the "throatpiece." Chimney-caps, when of good pattern, serve to keep currents of air from driving into and down a chimney. Thus they help to prevent "smoking."

The top of a chimney requires to be above all ridgepoles, gables or other obstructions to the free flow of air past it. The limbs of trees occasionally interfere with proper chimney draughts, and then ought to be removed.

Methods of Warming Rooms

Open grate fires have above been said to be by far more wasteful of fuel than are the other appliances used to warm our rooms. They are not a suitable means for the exclusive heating of houses and other buildings during the severe winter of our Northern States. Not only do they waste the heat of the fuel, but the scanty heat which they yield to a room cannot be well regulated and is not uniform. They do not ordinarily provide for purity of the air which they cause to be drawn into a room, and they allow the ashes of the fire to enter the room that they warm. Furthermore, a certain amount of gas can escape at times out of almost any ordinary grate and enter into the air of the room.

Open grate fires, however, furnish very valuable ventilating flues wherever there is no other special means of removing the bad air from a room and where at the same time there is abundant warmth supplied from other sources. The same purpose can equally well be served by burning lamps or gas flames in the back and upper part of the grate or in any suitably placed flue so arranged as to produce an upward draught out of the room by means of the heated air which rises out through the flue. A fire fed by coal or wood is much more agreeable to the æsthetic sense than a gas flame. As for the "fire-logs" on which minute gas flames burn in more or less successful imitation of burning wood, it may be said that they are usually placed too far out on the floor and not well enough back under the flue which they should heat and cause to ventilate the room. Thereby, unhealthful gases escape into the air of the house.

Open fires heat the fireplace somewhat and make that part of the wall warmer which is near the flue. This heats the room only slightly. Most of the heat that is got from open fires, sunk into the wall as they ordinarily are, comes by radiation of heat from the fire. Hence, in constructing a fireplace, we choose (for the backing) material that conducts heat poorly and thus does not waste it into the outer wall. According to all authorities, bricks (and fire-bricks) are several times better than stone, slate or marble, and probably more than fifty times better as non-conductors than metals. Hence as little as possible of iron or other metals should be used in the back and walls of a grate. Earthen materials are better.

The sides of a fireplace (technically called "covings") should not be sunk straight into the wall, but ought to flare out into the room. The most economical angle that these side walls can make with the back of the grate is regarded as about half-way out from a right angle, or say at an angle of 135 degrees. In Fig. 17, this angle is represented as one of 120 degrees. If the top of the fireplace slants upward so as to throw heat into the room, the construction must be such that gas is not sent out beyond the flue so as to come into the room instead of being carried off up the chimney. As a precaution against fire, it is well to have air-spaces at least two inches thick and somewhat more than thirty inches high built in the brick that are around the fireplace (see Fig. 17); for air is a very much poorer conductor of heat than fire-brick or anything else that we can use.

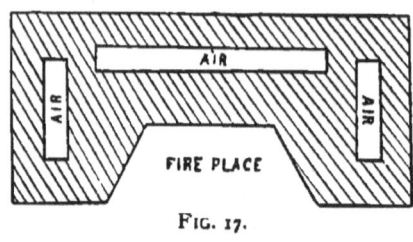

FIG. 17.

Fireplaces which are set out somewhat from the wall, like the various modifications and improvements upon the Galton grate, allow much more of the heat produced to enter the room. In these, when properly constructed, fresh air can circulate behind and come out into the room, conveying much warmth to the air and thus getting much more heat from the fuel. Such a grate (that of **E. A.**

FIG. 18.

Jackson) is shown in Fig. 18. Here the material may be rough metal if thick, perfectly cast and never made very hot. The firepot should be lined with fire-brick.

The contrivance known as a "Baltimore heater" or any modification of it adapted to a grate or stove (by which the air of any living-room is heated and carried up to warm a room above) cannot be hygienically commended. Such arrangements are sure to carry up air that is bad as well as warm. They are also apt to use much coal. When the mechanical parts of these are out of order, poisonous gas will escape into the air of the upper rooms heated by such devices.

Franklin stoves are akin to the modernized fireplaces. They are essentially fireplaces set out from the wall. Hence the cheerful effect of an open fire is had with some of the greater economy of heat that a good stove secures. The fire-containing portion of such Franklin stoves should be lined with fire-brick. The outside should be of soapstone. In these as in all stoves, *dampers* between the fire and the chimney may be a source of great danger. The connections between the stove and the chimney must be gas-tight and so arranged that no gas can escape out of any piping or joints and thus poison the air of the room. They must not be heated very hot, or they make the air disagreeable. Vessels of water should usually be on or near them as with ordinary stoves. Wire guards are useful things to have at times in front of all open fires in order to prevent coals from flying far out and causing damage from fire.

Stoves in which the fire is closed in by tight doors and iron-work, and where also the coal is supplied by an automatic, "self-feeding" arrangement, are much more economical of coal than the various grates and open stoves. Such stoves need coal of good quality, free from rock and slate and which does not "coke up." They are so economical, both as regards their first cost and the expense of supplying them with fuel, and are so convenient, that they inevitably commend themselves to a great portion of our population. Hence it is in the interest of health to indicate the few dangers that are associated with these, and the most important precautions for their use.

All stoves should be so well constructed that **no dampers** *are needed between the fire and the chimney.* This can be effected by having the doors so tightly fitting that the fire can be regulated entirely by means of the doors and the valves in them. Such perfectly fitting doors add to the cost of the stove. There are so very many kinds of stoves in general use that a complete mention of the merits and demerits of each variety would be less practically instructive than to have classed all alike as regards the harmfulness of any dampers present in the stove-pipe. Their mechanical construction commonly allows, even with the tightest pipes and joints, some leakage of gases. This is aggravated by preventing the free escape of these gases.

Base-burning stoves are usually defective in this regard. The shut-off valves of these and the pipe-dampers of stoves in general cause much dangerous gas to enter the air if they be stopped up as soon as coal is put on a fire, as is ordinarily done at night where fires are not lighted afresh every day. The practice of opening the front and top of a stove to suppress the fire is apt to allow harmful gas to enter the air of the room.

Stoves need to have the fire-pot well lined with fire-brick or similarly good non-conducting mineral substance. Then the outer air, that comes near the stove, is not heated so as to cause unpleasant odors to arise from the burning of particles of organic dust. Other objections to overheated iron have already been mentioned (see page 165). A cylindrical sheet-metal "jacket" or mantle around a stove and nearly reaching the floor, so arranged that air can enter the space between it and the body of the stove, is an aid to the equable warming of the room. The air between is caused to rise by being heated, and fresh air then enters from below so that the entire air of the room is thus made to circulate better than is the case if no such device is used. A still better plan is to have the fresh air enter from outside as indicated by Fig. 12 (on page 96). Fig. 13 shows a "jacketed" wood-burning stove.

Stoves of economical construction that are set up in the ordinary manner do not require enough air for the combustion of their fuel to secure a complete **ventilation** of rooms in which they are used and in which a number of people are breathing and lights are burning. Open grates are superior in this respect; for they carry large quantities of warmed unburnt air up the chimney. Stoves can be adapted somewhat to effect the same result by arranging a ventilating opening into the flue at the lower part of the room and beneath the entrance of the stove-pipe. This can be regulated by a perfectly fitting valve.

An excellent pattern of domestic stove, that suffices for the hygienic warming of a small living-room of a workingman's family, is shown in Fig. 42. The same stove serves for cooking food at all times of the year. It carries off the odors of the food that is being cooked, and can readily be adjusted in a moment so that, in summer, not much warmth is given off into the room.

All combustion of fuel in a stove or other heating apparatus not only uses up oxygen, but also **gives off carbonic acid gas** and other products, some of them very poisonous. This repetition of a fundamental fact deserves to be emphasized for the reason that dealers in stoves, as well as the manufacturers who produce such wares, induce people to buy certain kinds of stoves that are rendered dangerous through lack of provision for removal of these harmful gases. Charcoal braziers, oil-stoves, gas-stoves, "patent-fuel" stoves (using charcoal or pressed carbon with oxygen-giving salts added) may all be classed under this head. These latter, called "safety fuels" or having various similarly attractive names have, like charcoal and gas-stoves, caused very many cases of poisoning.

The interests of trade cause the dealers to state that their fuels are harmless. Such things can be very harmful, and should never be used for warming rooms unless the gases resulting from combustion are provided for by flues that efficiently remove these noxious products to a distance from the room that is being warmed, and do not allow them to escape and contaminate the air. The same necessity exists with regard to gas-stoves and the other stoves and heaters that warm by burning fuel in a room. (See Fig. 19. The gas-burners are there represented in the lower third of the diagram.)

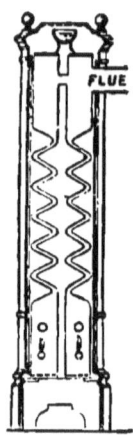

FIG. 19.

Unless water is furnished as, for instance, in open dishes in rooms, all simple methods of warming buildings tend to cause the heated air to be too dry. An exception to this rule is that, in hot-air furnaces (shortly to be spoken of), the use of water-pans in the hot-air chamber rectifies the deficiency provided that the furnace be properly constructed and well attended to. The customary, unhealthful dryness results because *a given amount of cold air can hold much less moisture than when the same volume of air is warm.* The air that enters a house in cold weather has relatively very little moisture in it. When this same air becomes comfortably warm, but yet has received no extra moisture, it is too dry for health or comfort, and is furthermore injurious to pianos, wood-work, etc. The amount of "relative humidity" (see page 17) in our heated rooms should not be less than thirty-five nor more than sixty-five per cent.

Water, therefore, needs to be supplied to the air in most of our warmed rooms in winter. Furnaces, as just said, if of the best quality and intelligently cared for, have an adequate automatic arrangement which gives off water-vapor in suitable proportions to the warm air before that is conducted through pipes into the rooms. All other usual means of heating need surfaces of water to be exposed somehow to the air of warmed rooms. Whether an open fire, a stove, steam or hot-water radiating coils be employed, none of them supply moisture to the air. Therefore a little moisture ought to be provided. The quantity needed varies of course with the weather and with the amount brought into a room as snow or dampness on clothing.

Flat pans of earthenware or non-rusting metal may be set about under furniture if it be desired to conceal them. Ordinarily they are put wherever they will be out of the way. Clean water is poured into these when the air is too dry. They give off moisture in proportion as they are kept warm by being near the source of heat. They should not be allowed to dry out through negligence.

The heating appliances above spoken of, while causing a movement of air and some natural ventilation, do not insure that the air which they cause to be drawn into a room is necessarily of good quality. The air that enters a steam-heated room is not at all pure, as a rule, unless by special means it is made so. This will be found more fully explained in later pages.

An open fire causes currents of air to be drawn into the room where it is burning. The air may be pure or impure according to its source. It may be the freshest and cleanest of sun-lighted out-door air, or it may come from foul vaults or from corridors that are thickly strewn with unclean dust and dirt from the street and possibly containing the germs of disease. This dust enters a room with the air drawn in. The importance of having the air supplied from the cleanest possible source is accordingly evident.

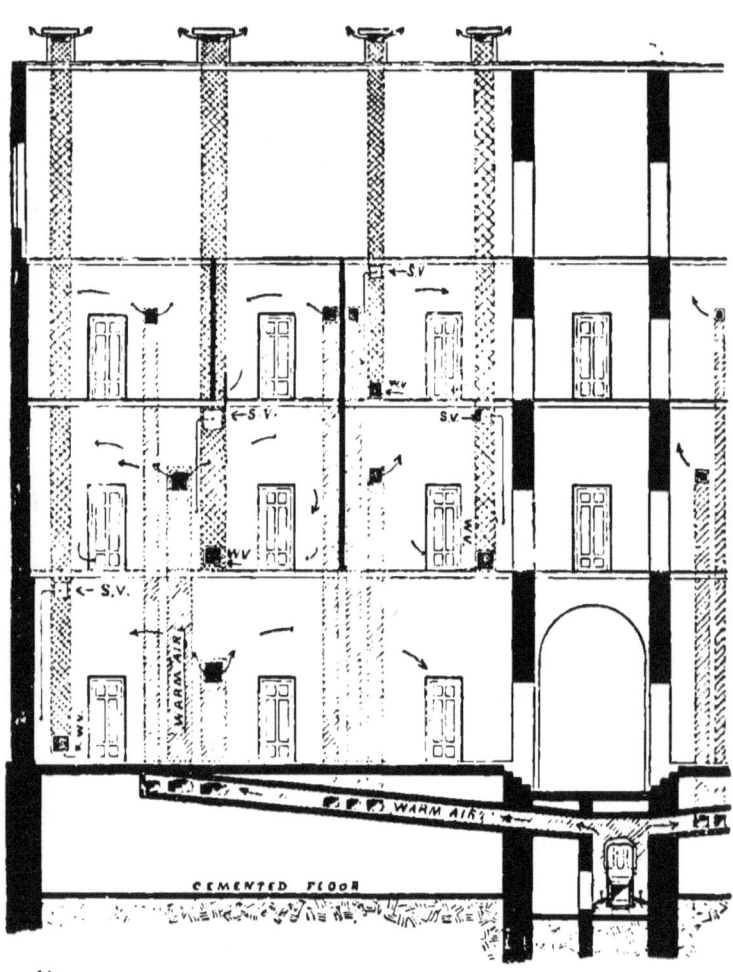

☒ = VENTILATING OUTLET FLUES.   W.V. = WINTER VENTILATION.
☒ = PIPES FOR HEATED AIR.   S.V. = SUMMER VENTILATION.

Fig. 20.

Combined ventilation and warming by heated air from furnace.
(After Gaertner.)

Hot-air furnaces, when well constructed in every respect and intelligently adapted for the building and situation in which they are used, afford—all things considered—the best single means of both warming and ventilating at the same time. The paragraphs just preceding this indicate some of the merits which a properly adjusted furnace must have in order to be considered hygienically fit for dwellings and larger edifices. Furnaces possess the great advantage of being comparatively inexpensive. Indirect heating through coils of steam-pipe—the only kind of heating that can fairly be compared with furnaces—is in every way more costly and difficult to attend to. Yet, if badly planned, defectively put up and shiftlessly managed, any system can be very unsatisfactory.

A hot-air furnace arrangement (see Fig. 20) comprises several essential features. The furnace is usually in the basement. Its doors, both that through which coal is thrown in and the one through which ashes are removed, then open into the cellar. The extra door or opening, provided for the admission of the air necessary to the combustion of the coal, opens also into the cellar, since the purity of the air that feeds the fire is not of material importance. [Of course the air in every part of our buildings should be as pure as possible; that is to be insisted upon at all times.]

From this furnace, a flue goes to the chimney. All of these parts must be in as few castings as possible, judiciously contrived and so well made that no gases leak out in any way. The parts last much longer if kept very clean and if the pipes are taken down before summer, then cleaned and left in a dry place. The flue should at the same time be stopped up. Moisture ought to be kept away from the furnace during warm weather. Some prefer that wrought-iron or steel be used for the fire-pots in which the coal burns.

Cast-iron is regarded by certain observers as being somewhat pervious to gases and hence a less healthful material for the purpose. Practically it is not found that any gas escapes through these if they be made suitably thick and no flaws exist. Cast-iron is the least expensive of these materials and is also very durable. For these reasons it is almost always used for the fire-pots. These are very often unlined, because thereby the heat goes more readily into the hot-air chamber than when lined with fire-clay. Lined fire-pots are best. When well made, these cast-iron furnaces answer every purpose. They should always be fully large enough.

Around all parts of this furnace, excepting the front portion (reserved for the doors just spoken of), a hot-air chamber is built, ordinarily of brick. This hot-air room should not be too small. It is usually not made high enough. In any case, it ought to be large enough to permit a man to enter by a small, tightly closing door, and to get about in it for the purpose of cleaning out the dust that gathers there. The hot-air chamber also contains a pan or, better, a carefully adapted series of pans holding a regulatable amount of water, automatically supplied by a pipe coming from a tank outside. The water supply must not be excessive.

This hot-air chamber and the furnace should usually be in or near the centre of the house or other building to be heated. Thereby the heat is as a rule more easily and evenly distributed as desired. The chimney then also, by being in the centre of the building, contributes somewhat to the warming of the rooms around it. It may in many cases be preferable to have the furnace and hot-air chamber somewhat away from the centre and toward that portion of the building which is most exposed to the prevailing cold winds of winter.

Into the hot-air chamber, as pure air as possible is received through a sufficiently large galvanized iron or other tube from a carefully chosen place out-of-doors. The best plan is to have this fresh air go to a fresh-air room before it enters the furnace chamber. This fresh-air room is in direct communication with the hot-air chamber and not at all open to air from the cellar. Very few people are inclined to make the outlay of money and effort necessary to insure that the air-supply is sufficient and constantly purified by the careful filtration that an ideal ventilation calls for. Hence especial pains must be taken in putting in the furnace, to see that there is ample provision for the entrance of air and that this is from the purest source available.

The outside opening of the supply tube for fresh air should be located a number of feet above the ground. Practical furnace-setters (that is, mechanics) prefer to put it only four or five feet above the ground. It should be in as clean a place as possible and far away from any garbage, drain-opening, sewer, vent-pipe or anything else that may contaminate the air. A fine wire screen on the outside serves to intercept coarse dirt and vegetable matter. Any screen, especially when clogged, lessens the flow of air.

Such a screen should slant considerably inward and downward, thus affording a larger surface. In the course of this fresh-air conducting tube, an air-filtering surface may be interposed, provided that some means of forcing the air through it be employed. This filter may be of cotton-batting or other suitable material, and other air-cleaners may be used as explained in the chapter on Ventilation. Such an air-filter requires a special arrangement of the air-conductor, and in certain conditions of the wind may prevent air from passing unless a blowing-fan (see Fig. 29) be used.

Settling-chambers serve to keep out considerable dust, but are not much used; for they add considerably to the cost, especially if a spray of water be used in them for arresting the dust of the incoming air. All air-conductors and hot-air chambers need to be cleaned at times. They should have regulating slide valves or other arrangements for lessening the flow of air through the tube, when this flow is excessive because of a strong wind blowing directly upon the outside opening of the fresh-air conductor. In some cases it is reported to be advantageous to have several (instead of one) of these large tubes for the inflow of air.

Such cases are afforded by large school-houses or other isolated buildings where four such tubes can enter (one from each side of the building) and where some one is attending carefully to the fire. Then the air can be allowed to flow in through the one of the fresh-air pipes that is exposed to the wind. The others are kept tightly closed.

According to practical furnace-setters, such complicated devices are not generally useful. Such experienced people find that a single fresh-air inlet answers best. It should receive its air from the west, northwest or north side of the building, to correspond to the prevailing direction of our winter winds (in most parts of North America). The size of this single fresh-air inflow pipe should be about three-fourths of the total area of the pipes supplied with hot air by the hot-air chamber.

Cold air, supplied to the hot-air chamber, very soon becomes warm. The temperature that all of this air there reaches is rarely much above $150°$ F., and is usually less than that unless the furnace be heated too hot. Probably many of the microörganisms, that chance to enter with the unfiltered air, are destroyed by the heat of the hot-air chamber, especially if it be not very dry. If the air be not overheated and not too dry, it is very agreeable, especially when it has been purified by careful straining before it enters the hot-air chamber.

Out from the hot-air chamber—perhaps through an intervening chamber where cold air can be further mixed with the hot air if desired—the warmed air is carried to various parts of the building by means of a series of pipes considerably more than nine inches in diameter and usually made of sheet iron. The arrangement of these must differ greatly according to the house or building for which they are planned. The colder parts of the house should have their supply from the upper portion of the hot-air chamber, since that is hottest. Most attention must be given to heating the lower floor and the colder side of the house. As above indicated, it is in some situations found quite necessary to arrange the furnace, hot-air chamber and fresh-air inflow pipe toward the northwest part of a building. Usually it is found best to have the long pipes going toward the east and south; while toward the northern and western side, the pipes should be shorter. All of these pipes must rise constantly; since the hot air, that they are to convey, tends to rise and not to move in horizontal directions.

Registers, similar to that seen in Fig. 22 (on page 183), with tight valves, are placed in the floor or on the wall where the hot-air pipes enter a room. Valves or dampers are also needed in the course of the hot-air pipes under certain circumstances, and especially so where the heat is to be regulated from the lower part of the house. It is usually regarded by furnace mechanics that it is best to have registers opening in the floor, after the fashion of that seen in Fig. 22. When low down on the wall, as in Fig. 23, they are less satisfactory. The location indicated in Fig. 20 is better. There they are placed higher up on the wall so as to be above the heads of people who may be in the room. In any case, the hot air will rise to the top of the room. We therefore gain by introducing it high up on the wall. The slats, which by being manipulated cause the heat to be shut off or let on, should as a rule slant upward when the register is partially opened. They thereby throw the heat toward the ceiling. When, for any reason, it is desired to throw heat (from a wall register) far out into a room, it is well to have a short, projecting board or slab above and another below the register.

With the hot-air arrangement seen in Fig. 20 is given a system of ventilation, the principles of which will be explained in the following chapter. If an open fireplace be in the warm inner wall in which the register is placed, and if in that fireplace a fire is maintained or gas flames are kept burning to draw air out of the room and up the flue, the arrangement affords a desirable complement to a system of hot-air furnace heating. We see houses made without fireplaces or ventilating flues and so very tightly built that no air can get out except very slowly. Such houses are not the easiest to heat by warm air; because, if no cold air or foul air can be carried off, it is not easy for warm air to flow in to take its place.

Certain systems of warming and ventilating buildings by hot air and which at the same time have "dry closet" systems combined with their hot-air flues have shown hygienic defects which are spoken of on page 99 and elsewhere.

Steam-heating is extensively employed, especially in large buildings. It is much more manageable than hot water or hot air, which require that the rooms, into which they are successfully introduced, be (at least obliquely) above the heater or furnace. Where steam is employed, the heat can be carried to a very distant room of an institution, or even to a remote building, in pipes which take up very little space, and whose heat can be controlled very completely. The steam can be made to warm intervening rooms as much or as little as desired.

A low pressure—of less than five pounds per square inch—is commonly employed in warming buildings by steam-heat. From the boiler, it is usual to have two wrought-iron pipes go out to make a continuous circuit, one pipe carrying out steam from the boiler and the other returning this steam as condensed (but yet hot) water to the boiler. There it is reheated to be sent out again as steam. The pipes through which this goes out from the boiler are necessarily larger than those which return the condensed steam in the form of hot water, since the water takes up much less space than when it is expanded into steam. If these pipes are covered with felt or other non-conducting material, less heat is lost from them than when the iron is wholly uncovered.

In the course of the steam-pipe circuit, or rather on side circuits from the main pipes, radiators are introduced in order to offer a large surface to the air and thus give off much warmth by radiation whenever the flow is not shut off by closing the inflow valve with which each radiator is provided. These radiators (see Fig. 21) are preferably made of rough cast-iron, because a rough metal surface radiates off heat much better than a smooth one. Lampblack or various white-lead paints as coatings cause more heat to be radiated from a given radiator than when bronze is used for coating the metal.

Usually the steam enters on one side of the base of the radiator, and on the other side the condensation-water pipe goes out. Single-pipe radiators can be used, the single pipes allowing the condensation-water to flow out along the bottom.

Steam that is superheated, as at a high pressure, does not cause the heat of the radiator to be proportionately increased although the return condensation-water is thereby caused to be hotter. According to a commission of experts, reporting to the Manchester Assurance Company and whose opinion is largely accepted as correct, high-pressure steam-heating pipes, being much hotter than where only low-pressure steam is used, are capable of causing fire in the wood-work through which the hottest pipes pass.

The warmth given off in condensation of the steam is what is depended upon for heating, rather than the heat of the steam as such. The steam in the usual two-pipe arrangement is first conducted by a main pipe, which has no stop-cocks, to the highest part of the steam-pipe system of the building. Thence it goes downward and backward to the radiators, where it is condensed (to produce warmth) and whence it is returned, as hot water, to the boiler.

The condensation of steam in the radiators produces a vacuum. To counteract the effect of the uneven pressure thereby developed, devices are applied so as to allow air to enter and prevent the escape of steam through the return hot-water pipes. Yet these contrivances are not always effective, and consequent startling "hammering" noises occur at irregular intervals even in some of the costliest steam-heated buildings.

The radiator gives out the heat *directly* into the air about it, but of itself it brings no air and no moisture into the room in which it stands. The radiator simply causes the air, which it has heated, to rise, and thus produces a slight circulation of air very much as an ordinary stove would do. It however does not remove any of the bad air out of the room, as a stove (or, better, an open fire) does through its draught. Neither, on the other hand, does it give off any harmful gases such as come from a defective or badly managed stove. A good hot-air furnace well supplied with pure, fresh air is decidedly preferable to the ordinary use of radiators as a means of warming and at the same time ventilating buildings of compact dimensions. When rooms are warmed by radiators as just described, we speak of the method as *direct* steam-heating.

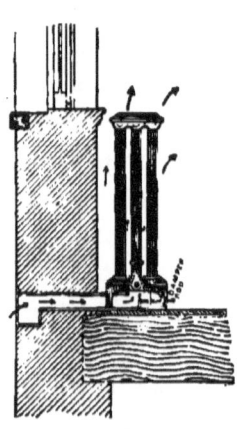

FIG. 21.

Radiators are much more suitable for warming rooms when arranged in what is called the *direct-indirect* manner (as illustrated by Fig. 21). Thereby, fresh air enters the room from out-of-doors through an opening in the wall and can be made to pass through an efficient dust-strainer if desired. The amount entering is controlled by the regulating damper. This air, as pure as possible, rises when heated, and—as a natural result of this—more fresh

STEAM-HEATING 183

air is drawn in to be warmed in its turn. Then it follows, in its circulation through the room, that air which has previously been warmed in the same manner.

Indirect heating is the term used to indicate such adaptation of steam-coils as is shown in Figs. 22 and 23. Steam

FIG. 22.

is turned on to heat the convoluted radiator pipes, and then these cause the inflowing fresh air to become warmed by contact with them. Therefrom it rises and enters as a warm current into a room or a series of rooms above. This air is of healthful quality, since it comes from a pure source unless the arrangement be defective in that very important respect. This air may be somewhat too dry, as explained on page 172.

In that case, the remedy consists in supplying moisture by pans of clean water or by other means.

In the indirect steam-heating arrangement shown in Fig. 23, the damper is represented as lowered so as to make all the inflowing fresh air pass between the heated radiating

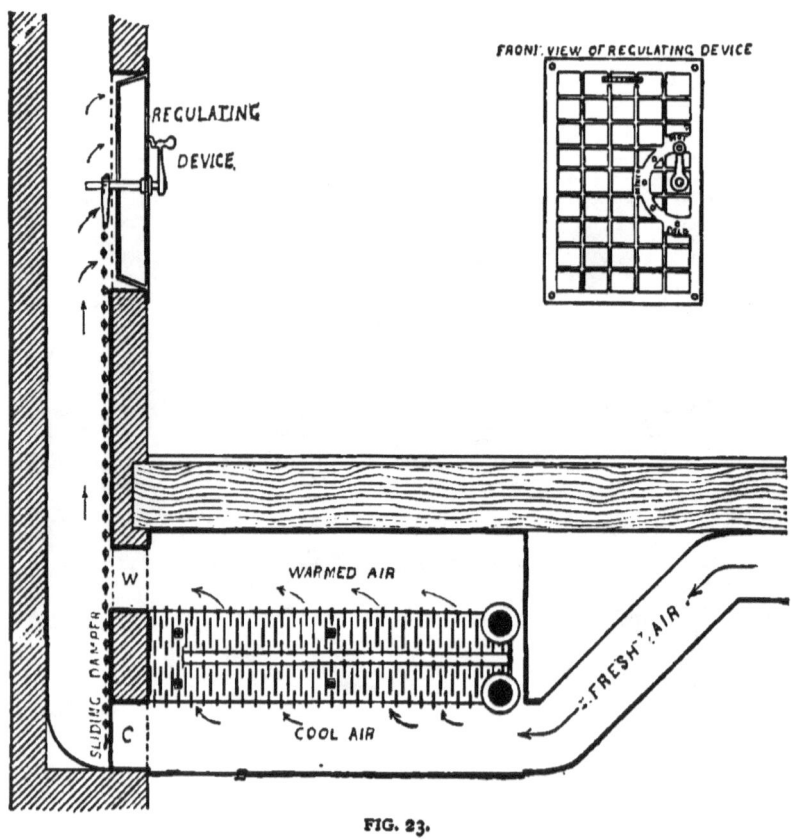

FIG. 23.

pipes. Thus the air becomes warmed in passing through. It then goes out of the opening IV and rises in the warm-air ducts. If the sliding damper be raised so as partially to close the opening IV, and to open C to the same extent, some of the cool air passes out at C and mingles with warm air. By thus mixing the warm and the cool air and by regulating the number of radiating pipes through which steam is passed, any degree of warmth in the fresh air sent into a number of rooms can thus be secured. This arrangement represents the best kind of steam-heating. It is however, as a rule, more costly than the other methods of heating so far considered, both as regards the necessary outlay for the entire equipment and in the expense of running.

In large hotels, extensive manufactories and other places where exhaust steam (reduced to a low pressure) can be had from boilers (used also for other purposes) and where a skilled engineer is regularly present, steam affords the best means of heating. The readiness with which it can be sent to a remote part of the building, and the promptness with which it can be controlled by turning it on or shutting it off entirely or partially, make it, if well arranged, the most satisfactory means of warming such places. It is, then, compact, prompt and manageable.

For dwellings, however, it is less satisfactory than warm-air furnaces. Hot-water heaters, if of the very best kind and well managed, are there preferable to steam. The original cost of hot-water piping and radiators for a given establishment is greater than that of steam; for steam, being hotter, requires perhaps only two-thirds as much radiator-pipe surface as is needed for a hot-water system.

Experienced scientific horticultural experimenters report that plants thrive as well with one of these two kinds of heat as with the other. The two appear to be hygienically nearly the same, with a slight preference to be given to hot-water heating, if the radiators are to be employed in the ordinary, *direct* manner. Hot-water heating is also excellent for the *direct-indirect* method shown in Fig. 21. For the *indirect* method (see Figs. 22 and 23), hot water is not satisfactory.

Hot-water heating depends upon the familiar physical fact that, in a circuit of continuous, vertically arranged

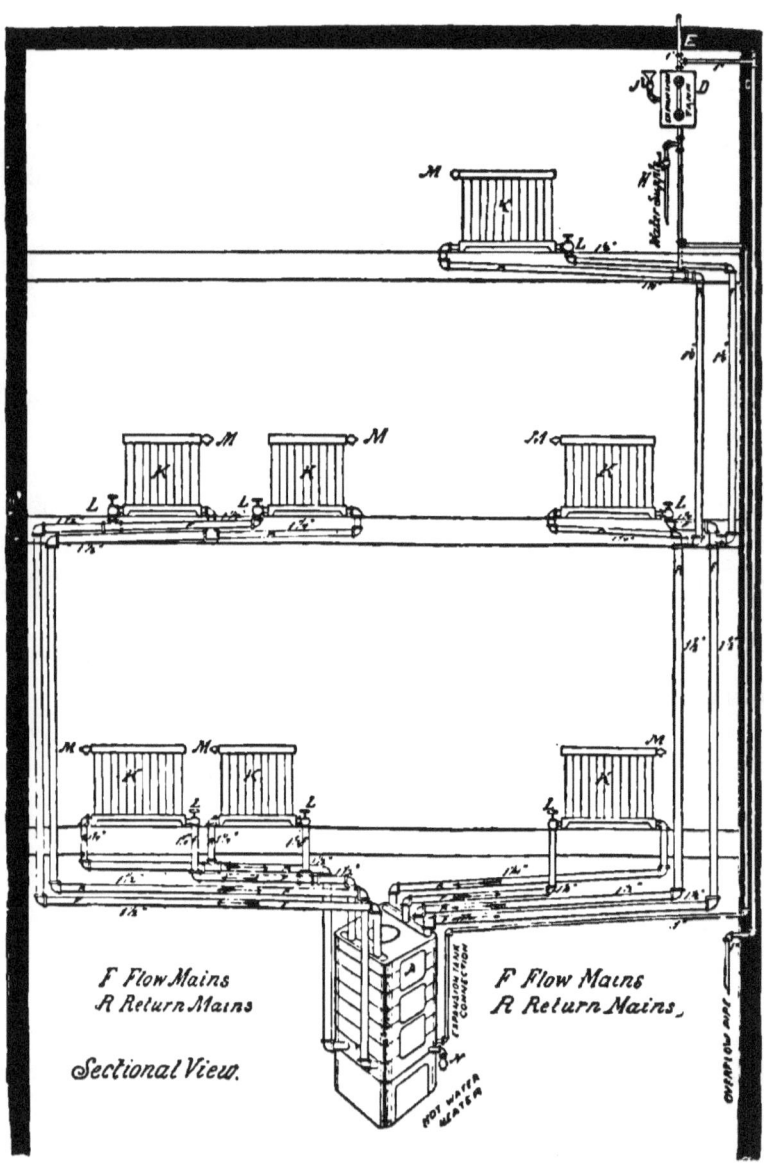

Fig. 24.

Hot-water system.

pipes, water that is at all warmer than the rest is thereby somewhat expanded and therefore lighter. Hence it tends to rise, while that which is cooler will settle to the bottom. If, then, any kind of good water-heater be in the central part of the basement of a dwelling, and from it a system of pipes be arranged somewhat as in Fig. 24, the water, when heated, will flow out through the pipes at the top of the heater and will rise to the highest portion of the pipe system. Thence it settles as it becomes cooler. The water that is coolest of all (and therefore heaviest) gravitates to the lowest part of the system to reënter the heater through the return pipes indicated in Fig. 24 by the letter R and by the arrows pointing toward the heater.

This water is thus in more or less constant circulation when the heater is working. A little evaporates from time to time. Very clear water is therefore poured in every few days to take the place of any that has evaporated. Freshly boiled water is slightly better for renewing the supply, as it has less oxygen than ordinary aërated water. Hence it is less likely to produce rusting of the iron pipes. The water is poured (or allowed to flow) into the *expansion tank D* which is to be kept more than half full. It ought to hold at least five per cent. of the volume of water needed to fill the entire pipe system. The top is partially open.

This tank must be above the level of the highest radiator of the system. It is connected to the pipes by a smaller pipe without valves or other obstruction to the free inflow and outflow of expansion-water. The tank allows for the expansion and contraction of the water in the pipes. It also serves as a security against any possible steam being pent up in case that the water become overheated. These details and their arrangement, as well as the sizes of the pipes used, are indicated in Fig. 24.

It is to be noted that the largest pipe needed for an ordinary dwelling is not more than $1\frac{1}{2}$ to 2 inches in inside diameter. Wrought-iron pipe, nominally called "inch-and-a-half pipe," is usually somewhat larger than indicated. Its internal area is a little more than two square inches, and every foot of it weighs less than 2¾ pounds. For every two feet of such pipe, there is a square foot of outside surface exposed to the air. From this surface, heat radiates into the air. If made "extra strong," the inside diameter of the pipe is less. For the branch to each radiator, a 1¼ inch pipe is large enough.

In summer it is commonly advised that the water be left in the pipes to prevent the exposure of the interior to the air and consequent probability of rusting. To avert danger of freezing, all water-pipes ought to be emptied if the house in which they are set is to be left unwarmed during cold winter weather.

A stop-cock at the lowest part of the system (N, Fig. 24) should be present in order to let off all of the water whenever necessary. An overflow pipe from above the expansion tank is also needed to obviate flooding by one of the mischances which may occur with such systems.

Radiators used for a hot-water system ought to be from one-and-a-half to two times as large as when steam is used. This is because the water is heated to a temperature usually below 200° F. (and ordinarily above 150° F.), while steam is always at 212° F., or higher. Because of the outlay for piping, it costs much more to introduce hot-water heating than any other. For indirect heating, as illustrated by Figs. 22 and 23, it is altogether too costly, and is besides less suitable than steam, which is much more promptly and easily controlled and utilized.

As is usual with steam-heating, so with hot water, each radiator (K) has a separate set of inflow and outflow pipes. A valve to shut off the hot water is with each radiator as shown at the letters L in Fig. 24. Radiators have air-valves at the upper part for letting off any air that may be present and which would stop the circulation of water. These air-valves (M, Fig. 24) should turn only with a key, such as is shown in Fig. 25. Otherwise there is always great danger of flooding the house with water.

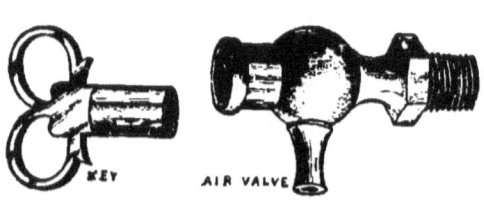

FIG. 25.

Hot-water heaters do not differ much. The principal element embodied in all is a series of convoluted tubes more or less modified. Through these the water flows, and around these the heat of the burning fuel plays in its course to the chimney-flue.

When they are well planned, hot-water heating apparatuses are easily managed, and also usually cost less to run than steam-heating systems or hot-air furnaces. This economy in working is, in the first place, due to the fact that a certain amount of heat-energy has to be expended to convert water into steam. In the second place, all heated bodies, that conduct heat from one place to another, lose more heat, in the process of conveying, when they are very hot (like steam) than when they are somewhat cooler—like hot water, for instance.

In an average room, there ought to be allowed from 30 to 33 square feet of (hot-water heated) direct-radiating surface for every 1,000 cubic feet of air that the room contains. It should be stated that if a pipe be (on its inside)—

  1 inch large, 3 feet of it give 1 sq. ft. of radiating surface.
  1½ " " 2 " " " " " "
  2 " " 20 inches " " " " "

Let it be assumed for instance that, in a given house in a cold region, a *reception-room* is exposed to the north and east. It is 14 by 20 feet square and 10 feet and 9 inches high. Hence its cubic contents are somewhat less than 3,000 cubic feet.

By reason of the room having a cold situation and being upon the lower floor, the allowance of radiator surface should be 1 foot for every 25 cubic feet of room space. Therefore 120 feet of radiator surface are to be introduced to warm the room. This may be divided between two radiators near opposite walls; or one radiator may be used (near the north wall) having 70 feet of surface, while the remaining 50 feet may be laid around the junction of the wall and floor. This latter arrangement adds to the cost, but is of great value as serving to heat the walls. It must always be borne in mind that cold and damp walls are most unhealthful. In some very modern buildings only the walls are heated, a suitable supply of slightly warmed air being introduced in addition for the purpose of ventilation.

A dining-room, if it has not an exposed location and is near the kitchen, or if its floor is warmed by being above that room, needs less heat. So, one foot of radiating surface is allowed there for every 33 cubic feet of room space. For this, two radiators are used, having either flat or round pipes.

In the middle of one of these radiators, there may be enclosed a polished brass (or other sheet-metal) cabinet for warming plates.

For *bed-rooms*, 1 foot of radiator surface is sufficient for from 40 to 50 cubic feet of room contents unless in exceptional cases where very warm rooms are desired. In a *nursery*, the radiator should have 1 square foot of surface for every 30 cubic feet of room space. As elsewhere, the radiator ought to be on the coldest side of the wall. It is better to have too much radiating surface than too little.

Hot-water systems require that the pipes rise vertically or have a more or less constant slope. Otherwise, the water does not circulate freely. Although very much inferior to steam-heat for heating laterally distant parts of buildings, hot-water systems are superior to furnace-heating for lower floors and exposed cold sides of houses.

A combination of a hot-air furnace, which insures a renewal of the air, may advantageously be made with a hot-water heater in the same apparatus. Or the two may be used separately, but so coöperating that hot-water-heated radiators can be employed upon the lower floors and on the colder sides of a building. In mild weather, the hot-water apparatus alone need be used.

Hot-water systems suffice to heat buildings even in very cold weather, as is seen from the extensive use of these in Canada. There the abundant movement of the air causes a considerable degree of natural ventilation.

Radiators warmed by hot water can be used for "direct-indirect" heating such as is represented in Fig. 21. Abundant fresh air warmed to any desired temperature can thereby be brought into a room.

To summarize and repeat somewhat, it may be stated that hot-air furnaces of the best quality (properly put up), if never overheated and always carefully supplied with fresh air from a pure source, give the best results in heating an ordinary house and at the same time ventilating it.

In very large houses, that are much exposed to cold weather, a hot-water system as an auxiliary is excellent for supplying equable, extra warmth by means of radiators used on the lower floor and on the bleakest side of the house.

For warming larger buildings such as, for instance, school-houses, a good furnace arrangement can be both economical and very satisfactory. This is notably the case with medium-sized buildings. For the largest structures, and especially when they are not compact, steam-heating by the *indirect system* (see Fig. 23) is the most satisfactory. It is usually more expensive than the hot-air furnace.

Exhaust flues for ventilating, that is, for drawing out the bad air, are a very desirable addition to all buildings. With heating, ventilation should be combined. The subject is treated further in the next chapter.

As regards the *comparative cost* of steam and hot water for warming, it may be said that steam usually costs more to operate. Some recent careful observations made at the Cornell Agricultural Station (Bulletin 41, August, 1892) showed that where there were many bends in the pipes and long levels, steam was considerably cheaper than water, regardless of the styles of heaters. Others have reached similar conclusions. In Massachusetts and elsewhere, however, hot-water heating has been found to be cheaper than the use of steam, when once the pipes and radiators were set. This is in conformity with what general theoretical conclusions allow one to suppose. To determine which is the better method for heating, one must carefully consider the situation, as hot water can be a more costly means of heating than steam.

Under the most favorable conditions for hot-water heating, it appears slightly less expensive than heating by hot air or steam when once the very costly piping is introduced.

The ingenious contrivances for regulating the heat supplied to all parts of a building by utilizing the automatic action of a *thermostat* or of various electric devices are not wholly reliable. The lowest priced of the good ones cost about forty dollars each. Such things are liable to get out of order and are of rather limited utility in their present imperfect condition.

Summer Heat, and Means for Lessening its Unhealthful Effects

The persistent, extreme heat of most of our summers causes oppression, lassitude, and diarrhœal and other diseases. Accordingly, any physical or other means that afford relief from these and other effects of prolonged summer heat must be declared a great boon to humanity. We suffer especially from the moist heat at times of prolonged "heated terms" of weather, because, with our habits of overeating and exercising more than is approved by the natives of tropical climates, our bodies then produce more heat than they can easily lose by radiation or by the evaporation of moisture. The prevalent diarrhœal diseases of summer are due to the fact that, unless great care is taken, bacteria and their more or less poisonous products increase in and on our various articles of food under the influence of the prevalent warmth.

The evaporation of water (as from water spray or fountains, wet cloths or other surfaces) cools the air, yet not notably so when the air is already very moist and the heat therefore most oppressive. The melting of large quantities of ice, the use of the improved anhydrous ammonia apparatus, and other devices for making ice and for cooling air, as also the employment of compressed air which, by its expansion, produces cold, are all employed. Yet they are not practicable except in a very limited way.

The immense majority, of the population cannot command such aids toward resisting the great heat of our summers. Hence recourse must be had to extreme moderation in diet and exercise. Work should be suspended during the midday hours in hot months, and usages, clothing and abodes must be as well adapted to the weather as is possible.

The walls of an ordinary house receive and retain an immense amount of heat from the sun. This heat they radiate off into the rooms to a very uncomfortable extent in summer days, unless the process be restricted by great thickness of the walls, by their excellent non-conductivity, or by an interposed layer of air between the inner and outer portions of double walls. This latter arrangement, if properly constructed, allows an upward current within the wall. Much heat thereby rises and is carried away instead of being radiated into the adjoining rooms.

Upper stories in any building are more uncomfortable in summer than are the lower ones. This is owing to the heating effects of the sun; for the roof, even if having two or more non-conducting layers besides being well ventilated, allows much heat to enter. Besides this, the air of the lower rooms, when it becomes warmed above the average temperature of the house, rises to the upper story.

Foliage and creeping vines, screens, awnings and the use of white or light colors (as absorbing less heat than darker shades) for roofs and the outside of houses, ward off the heat effects somewhat. A careful choice of a location and a proper construction of buildings prove always of much value. To the laboring poor of cities, however, these aids are not usually available. They are better off in summer if they then begin work very early, take a long rest at noon and resume work later in the day.

VENTILATION

All people, especially when using the muscles, excrete a considerable quantity of carbonic acid gas. This is given off almost entirely from the lungs. The hourly amount may be estimated at not far from 1,350 cubic inches, or say three-fourths of a cubic foot. Children of course produce less of this than adults. The amount given off during sleep is much less than when one is at work. We may consider air to be pure when, in 10,000 parts, it has no more than from 3 to 4 parts of carbonic acid gas. (See page 13.)

An adult requires 1,200 cubic feet of such pure air every hour for breathing, in order to supply the system with oxygen so that it is enabled to excrete the above-specified amount of carbonic acid gas in the exhaled breath. If less than this volume of fresh air be allowed for each person, the health and efficiency suffer in the end. Practically, it is found better to allow more than this for each individual, as will shortly be indicated.

From the bodies of animals, various other *gaseous* products are exhaled. They do not appear to have any considerable hygienic significance. (See page 16.) They are very different from bacteria and dirt in the air, which can be very harmful. Certain irregular and unusual gaseous and other contaminations can be present. Accordingly, the air of rooms used for some industries needs to be tested especially for the chemical or other poison which is particularly liable to be in such air. In localities where coal that contains much sulphur is burned, sulphurous acid (which further becomes sulphuric acid) is present at times to an unhealthful extent. Our coals vary greatly in respect to the amount of sulphur that they contain. In England, sulphur gas has become a serious contamination of the air. In Manchester and London, the amount of sulphurous acid detectable in the atmosphere during foggy weather in the worst districts, has been reported to be increased at times to thirty-four and fifty times the ordinary amount found in the air of those cities.

Besides giving off gaseous excreta, people who enter a room may bring there the microörganisms of disease or of organic decomposition. Such causes of disease are liable to be present in unclean and unventilated rooms. Hence the further necessity of purifying the air by laying the dust and cleaning it out by moist cleansing. If fresh, pure air be introduced into a room containing much bad air or unclean dust or both of these together, much of the dust is thereby removed from the room, and the impure air is replaced, in part at least, by more healthful air.

Carbonic acid gas is properly taken as a guide to the degree of impurity of the air; for it is certain to be quite accurately recognized by a careful test (see page 14) in whatever amount it be present. Furthermore, it is the most constant and inevitable contamination given off wherever human beings or animals are present. All combustion produces it, and, as explained on page 136, this gas comes in great quantities from all means of artificial illumination other than the electric light.

Other means than chemical tests for determining the degree of impurity of the air are less exact. The sense of smell reveals organic exhalations, especially when the air is moist. It aids to the recognition of certain gases, yet does not detect the most poisonous ones. Our senses are too vague in their interpretations to afford a reliable means of detecting air-impurity unless occasionally to exceptionally endowed persons or in very marked instances.

Microscopic examination of the air by studying an exposed glass slide, having upon it a drop of glycerine, reveals much; but this gives very slight aid to hygiene. More may be said for the various methods of bacteriological examination of air. Yet, in the majority of cases, the chemical test for carbonic acid gas is the best single standard to use for judging air-impurity.

The *Wolpert* test (see page 15) is rapid and quite useful; yet it usually reveals less carbonic acid gas than is actually present, and the extent of this discrepancy may be equivalent to the full amount of the gas in question that is present in ordinary air. This is, then, a good means to use where the air is grossly contaminated with that gas, as is common in some churches, badly ventilated offices and public buildings. For greater accuracy, a chemical test is indispensable.

It has above been indicated that 1,200 cubic feet of pure air (that does not contain more than 4 parts of carbonic acid gas in 10,000 parts of air) ought to be supplied every hour for each person in a room. Our ordinary city atmosphere is very apt to prove rather more contaminated than this if samples (for testing) be taken at random from crowded neighborhoods in manufacturing districts. Furthermore, pure air introduced into a room may not become evenly diffused and may fail to be so distributed throughout the room as to drive out or dilute all of the impure air.

For school-rooms, therefore, the lowest standard amount of fresh air to be supplied every hour for each pupil is set at 1,800 cubic feet. This is at the rate of 30 cubic feet per minute. Some schools receive twice this amount of fresh air for each scholar, and numbers of schools have 45 cubic feet a minute allowed for every child that the room can accommodate. Unfortunately, very many schools are exceedingly deficient in this respect. When the pupils are not children, 45 cubic feet per minute ought to be the lowest amount supplied for each individual.

For court-rooms and other **assembly rooms,** especially if they are to be occupied continuously for several successive hours, no smaller allowance of fresh air should be made than 3,600 feet an hour, or 60 cubic feet per minute, for every person of the largest number present at one time. Somewhat more than this amount of air is required to replace that contaminated by every average-sized *gas-burner* (or lamp) that does not have a proper flue arrangement (see page 135) for carrying off the waste products of its combustion.

For every cubic foot of illuminating gas that an ordinary gas-burner consumes in an hour, we should provide at least 800 cubic feet of fresh-air inflow. Hence every five-foot gas-burner (as well as each lamp that gives nearly as much light) ought to have supplied for it while it is being used for lighting, no less than 4,000 cubic feet of fresh air per hour. Some observers consider that this allowance is not large enough. The more fresh air a room receives and the more completely all contaminated air is drawn off by suitable means, the more healthful is such a room.

Mechanical means of ventilation, in our most hygienically constructed buildings, cause the air to be completely changed every seven minutes and at times even more rapidly than that. This mechanical ventilation ought to be so well arranged that no uncomfortable currents of air are experienced. In our ordinary rooms, however, where no provision for ventilation exists other than such natural means as doors and windows, draughts are felt if the air be changed more often than two or three times in an hour.

Accordingly, the smallest permissible **room space** to be allotted to an adult, in an average room where no good special facilities for ventilation exist, should be set at no less than half the 1,200 cubic feet of pure air needed every hour; that is, every adult needs at least 600 cubic feet of room space. The smallest school-room space provided for each child ought to equal or exceed 250 cubic feet, even if there be adequate ventilation. If less than this be allowed, the final result is almost certain to be deteriorated general health or lessened capacity of the system to resist infectious disease.

In all closed rooms, each individual requires at least 1,000 cubic feet of space, exclusive of that taken up by furniture. More than this is desirable, and in wholly closed sleeping-rooms more than 1,000 cubic feet ought to be allowed for children and adults alike. If, in case of infectious disease, more than this cannot be had indoors, the patient will generally do best when treated in large airy tents which allow very much more fresh air. For workshops where, as is usually the case, even less than 1,000 cubic feet are allowed for each person, electric lighting is very desirable as causing no contamination of the air. If gas be used and no suitable means exist for carrying off the products of its combustion, the air is thereby rendered very unfit for breathing.

Open windows and doors ordinarily insure an exchange of air between a room and the atmosphere outside. Where there is absolutely no breeze and when, as in the closest days of our summers, the temperature is the same inside a building as it is without, the unaided natural process of diffusion and purification of the bad air is at best a slow one.

In winter, much air gets in through crevices and openings. Through walls, some air enters, especially where the building material is very porous and when also no very impervious layer exists in or upon its substance. These natural means are the only ones used in most buildings. They may, however, be quite inadequate as a rule; for they depend upon the weather, which is a very uncertain thing. Furthermore, the air which enters through a window or a door may be very impure or may blow unpleasantly upon people.

Artificial ventilation is an invaluable means of increasing the fresh-air supply in crowded rooms and removing vitiated air. By the use of intelligently adjusted contrivances, the air of a large and crowded room may in any weather be so purified by frequent and yet healthful renewals that the accommodations of that room are thereby practically several times increased. Whatever means be employed to renew and purify the air of a room, great care must be taken to see that *no draughts* of air stream directly upon people.

Artificial ventilation methods may either be directed to the removal of vitiated air from a room or building, by mechanical means or by heated flues; or fresh air may be driven in to displace the used-up air which is already in the room. Another, and usually the best way of all, is to combine the two preceding methods. This combined method may have the air driven in by mechanical means (such as blowers or fans), or the tendency of air to rise when heated (as by steam coils or hot-air furnaces) may be found sufficient to send in abundant fresh air from a pure source.

A very satisfactory way of drawing out the used air from the rooms is to introduce into the centre of a building, such as for instance a school-house, one or more large ventilating chimneys. (See Fig. 26.) Each of these has a special stove fire in the lower part which by its heat causes the air to rise within. Each is also arranged so that no air enters excepting such bad air as is drawn into it through flue-openings in the lower parts of the rooms which it is to ventilate.

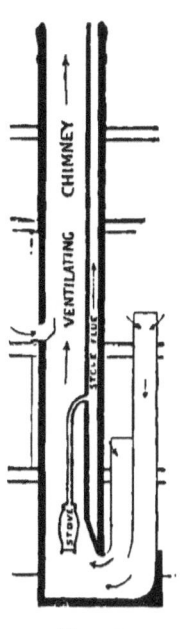

FIG. 26.

In winter, the heat is in some cases introduced into such ventilating chimneys by carrying the smoke-flues from room-warming stoves or furnaces up through these chimneys. Yet the gain therefrom is not so great as it may at first appear; for a considerable portion of the chimney-flue is taken up by the introduced smoke-pipe, and the friction (obstructing the upward flow of air) is thereby greatly increased. The efficiency of the chimney is of course lessened by whatever is put in it. When the weather is warm and no heat is needed for the rooms, only the special chimney stove is used. At such times, any smoke-pipes that may be present are purely obstructions.

A ventilating chimney that is square is cheaper to build and also causes less loss from friction than one of the same cross-sectional area that is oblong. The higher a chimney is made and the hotter it is kept inside, the better does it draw air out of the flues.

A ventilating chimney $4\frac{1}{2}$ feet square has a cross-sectional area of $20\frac{1}{4}$ square feet. Allowing for considerable loss by

FIG. 27.

friction of the rising warm air upon the walls of the chimney, the upward movement of this air when properly heated may fairly be expected to be about 720 feet in a minute. That is, an *anemometer* or wind gauge (see Fig. 27), when held for the same definite time in several parts of the upward current of the chimney, ought to indicate an average movement of 12 feet per second. This would be a movement of 14,580 cubic feet every minute. If the ventilating openings in the rooms offered no frictional resistance to the outflow of air, this volume of air movement up the chimney of a given school-house would be equivalent to between 29 and 30 cubic feet of air removed for each one of 500 pupils. In practice, it is well always to allow for considerable friction whenever outlets or bends come in the way of a current of air.

Drawing the air down out of a room as indicated in the descending flues entering from the lower rooms, into the ventilating chimney as shown on the right-hand side of Fig. 26, may give a slight saving of heat in cold weather. By going in a roundabout way into the chimney, this air warms somewhat any colder parts of the building with which it comes in contact. In some of the variations of the above given, very widely used method, this principle, of economizing the warmth, is carried out in too thrifty a manner. The results may be very unsatisfactory, and the ventilating flues can harbor and spread disease if these flues are introduced between floors or in any place where they cannot readily be cleaned out. It is also very undesirable that they be connected in any way with "dry-closet" systems as indicated in other parts of this book.

The cost of this hot-air shaft system of ventilating buildings is practically less than that of mechanical ventilation (by means of fans and blowers), especially where the large space required for the chimney is of no consequence. Because of its cheapness and generally satisfactory working, it is used in some of the most recent large school-houses, even when they are heated by the indirect steam-heat method that is shown in Fig. 23. A common size for such ventilating chimney-flues in school-houses is three by six feet. The flue for ventilating toilet closets is usually made somewhat smaller than this. To heat such a flue properly, at least one ton of coal per month should be allowed, although some tradesmen claim to have stoves that produce sufficient upward draught with less than half this amount of coal.

Heat, therefore, when properly managed so as to draw air out, causes an efficient ventilation of our buildings and rooms. Even in its ordinary activity the principle is operative in ventilating buildings. Whenever an opening exists at the upper part of a house, for instance, the warm air,

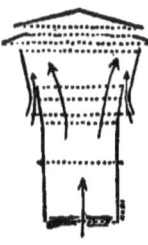
Fig. 28.

rising within the house, tends to flow out through the opening. Thus a natural ventilation is secured since air flows in to replace that which rises. Cowls or caps (see Fig. 28) of round, angular and various other shapes are used to protect openings at the top of flues. While they keep rain and various large objects out, they do not improve the ventilation. They rather obstruct the outward movement of the currents of air. Ventilating chimneys and pipes ought therefore to be as open as possible at the top.

The simplest way of drawing air out of ordinary livingrooms in order to ventilate them by the inflow of fresh air (replacing that which is drawn out), is to have a fire in a flue leading upward and outward. An open-grate fire, as already explained, is very valuable in this respect. We find it equally efficacious and more convenient (although less pleasing to the eye) to have gas or other flames burning in a suitably arranged flue. The proper location of such ventilating flues is explained on page 208. Having a flue or flues of sufficient size, and using heat enough, we can in this way draw the bad air out of any room.

This common, easy and effective method is known as *exhaust* ventilation or *aspiration.* When working well in a tightly closed apartment into which no air is driven, it tends to create a slightly lessened pressure of the atmosphere in the room from which air is drawn out. This indicates the chief objection that can be made against the exclusive use of this method, whether hot-air, air-driving fans, jets of spray, steam or other means be used with a flue to *draw* AIR *out* of a room. It is obvious that the ordinary air, which flows into rooms to replace that which is thus drawn out, may be unclean and impure at times, coming—as it does, when no especial precautions are taken—from the nearest source. If the neighboring corridor or room be loaded with unclean dust, that is liable to be drawn in with the same readiness as the purest air from outside. So, when air drawn in promiscuously will probably be impure, it is especially important to select the supply from the purest possible part of the neighboring air. This then is driven into the rooms either as the hot-air current of a furnace, or mechanical means are used to propel currents of air into the interiors and thus insure their ventilation.

Mechanical means of purifying the air of rooms, by driving quantities of fresh air into them, furnish a very reliable and constant supply; but at the same time the cost of running them usually proves greater than the estimates made beforehand. The most common device is a fan of some sort (see Fig. 29) that drives air through a tube in which or in front of which the inclined planes of the fan are rotating.

FIG. 29.

For forcing large volumes of air rapidly through comparatively small tubes, blowers are used, of the Sturtevant pattern (as indicated on a very small scale at the right-hand lower corner of Fig. 30). These blowers take air in at the side and force it out centrifugally by the rotating (within a drum) of flat sheets of steel arranged and moving very much like paddle-wheels on side-wheel steamboats. Thereby the air can be driven, with great force, through a ventilating flue. The propelled air is then always under at least a slight pressure.

It is hygienically best to have the conducting flues and the blowing machines larger than estimated necessary for the work. In all cases, the current on entering a room ought to be no stronger than six feet per second. If stronger than this (and at any rate if exceeding ten feet per second) undesirable draughts are experienced. In the interests of economy, also, it is found best to have a fan or blower considerably larger than appears fitted to supply the minimum amount of fresh air required. By making the flues and all mechanical parts so ample that abundant fresh air is secured while running such appliances at a moderate speed, better results are got than when they have to be worked at or near their utmost limit.

Using such powerful means to drive fresh air into all parts of a building, there is a distinct gain in that the pure supply can be drawn from such a height above the ground as we choose to take it. With simple hot-air furnaces, it is not as a rule feasible to take in this out-of-doors air from a point much more than five feet above the ground. Otherwise, backward currents may result. Thirty feet above ground is, generally speaking, a suitable level for the fresh-air intake. At that height, the outer opening of the downward-drawing tube, commonly used for the purpose, is below the tops of house-drainage "risers" and smoke-chimneys in cities, while considerably above the level of the worst (coarse) street dust. Every situation needs, however, to be judged by its own peculiar conditions. The longer and smaller the inflow pipe, the greater its frictional resistance to the drawing in of air and hence the greater the cost. If the desirable introduction of an efficient air-strainer is added, this increases the resistance, and consequently the cost of running. Wherever possible, the fresh-air inlet must be far away from foul-air outlets and chimneys. (See Fig. 30.)

For filtering air perfectly, the very finest tissues are needed. Fine cotton-wool is excellent for this purpose and can, for a time, hold back bacteria better than any sheeting, muslin or gauze. It is well that as large a surface of the filtering substance as possible be exposed to the air. It must often be renewed ; otherwise, the abundant dust of the atmosphere speedily clogs up such tissues and offers a formidable resistance to the passage of air. As moisture is the most effectual practical means of arresting dust and bacteria, sprays and moistened surfaces have often been used for this purpose. An interesting account of a seemingly very successful adaptation of all these principles by Mr. Key for the Victoria Hospital in Glasgow can be found in *Engineering* for August 28, 1891. This is mentioned because it appears to be much less costly in its practical operation than similar ones in our country prove to be.

When air is thus drawn in, the mechanical means for driving it along should be as near the inflow pipe as the satisfactory disposition of the apparatus permits. Thus if, as is usual, the blower works also to drive the air through steam-coils for the purpose of warming it, the heating and mixing arrangements (shown in Fig. 23) ought to be so placed that the blower or fan *drives* air upon them and does not *draw* air from the coils. Fig. 30 shows the proper relative position of the different parts. In the former way, it is always very easy to mix in colder air with the warm air by merely regulating the position of the "sliding damper" or any of the similar appliances which ingenuity adapts as best for a given situation.

This mechanical method of ventilating buildings is more expensive to run than the warm-air ventilating-shaft system spoken of on page 199. The permanency and general reliability of the latter plan commend it where it is practicable.

Furthermore, it does not require so great intelligence on the part of the care-taker of the building as is needed for the machinery of most of the mechanical systems, which are necessarily more complicated and hence liable to get out of order. Some agents of fans and blowers claim that their apparatus will supply, to a ten-room school-house, 20,000 cubic feet of air per minute at an hourly cost of five cents or less. Practically they do not effect this. Trial is apt to

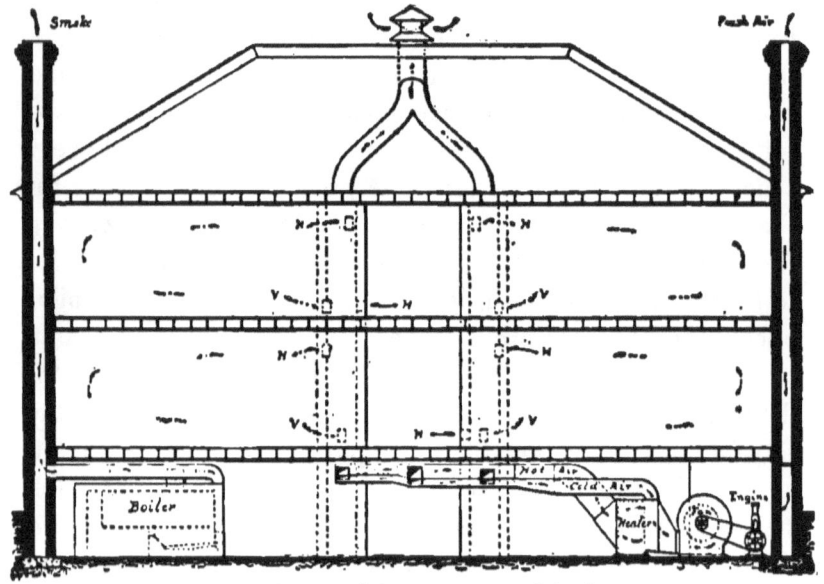

(The air enters at the top of the rooms, as explained on page 208.)

FIG. 30.

show that the cost is several times greater. The highest amount of air that can be got under favorable circumstances, may be set at 10,000 cubic feet of air per minute for each "horsepower." One horsepower as used for such devices should not be figured at less than nine or ten cents per hour. In practical working, the best makes of blowers need about four horsepower to supply an inflow of air slightly larger than is taken out by a ventilating chimney such as is specified on page 200.

Electric motors, even if larger than needed, are not so satisfactory in most cases as vacuum engines or such steam engines as are commonly used for running these blower fans. Water motors, wherever available and economical in use, have the great further recommendation that, after being used for power and for steam, the water from these can be utilized to flush water-closets and thereby maintain the best hygienic condition of the building. Some superintendents of water-works are, however, apt to regard hydraulic motors with disfavor and hence manage to put practical obstacles in their way.

The amount of fresh air that comes in through ventilating flues is satisfactorily measured by means of delicate *anemometers*. (See Fig. 27.) An instrument of this sort is to be held at each test and at each of the separate trials in the test always for the same given time in various parts of the current of air. If then the several readings of a given test be averaged, very reliable results are secured by a person who is at all familiar with the use of this delicate recorder. Multiplying the average velocity of the current by the size of the flue through which it passes, the amount of inflowing air can be accurately estimated. Very *delicate vanes* can be made by carefully weighting toy-balloons or by fixing feathers, mica sheets, etc., to a wire or needle balanced on metal or glass. Thus, the least movement of air may be revealed. Down, the smoke of burning "joss-sticks," smoke of powder or of pungent substances and similar visible light particles aid the recognition of air movement.

Studying the movement of such indicators in rooms under various conditions, we are enabled to form an idea of the most effective and at the same time most economical location for placing the openings through which fresh air is to flow in and contaminated air is to flow out. It is found that, although the carbonic acid gas breathed into the air is heavy, it does not at once fall toward the floor. It tends to rise with the other impurities of the breathed-out air, provided it be warmer than the neighboring air. Otherwise it sinks. It is the temperature of the air that has most influence upon the movements of the exhaled breath when no external influences, such as draughts for instance, are acting upon it.

Fresh air that is sent into a room through a ventilating flue in winter, should preferably come in at the *upper* part of the wall; for, being warm wherever it comes into the room, it rises to the ceiling and draws up bad air with it. If, however, at the same time an unclosed opening into an open outlet flue exists on the upper part of the wall the fresh air tends to flow out at once into that without circulating through the room. Under such circumstances the incoming air fails to purify the contaminated air that may have stood long in the room. Furthermore, a very rapid outflow and waste of heat is an economic loss.

The winter outlet for ordinary purposes of ventilation should accordingly be at the *lower* part of the room, as is the case with a flue used for an open grate fire. Fig. 31 shows the winter plan and Fig. 32 the summer arrangement. The difference between the proper location of winter ventilation and that for summer is likewise shown in Fig. 20. It is, however, always desirable to have a ventilation outlet at the upper part of a wall or even in the ceiling. In winter this is usually kept closed. It ought invariably to be so arranged that it can at any time be opened in order to let out rapidly any uncomfortable excess of warmth, and especially so when such warmth is due to the heat of gas flames.

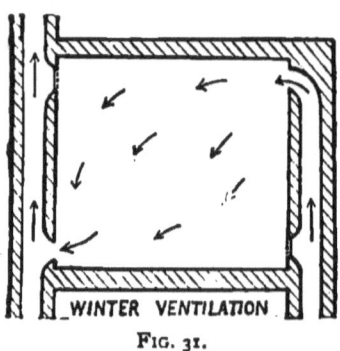

Fig. 31.

This illuminating-gas heat rises toward the ceiling, and has in it various harmful gaseous products which ought not to be allowed to mingle with the body of breathable air in the room. If gas be used abundantly, the gas-burners require (above and near them) special outlet flues for their harmful products. Where such outlet flues do not exist especially for the burners (see Figs. 16 and 19), a ventilating opening in the ceiling overhead or upon the upper part of a wall is of great value.

In summer it is desirable to keep the rooms comfortably cool. When fresh air then comes in through the ventilating supply ducts, it is found best to have this enter the rooms from the lower part of the wall as shown by Fig. 32. The air of the room is warmed by the body warmth of the people present, and heated by the sun's rays if they enter. Thus

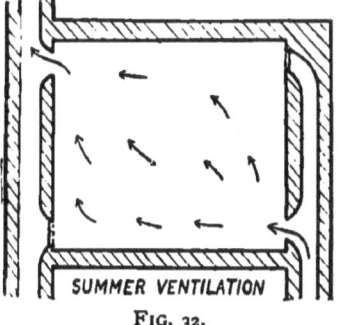

FIG. 32.

becoming lighter than the cooler air which enters, this impure air flows upward and outward. While in winter the chimneys are warm and dry because of the fires, they may in summer be colder than the remainder of the house. Air may therefore at times descend chimneys and flow out of them into the rooms with which they are connected. It is accordingly desirable, in the absence of other heating means, to use burners for warming flues and ventilating chimneys so as to cause an upward current in these flues when they are relied upon to draw bad air out of rooms.

The inner wall of a room is always to be preferred for both inflow and outflow openings and flues. The warmth is there usually more even and permanent, and it is also in general the best location for a chimney. The movement of the air within the room is most satisfactory when the warm air from the heater enters at the upper part of the wall; and this air (after circulating about) is to be drawn out on the same wall nearer the floor. This is indicated in Fig. 33 (a school-room) where the outlet is under a platform. The principle is associated with the name of Mr. Briggs, and is always valuable where suitable exhaust flues exist and are properly used. This has been demonstrated by repeated and long-continued use in various highly satisfactory buildings. It is the most economical way of utilizing the indirect method of steam-heating or furnace-heat and at the same time ventilating rooms.

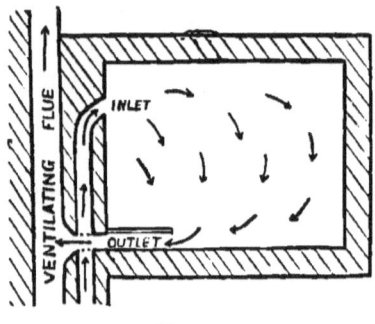

FIG. 33.

For ventilating large and very high rooms and also warming them for a short time to a not very high temperature, as in the case of churches, it is found that air from numerous small openings in the entire floor effects this very evenly. In such a case, the basement must be dry and warm before the hour or more for which the room is needed. In the buildings where this plan has been carried out in its fulness, it has proved quite expensive for the brief time that it was used. If by such means the floor be honeycombed and very uneven and irregular, cleaning may be obstructed and thereby a hygienic defect introduced.

In mines, ventilating shafts or equivalent means of renewing the air should always be introduced wherever necessary. A fire in or at the top of a shaft helps to establish the healthful upward current. For a blind tunnel being driven into the solid rock and where of course no natural ventilation exists, compressed air forced in through pipes, for the purpose of running the power drills, furnishes air to breathe and to drive out the poisonous products of the explosives used. Some sort of ventilation is necessary if men work steadily in such places. Good ventilation is not only indispensable to the health of the miners, but also proves economical for the employers. It enables them to get more and better work done.

In the States where "fire-damp" (carburetted hydrogen) occurs in coal mines, legislative enactments usually require that, for each miner, at least as much as 100 cubic feet of fresh air is supplied every minute. Several times that much is desirable, especially in mines where the dangerous gases are very abundant.

On a steamship which is steadily propelled against a wind or through a calm, such devices as the "blower" shown in Fig. 34

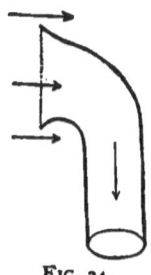

FIG. 34.

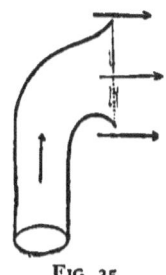

FIG. 35.

turned against the wind can cause fresh air to be driven into the interior of the vessel at the rate of a number of feet per second. At the same time, similar contrivances, turned away from the wind (see Fig. 35), cause air to be drawn out of the interior of the vessel. The fresh-air draught created in this way may be altogether too strong for health. In every case, great care ought to be taken to diffuse the powerful incoming current gently and equably over all parts of the staterooms or steerage. Shipbuilders and seamen do not usually attend with sufficient care to their respective duties as regards this very important matter. We therefore see some passengers and sailors deprived of sufficient air, while others, especially in the upper berths, have draughts blowing directly upon them. In both ways the health may be unfavorably affected. For men-of-war and other ships that are to lie at anchor, mechanical means of driving fresh air throughout the vessel are also needed.

FIG. 36.

Flues and air-conduits should, as already said, be at least large enough for their purpose. The inside of all pipes ought always to be smooth. All contractions and bends cause waste by the retardation that comes from friction. For turning off a current or a portion of a current in a side direction, a gradual, smooth curve (see Fig. 36) is better than a sharp bend. If flues be not already properly built into the wall, galvanized-iron tubes (see Fig. 36a) may be used to help out the ventilation. Like all flues these should be perfectly tight. Especially must they be free from any contact with plumbing waste-pipes, whether these be defective or not. Inspection of even the most costly dwellings reveals at times very glaring offences of this sort.

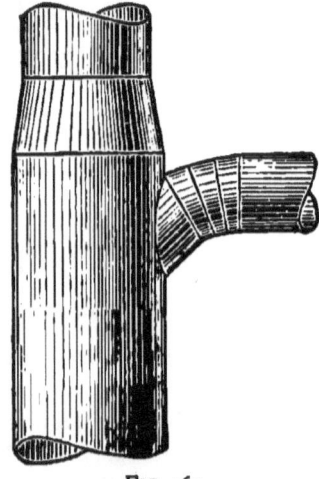

FIG. 36a.

To test for the existence of such dangerous conditions, use is made of a little furnace and fan-blower driving pungent smoke into the soil-pipe at the roof. Such smoke flows out through any leaks in the drainage system. It sometimes reveals very unhealthful faults of construction and repair where the hot-air furnace or the ventilating flues are in communication with badly leaking soil-pipes. It is best that ventilating pipes be so arranged that they can be well cleaned at frequent intervals. Otherwise they may become loaded with dust and abounding in unhealthful dirt that can be drawn back into rooms in case that the current of air happens to flow backward.

It is proper here to state that not only humanity but also the interests of self-preservation should compel an allowance of more air-space than is usually given to stabled animals. Without fresh air and light, all domestic animals languish and become more readily a prey to diseases. These diseases may spread to human beings. Wise regulations by a very few of our leading cities require that all stables for cows contain at least 1,000 cubic feet of space for each animal. Wherever possible, several times that much should be allowed.

FOODS

To compensate for the constant waste of the body, new substance must be supplied for the nutrition of the various parts. This necessary addition is effected by the system through the use of foods. From the healthy digestive organs the greater part of the food swallowed is absorbed in a more or less changed and fluid form. Finally, under the influence of the cells in the several organs, the nutriment is converted into new tissue, body warmth and work.

The indispensable food elements required for maintaining the perfect balance of the intricate human organism are water, salts, albumens, fats, and carbohydrates (the latter being usually in the form of starch and sugar). While the daily amount of these that one needs may vary much, there is a normal allowance below which it is not wise to restrict the food quantity under ordinary conditions of health and activity. The figures of Voit and Pettenkofer are still generally accepted with slight modifications, and give the standard chemical requirements of a normal diet.

These observers consider the amount needed daily by an average workingman weighing not much over 150 pounds, as nearly the following: Albumen, $4\frac{1}{4}$ oz.; fats, $2\frac{1}{4}$ oz.; carbohydrates, 1 lb.; water, 2 qts. +. This estimate (in avoirdupois weight) is considerably below the actual figures which we derive from analyzing the carefully arranged data of some establishments where it is known just how much the average diet of large bodies of laboring men amounts to. Thus, recent statistics from the enormous cast-steel works of Krupp show that each man there receives an allowance greatly exceeding this, especially in the non-albuminous elements of the diet.

At the above-designated model establishment, a practical school is maintained for teaching cooking and housekeeping to the daughters of families connected with the works. The diet of these girls (14 to 18 years of age and weighing on an average nearly 100 pounds) contains : Albumen, $3\frac{1}{2}$ oz. ; fats, $2\frac{1}{2}$ oz. +; carbohydrates, 14 oz. (avoirdupois). Upon this diet, the girls thrive, and their weight appears to exceed the general average of their age and sex.

When there is a great strain upon the body, as in the case of nursing women or of men laboring hard, the above allowances should be exceeded. Especially then are more fats desirable. Old and inactive people need less than the above-indicated amount of food. The tendency among the luxurious and well-to-do classes is to eat too much. This, with the absence of sufficient gentle bodily exercise, contributes to cause some of their ailments. Intemperate excess in eating should receive a share of the condemnation lavished by zealous reformers, but whose strained energies seem concentrated exclusively on preventing all use of alcoholic beverages. The general effect of overeating is to lessen the health and to shorten the life. Very old people have rarely been heavy eaters.

Whenever the food is actually insufficient for keeping the various parts of the human body in a normal condition, the stored-up fat of the system is taken out of the tissues and consumed first. Yet the nervous system loses in starvation only a very small percentage of its abundant fat. The fixed, organized albumen of the tissues is then given up only in scanty amounts corresponding to that portion of the body-cells that is used up.

Albuminous substances (called also " proteids ") are indispensable tissue-forming constituents of our food. While albumen is capable of conversion into fat in the body, the carbohydrates (starch and sugars) and the fats are incapable of conversion into albumen. This is because nitrogen, the distinguishing chemical element present in albumen, is wholly absent from the carbohydrates. These latter, however, containing carbon, hydrogen and oxygen, can become converted into fat in the body.

Like fat, the carbohydrates by being consumed (or literally *burned up*) in the system can produce the greater part of the heat and work of the body. It is the combustion of these non-nitrogenous substances in great part, and not largely the using up of albumens, that, under the best health conditions, produces work and heat. This is shown by the fact that, when we work, the excretion of carbonic dioxide is distinctly increased, and that then the excretion of nitrogen depends upon the amount of albumen in our food.

In an average mixed diet, sufficient salts (phosphates, chlorides, carbonates, sulphates, iron salts,. alkaline earths, alkalies, etc.) are afforded. Water enters largely into the composition of our foods, and the remainder needed is supplied by that which we drink. As will be explained later, the purer the water, the better must it be considered for the health. The less a water has of mineral ingredients, the more suited is it for the table or for any other uses.

A mixed diet is the best for maintaining the health; exclusive use of any class of foods is to be avoided. In the adaptation of a mixed diet, the fats and special fat-forming elements need most to be modified according to the individual and the amount of work and heat demanded. Working in cold weather, one needs much more fat than in warm seasons. In hot summer weather, fat is not generally relished so well as in colder times of the year. Hence we should in summer use less fat and more in proportion of the most easily digestible of the starchy foods, such as rice and wheat bread. The latter furnishes also considerable albuminous substance as well. Unlike fats, the amount allowed of lean meat, if always eaten in moderation, need not be very much lessened with the coming of the warm season. This is because nearly as much albumen is then needed for the absolute repair of the waste of nitrogenous tissue.

An excess of fats in the food tends especially to produce an increase of stored-up fat in the system. Contrary to Ebstein, it is generally regarded that the fat eaten as such is more apt to be stored up than is the fat formed in the system from the non-fatty elements of our diet. Yet, if it be desired to lay on fat, the albuminous substances and also the starches and sugars in the food must be increased as well as the fats.

This is because the tissues need to be kept up to their healthy condition by being allowed as much albumen as they can well take care of. At the same time the uneconomical conversion of this into fat is lessened by giving an excess of starchy foods. To produce a laying on of fat from eating starchy (or other carbohydrate) food, we must allow nearly two-and-a-half times as much as corresponds to the consumption of fats in the system. It is better that starchy and sweet foods be not eaten in any considerable quantity when the stomach is already quite full of meat.

Although fats are more costly, it is not well to substitute the carbohydrates in too great a degree for these. Starches and sugars afford a more favorable medium for the growth of intestinal microörganisms with their consequent fermentations and gases of decomposition. Thence catarrhal conditions and diarrhœas are apt to result, especially in infants. The babe that thrives with milk and cream or cod-liver oil is apt to become ill if fed on starchy food.

The human system is a very perfect mechanism, and can by its vital processes avail itself of and manifest in work nearly one-fourth of what physicists term the caloric and potential energy of the material taken in as food. This is mechanically a much more perfect result than the steam engine gets out of the fuel which it uses. Practically it is not wise for individuals to estimate the value of foods by considering only the exact chemical composition. Foods that are chemically equivalent are not of necessity equally nutritious. (Compare tables on pages 218 and 220.)

Those who construct diet lists purely on a chemical basis do not appear to realize how important it is to consider the condition and activity of the digesting and absorbing mucous membrane. The individual peculiarities and the state of health, the preparation and quality of the food,—all affect the question. The albuminous matter enclosed in an indigestible cellulose coating of an insufficiently cooked vegetable cell is very much inferior, as food, to the more absorbable elements of good meat. If too much food be in the stomach, the system can utilize, for nourishment, less of this food than when a small meal is eaten.

Meat digests best when no other food is with it in the stomach. The healthy condition of the digestive apparatus is essential to the best digestion. It is not desirable to say that such and such a meat or other article of food is digestible in two or three hours or any other time. There is very little definitely known to enable us to say how it will be in a given case. The experience of any individual as to whether a food "agrees" or "disagrees" is a better guide for that person than any tables which can be offered.

The method of cooking affects the digestibility of foods to a great extent. If soaked in fatty sauces and abounding in the aromatic, savory substances coming from the action of high heat upon fatty tissue, a meat may give evidence of remaining in the stomach for twice the three hours (more or less) that it requires for digestion when cooked very plainly and when only a little is eaten.

We can however speak more precisely when it is a question of the **absorbability** of food. Thus we find that of various kinds of food received into the stomach a varying amount is taken up and assimilated by the system. From figures given by different authors it may be regarded that, of the following foods, the **percentages assimilated** after they are taken into the adult stomach amount to :—

	OF THE DRY SUBSTANCE.	OF THE ALBUMEN.	OF THE FATS.	OF THE CARBOHYDRATES.	OF THE SALTS.
Meat	95.4%	97.4%	83.4%	. . . .	85%
Eggs (boiled) .	94.8	97.4	95.5	. . . .	89
Milk	92.3	93.5	96.7	. . . .	51.3
White bread . .	95	78.2	. . . . . .	98.8%	. . . .
Split peas . . .	90.7	82.5	. . . . . .	96.2	. . . .
Macaroni . . .	95	84.2	94.2	97.8	79.2
Rice	95.9	77.2	93.1	99.1	85
Potatoes . . .	90.5	67.8	96.2	92.4	84.2

Common salt is the one relish that is actually indispensable to health. In an exclusive meat diet, this is abundant; yet lime and potash salts are there deficient. On the other hand, common salt is not sufficiently abundant in vegetables. Hence the propriety of adding this to the food. Cooking may lessen the lime-salts of milk by driving off the carbonic acid gas which held some of these salts in solution.

Human beings are not mere digestive machines. The will and fancy count for much, and destroy the value of a purely chemical standard. These factors also require that food shall be savory and varied as well as wholesome. Furthermore, people demand the addition of other and innutritious substances to the diet. Of these, the various **spices and condiments** are fortunately not used here as much as among some other nations. The desire for alcoholic liquors and the less flagrantly harmful kindred luxuries—tea, coffee and tobacco—seems to be universal. These are all prejudicial to the health, and the human races would be stronger if such substances were unknown.

Animal food appears in general to be more nutritious and better utilizable than vegetable food. Yet some very nutritious foods (such as cheese, lobster, etc.) may prove difficult or even painful for the stomach to digest. Cooking may increase or lessen the digestibility of a food, its nutritive value being perhaps unchanged. Cooking makes tough meat more digestible. Tender meat digests equally well whether raw or cooked.

Meat (including the flesh of fish) is the main reliance for supplying the albumen needed by the human system. It comprises in its substance nearly everything required for the nutrition of the body. The bones, however, are not digestible and absorbable. If eaten, they do not contribute to the bone substance of the body.

From the table on page 220, we see that the chemical composition of the different meats varies somewhat. Yet from a commercial or a hygienic point of view, these differences are less important than is the amount of fibrous tissue and the tough envelope (*sarcolemma*) around the muscle fibres. The toughness, that these elements cause, is lessened when the meat is kept for some days or weeks. This is because of the softening action of the dilute lactic acid, formed in the meat when kept, and which is so important in making game and other meat more tender by keeping. Vinegar and other dilute acids are often used for the same purpose.

Fish in general has less of this fibrous substance. It is best eaten in a fresh state. Fish-meat is also quite perishable, abounding in bacteria as it often does. It needs to be well cooked. Salmon, eels and similar fish have a considerable percentage of nutritious fat which, however, makes these fish difficult of digestion for many persons. The herring is the most valuable of the fat fishes. Oysters and other shell-fish afford much less nutriment than they are usually thought to yield. If from filthy waters and eaten

Chemical Composition of Animal Foods
Expressed in percentages

	Water.	Albumen	Fat.	Carbohydrates (etc.)	Salts.
Human milk (average)	88.00	2.00	3.60	6.00	0.40
Cow's milk "	87.50	3.45	3.70	4.70	0.65
Goat's milk "	86.50	4.00	4.00	4.70	0.80
Butter (unsalted)	14.60	0.75	83.55	0.90	0.20
Cheese (medium fat)	42.20	29.50	22.00	1.80	4.50
Beef (average)	72.00	20.95	5.85	0.32	1.15
Beef (corned)	58.30	30.00	8.20	....	3.50
Veal (average)	75.00	19.50	4.30	0.20	1.00
Mutton (average)	75.25	17.20	6.30	....	1.25
Pork (fat meat)	47.40	14.54	37.34	....	0.72
Pork (lean meat)	72.57	20.25	6.81	....	1.10
Venison	75.76	19.77	1.92	1.42	1.13
Blood (of ox)	77.34	20.87	0.97		0.82
Oysters	89.70	4.95	0.37	2.63	2.35
Salmon (California)	61.80	20.15	15.70	....	2.35
Herring (fresh)	74.64	14.55	9.03	....	1.78
Mackerel (fresh)	71.20	19.36	8.08	....	1.36
Trout	77.51	19.18	2.10	....	1.21
Hen's eggs	73.67	12.55	12.11	0.55	1.12

Chemical Composition of Vegetable Foods
Expressed in percentages

	Water.	Albumen.	Fat (oils).	Carbohydrates, etc.	Salts.
Spring wheat	11.80	12.25	2.05	72.20	1.70
White bread	35.59	7.06	0.46	56.90	1.09
Oatmeal	10–13	12–19	5–7	70–74	1–2
Cornmeal (maize)	12.65	9.35	7.40	69.50	1.10
Rice	12.58	6.73	0.88	78.98	0.83
Potatoes	74.98	1.88	0.16	21.92	1.06
Dry beans	12.04	24.02	2.07	58.25	3.62
Cabbage	87.06	2.74	0.63	8.45	1.12
Apples	84.76	0.37	....	14.35	0.52
Grapes	78.17	0.59	....	20.71	0.53
Bananas	79.36	4.85	0.53	19.69	0.97

raw, they introduce an element of danger by carrying harmful bacteria. Chemical poisons are also contained in them at times. Fish-meat, when white, although containing considerable water, is yet a good substitute for flesh of animals and may be recommended for albuminous diet to those who enjoy fish and digest it easily.

The prejudice existing against veal as an innutritious meat is not justifiable, provided that the calf has not been killed till several weeks after birth. Meats and fish that have been "preserved" by drying or other means have the nutritive value of the fresh product; yet the processes usually make these less digestible. In the process of "corning," *trichinæ* that may be present are believed to be speedily killed if in the outer parts of the meat. It takes weeks for the pickle to penetrate in such strength as to kill those trichinæ that are an inch deep in the meat. Tubercle bacilli and others can live for months in the strongest brine. Hence salted pork or beef always requires to be cooked.

The process of preservation by "smoking" meat, etc., is regarded by many as speedily killing trichinæ and other microörganisms by the drying and by the creosote of the smoke used. Yet it is always advisable to cook such food, since recent experiments have shown that bacteria of various kinds survive "smoking." Bacon should always be well cooked.

Preserved meats that give an *alkaline* reaction to test paper are to be suspected as being prepared from unwholesome raw meat. *Salicylic* acid is often introduced into preserved food of all sorts. Its presence is hygienically undesirable, although it is a valuable preservative. To detect it, the delicate violet reaction with chloride of iron is relied upon. Dry cold affords the best means of preserving meat.

In canned meats, we do not fear disease germs. The heat of the process that suffices to preserve the meat will have destroyed bacteria. Metals, and particularly **lead**, may be present, especially if the contents have been allowed to remain long in the can after opening. For examining canned food we first employ a good magnifying glass for detecting particles of lead, etc. Then the meat is analyzed in the usual way for lead. (See page 252.)

Meat extracts, prepared foods, proprietary beef preparations, etc., have for the usual conditions of health or disease little or no hygienic superiority over the cheaper domestic preparations such as scraped beef, broths, etc. The much advertised articles are usually inferior and lacking in the merit that they are claimed to possess.

Meat from various birds is much like other flesh in chemical composition. Yet their muscles are less bound in fibrous tissue than is the case with other meat, and hence are more delicate. Although rich in albumen, this meat is relatively deficient in salts and fat. Grain-fed fowl are best. An odor of decomposition, bluish color or spotting of the skin should cause the poultry having it to be rejected.

The internal organs of slaughtered animals have, with the exception of the lungs, nearly as much albumen and fat value as ordinary meat. They are to be classed with it in nutritive worth. Sausages are nutritious but are often made of diseased meat. In any case, they should be well cooked. According to Ostertag, the addition of more than two per cent. of flour to sausages deserves to be considered an objectionable adulteration.

Dangerous Parasites in Meat

Trichinæ enter the human system almost always through uncooked pork. They are found in lean pork and very rarely indeed in the fat substance. They are minute worms, less than one-eighth of an inch long when full-grown. The female is much larger than the male. These worms lie coiled up (see Figs. 37 and 38), immature and inert, in the muscle substance of pork and surrounded by an oval capsule visible to the naked eye. This is apt to appear very white, owing to the infiltration of lime salts into it.

These worms mature in about two days after they have entered the bowel with the lean pork that is eaten. Then they propagate and, within a week, more than a thousand minute embryos result. These new trichinæ burrow through the bowel wall and reach muscles in which they appear just like the original ones in the pork from which they originated. The prolonged, slow burrowing of very many thousands of these causes the muscular pain and other symptoms. If only few trichinæ are present, the trouble is often mistaken for rheumatism.

FIG. 37.

To prevent this disease, care is required to see that swine do not get it by eating rats or other animals (or offal from swine that are trichinous). *Pork should not be eaten unless it has been well cooked.* If it be cooked so that the interior in all parts reaches a temperature of 140° F., this will have killed the trichinæ. If pork has been eaten that is suspected of containing these worms in a live state, prompt and thorough purgation will ward off much of the danger.

FIG. 38.

Meat should always have been inspected by faithful and competent officials whose work is "controlled" by occasional independent tests. An ordinary microscope, magnifying fifty times, suffices for the purpose of examining pork (or other meat) for trichinæ. A dozen or more half-inch pieces are cut thin (as by curved scissors) from the belly muscles as well as from the diaphragm and deep throat muscles. Each piece is then torn somewhat and, in a drop of glycerine or of potash solution (but preferably without the addition of water to fresh pork, according to Johne), is pressed between two pieces of glass. A low power of the microscope suffices then to detect the minute worms. If the pork has been smoked (ham or bacon) it must be soaked for a few minutes in weak acetic acid. Other harmful parasites may be recognized at the same time.

Fig. 39 (after Leuckart) represents a piece of lean meat from a **measly** hog. The little *cysticercus* cysts which cause the disease are there shown of life size. They may, however, be a trifle larger or smaller than there given. If meat which contains these be eaten uncooked, they are liable to develop into *tapeworms* in the intestine. If one of these little bladders be pricked and then examined between two pieces of glass, with the aid of a microscope or a strong lens, a characteristic circle of hooks is readily seen. Not only tapeworm but also *hydatid* tumors can come from eating beef or pork that has not been cooked well. It may here be mentioned that tapeworms may result from careless contact with dogs or from drinking uncooked water that comes from a place frequented by dogs.

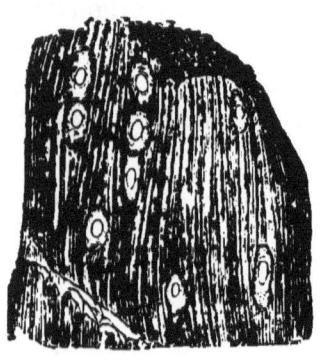

FIG. 39.

Tuberculosis is the most notable of the bacterial diseases that occur in the meat of cattle and hogs. Even more than from three to five per cent. of the average slaughtered cattle reveal the characteristic nodules of tuberculosis, and often the disease is still further advanced. In some regions, more than one-fourth of the cattle have this disease. The glands and membranes about the intestine should be carefully examined in all cases. Also the inside and outside of the lungs. If the muscles are not affected —and they usually are not—it is regarded as not necessary to condemn the meat merely because lungs or glands are infected. Yet, owing to the possibility of infection, such meat must be well cooked; for thorough cooking destroys the harmfulness of those germs that may be present in the meat. Calves are much less liable to have the disease than are older cattle. Sheep have it much less than cattle, and goats almost never have tuberculosis.

Animals that have died of fever of any kind must be condemned as unfit for food. Beef from a cow that has died of *calf-birth fever* may cause serious diarrhœal and other symptoms. Cooking does not destroy the poison of this meat. Bollinger, Ostertag and others have published enumerations of several thousand cases of illness caused by eating such meat. "Joint disease" should cause meat to be condemned.

The carcasses of animals that have died of *splenic fever* must be burned up or buried very deep, as the disease is very dangerous. In this disease, as also with *glanders* or *farcy*, care should be taken to avoid infection from handling. Inspection enables an examiner of any skill to detect these and other unusual appearances, such as the little, yellow grain-like points as well as abscesses caused by the same microörganism (*actinomyces*) that produces "lumpy jaw" in cattle and hogs. Meat having these present must be condemned.

When meat, upon being cut, is "watery" or even bloody it is at least inferior and probably from a diseased animal. Such meat is particularly apt to decompose speedily. Reddening, swelling and thickening are the first signs by which meat from an inflamed part is recognized. The other signs are so obviously unlike the appearances of sound meat that the least care allows them to be recognized. Swollen and dingy-looking meat is to be suspected. So, too, is that which is yellowish-waxy in appearance. "Blowing up" meat, by forcing in air through bellows or by other less cleanly means, may drive in bacteria from outside. The meat then does not keep so well as it otherwise would.   The object of treating the meat thus is to make it seem more tender and to increase the bulk.

Bad meat is altogether too often put into sausages. At times the organic poisons called *ptomaïnes* are developed in sausages. In such cases the meat decomposes and produces these poisons owing to bacteria present. Cooking kills the bacteria and arrests the process, yet cooking does not necessarily destroy the poison already formed by the activity of the bacteria.

"**Gamy**" **flavor** of wild fowl and other meat that has been kept rather long after being killed, depends upon the added taste imparted by the gases and other products resulting from the activity of millions of bacteria that develop in the intestines and on other moist surfaces of the bird or other creature. These products of decomposition, in limited quantities at least, do not appear to derange the health of gourmets who are used to them. Yet meat having these bacteria or their products present should not be approved; for many people cannot tolerate such tainted meat.

Microörganisms grow most rapidly when the food upon which they fall is moist. The dryer and cooler it is, the less do they thrive. This explains the great importance of keeping ice-chests and refrigerating rooms very dry. Freshly slaughtered meat should be kept in dry, artificially cooled rooms for a few days.

Food animals need to be carefully watched during life, and examined by experts before being slaughtered. After that, the meat should be inspected faithfully by people skilled in detecting the evidences of disease. The health of all demands that private slaughter-houses be abolished or constantly supervised. General public slaughter-houses constantly supervised are best. In any case, the official inspectors must be wholly independent and beyond any control of butchers or drovers.

Eggs, as shown by the analysis given on page 220, are quite nutritious. Yet in that respect they are inferior to good meat. The egg of an average hen has no more food value than one-third of a pint of milk, and lacks the sugar of the milk. One dozen of eggs have only a trifle more food value than a pound of fat meat.

Milk is an emulsion of fat (in globules of varying size) in a solution of albumen (chiefly casein), milk-sugar and salts. See analysis, page 220. The proportion of each of these in cow's milk varies greatly according to the breed of the cows, their age, the time since the birth of the calf, the food, etc. It should have over three-and-a-half per cent. of fat. Some dairy cattle yield much more than this. The specific gravity should not be less than 1,028, nor more than 1,036. The average may be given as a little over 1,030. If lower than 1,028, and the cream be scanty, we should suspect adulteration with water.

While cow's milk is neutral in reaction, human milk in health is alkaline. The latter has less albuminous matter and a smaller amount of salts than the former. The addition of a little sugar and water renders cow's milk more like human milk. A little cream is also needed with the watered cow's milk unless that be unusually rich. The milk of mares and she-asses resembles human milk more than does that of cows. That from the last part of a milking is much richer in cream than the milk which comes first from the udder.

Particularly when used for **babes,** milk should be very fresh, from perfectly healthy cows and supplied by honest and careful people. This is not only because of the constant danger of adulteration, but also because bacteria of various kinds enter the milk unless the most intelligent care is exercised. When once in the milk, these microörganisms can increase rapidly, especially if the milk be kept warm. These cause milk-sugar to become lactic acid with the formation of carbonic acid and other products. Lactic acid and also other acids and coagulative ferments convert the casein into cheese which, in the milk thus soured, separates and carries nearly all of the fat in its mass.

To prevent these undesirable changes, the udder should be cleansed before milking, and the hands of the milker and the pail or other receiver should be very clean. The milking must be carried out with the strictest cleanliness. At no time during or after the process should dirt be allowed to enter the milk. Observing these precautions and cooling the milk as soon as possible, the danger of contamination and rapid spoiling is removed.

Disease germs usually get into milk because of the use of bad water for adulteration or for rinsing out pails, cans, etc. Carelessness allows harmful bacteria to enter in other ways. Numerous cases are reported where typhoid fever, cholera, scarlet fever, foot-and-mouth disease or other disorders have been caused by the use of infected milk.

Of the various disease bacteria that can live in milk, the most notable are those of tuberculosis. Many dairy cows have this disease. Milk being produced in part by a breaking down of the cells of the milk glands, the bacilli of tuberculosis are often carried into the milk from unrecognized cases of this disease. The udder of a tuberculous cow reveals to the touch a notable hardening and enlargement of a portion (or portions) of it. It is rare that all of the udder is thus affected. It is every year becoming more and more certain that the germs of tuberculous consumption can enter the human system through the use of such milk.

The best (laboratory) means of recognizing the presence of the peculiar bacilli is to inoculate some of the doubtful milk into guinea-pigs. These animals are very sensitive to the disease and die from it if the milk contain many of the bacilli. In the organs of the dead guinea-pig, these typical bacilli can then be found in great numbers.

EXAMINATION OF MILK

To ascertain the number of ordinary bacteria present, we take up a drop of the milk by means of a heat-sterilized pipette. We can still further divide this drop by mixing it with a measured amount of water that has been sterilized by boiling. The drop of milk is added to some of the usual sterile nutrient gelatine (spoken of in the chapter on Bacteria) in the bottom of a test-tube. This gelatine is softened by previous gentle warming and is agitated slightly so as to mix into it the milk. Then the test-tube, closed with the usual cotton plug, is left to lie nearly level on its side in a shaded place that is not warm.

If more than 500 "colonies" of bacteria appear from the original drop, the milk is not of high quality as regards freshness or cleanliness. Low-grade city milk may have more than a thousand times as many germs as that in each drop. Such inferior milk is undesirable, even when cooked. Occasionally a potent organic poison (*tyrotoxicon*) occurs in bad milk, as also in cheese and ice-cream made from such milk. This poison is due to the action of some bacteria.

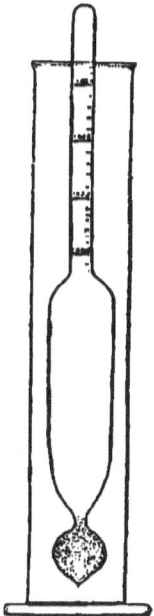

FIG. 40.

Skim milk, best obtained by rapid removal of nearly all of the cream through use of centrifugal *separators*, is a very cheap albuminous food. It however may have much less than half of one per cent. of fat. This makes it an imperfect food, and children fed with it should have fat besides. Unsterilized water is also added at times to the original milk from which such skim milk is derived. (See Cornell University Agricultural Bulletin, No. 39, 1892.) This water introduces the danger of contamination. If no water be added, the removal of the cream causes the specific gravity to be as high as 1,035 or 1,038.

For ordinary purposes, we can sufficiently well detect the *adulteration* of milk by using a *lactometer* indicating the specific gravity of the fluid in which it floats. (See Fig. 40.) It is adjusted to 60° F., and should have a scale that is accurate from 1,025 to 1,040. This need not cost much more than half a dollar. At the same time, a *creamometer* should be used. This is an upright graduated glass tube two inches or more across and in which the milk is to stand for 36 hours or more at the average comfortable room temperature. Yet cream rises more rapidly if the temperature of the milk be quickly lowered and kept low (40° F.) for hours.

The creamometer scale being arranged in hundredths (the zero at the top and the hundred at the bottom), a good milk should yield at least ten per cent. of cream. If $\frac{10}{100}$ of cream rise to the top of the standing tube of milk, that indicates a little less than 3½ per cent. of fat in the milk. $\frac{15}{100}$ of cream mean nearly 4¾ per cent. of fat, which is a high proportion. The Soxhlet and other methods requiring laboratory facilities are to be employed when very exact results are called for. Bulletin No. 13, U. S. Department of Agriculture, 1887, also the fourth annual Report of the Board of Health of New York State, may be referred to for further details.

No chemicals should be added to milk except upon medical approval. *Salicylic acid*, the most objectionable preservative chemical added (usually in the strength of one-twentieth of one per cent.) is detected by the production of a purple or violet color on the addition of a few drops of chloride of iron. For the test, it is best to remove the casein and fat by the use of sulphuric acid, then to filter and shake the filtrate with ether. This ether is then poured off, evaporated, and the residue tested with the iron chloride.

Soda is often used to lessen the acidity of soured milk. Yet it favors the increase of bacteria, and the milk dealer should not use it. It causes milk that is long cooked to become darker by the change of milk-sugar into caramel. Milk that shows an acid reaction on standing a while in a room of ordinary temperature is not suitable for feeding young children.

Since bacteria thrive so well in milk and rapidly spoil it, heat is much used to kill these microörganisms and thus "sterilize" the milk. All proper condensed milk has undergone this process to a sufficient extent. Any disease bacteria that are liable to be in milk die in a minute if the milk be heated to the boiling point. Even the temperature of 165° F. will have the same salutary effect if the milk, in which these disease germs are, be kept at this degree of heat for ten minutes. *Pasteurization* of milk is a valuable process. It is explained later, in the chapter upon *Bacteria*.

A higher heat, and that much more prolonged, is needed to destroy the various bacteria that cause souring and other changes. If, as is usually the case, the milk have hay dust and bits of manure present, hours may be required for the boiling to have killed all bacteria. When all bacteria in the milk (and in its container) are destroyed and it is so protected that no other bacteria can enter, the milk will keep for an indefinite period. The more strictly clean the milk is, the less time is required for sterilizing it by heat. The carefully managed milk establishment of Bolle, in Berlin, shows how well the business ought to be conducted.

The cows of the establishments that produce the best sterilized milk are very clean. So, too, are the hands, boots and clothing of the milkers. The pails and other receptacles are cleansed by hot water or steam. Care is taken to keep hay dust out of the air. The fresh milk is received into the steamed receptacles in which it is to undergo sterilization or to be transported in its unsterilized state. Such milk from healthy cattle is, however, better when unsterilized and will then keep much longer than inferior milk.

Sterilized milk is, in the opinion of most physicians, less digestible than good milk in its fresh, natural state. The changes in its casein and other elements and the partial precipitation of lime salts make the cooked milk a less satisfactory food. Yet, because of the bacteria that are swarming in low-grade milk, it is generally well to recommend that milk be boiled in summer unless fresh and of unquestionable purity. On carefully sterilized milk, children can be reared very successfully, even from birth. Yet fresh, pure milk is better, just as human milk, if healthy, is the best food of all for babes.

For home sterilizing of milk, it is well to recommend small, clean bottles standing in a wire rack or basket. After the bottles are filled, their mouths are plugged with cotton. Then they are heated in steamers of any kind or in hot water (at a temperature of 180° F. or more) for half an hour. After this, the milk should be cooled unless to be used very soon. With this brief heating, ordinary milk will not keep long.

It would be well if the milk inspectors of cities could

supervise the dairies and cattle-stables that supply milk. In nearly all of our cities, dangers to health exist in the shape of crowded, filthy stables and sheds where diseased cows, feeding on the refuse of distilleries, vinegar works, etc., furnish milk that finds ready sale among thousands of families.

In Chicago, New Jersey and elsewhere recent extensive movements have begun to improve these unhealthful conditions. The Boston milk-inspection law is one of the best. It is important that cattle have daylight supplied them. At least as much as one thousand cubic feet of space should be allowed for each animal. That is a very scanty allowance.

Koumiss is an alcoholic drink which some pastoral tribes of oriental lands prepare by causing the milk of mares to ferment through the introduction, into the milk, of certain kinds of bacteria and yeast. Among us a similar beverage is made from cows' milk to which a little cane-sugar is added and then common yeast planted in it. [See "The Fermentations of Milk," by Conn, 1892, issued by U. S. Department of Agriculture.] Such fermented milk is furnished under various names energetically advertised.

By the conversion of some of the sugar, more than one per cent. of alcohol is present in these preparations. The casein of the original milk is somewhat changed (peptonized) and is in much finer lumps than in ordinary coagulated milk. Although some people dislike and cannot tolerate these preparations, others find them agreeable and apparently of some nutritive value. Yet all impartial analyses show that "koumiss" is not sufficient for exclusive nutrition of the body.

Butter is chiefly composed of the fat of milk, the casein around the globules of fat being broken away by churning and these very many minute fat globules being then compressed into large masses. With the fat of butter is a varying, small percentage of water and a small amount of the other milk elements. (See analysis, page 220.) These make it a fertile soil for bacteria to thrive in, and millions of these may be found in an acorn-sized piece of ordinary uncooked butter. Disease-producing bacteria can remain alive in and on it for days. Hence the origin and cleanly treatment of this, as of other dairy products, are of great importance.

Butter of good quality is an agreeable and wholesome fat, yet it is costly as compared with the other fat foods. Good olive oil, even, can be bought by the gallon in our large cities for less than the price of its equivalent of the best butter. Much refined cotton-seed oil is used for adulterating and imitating butter.

Artificial butter (*oleomargarine*) is made in immense quantities; but this product is largely driven out of the market owing to the present unjustly severe laws. The best of it is more wholesome than some of the stuff which is sold as genuine butter. Whenever this artificial butter is allowed to be made, the process of manufacture should be carefully controlled; for sufficient heat is not always employed in making this. Unprincipled people may use inferior or refuse fats and cheap vegetable oils. The product is then unwholesome.

Cheese gives a very concentrated nutriment which is comparatively cheap. It is prepared by causing rennet or acid to precipitate the casein of milk, and this carries with it the fat. In such varieties as Neuchatel cheese and cream cheese, extra cream is present. Parmesan cheese and "skim-milk cheese" have had some of the cream removed from the milk before the cheese-making began. Delicate flavors in cheese depend upon refinements and great care in manufacturing. Some are due altogether to the milk coming from special pastures. From skim-milk, to which cheap fats have been added after being sterilized and deodorized by long steaming, successful imitations of good cheese are made in various portions of the United States.

All the remarks made above regarding the need of care and cleanliness in obtaining, handling and treating dairy products, apply also to cheese. If decomposed by bacteria, it may develop the organic poison mentioned in speaking of milk. The outer part is the most unclean, and may contain lead (from tinfoil) and other metals. Cheese should not in any case be eaten to the extent of more than seven ounces in a day. For those with whom it agrees, it makes an excellent addition to a starchy diet such as hominy or bread. The belief that small quantities of cheese may then aid the digestion of other foods, seems well founded.

Cereal foods have considerable similarity of composition. Outside of all grains of wheat, etc., is a firm layer of indigestible woody substance, silica and other elements. The inner part of these grains consists almost entirely of starch cells. Next to the starch and between it and the tough outside layers is the gluten (albuminous) layer. In milling, the starch readily pulverizes into flour of the whitest sort. The outer parts of the grain form bran, which is tough and indigestible. So it is not desirable that this remain in the flour. (For composition of wheat, see page 220.)

Very white flour, such as that made from winter wheat, is preferable for pastry, yet has less of the albuminous element, gluten. Spring-wheat flour is yellower because it has more gluten, and this makes the flour have a greater nutritive value. Until the introduction among us of the Hungarian (high-milling) process, in 1873, fine white flour could not be produced from spring wheat. A bushel of wheat, weighing sixty pounds, yields a little less than three-fourths its weight of white flour.

If, for the sake of its superior nutritive value, all the gluten is kept in the flour, it should be thoroughly pulverized in milling, as otherwise it is not well absorbed. The indigestible, branny elements of the outside of the grain, if present in the flour, interfere greatly with the absorption, into the system, of the starch and all other elements of cooked flour or bread. For porridge, "stirabout," etc., it is well that the crushed wheat, oatmeal or flour used should be quite finely ground up in milling, if the full nutritive value be desired.

In order that such foods be well digested, it is necessary to cook them so as to rupture the envelopes of the minute cells which contain the starch and other substances. Bread is the most common form in which we use these foods. Gluten must be in the flour in order that the well-kneaded dough-mass, into which the flour is made, may hold together and "rise" when bubbles of gas are formed in the dough-mass and expand it. Flour made from wheat or rye is preferred for bread-making, as these grains have much gluten. These flours may be mixed with other, less glutinous, flours if desired. The most commonly used gas for raising dough is carbonic dioxide, which is there harmless.

This gas is usually produced by the action of a small amount of yeast thoroughly worked into the dough by kneading. At an overwarm room temperature (between 77° F. and 95° F.) the diastatic ferment contained in the flour effects the conversion of a small portion of the starch into dextrine and maltose. Under the influence of the warmth these substances are in the course of a few hours further converted into lactic and butyric acids by the living yeast cells present. Besides other products of this fermentation, some alcohol is formed and also much carbonic dioxide, which is evenly distributed throughout the loaf if the dough has been well kneaded.

By means of an oven heated to more than 390° F., the bread is then baked. The gas thereby expands, but the resistance of the firm crust formed keeps this gas and most of the water from escaping. The crust is due to the action of the heat in coagulating the albumen of the gluten, which also in part forms a new combination with the starch. The heat of baking causes the conversion of a portion of the starch into dextrine and other very digestible forms of carbohydrates. This occurs especially in the brown crust. *Bread is in most cases insufficiently baked.*

As a substitute for yeast, older "sour dough" (kept over for the purpose) may be worked into the dough and be made to act as a leaven for "raising" the mass. This sour leaven gets its sourness from lactic and acetic acids formed when it is kept over and due to the presence of numerous microörganisms capable of inducing a fermentation somewhat different from that caused by pure yeast.

These fermentative processes cause the chemical conversion of from 1.5 to 3 per cent. of the starch. There are some who fancy such processes to be objectionable and who advocate the use of commercially produced gases introduced into the bread, instead of using yeast. No wholly satisfactory substitute for yeast, as a leavening agent, has yet been produced.

It may here be said that the high heat of the baking oven, maintained for less even than the usual time of an hour, surely kills the yeast cells and any other living microorganisms that in any way chance to get into the dough. Yet bread, especially when moist, furnishes a fertile soil for the growth and transportation of various sorts of microorganisms that may come from the air, from unclean hands, etc. During the European epidemic of 1892-93, numerous cases of cholera were traced to the eating of bread and other foods infected by careless people.

Instead of using yeast for raising dough, the desired gas can be produced when an alkali, such as bicarbonate of soda, is well mixed through the dry flour, and then sufficient acid is added in the water which we mix with this dry flour to make a dough. Almost any acid of pure quality may be used to bring about this chemical reaction and thus produce the desired carbonic dioxide gas. The various **baking-powders** furnish these (acid and alkaline) chemical substances mixed in suitable proportions; but more than a third of all the baking-powders sold in America are estimated to be compounded of harmful chemicals!

The safest and best acid ingredient for these is good cream of tartar (commercial bitartrate of potash). Carbonate of ammonia is less desirable, yet is permissible. The use of bi-sulphate of potash is undesirable because of the purgative tendency of the salts produced in making the bread. Baking-powders containing alum or alum-phosphate are objectionable and ought to be prohibited.

Since nearly one hundred million pounds of baking-powders are presumably consumed every year in North America, it is proper here to indicate that this very important subject can be further studied in part in elaborate reports issued by the Canadian Inland Revenue Department, and by the U.S. Department of Agriculture. All baking-powders should, under penalty, be required to have their composition indicated by an accurate label attached to every package sold.

In general, baking-powder may be said to be less healthful than yeast for bread-making. The addition of a little salt and also of milk improves the quality of bread. High-grade wheat produces bread of better quality than comes from inferior grain. There is very little or no adulteration of flour with inferior substitutes. Such things usually cost more than flour. Potato starch is added to bread by some bakers.

The use of diseased grain and of salts of copper, zinc, etc., to rehabilitate bad flour seems very rare among bakers. Lead-poisoning may be feared where that metal has been used to fill up flaws in mill-stones. The presence of alum in bread is always undesirable. Alum in any considerable amount is recognized by moistening well the suspected bread or flour with logwood water (made by steeping logwood chips thoroughly in pure, soft water that has been boiled, or preferably distilled). Alum in bread thus tested causes a bluish or lavender color.

Old bread loses water and becomes dryer; yet the crust becomes more moist at first. New bread is wholesome if not so moist as to be clammy. It is best when dried by heat and then toasted slightly over coals or above a hot stove. Much of the starch is thereby converted into dextrine and thus rendered more easily digestible.

Wheat-flour and water, mixed to a thin, unleavened dough

and then baked, make a very nutritious food, as seen in the form of the various "crackers," biscuit, cakes, etc. The same may be said of very simple pudding, such as "duff," etc., if not very moist and soggy and thereby less digestible. *Pastry* and other "rich" foods are more or less indigestible owing to the excess of fat through all parts and surrounding the otherwise nutritious vegetable cells. Macaroni and "nudels" make a valuable food; when eggs are used in their preparation, these foods may be regarded as having nearly as much nutritive value as meat.

Indian corn (or maize) is the most used of the other cereal foods. The meal (and also *hominy*) made of it needs to be cooked long and well. If made with milk into "mush," it is like the Italian *polenta*. If cheese be eaten with this, a complete food is had at a very low price. The "hog-and-hominy" of the Southern States may also be considered a fairly complete food. Johnny-cake, corn-pone, corn-bread, tortilla, and other cornmeal products are excellent foods, yet incomplete. They need the albumen and fat of a little meat added in order to make a proper diet.

Rice is a similar starchy food, having less albumen and much less fat. It is very digestible when simply cooked. In this and in such bland and purely starchy foods as sago and tapioca, boiling causes the starch cells to swell up and burst, taking in from four to six times their weight of water.

Potatoes are very valuable as furnishing a palatable starchy food at an extremely low cost. Being very deficient in albumen and fats, potatoes furnish only an incomplete food. They require to be cooked quickly and well with good heat. If boiled, they should not be peeled till after they are cooked. They are made less digestible if butter or other fat is mixed or melted into them.

Beet-roots have considerable sugar, and carrots and parsnips have nearly as much. The usual edible roots as well as other vegetables and " garden truck " have comparatively little nutritive value for human beings. Their salts and stimulating flavors are what recommend them most. Of these vegetables, cabbages are perhaps the most important. They should be very thoroughly cooked. Their comparative chemical value is shown on page 220.

If eaten raw and unclean, vegetables may be the means of introducing tapeworms and other parasites into the digestive canal. Hence lettuce, radishes and other salad eaten raw must be very carefully cleansed. The health value of such vegetables is often overestimated. Cucumbers, fresh or pickled, may, like these others, be mentioned as being quite innutritious and needed only for capricious appetites. They serve however to increase the bulk of the excrement and, by irritation of the bowel, appear to lessen constipation. Green peas and string beans have somewhat more nutritive value than other ordinary green vegetables. Onions and garlic are not to be recommended as either very digestible or very nutritious.

In view of the prevalent idea that tomatoes, when eaten, cause cancer, it ought to be stated that they neither provoke the disease nor are they in any way injurious to people in whom cancer is already developed. Tomatoes are wholesome and agreeable to most persons. It is well that the peeling always be removed. These vegetables are preferable when cooked. They lose none of their salts or other nutritive substance by being canned.

An excellent, simple way of detecting the presence of copper used in poisonous quantities for the purpose of giving a green color to vegetables, that are " put up " in bottles or canned, is to leave, for a short time, a bright steel surface (such as a polished knitting needle or a penknife blade) in the fluid that the peas or other vegetables have been standing in within the can. Copper, if present, is then visibly deposited upon the steel surface. Tin may be present, but is not poisonous in small quantities. Lead, however, is dangerous when present. The test for these metals is given on pages 252 and 253.

Fruits and berries contain varying, small amounts of nutritive substances, chiefly sugar, with some salts and much water. They tend to stimulate the appetite, yet disagree with some people. Strawberries may be quite unclean by reason of the presence of soil bacteria. Dried, preserved or canned fruit contain all the important nutriment that was in the fresh fruit of which they were made. Canned fruit and other foods should be promptly removed from the can when it is opened. Rubber rings used for preserve jars and bottles should be soft, elastic and light enough to float on water. Antimony is present in much red rubber. Red lead may also occur, and zinc is almost always present in gray rubber rings and similar articles.

Mushrooms contain considerable nutriment, but are used almost altogether for their delicate flavor, to afford a relish to other foods. There is no reliable chemical means of recognizing the poisonous character of certain mushrooms. In general, the highly colored ones are poisonous. Among the more accessible of the books illustrating limitations of the above rule may be mentioned an article by Dr. Taylor reprinted from the U. S. Department of Agriculture report for 1890. Also a New York State publication for 1893.

Bananas are all the time becoming more and more cultivated in our Southern States and elsewhere. Thirteen million bunches are imported into the United States yearly. Besides furnishing a valuable food, one acre planted with banana or plantain yields more than 300 pounds of fibres from which a fine, muslin-like cloth is manufactured. The nutritive value of bananas is considerable, as can be seen from the analysis on page 220. The hydrocarbon elements consist largely of sugars.

In hot countries, various vegetable oils become an important addition to foods, in place of animal fats. The high value of the olive may here be indicated. As an adulterant of other oils and of lard, cotton-seed oil when refined is very extensively used. Although inferior in nearly every way, cotton-seed oil has not yet been shown to be unhealthful.

Dried peas, beans and others of the foods called *leguminous* have more than twice as much albumen as is found in the cereal foods. They are also rich in carbohydrates. Hence they appear to furnish a very nutritious food when fat is eaten with them, as in the form of "pork and beans" or bacon and peas. Yet these are not wholly satisfactory, although dried peas and beans are often recommended in dietaries (because of their having more chemical food value than meat). Their use is somewhat limited, owing partly to the fact that they cannot so easily be well cooked as other foods. Furthermore, their albumen, although equally absorbable and quite as nutritive as the gluten of wheat-flour, is in the form of *legumin*. Since this is not like gluten in adhesiveness, pea meal and bean meal are not fit for bread-making.

Salt is required with all vegetables. Fortunately, its cheapness does not encourage adulteration. The frequent addition of sulphuric acid or hydrochloric acid to *vinegar* is harmful only because very *impure* acids are apt to be used for the purpose by the unscrupulous dealers. Mustard (like pepper and other *spices*) is very often adulterated.

Here, as with other foods, the use of the compound microscope (magnifying from 40 to 150 times) is a valuable aid, a minute amount of various unquestionably pure specimens and also of any probable adulterants being used as checks and guides under the microscope lens. Comparing the suspected specimen with these, a definite determination of its purity or impurity is easy.

Stimulants and Sedatives

Tobacco contains various complex elements and notably *nicotine*. This is a colorless, nitrogenous, alkaloidal poison which, when not combined with acids, is rather volatile. Nicotine, with an aromatic oil of tobacco and some bases formed in burning, causes the familiar nausea, vertigo and depression occasioned by the use of tobacco. Habitual users of it lose much of their susceptibility to these unpleasant effects, and then its agreeable excitant or sedative influence is experienced. From prolonged, excessive use and by swallowing it, tobacco causes indigestion and also inflammation of the exposed mucous membranes of the throat and other parts.

Over-use of strong tobacco tends to impair the nutrition, especially of the nerves; so that, for example, enfeebled and irregular action of the heart occurs ("tobacco heart," "trotting heart"). The vision may also be affected. Color-blindness and, in extreme cases, serious nervous diseases may be caused by this widely used poison. On the whole, *the use of tobacco, even in moderation, is harmful* as regards its final effects; although in favor of "chewing," it may be said that tobacco has a slight antiseptic value.

Pipes with long stems that are frequently cleaned, and especially the "hookahs" or water-pipes used by orientals, are preferable to cigars or short-stemmed pipes. The highest-priced cigars do not necessarily have any less nicotine than the cheaper brands. The inhalation of tobacco smoke is a pernicious habit, as practised by habitual smokers of cigarettes; it can, however, afford relief to asthmatic people.

Coffee and tea, as consumed in beverages, contain little or no nutriment. The sugar and milk, commonly taken at the same time, are of course to be considered as nutritious foods. *Theine* (in tea) and *caffeine* (in coffee) are alkaloidal substances giving to these their peculiar qualities. When used in small quantities, these serve as excitants to stimulate the tired energies. If used in large quantities, they tend to injure the nervous system. This was very emphatically stated by Hahnemann many years ago.

The ancient view, that these drugs lessened the need for food or that they even improved nutrition, is incompatible with the most recent scientific knowledge. Coffee and tea add nothing to the real strength of the system. There are times when such stimulants are (like their near relative, alcohol) of use in producing work by inciting the system to further waste. In favor of tea and coffee it may be said that they lessen the craving for alcohol and are very slow in producing harmful effects if used in great moderation. The astringent principle, tannin, is considerably less abundant in black teas than in Japan teas and green teas.

Fig. 41, originally in Money's work on *Tea Cultivation*, gives an accurate idea of the proper shape and appearance of tea-leaves. By comparison with this, the genuineness of a given specimen may be determined. *Spurious teas* are not at all common with us; yet exhausted leaves are occasionally treated with Prussian blue, etc., and sold as good tea.

FIG. 41.

a, Flowery Pekoe ; b, Orange Pekoe ; c, Pekoe ; d, Souchong 1st ; e, Souchong 2d ; f, Congou.—a, b (when mixed), Pekoe ; a, b, c, d, e (when mixed), Pekoe Souchong.

If there be another leaf below f, and it be taken, it makes Bohea.

Each of these leaves was first a Flowery Pekoe leaf (a) ; it then became b, then c, and so on.

At the base of the leaves c, d, e, f, exist buds 1, 2, 3, 4, from which new shoots spring.

Coffee is very extensively adulterated, especially when already ground by the seller. Even the unroasted coffee-beans are skilfully imitated. A microscope, magnifying as much as 150 times, is of extreme value as an aid to the recognition of the exact character of adulterated coffee and cocoa products. For further details and a mention of the sources of original information concerning this subject, the reader is referred to the U. S. Agricultural Department Bulletin No. 13, 1892, on tea, coffee and cocoa.

Cocoa is usually better than the various "prepared cocoas," chocolates, etc., made from it by the use of alkalies and the addition of wheat-flour or sugar and too often harmful chemicals besides. "Digestible cocoa," "soluble cocoa" and other preparations usually lack the qualities that they pretend to possess, and may contain magnesia and soluble alkalies. Simple finely-ground cocoa-beans, without the husk or shell, have a more delicate aroma and are more healthful than most of the vigorously advertised preparations. Good cocoa and chocolate possess gently stimulant properties, similar to those of tea and coffee, yet the former are milder, and have a considerably greater nutritive value.

Alcoholic Liquors and their Effects

Alcoholic beverages contain a varying percentage of alcohol. They are commonly derived from fermentations of grains or of sugary fruits and vegetable juices. The stronger spirituous liquors are usually obtained by direct distillation from other alcoholic fluids. The amount of alcohol present in beers varies from 3 per cent. in light beers to over $8\frac{1}{2}$ per cent. (by volume) in strong ale. Ordinary wines have from 5 per cent. in "fruit wines" (or even less in "home-made" wines) to 15 per cent. in a very strong French wine. The average California wines (including champagnes) have from $9\frac{1}{2}$ to 12 per cent. by volume, yet some have more and some less than these amounts. Sherry is usually "fortified" by the addition of alcohol. The American sherries, like the foreign ones, show over 16 per cent. of alcohol. Some (genuine) port wines have more than 20 per cent. of alcohol; yet the American wines classed under that name show less than that, with the exception of a few of the California ones.

Distilled and other strong liquors have usually not far from 50 per cent. of alcohol. All of these differ greatly in their quality according to the substances from which they are produced and also according to the process employed, their age and other elements. Great outlay of skill, study, labor and means is required to achieve the excellence of the best products. Yet the lower-priced alcoholic beverages such as, for example, beer and rum, may be cheap and yet not harmfully adulterated.

Alcoholic beverages are often watered. *Imitations* are common, and liquors are frequently sold under the representation that they are of better quality than they really are. *Sulphites* are often added to wine for the sake of preserving it. *Salicylic acid* is still more liable to be found present. This is also often employed, as a preservative, in bottled beer. The use of poisonous and other chemicals as a substitute for hops is not so common here as is generally assumed. More harm is liable to result from the use of leaden pipes and faucets for beer. Our American beers are quite often inferior from the substitution of glucose for malted barley in the breweries. This cheapening may also introduce some *fusel oil*.

American wines seem freer from "plastering" than many European wines are. Our sweet wines are very variable. In some of these and in some "California port," the chemists show that very little pure grape-juice enters. *Cider* is a very variable drink which usually has less than six per cent. of alcohol. With proper attention to cleanliness and sorting the apples of which it is made, it can be a much better beverage than it usually is.

Fusel oil is the most harmful substance to be feared in spirituous liquors of low quality, such as "high wines" and potato spirits. Fusel oil consists of amyl, butyl and propyl alcohols, which are less vaporizable than ordinary (ethylic) alcohol. With care, this dangerous substance can be prevented from being carried over in the distilling process. Redistillation, and the changes taking place when liquors are kept for years, lessen the amount of fusel oil present. This harmful substance gives an unpleasant odor (and taste), which aids the recognition of it when a little is caused to evaporate from the palm of the hand.

A hygienic estimate of alcoholic beverages involves several considerations:

They are not valuable as foods, since they contribute very little nutritive substance to the system. Wines have a little sugar and other carbohydrates. Beer contains some albuminous matter and a small fraction of the amount of carbohydrates present in the same weight of bread.

If these beverages are drunk in the small quantities in which their use is considered permissible, the alcohol is in great part oxidized (or "burned") in the system. A little actual heat is thereby developed. Furthermore, the consumption of fat to produce heat is, in a corresponding way, lessened. Although not desirable for the system in health, alcohol is thus of real value in disease where the assimilative functions are impaired. Yet alcohol does not, as was formerly supposed, lessen the need of the healthy system for more substantial food. It seems to lessen the amount of albumen taken up from the digestive tract, or causes the albumen of the system to become changed to fat.

Much more valuable is the stimulative power of alcohol. This at times is a great aid to incite the heart and nervous forces to fresh effort. As with all stimulants, however, a reaction may be expected after the use of alcohol. Even the feeling of warmth caused by alcohol is not real warmth added; it is simply the *sensation* of warmth upon the sensitive nerve ends and due to the flushing of the enlarged small blood-vessels of the surface with warm blood from the deeper parts of the body. This means a *loss* of heat rather than a gain.

Alcohol accordingly does not aid us to resist the effects of cold, except for a very brief time. The heat, alluded to above, as produced by the burning (physiologically speaking) of alcohol within the body is slight compared with the great direct waste of heat that it causes and the loss to the system through impaired nutrition induced by alcohol.

It is possible that a small amount of alcohol stimulates the digestive apparatus, of some persons at least, to the secretion of digestive juices. The *diastase*, from the malt of beer, can aid the digestion of starchy foods. It is well known that alcoholic drinks can at times stimulate people to notable mental and physical achievements. Yet here again the inevitable reaction manifests itself in the form of after-effects. These, however, may in some cases be considered as more than compensated for by the success of the stimulation. The habit of ether-drinking, for the sake of the rapid and brief stimulus, seems wholly reprehensible.

Over-use of alcoholic beverages, especially if persistent and long-continued, unquestionably causes digestive, nervous and other disorders, and lessens the natural resistant power of the system to various diseases. The children of drunkards seem inferior and predisposed to epilepsy and other diseases.

Harmful substances, said to be frequently present in various liquors, are often asserted to cause more harm than the alcohol itself. This is hardly true; although half of the whiskey produced here is "compounded." Some liquors, such as genuine absinthe and some other cordials, include ingredients in their regular composition that are regarded by most expert authorities as being harmful and tending on long use to result in positive injury to the system.

As for the numerous vague and general charges, provoked by a few genuine and specific cases of fraudulent mixing in of more or less poisonous drugs, it may be said that they seem exaggerated. Among the worst substances to be suspected in this connection are turpentine, picric acid, picrotoxin, Cayenne pepper, aloes, alum, tannin, logwood. The latest publications of the special agents of the U. S. Government do not allow one to indorse the newspaper statements of the very dangerous adulterations of our liquors in general; although the dealer's guaranty gives little certainty that the article is genuine. Adulteration and "compounding" are very common; yet the counterfeits are rarely very poisonous. Genuine goods are, however, preferable.

In Canada, the latest statements from the laboratory of the Inland Revenue Department show that there also the presence of these substances is rare in liquors. The small amount of *fusel oil* present in some crude liquors is a harmful element. Equally so are such drugs as are added to some of the proprietary and other "medicinal" wines. *Coca* is one of these drugs, and should be used only in definite, known quantities, if at all, and under strict medical control. The good wines and other liquors need no advertisement, and are best when bought directly of reputable dealers. Labels are usually not to be trusted.

"**Moderate drinking**," like excessive use of alcohol, must be regarded as harmful or at least liable to become so. The tippler errs who fancies that, by using only expensive liquors, he escapes the dangers to which a poorer drinker is exposed. Even the milder alcoholic beverages are not only unnecessary, but probably injurious in the long run. The more or less reliable statistics of temperance agitators and institutions seem to prove this. The keenest and most studious life-insurance examiners are inclined to reject applicants who in each day consume more liquor than is equivalent to one-and-a-half ounces of alcohol. Insurance companies, which reject alcohol-drinkers, show a lower rate of mortality among their "risks" than do the companies that are careless in this respect. Section 39, Chapter 401 of the New York laws of 1892 makes it a misdemeanor for a common carrier to employ in any responsible position "any person who habitually indulges in the intemperate use of intoxicating drinks."

Opium-eating.—It is altogether too easy for people to procure stimulating, anodyne, sleep-producing and other harmful drugs that the most careful physicians use only with extreme precautions. *Morphine* is one of these. Like alcohol, morphine (or opium) is a stimulant when only small doses are taken. Larger doses cause the narcotic effects to be manifested. Opium (or morphine), being more secret, convenient and elegant than alcohol, seduces many people. In the end, the will-power becomes paralyzed when it comes to the question of resisting the pernicious drug. The result is a gradual moral and physical degeneration.

Too often the beginning of the "habit" of the drug is due to the careless readiness of a physician to use morphine for the relief of pain in simple cases where the drug is not indispensable and where other means would effect the relief, even though requiring more time and effort on the part of the physician and making less impression upon the mind of the patient. It is desirable that rigorous legislative enactments be enforced to restrict the sale of these drugs; for, if we can trust our evidence, opium, morphine and other dangerous and poisonous substances are dispensed without prescriptions oftener than druggists admit.

FOOD PREPARATION AND ADAPTATION

ELSEWHERE in this book, the important fact is explained that great cold does not kill all the harmful bacteria that may chance to be on or in unclean food; yet the cold of a proper ice-chest will act to prevent increase of bacteria of any kind that may be in milk or on other food.

Because of the danger that with uncooked food we may introduce into our systems the minute organisms that cause more or less serious disease, it needs to be repeated here that *it is safest to cook all that we eat and also the water or milk that we drink*, if any uncertainty exists as to their purity.

The heat of thorough cooking not only destroys any living thing that may be in or upon our foods, but the effect of the heat is also to make vegetable matters and tough meat much more digestible than when raw. A further advantage of cooking is the development thereby of aromatic and other products agreeable to the taste and hence serving to promote the appetite as well as the secretion of digestive juices.

In the preliminary preparation of articles of food, the indigestible parts are to be removed so far as is easily possible, in order that what we eat may always be unirritant and readily assimilable. The pounding of tough meat renders it somewhat more tender and digestible. It is well to have removed the hulls and outermost parts of grains, the woody matter of vegetable coatings and the sinews and tough fibrous membranes in and around muscles and fat of meat. All such indigestible parts lessen the alimentary value and impair the absorbability of foods when they have been taken into the digestive tract. Whatever we eat should generally be finely divided before it enters the mouth. Food ought to be well chewed before it is swallowed.

Fig. 42 is introduced as illustrating a scientifically constructed cookstove for a workingman's family. It is made by the Kaiserslautern foundry in Germany. It is so arranged that it suffices for warming a small room (of 1,750 to 2,000 cubic feet) in winter. Yet in summer the heat can be carried off up the chimney so as not to heat the living-room. Furthermore, the stove efficiently draws off the steam and odors of cooking, taking them up the chimney.

Fig. 42.

The air of the room is not only warmed whenever desired, but is also renewed by the skilful introduction of large flues occupying the entire back and right side of this stove. The large single door on the front opens into the oven. On the left of this is the fire-pot. From that the heat goes directly to the right, then downward and finally is made to circulate entirely around the oven. Unlike ordinary stoves, the top is here cased in, as shown in the illustration, the doors of this upper part being of glass.

It is wisest and in the end most economical to have good stoves or ranges. The fuel should be of the best. Utensils should, so far as possible, be convenient, of approved quality, and carefully kept in a cleanly kitchen or where they can be most promptly found at hand. Although burnished *brass and copper* are very pleasing to the eye, they are not to be recommended for saucepans or for any use where the food remains in contact with the metal.

Fats are liable to attack these polished copper surfaces. Vegetable or other acids, such as vinegar, may also act upon copper and brass pans, etc., causing copper salts thereby to be formed to a slight extent. These salts may be very poisonous. Carefully tinned ironware is excellent, yet tin is apt to have lead in it. Hence, inferior qualities of tinware are unsafe, and the same may be said of the common glazed metallic ware.

Lead is an ingredient of crystal glass and of most of the enamel used, upon crockery and other porcelain articles, to make these porous vessels impervious to moisture. In some cheap or insufficiently burnt earthenware, this lead glaze is badly prepared. Such vessels, when used for cooking purposes, may give off this poison to the food. Bottles and cooking utensils should not be cleaned by shaking shot in them, as cleaning by this process may cause lead to remain on the surfaces.

To test such utensils, fill them nearly full of strong vinegar to which a little salt has been added (not much more than a drachm to the pint). Boil this for an hour, adding a little boiling water now and then to replace that constantly being lost by evaporation. After the vessel and the contents are allowed to cool somewhat, the vinegar is filtered. Then *sulphuretted hydrogen* is added. If any brown or black discoloration or precipitate appear, this should be tested further to determine definitely whether *tin, copper* or *lead* is present.

The precipitate caused by adding the sulphuretted hydrogen (to the vinegar boiled in the suspected dish) is filtered in the usual way upon filter-paper in a funnel. The filtrate is then washed with water containing a little sulphuretted hydrogen. Then the funnel is stopped at the bottom by means of a bit of rubber tubing clamped or tied at the lower part. Without removing the precipitate from the funnel, **yellow** *ammonium sulphide* is poured in and allowed to act on the precipitate for an hour. This is to dissolve any tin that may be present.

After an hour, the bottom of the funnel is opened : the ammonium sulphide (which can, if desired, be tested later for *tin*) is thereby allowed to run out. The precipitate remaining on the filter-paper is washed with water that contains a little ammonium sulphide.

This precipitate, together with the filter-paper used to filter it, is put into a small porcelain evaporating dish, the whole of the precipitate covered with strong, chemically pure *nitric acid*, and this dish is heated on a water-bath until the entire contents are dissolved.

After filtering this, we add *sulphuric acid* sufficient to produce the white precipitate of sulphate of *lead* if that metal be present. [One part of this lead sulphate (dried, washed and re-dried, then heated to a glowing temperature in a porcelain crucible) corresponds to 0.683 parts of lead.]

Ammonia, in excess, is then added to the filtrate from which the lead sulphate has been filtered out. If this excess of ammonia produces a blue color, *copper* is present. A very delicate test for copper is to add acetic acid and solution of *ferrocyanide of potash* to a portion of the solution. The reddish-brown ferrocyanide of copper results, if copper be present.

For baking meat, the heat should be greater in the beginning than is desirable after the meat has been baking for a few minutes. The heat of the oven causes at first a speedy evaporation of water from the surface, with consequent contraction of the outer part of the meat. At the same time, other changes occur.

Especially does the development of aromatic odors from the fat take place and add to the agreeable taste developed by cooking. With the contraction and drying of the outer layers exposed to the heat, there is formed a more resistant coating on the outside. After the coating is formed it prevents the juices of the meat from escaping to any great extent.

As meat is a poor conductor of heat, the heat enters but slowly into the interior. So far as it goes, it tends to convert the tough connective tissue into more tender and gelatinous forms, coagulating the albumen and lessening the red color of the blood pigment. If a piece of meat be heated throughout to a temperature of 160° F. or very nearly that, the red, bloody appearance is no longer present. For an ordinary joint or roast, more than two and one-half hours of the usual oven heat must be allowed in order that all the inner portions of the meat have reached the temperature of 160° F.

This degree of heat suffices to kill all dangerous parasites that are apt to occur in our food. Even trichinous pork and tuberculous beef are not dangerous after *every part* of the meat has been exposed for five minutes to such a heat. It is obvious that underdone ("rare") meat ought not to be eaten when evidence exists that it is diseased.

The sauces and gravies that are produced from baking and roasting meat have fats, fat acids, salts, "extractives" and the heat products (of gelatinous and fatty elements) which give the flavor, but which are not always well borne by people of delicate or impaired digestion.

Although tender, lean meat from a young and healthy animal is more digestible when scraped and eaten raw than when such meat is cooked, it may be said that, in general, cooking increases the digestibility of meat. Roasting on a spit before a fire gives the meat, especially of fowls, a very agreeable flavor.

Broiling is a similar process and equally effective. When, however, the meat is cut very thick and the centre remains red after cooking, the inside has not been sufficiently heated by the fire to insure the certain destruction of all possible parasites. Hence the importance of careful, skilled inspection of meat that is to be broiled in thick slices and eaten in a half-raw condition.

For frying food, the hot fat used should be at a temperature of from 380° to 400° F. A piece of bread changes its color at once if thrown into such hot fat. The fish, veal or other meat put into this, cooks rapidly with a crackling or "sizzling" sound which comes from the small amount of water that is on and in the substance of the cooking food. This water is suddenly converted into steam, a little at a time, and thus the hissing noise results. In this way the food is cooked by the steam of its own contained juices. No fat enters a piece of frying fish, for instance, so long as the heat of every portion of the surrounding fat is greater than that of boiling water. The outside is browned by the great heat of the boiling fat. Yet, however well fried, such food should not be "warmed over," as the small amount of fat adherent to the outside is thereby driven inside.

A *dry fry*, as by putting steak, etc., on a hot frying-pan or other surface, is more healthful when the heated iron surface is not greased over. The side of the steak next the frying-pan, being cooked first, cools when the meat is turned over to cook the other side. With this cooling, any adherent fat tends to enter the meat and make it greasy. All fried food necessarily has a varying amount of fat about its outside. Hence it may be somewhat indigestible on that account. Yet there is a great difference in digestibility between properly and improperly fried food.

Boiled meat has not in its substance so much of the natural salts and juices as would be present in the same piece if cooked by dry heat, as in baking. The savory elements and "extractives" are also less abundant in boiled meat. Very little of the albumen is lost, however, by going off into the surrounding water. Yet this water contains whatever has been lost from the meat. Hence it can be used for soup-stock. The lower the temperature of the hot water in which the meat is cooked, the more does the meat lose from its substance.

As the use of water that is actually boiling acts better than that of a lower temperature to seal the outside of a piece of meat and prevent somewhat the waste of salts and other principles from its substance, it is usual to have the water as hot as possible for the first few minutes after the piece of meat is put in to boil. Then the temperature of the water is allowed to sink somewhat; for, under this lower heat, the meat is cooked more evenly throughout.

Boiling causes the centre of the piece of meat to be heated more speedily and thoroughly, in a given time, than does a dry heat, such as that of baking. Yet considerably more than two hours must be allowed for the temperature in the middle of a seven-pound piece of meat to have got within fifteen degrees of that of the water in which it is being boiled.

Soups are richest when the meat and bones are first put into cool water. They should later *simmer;* but the water must at no time reach the boiling point, if much of the strength of the meat is desired in the soup. Ordinary thin soup has almost no nutritive value. The various proprietary bases of soup, "meat extracts," and so on are not so desirable as the ordinary broth which comes from the gentle boiling of meat. Bones, gristle and tough meat on long cooking in water that does not rise at any time above the temperature of 155° F., make a strong gelatinous soup. This is in reality quite nourishing; for the gelatine in it has some value as a nitrogenous, tissue-restoring food; yet it is incomplete even as an albuminous food, being decidedly inferior to the albumen of lean meat. The meat salts in the soup are of considerable value. *Tripe* is rather gelatinous and very easily digestible, requiring less than half the time needed to digest average beef.

The harder **eggs** are made by means of boiling, the more solid is the densely coagulated albumen, and the less readily can they be digested. Such hard-boiled eggs digest better when chopped or chewed into fine pieces. *Poaching* is the most delicate and digestible way of preparing eggs. The eggs to be cooked in this way are opened, then dropped singly into boiling water and removed therefrom as soon as the albumen is coagulated to a bluish white (not yellowish) color. Greasy methods of cooking eggs are not to be recommended. Omelettes should not be very dry.

Recent attempts have been made in various places to revive the older-fashioned apparatuses for cooking meats and other food at temperatures below that of the boiling point of water. Roughly speaking, we may say that the boiling point of water diminishes by about one and a half degrees (Fahr.) for every thousand feet of altitude above the sea-level. Hence the processes of cooking have to be somewhat modified among high mountains.

When the water in the cooking vessel is at about 202° F., it requires a little more time than usual to cook meat, and at least one-fourth longer to cook potatoes or dried vegetables. While vegetables in general require the water to be as hot as possible in order that they become well cooked, meat is considered by some to be more palatable when cooked at the temperature of 200° F. or less. There is a considerable economy of heat when we do not have to convert water into steam.

The "Norwegian sauce-pan" is adapted for cooking on high mountains or elsewhere that the heat is, from necessity or choice, below 212° F. The more primitive forms of this appliance comprise some sort of woollen-covered sauce-pan kept in a non-conducting box after being well heated. The same sort of cooking can be carried out by using a sheet-iron oven covered with felt, asbestos or some cheaper substance which is a good non-conductor of heat and not liable to catch fire. A layer of water, even, may be adapted for the purpose. This oven-box, whether large or very small, stands by itself, on a rest, or may in any convenient way be kept a foot or so from a table or the floor, so that a lamp or gas-burner beneath can be used for the desired heat.

There is a door through which the dishes of raw food can be placed upon the shelf or shelves within the oven. There should also be a small round opening on the top or side. It is closed by a cork stopper. Through this latter, a thermometer can be fastened so that it records the inside temperature, which must not be allowed to fall below 160° F. for cooking meat. The same degree of heat is excellent for sterilizing milk; yet more time is then of course required than when the temperature used is that of boiling water. This oven is useful for foods that need a slow, long cooking at a moderate temperature, especially in summer and where other fuel than oil is scarce.

For cooking vegetables it may in general be said that boiling water is none too hot. The common error is that they are not cooked sufficiently long and well. Thorough cooking causes the starch cells to swell and thus rupture their cellulose walls and tough framework. The starch, thus opened to the action of the digestive juices, is in part further converted by the heat and made more digestible. In boiling potatoes, it is well to add salt to the water, as this is a necessary substance that is not sufficiently abundant in potatoes.

To cook leguminous vegetables (such as peas and beans) soft water is preferable to hard water; for the lime-salts of the latter tend to form an insoluble combination with the *legumin*, the albuminous element of these foods. In cooking dried peas and beans, the water into which they are put should be at first cool and only very gradually raised to a high temperature. Proceeding thus, and cooking them for a long while, these very nutritious vegetable foods are made more digestible than if carelessly cooked. Pea-meal, even if prepared by using a "coffee-mill" in the kitchen, is more digestible and nutritious than are whole peas. Mashing through a sieve also improves them.

Green peas, string beans, cabbage and *vegetables in general must be thoroughly cooked;* cooking them well, we increase their digestibility. **Steaming** is preferable to boiling as a means of cooking vegetables when it is desired that their salts and flavors be retained in full strength instead of going off into the water as they do when boiled.

Toasting improves the digestibility of ordinary bread. So many people are ignorant of the proper way to toast bread, that it may be repeated here that the bread, if at all moist, needs in all cases to be dried near the fire just before toasting. The toasting should only brown the bread, and in no case blacken it. It is often best to toast bread on a broiler placed on top of a hot stove and without removing the stove covers.

Coffee is so universally used that a few words may be said as to its proper preparation. It should be roasted at a temperature not exceeding 425° F. until brown, and not blackened at all. It is best when freshly roasted, and should be finely ground immediately before preparing the beverage. For this, a gentle temperature is best. Prolonged boiling drives off the aroma. The pot is to be scalded out beforehand.

Tea should not be "steeped," because long standing in hot water causes tea to yield up its astringent and unhealthful tannic acid to the water. Very hot tea is injurious to the mucous membranes of the throat and digestive apparatus.

The temperature of the food swallowed ought not to be very much higher than that of the body. This rule should be borne in mind particularly in the feeding of infants. The habitual use of very hot or very cold foods and drinks tends to induce organic disease of various organs and especially catarrh of the stomach. Even the hard enamel of the teeth is considered liable to injury from extreme temperatures in the food as it is eaten.

While it is not desirable to fix an arbitrary limit, it may be said that food which is not above the temperature of 110° F. is not too hot for an adult to eat. For infants the temperature of milk or other food must not be above 100° F. when it is given to them.

Spring water has an average temperature of from 44° to 58° F., in its natural state. Health requires that the water or other liquid drunk should have a temperature of at least 53° F. It is more healthful if the temperature is several degrees higher than this. The instinctive desire for cool drinks when we are very warm is not to be gratified by copious draughts of very icy water. It must be remembered that unaided instinct is not always the safest guide.

Ice-cold water is not only prejudicial to the best health, but also is not favored by people of the most delicate tastes. Although it is not uncommon to drink champagne or beer cooled to 45° F., white wines (that do not foam) please the palate much better when warmer than that. The best judges prefer red wine when it has a temperature of about 65° F.

Coffee and tea are also agreeable when about as warm as that, and are apt to prove unhealthful if habitually taken much hotter than 115° F. Some of the stomach trouble caused by these drinks is often due to swallowing them when they are very hot. Milk just taken from the cow may be said to average nearly 94° F. At this temperature it is very digestible. It should not be drunk when it is much cooler than 60° F. It may cause gastro-intestinal and other disorders if swallowed in large quantities and very cold.

General Considerations regarding Eating

For infants, fluid foods, such as milk, are best. With adults, however, the case is different. Even a pap-like consistency of the food is undesirable for prolonged use. While much water is needed daily for the body use, an excess of liquid at meals and in and with the food appears to be in general detrimental to the health. That the solutions of salts and other substances in the system may not lack water, we should drink from time to time between meals.

It is well to make it a rule always to drink a little pure water on rising from sleep and also on retiring, in case that enough fluid has not already been taken into the body. Alcoholic drinks should not often be taken into an empty stomach. If water be needed, it should generally be taken before a meal rather than when the stomach is full or receiving food. Yet this is not meant to say that we should not drink with meals when we are very thirsty or when the food is very dry. Within four hours after a meal, as a rule, it is well to drink some water, as an unhealthful concentration of the urine and the body fluids is thereby prevented. No considerable amount of soup should be taken with a full meal of other food.

Extremely condensed foods may be so adjusted as to supply the needs of the body; but when they are used exclusively, one is liable to eat too much of such concentrated foods if they are palatable. It is well to have the food sufficiently bulky to produce a sense of satiety when enough has been eaten. Hence it is best that the nutritious elements be diluted, so to speak, by the presence of inert and innutritious substances that cause the volume of the food to be enlarged. Such a suitable condition of the food is produced by the substances usually eaten in the ordinary mixed diet that has abundant vegetables. Not to consider the extra water required by the body, the total bulk of the nutritious and innutritious elements in the food needed in one day by an average man at work may be estimated at somewhat less than three and three-fourths pounds.

The principal meal of the day usually ought not to comprise more than half of the entire daily food. The remainder is to be taken at intervals during the day. If only one or two meals are eaten in a day, the necessarily large amount then swallowed not only impedes digestion by reason of the large mass, but in most cases tends also to distend the stomach too much. A permanent dilatation of the stomach results if the habit of overfilling it with food be persisted in very long.

Especially with heavy eaters, do the *digestive organs need some rest* during the day and at night. Hence numerous, frequent meals are not, as a rule, to be recommended. The stomach ought to be allowed to rest for at least five or six hours after the appetite is fully satisfied. Yet no rule is absolute. Habit counts for much. Regularity is, in most cases, of advantage. In general, three meals a day are enough for adults; yet some seem to need four, and five even may be allowable when one is recuperating from an illness. Laborers, especially if at manual work for many hours, need more abundant meals than people engaged in strictly sedentary work.

Dinner may, for manual laborers, be at noon-time, as a rule; but in that case at least a brief rest should be had after the meal. For brain-workers, the heaviest meal of the day serves best when taken after the effort of the day's work is over. It is well to rest for a while after a substantial meal. Mental or emotional activity, during or near the time of eating, impedes digestion. The stomach needs to have received some food before work is begun. The first meal after arising from sleep ought to be a light one, although having an abundance of the albuminous elements of the daily food. At dinner, the main part of the day's fat food should be taken.

Very rapid eating is liable to result in confirmed "dyspepsia." It is more healthful to allow sufficient time for chewing the food and having it mingle thoroughly with the digestive juices. The question as to whether a very small amount of good *wine*, taken with a meal, aids in any way the digestion of food, is not yet settled. Probably it does so, especially when fat has been eaten. A large amount of wine and other liquor is unquestionably harmful. *Beer* at meals is considered by the highest, unprejudiced authorities of beer-drinking countries as hindering stomachal digestion.

The use of "cocktails," "bitters," "appetizers," or other alcoholic stimulants just before a meal is reprehensible. In the first place, such things do not accomplish what they are supposed to. Secondly, they may provoke catarrh of the stomach and permanent weakening of the digestion. Thirdly, alcoholic beverages drunk when the stomach is empty are uncommonly liable to produce liver disease. Sir Henry Thompson, in his excellent little book on *Food and Feeding*, condemns the practice as "a gastronomic no less than a physiological blunder, injuring the stomach and depraving the palate."

Infant Feeding

The young infant needs relatively more nitrogen and carbon in its food than is required later in life; for the little body, besides having to develop flesh and other new tissues for its growth, loses heat disproportionately fast. Hence it must have much fat to burn up for producing the heat. In the early weeks, the digestive secretions of the infant are quite unlike those of the adult. Starch is then indigestible. The first set of teeth is not developed till in the third year. Hence, and for reasons previously given, milk is the most suitable food for very young children.

Milk from the breast of a healthy woman is the best food for a babe. *It is better for the mother that she suckle her own new-born babe.* She should at least do so for the few weeks that she is resting after child-birth and while the naturally enlarged womb is returning to its ordinary size. As soon as the new-born child cries after its first sleep, it should be suckled. If mother's milk then be lacking, a little diluted cow's milk, properly sterilized, and then skimmed, may be given. In the first day of life, food is needed only two or three times.

After that, the infant requires to be fed at least seven or eight times in twenty-four hours. That is, it receives milk every three hours with only one feeding during the night. To this latter point the babe can easily become habituated without injury to its health and with pronounced advantage to the mother. If it appears to be hungry oftener than once every two hours, either the child is ill or the quantity or quality of the milk is deficient.

The most reliable estimates assume that of mother's milk at each meal the healthy nursing infant receives probably from one-fiftieth to one-fortieth of its body weight. Cow's milk is unlike woman's milk. (See table on page 220.) When cow's milk is used as a substitute for milk from the human breast, this milk ought to be sterilized by heating, as explained on page 231, unless very fresh and from the purest source.

When it is used for feeding an infant during the first months of life, average cow's milk ought to be **diluted** at least as much as follows:

COW'S MILK (REQUIRED DAILY).	AGE OF BABE.	PROPORTION OF WATER.
½ pint	3 days.	1 part milk to 3 of water.
1 "	3 weeks.	1 " " " 2 " "
1½ "	3 months.	1 " " " 1 " "
1 quart	5 "	4 " " " 3 " "
1 " (or more)	7 "	3 " " " 1 " "
3 pints	9 "	10 " " " 1 " "
	11 "	Undiluted milk.

The above daily amount may be slightly exceeded. The usual tendency is to give too much. The bottle should be held so that the babe swallows no air. Very fresh cream may be added in very small quantities. But it is better to have very rich milk. Water can be given besides, especially if the weather or rooms be dry and hot. In any case, this water should have been boiled unless unquestionably pure. So, too, is boiling necessary for the water used to dilute the milk unless the milk is to be sterilized; then both can be sterilized together after the water is added. The artificial food should have a temperature of about 98° F. at the time when fed to the babe.

It is important, from a hygienic standpoint, that the milk in the nursing-bottle be thrown away after each nursing and that the bottle be rinsed with boiling water. Shot should never be used to clean out such bottles. The rubber-nipple arrangement must be rinsed well at the time when the bottle is being cleaned out after using. It can lie in a saturated solution of *boric acid* before use.

From one to two per cent. of sugar may with advantage be added to the milk prepared for babes. Milk-sugar is preferable to cane-sugar. Little packets of this can be weighed out by a druggist so that one contains just the proper percentage of sugar for one day or one meal as the case may be. (100 grains may be added to each pint.) It is well to advise against using too much sugar.

An excess of sugar is what makes ordinary condensed milk objectionable. If (as is the case with the best brands) the milk is heated in condensing so as to have destroyed all tubercle bacilli, and if it is not oversweetened, condensed milk is quite a good artificial food, especially for hot climates. Some very strong and healthy children have been reared entirely upon this food. It must be sufficiently diluted with pure water immediately before using. When travelling, it is well to cook the water used for diluting condensed milk. A spirit-lamp is convenient for this purpose.

At the end of the twenty minutes required for the babe to take its meal from the mother's breast, the nipples should be rinsed with boiled water (or boracic acid solution) and dried with a clean cloth. If corsets be worn, they are to support the breasts from below and must not press upon the nipple. The welfare of the infant makes it desirable that any attempts to wean be deferred till after the heat of the summer and early autumn.

Starchy foods are not fitted for infantile digestion. Yet strained barley-water (made by taking whole, unground barley-grains and boiling them) aids the digestion of cow's milk at times if such barley-water be added to dilute the milk. Although undesirable as a food in early months of life, starch serves as a food for young children provided that it has previously been converted into *dextrine* and other more digestible substances. This desirable action upon starch is effected by very thoroughly roasting or baking any good flour. Such baked flour is the basis of most of the proprietary foods. Their high cost is quite unwarranted, since the same products (or rather their counterparts) can be purchased at a fraction of the high prices charged for the proprietary article.

Let no mother take up the use of such advertised articles in the belief that milk is not an all-sufficient food for her babe till the first year is nearly past. A minute amount of iron may at times be needed in addition. Raw bread, biscuit, crackers, and vegetable food in general cause most of the digestive disorders of early life. It is more desirable to improve the quality of the milk given (if it seem unsuited) and to attend to extreme hygienic cleanliness of that food, than to add other articles to the diet.

By the end of the second year, the child has all of its first set of teeth excepting the posterior molars. Even these may then have appeared. Yet its delicate and immatured digestive organs cannot so well dispose of tough and fibrous food as they can later in life. So, too, sour or sugary foods (or confectionery) or things abounding in starches are to be allowed only cautiously. Milk and other animal foods are still preferable to vegetable foods even till after the fifth year. It is best that these latter be not given in excess, and they should always be thoroughly cooked.

The complex diet of the adult is not proper for the young child. Especially should stimulating beverages of all kinds be excluded. Water and milk (both boiled if not absolutely pure) are all the drinks that the child needs. As many as five or six light meals slowly eaten may be given, but only pure water should be allowed between meals. The child should drink just as much of this as it desires.

DIET

MODERATION and abstemiousness in eating as in the use of stimulants and of all other things seems to be the prominent factor that rules among long-lived people and races. As has already been indicated, overeating is accountable for many ailments, especially among those who do not exercise at all.

A purely vegetable diet is as undesirable as an exclusive use of meat and other animal food. After the first years of life, *a mixed diet is best* for all ages and conditions of people. In ordinary life, we can only approximately estimate how much a person eats. There the main thing is to see that poisonous or even mildly harmful things are avoided, that one has what one likes, and that at the same time this contains enough nutriment but still no excessive amount of any food. The tables given on page 220 serve as a guide for estimating the chemical value of such foods as are included there.

In the main, the proportions proper for the daily diet of an individual correspond quite closely with those given on page 213, if provision be made for an increase of fatty elements when needed. For institutions and places where food is prepared week in and week out for the same persons taking no food whatsoever besides, careful measurements and chemical estimates furnish very important aids.

Koenig's figures given in his well-known tables still remain the basis for almost all such estimates. An instructive little book, giving some low-priced dietaries for families, is that of Mrs. Abel (on economic cooking), published in 1890, by the American Public Health Association. In that book, the word "proteid" is used to indicate albuminous **food** principles.

Practical physicians realize that it is well to regard the human body as more than a mere machine for getting work out of food. It seems to them proper always to take into account the individual peculiarities and other *human* factors. It is therefore quite unwise to consider the mere chemical value of foods as the only thing of importance.

Chemical standards are furthermore misleading if followed without discrimination. Meats differ much according to the animal from which a certain cut is taken. Beef from northern range cattle is not the same as that from the stall-fed steer. Both are decidedly superior to the beef of the great southwestern grazing regions. Considerable variations occur with other meat, irrespective of the general fact that fat meat is economical, as having fat in its tissue where most lean meat has water. Other food products can also vary greatly.

In pregnancy, the diet, owing to the peculiar condition, needs to be very simple yet nutritious. Albuminous substances should abound, since much new tissue has to be formed. The use of sour and highly spiced food should be restricted, and the fat supply need not be large. A tendency to a constipated state of the bowels is commonly present and needs especial attention. For the first three days after labor, the diet should embrace only light food, as toast, poached eggs, soups, etc.

When the child is born and deriving its nourishment from the mother's breasts, she needs copious supplies of albuminous and other foods and as much fat as is well digested. Rich, pure milk taken on retiring helps to supply this fat. If any considerable amount of peas and beans or of the less valuable green vegetables be taken, indigestion is apt to result and the quality of the milk may thereby become injured. Green fruits, sour things, spirits, inferior beer and wine may have the same effect, especially if these be not part of the habitual diet. Liquids should be given in abundance to the woman who is nursing a babe; yet the use of alcoholic liquor should in any case be very limited. Coffee and tea if taken should not be strong.

Because of the great strain upon the system, several **extra** meals may be allowed. They must, however, be very simple. Particularly with *wet-nurses*, is any unwonted elaborateness of food to be avoided. Rich foods are quite undesirable for such women. The absence of restraint with an abundance of " good things " may cause the milk of wet-nurses to become unfit for their nurslings.

In old age, the digestive power is weakened. Other organs, including the muscles, are then feebler and almost always have less work to do. Besides therefore requiring less food for the muscles and actually being able to use up less nutriment in work, there is much less food needed to repair the relatively small waste of the system in general. In the aged, there is no new-tissue formation. Old people ought to be exceedingly careful to avoid overeating. They need considerably *less food than in middle age*, and any excess is particularly harmful.

A simple and limited but nutritious diet is best for the aged. Tough, fibrous food, especially the coarser vegetables and coarse parts of meat, are to be avoided. Fat should be eaten somewhat sparingly, as its absorption is usually more restricted in old age. As the nervous system is also weaker, mild alcoholic stimulants may then very properly be given regularly and in great moderation. Yet this must be always with recognition of the fact that the blood-vessels, especially of the brain, are deteriorated in advanced years, and quite liable to give way under strain if very much of a stimulus be given at once in any shape.

In summer we do not need much less albuminous food than in winter; yet it is more important to guard against an excess in hot portions of the year and in hot climates. Any superfluous meat or other highly albuminous food is then very liable to become converted into fat and heat. For supplying the general needs of the body, bread, rice and various other foods having much digestible carbohydrate substance that is well cooked should be chosen in preference to fats.

Fats are not as well absorbed nor so agreeable in summer as in winter. The digestive tract is, in warm weather, quite sensitive to unwholesome and improperly cooked foods. This is partly because of the greater number of bacteria that then enter with the food and increase and cause trouble with any excess of indigestible food. It has already been emphasized that vegetable food when uncooked is much less suited for human diet than when thoroughly cooked.

Fruit is most healthful when ripe, but not over-ripe. Raw food should be very clean. Lettuce, for example, ought to be carefully picked apart, leaf by leaf, and rinsed. The hands must be clean before touching such food. As already explained, water and other beverages may be cool, but icy drinks are unhealthful. The ice should be from pure lakes or artificially made of distilled water. Water, unless coming from an exceptionally pure source, should have been well heated, as by boiling or distillation, before being drunk.

Diet in Disease

There are comparatively few diseases in which diet is not of vastly more importance than are medicines. Hygienic management of the diet in serious disease-states involves a consideration of the previous habits as well as of the present condition of the vital powers. Especially must the digestion be considered, since it is in disease less able to utilize the food properly than in health.

In fevers where the process is acute, rapid and continued, the wasting of the body substance may be speedy and excessive, as regards both water and solids. Even though, as is usual, very little food is then taken into the body, the waste of nitrogen may in fevers be twice as great as in health. The carbon of the body is destroyed to nearly the same extent. Hence the weight diminishes so fast that the loss may be a pound or more every day.

This soon becomes serious, and, if it goes very far, death

is nigh. While the diseased condition is present, the serious loss of the body substance cannot be repaired so readily as could a similar waste in health; for not only is the stomach more sensitive and its absorptive capacity diminished, but in the worst cases the secretions of the enfeebled digestive tract are almost wholly inactive.

Experience in many cases, as well as experimental proofs, warrant the view that no aggravation of a general fever or other harm results upon the intelligently managed giving of food. Of course, common sense must be used, and the peculiar features of each case are to be considered. When the stomach or intestines are notably diseased, or if peritonitis be present, very delicate food is necessary. In children, as in adults, we find that when the body is being wasted, the excretion of carbon and nitrogen does not increase in proportion to the amount supplied by judicious feeding. This means that the food does not serve to feed the system and is to a varying extent wasted.

Pure water is the first need of the fever patient and should be given without stint, in small amounts frequently repeated. In cholera, where the sufferer seems actually to dry up before our eyes, the most approved modern practice is to give sterilized water (with a little salt) under the skin (or in the veins) when it cannot be retained if taken by the mouth. Milk has the advantage of supplying much water and at the same time is very nutritious. Yet common milk, because of its many bacteria, may be far from being a fit food. So, milk should be from very reliable dairies. It requires to be sterilized if at all old or of doubtful quality.

The food chosen must be as delicate and unirritating as possible. Garden vegetables are to be avoided. Fat should be used sparingly in acute fever cases. Starch then digests better in many cases when malt (as in the form of a reliable malt extract) is given with it. Chemically pure malt-sugar (maltose) and pure glucose are very absorbable and may be given in small quantities. Gelatine used moderately is well borne and gives some nutriment, although it is an insufficient food, as has been explained above.

Peptones and proprietary prepared foods in general are better for rectal use than for feeding by the usual means. Better are scraped meat, broths delicately prepared with gentle heat, eggs poached or simply the whites of eggs stirred up with ten times their bulk of water. Barley-gruel or sago long cooked are well borne by most convalescents. Whey-puddings even are well digested by weak stomachs that crave a change. Highly spiced dishes and the messes prepared by most pretentious cooks are to be shunned.

In serious fever cases and in instances of considerable debility, whiskey or brandy as well as rum (with or without milk and soda-water) prove very valuable. Alcohol does not increase the heat of the fever. In general, the liquor that is most agreeable is best. American-made "brandy" is usually unsatisfactory. In fevers, seltzer-waters are very agreeable. Acid drinks are then both pleasing and beneficial. Some find dilute (chemically pure) hydrochloric acid preferable to lemon juice as an addition to cool water for the preparation of such drinks. For cleansing the dry, thickened tongue, bits of lemon are useful; but water made slightly alkaline by the addition of bicarbonate of soda is more effective.

Where the stomach is greatly irritated and rejects everything swallowed, *ice* (from pure lakes or made from distilled water) should be crushed fine and swallowed in small bits. This often suffices, even without giving chloroform-water at the same time. Barley-water (that has been well cooked) is then much better borne than milk. It is desirable at times to dilute the milk with lime-water, artificial vichy-water or pure water, especially if diarrhœa be present.

In nearly all diseases, *pure milk* affords a most reliable food. Typhoid cases usually thrive upon it. It is valuable in other diseases in and near the alimentary tract, where a very absorbable food is needed that causes no irritation. Then especially should all vegetables be avoided, and of fruits only the juice can be allowed. In convalescence, much albuminous food ought to be given.

In certain chronic diseases, such as tuberculous consumption and other wasting diseases, no large amount of albuminous substances is needed; for the waste of the body is increased when such food is in excess of the actual need. Yet fats in abundance and other non-albuminous foods are very important in chronic diseases. The value of cod-liver oil in such cases as it agrees with is a very familiar fact. While pure butter and olive oil are very valuable fats, they should not be soaked into the food in cooking or by putting fats upon hot food that they are liable to soak into.

Dyspepsia is such a vague term that it is necessary to recognize the general nature of the deviation from health before the diet can be properly regulated. An irritable, inflammatory disorder is very different from a bloodless, chronic, toneless stomach enfeeblement. This latter sort will allow the use of stimulants in moderation and as much albuminous animal food as can readily be absorbed.

If the appetite be capricious, as in a neurotic case, foods may be tolerated which are usually rather indigestible. If the case be of the *torpid* sort, scraped lean meat as well as tender poultry and game are very useful. We even see such cases at times able to tolerate boiled ham finely divided! Yet such things should be allowed only as occasional relishes and then experimentally. If the appetite of such "dyspeptics" calls for it, it is quite proper to sanction almost any food that is desired and at the same time is well borne. Delicate spices may be allowed, and also salt.

If the case be "gouty," as shown by rheumatic pains, the familiar brick-dust sediment of urine, etc., the common table-salt may have chloride of lithium added to it in equal parts and the mixture used from a salt-cellar upon food instead of the ordinary salt. Alkaline waters, such as vichy, may be given between meals and on retiring. A few drops of hydrochloric acid may be taken at the beginning of the meal unless the acidity of the stomach be excessive. Artificial and concentrated foods are in this stage undesirable. Fresh air and gentle exercise in the sunlight are very important aids to improvement. Further consideration of the diet suitable for gouty cases will be found on page 276.

If, however, the condition be one of *irritation and inflammation*, stimulants are to be used only very cautiously, and the food should be carefully considered so as to eliminate anything irritant. Vegetables are here usually undesirable because of their especial liability to gaseous and acid fermentations in such cases. Bread should be dried and then toasted and soaked in hot water or weak tea. Soups with barley, rice, macaroni and other mild food substances are here of use. When flatulency is present, it may be ascribed chiefly to the gases of fermentation.

Vegetables in general tend to aggravate this condition. So does an excess of fat and likewise starchy food when imperfectly cooked. Fruits are not to be used very freely, especially when abounding in sugar or fibrous substance. Rich, fat sauces and gravies are objectionable here as in nearly all other conditions of health or disease. Water should not be drunk at meals in these cases. Yet a large cupful of warm water taken before meals and at night before sleeping serves a useful purpose. If the dyspeptic or other symptoms, such as acne eruptions on the face, appear to be due to defective teeth, the services of a dentist are needed.

Habitual constipation is so prevalent among all people of all races and classes, that a few words of hygienic suggestion are here in place. The habits and diet need to be regulated. The frequent use of medicines, even if they be such approved and valuable ones as *cascara sagrada* and other mild laxatives, is to be restricted. The popular use of much-advertised pills and drastic purgatives, as well as the habit of resorting to injections, is harmful and, in the end, makes the condition worse than in the beginning. The custom of allowing several minutes after the morning meal, with unvarying regularity, for the purpose of encouraging a movement of the bowels, is a most valuable natural aid. False modesty should not interfere with this nor cause one to resist a prompt and proper relief whenever nature gives an indication that a movement of the bowels is desirable.

Abundant pure cool water should be drunk, especially in the morning on rising from sleep. Yet this is not meant to encourage the use, other than occasionally, of bitter or other purgative waters. Sufficient fats should be eaten. Although buttermilk often serves to secure a relaxed condition of the bowels wherever it is well borne, it must be remembered that such changed milk acts because of its numerous bacteria and their products. Hence the original milk from which it is derived should have been from a pure source.

Figs, prunes and other dried or fresh fruits, excepting huckleberries, have a general tendency to relax the bowels as well as to increase the volume of their contents and to stimulate the intestinal muscular movements that tend to expel the contained food residue. Wheatmeal bread, rye-bread, oatmeal, and other vegetable foods containing much waste matter, act in the same way, and are to be recommended in cases of constipation if they do not cause irritation.

If a tendency to hemorrhoids be present, large, rapid and heavy meals should be avoided. Spices, especially pepper, as also strong coffee and other stimulants are bad for those having such a tendency. Unripe fruits, salads, cabbage, beans and peas are not desirable articles of the diet for these cases. The diet should, in brief, be simple.

Gentle exercise, that brings the abdominal muscles into

activity, is advisable. Horseback exercise is not so good as walking. It is not advisable to walk long distances in warm weather. Cane-seated or hard-seated, unyielding chairs are to be preferred to warm, upholstered cushions. If the necessities of the case call for a resort to the use of the customary injections, these are to be small and slowly introduced. Cool or cold water is in the main to be preferred to other fluids used.

In rheumatic or gouty cases, diet and dry warmth are of extreme importance. An abundance of pure water should be drunk, yet not an excess as in "water cures" which saturate the system with water. If the only water to be had is impure or abounds in lime, it should be boiled. The lavish use of alkalies is not desirable. They should be taken only in small quantities. (See page 273.) Overeating and the use of alcoholic liquors are regarded as causing these diseases. Mental and physical strain seem to have the same effect under some circumstances; while temperate living, gentle exercise and out-of-doors life in dry, sunshiny weather appear to lessen the tendency. (See page 38.)

A mixed diet is the best, and the patient must be kept well nourished. Sugar should be used very sparingly, and sugary fruits are undesirable. Starchy food should not be taken in unusually large amount, and pastry is to be avoided. Cheese and very concentrated albuminous foods are not to be advised. Ebstein's view, that fats are here of value if well borne, meets the approval of many. Sweet wines, strong wines such as port, and especially strong malt liquors are generally regarded as potent in causing gout and rheumatism. The patient is to be cautioned against using such things to any extent. Champagne seems to be here, as in general for all other healthy or diseased states, the worst possible beverage. It is usually inferior.

Warm clothing, so adjusted as not to cause sweating and chill, is necessary. The general location, as also the walls and basements of buildings in which the rheumatic person lives, should be very dry. Observance of the principles above indicated aids to prevent the development of a tendency to these diseases. Temperate living and the regular, free use of pure drinking water afford the best safeguards. It is proper to advise against the use of the various open or secret preparations of colchicine and other strong and dangerous drugs used against these very common diseases.

Kidney disease, when chronic, requires that the entire body be as well nourished as possible, yet with extreme care to avoid excesses or even slight indiscretions in diet. The diseased state of such important organs makes it difficult to keep up the nutrition of the system. Long experience teaches that we must not take away the albuminous foods; but it is wise to restrict these, while not making very great changes in the usual diet unless that be excessive.

Alcoholic and other stimulants are to be avoided, and powerful drugs used only when extreme need arises. The best drink is pure water; yet that should not be drunk in excess. Many a case has had a too early, fatal ending because of "water cures" where large amounts of (usually) very good water are swallowed in a very injudicious manner. These diseases differ much in their character. The food that suits one given case may not be good for all.

Milk, as proved by the prolonged observations of all able physicians, is usually the best food. The use of rich, pure milk taken at intervals of two or more hours, in small portions to the extent of two quarts or more daily, and with it bread to satisfy the average appetite, gives nearly enough food and proves usually to be a very valuable diet for such cases. If meat and albuminous vegetables are added, this must be done cautiously. Fat should also be given if well borne by the stomach.

The value of free movement of the bowels must not be forgotten at any time. An "easy" condition of the bowels tends to lessen the amount of water and consequent pressure in the passively congested veins of kidney disease, as also in heart disease and other troubles of the circulation. Eggs are for such diseases a much better food when cooked than when raw. Food for people with kidney disease should be simple, well cooked and otherwise digestible. Warm baths, gentle exercise, warm and dry dwellings, together with carefully adjusted clothing such as will maintain the warmth and yet not induce a chill from perspiration, are all important in the care of these cases. Cases with marked kidney symptoms may live for years if due attention be given to hygienic management.

In diabetes, it is desirable to lessen the starchy and sweet foods, but not wholly to restrict them. In every case, it is well to be gradual in enforcing the exclusion of such things from the daily food. An abrupt and complete change to a meat diet (from which everything else is excluded) may cause the dreaded brain symptoms of diabetes to come very speedily. Even a few ounces of bread may be allowed in mild cases.

It is better of course that ordinary flour be replaced by gluten in the bread, so far as the patient will tolerate this. Yet the rigorous exclusion of a food because analysis shows it to contain carbohydrates is not usually the wisest plan in cases that are seen early in their course. Thus the sugar present in milk, while causing us to recommend that not much milk be used, should however not lead us to prohibit its use altogether. Koumiss and other fermented milk have less sugar than the milk originally contained.

The bulky vegetables and roots in general (such as parsnips, carrots, beets, etc.), as also potatoes, are to be *prohibited*. The green vegetables (such as spinach, lettuce, water-cress, and also radishes, may be *allowed*. Champagne, sweet wines and cordials, as well as most kinds of beer, should be strictly excluded. Chocolate has too much sugar to be permitted. Yet the small amount of sugar in cocoa infusion should not cause it to be excluded altogether. No sugar is to be allowed with tea and coffee. The use of *saccharin* for the sweetening of drinks is generally approved. It contains no carbohydrates. One grain of it serves to sweeten two cups of tea or coffee. Honey should be excluded ; but glycerine may be used for sweetening.

Sour fruits, almonds, almond-meal bread, gluten bread and bran bread are useful and may be ingeniously adapted, but do not always enable the patient to bear satisfactorily with the total deprivation from the use of ordinary bread, meal and starchy foods. Of the two most recent products introduced as substitutes for ordinary bread—bread made from the *soya* bean and that made from *aleuronat*—the latter seems preferable. Ebstein and others report continued satisfaction from its use. Meat, with as much oily and fatty food as can be borne, must form the main part of the diet in cases of diabetes. Since much water is needed, that should be of good quality. Gaseous waters are allowable.

For fat people who wish to reduce somewhat their excessive amount of fat, the " Banting " method is the most martyring. It may be dangerous if carried very far. It calls for an excess of lean meat or white fish in the food and does not permit much fluid. A little red wine and rum or brandy may be taken. Very little fat, starch or sugar should be allowed. The results may be very successful in lessening the amount of fat in strong, suitable cases. But much determination and will-power are necessary with this method. It is apt to cause indigestion and more or less derangement of various organs of the body.

Ebstein's method is a little better for those who can digest considerable fat. The allowance comprises much more fat than is eaten by the average person. Very little starchy food should be taken, and all sweets or sweet fruits ought to be avoided. The amount of albumen is also made very small.

Voit's method, as applied by Oertel, Schweninger and others, allows considerably more albumen than the healthy body requires. The amount of fat in the food must be quite small, and very little starch or sugar is eaten, less than a quarter of a pound being allowed in a day. Delicate vegetables, having very slight nutritive quality, and fruits that are not sweet can form a portion of the diet; for they produce a sense of "fulness" without adding to the nutrition of the body except by their salts. This method is better than the two preceding. Liberal exercise is advisable with it.

Some of the "cures" practised at various continental European "watering-places," as for example at Carlsbad, are serviceable in reducing fat, simply because they are *starvation* processes which people tolerate as they would not at home. Those who are heavy eaters, yet living a sedentary life; people absorbed in affairs who are so indifferent to every advice as to neglect all exercise, even rejecting every opportunity of enjoying the most valuable of all usual exercises—namely, that coming from a brisk walk in the open air—such persons often profit by these water cures.

In these hygienically favorable, park-like places, they follow the fashion that prevails there and accordingly exercise somewhat. This is partly because they are influenced by example, and partly by reason of the fact that they find little else to do. In any case, they get some physical exercise. This, with the restricted diet, tends to reduce their excessive fat. The results are not always beneficial. Some come away in a shattered condition. Especially where heart-disease or other organic trouble exists, should careful consultation with impartial, competent advisers be had before any unusually rigorous procedures are undergone.

It is in general best to "make haste very slowly" in attempting to reduce superfluous flesh. Enough has been explained above to indicate that the reliance must be upon diet combined with exercise. Sufficient time however should be allowed for nature to do the work very gradually. The essential principle is that the body substance must be used up slowly in the vital processes, and not quite enough nutriment supplied in the food to restore the excess of fat.

It is of prime importance for the future health to avoid violent exercise if the previous life has been purely sedentary, and particularly when one is not robust. One should begin with gentle exercise such as walking in the open air at as rapid a pace as is comfortable and does not make the heart-beats irregular nor cause them to increase very much. Gentle exercise is to be advised even in heart-disease. Walking briskly with the shoulders squared back is a more valuable exercise here than either bicycling or horseback riding. Yet these, too, are excellent exercises. The amount of physical exertion is to be increased gradually, with a careful avoidance of excess or severe fatigue.

At the same time with the increase of exercise, the diet is lessened. The food is very gradually reduced in amount. Less albumen is eaten daily than before and very much less of fats, sugar, sweet fruits or starches. No excess of water should be drunk. No alcoholic liquor is advisable; and sweet wines, beer and chocolate, as also sweet foods in general, cakes, puddings and pastry are to be avoided. Bread and butter, potatoes, hominy and rice make fat, and hence should be eaten only sparingly. Early rising and cold bathing (while at the same time swimming for exercise, if possible) are to be recommended. High mountain residence is of some value, but probably most so by reason of the more nervous activity that it promotes and which increases the vigor and also the extent of the exercise taken.

Lean people, who wish to accumulate fat, are to live a more inactive life and to prolong sleep and rest as much as they can. They are not to exercise much. The more restful they are, the better it is for the accumulation of fat. Water, milk, chocolate, strong beer, ale and porter may be taken liberally between meals and on going to bed. Five or even six meals may be taken during the twenty-four hours. Some hominy and milk or butter and toasted bread with sweetened coffee and milk (also perhaps a little meat) may be taken before rising. Oysters are desirable when eaten raw. Bread and rich milk or other desired food should be taken shortly before going to bed if this late eating agrees with the digestion.

No less than the usual allowance of meat should be taken, and with it all the fatty food that one can well digest. Bread, especially when well toasted, sweet fruits, such as figs, plums and bananas, if desired and well borne, are all of value in aiding to lay on fat. A dry and cool seashore region or at least one having cool nights is favorable. A malarial district is particularly to be avoided.

Drinking-Water

Nearly two-thirds of the substance, by weight, of the human body is in the form of water included in the composition of the tissues. Lean muscle substance contains 75 per cent. of water, and the blood has 78 per cent. To supply the daily needs and replace the water lost by excretion, an adult has to take into the body perhaps more than a gallon of water daily. Severe labor, especially in warm weather, may cause over half as much again to be needed. With the food, we receive perhaps half of the needed amount of water; yet the water consumed in and with the food may often be considerably less than half of what the body needs. Water and other fluids make up more or less sufficiently the balance needed.

In any case, enough should be drunk to prevent the urine from becoming so concentrated that it has, at the body temperature, a specific gravity much above 1,020, as is readily recognized by the ordinary urinometer. Every portion of the water that one drinks should be exceedingly pure. The fewer bacteria present, the better; and none of these should be of harmful kinds.

If not from the purest source, drinking-water should have been boiled. The process of boiling renders it healthful, even though it have been badly polluted by any organic filth. Yet boiling does not very much lessen the amount of any (non-gaseous) chemical substances present other than lime and magnesia carbonates. *Boiled water is palatable to those who are used to it. It is hygienically preferable to any filtered water.* The porcelain or "porous clay" filters, the only ordinary kind that should be at all relied upon to remove all bacteria, are so slow in their action that they cannot be intrusted to all servants. Filters are more fully considered in the following chapter. The great hygienic value of distilled water is also indicated there.

People reason wrongly who infer that we receive important nutritive substances from natural waters that can be got in no other way. Nearly five per cent. of the body weight is composed of salts. In the $2\frac{1}{2}$ or 3 pints of urine coming daily from a healthy adult, there are contained nearly 1,000 grains (or more than 2 ounces) of solids consisting chiefly of the salts produced from the combustion and waste of the body tissues.

The daily allowance of drinking-water for a healthy adult averages less than one gallon. Now, the most liked of the pure natural waters, sold in bottles or in bulk, and which many of the most careful people use regularly as an ideally healthful beverage, contain in one gallon only from 1 to 10 grains of salts of any and all kinds. A mineral water that has more than 100 grains of salts in the gallon is a very "strong" water and should be used only very sparingly. We repeatedly see digestive and other disorders induced by indiscreet drinking of large quantities of such waters. It would require enormous quantities of ordinary waters to supply all the salts needed by the body. For these reasons it is clearly unwise for us to rely largely upon drinking-water for supplying the salts needed daily to replenish the body loss.

In a mixed diet, all the salts needed are supplied in ample amount; yet it seems desirable to prescribe at times certain very carefully selected waters in particular ailments, where the case is under trained observation. The various advertised waters are almost always inferior to their pretensions. This is notably the case with the "natural lithia waters." Salty waters are not at all desirable, and the half-ounce of common salt needed daily can perfectly well be taken in and on our food.

WATER AND WATER SUPPLIES

THAT all of the water supplied must be of the very best quality is one of the uncontested and fundamental truths of hygiene. Even those who profess to believe that contaminated water is not necessarily a cause of disease, admit that the purest water is the best for all purposes.

The majority of a population are imprudent and liable to drink cool and agreeably tasting water coming from any hydrant, however dangerous the water may be at a particular place and time. Whether it be used to wash floors and sprinkle streets or to cleanse vegetables and for the various domestic and manufacturing purposes, the water should be pure. It deserves to be mentioned here that various independent and wholly reliable observers have reported cases of more or less familiar diseases due to bathing in impure water. Even for the use of domestic animals, water ought to be of good quality.

Lead is a chemical that we must always zealously guard against in our drinking-waters; for, if even a very small fraction of a grain of lead be in every gallon of water, this will in the end be harmful. The presence of copper is less common, but is bad in any case. Iron salts, occurring as they do in many waters of deep origin, are undesirable when present in any considerable amount. So, too, are alkalies. In some parts of the dry regions far west of the Mississippi River, the water is often undrinkable because of its great alkalinity. When lime and magnesium are very abundant in a water, it is called *hard*. Hard water may be valued by some stock-breeders as making their colts and calves develop firmer bones. Yet for domestic and industrial purposes, such hardness is a serious drawback which usually proves very costly.

Lime is the main cause of hardness. The sulphate of lime, together with some of the carbonate of lime, tends to form a hard scale on boilers, partly because of the evaporation of the steam. This *scaling* is a great annoyance and also increases the liability to explosion through stopping up pipes of boilers. Of these two salts, the carbonate is the less soluble; yet its solubility is much increased by the presence of carbonic acid gas in the water. This gas is present in natural, untreated waters and is driven off by boiling. Of the total lime and magnesia present, it is usual to class as *temporary hardness* that portion which can be precipitated by boiling. The remainder is called *permanent hardness*.

To reduce its hardness, water is at times boiled before using. This lessens the liability to the formation of scale in boilers. It also improves water for drinking and cooking purposes. By this heating, the carbonic acid has been driven out of the water. Consequently a considerable portion of its lime carbonate is no longer in solution and can be removed by straining. The usual and cheapest way is to reduce the amount of temporary hardness by the addition of freshly prepared milk of lime. The process must always be done in the cold.

To counteract the permanent hardness (that due to the presence of the sulphate of lime or magnesium), we have to add carbonate of soda. Of this, there are needed 2.8 parts of crystalline carbonate of soda (sal soda) for each part of the *sulphates* of lime or magnesium. For each part of the *carbonates* of lime or magnesium, 0.56 parts of fresh quicklime must be allowed. This use of lime actually lessens the total amount of lime *dissolved* in the water, because that which is added takes up the carbonic acid.

By such precipitation and also by sedimentation induced at times also by the addition of alum or of iron, turbid waters can be rendered purer. These added salts form hydrates and, to a certain extent, organic compounds which mechanically carry down minute particles and a varying percentage of microörganisms. If the precipitate falls upon sand or broken coke, etc., it there forms a felt-like coating through which only a few bacteria can pass and which holds back suspended particles.

This fact explains the action of several kinds of large filters, all very much alike and which may be used for communities of considerable size. Their value lies in the *mechanical* separation of particles of matter that are in suspension. When of good quality, they hold back a very large portion of the disease-producing bacteria that may be present. Yet a few of these harmful germs may pass through by reason of imperfect filtration; for the minute amounts of chemicals used are quite insufficient to destroy the disease germs. Some of these harmful bacteria also get through because of flaws that occasionally occur in such filters. Not even permanganate of potash (so effective against organic matter, ammonia, etc.) nor any other chemical—if used in the very weak proportions permissible from a hygienic standpoint—can be relied upon to insure the speedy death of all harmful germs in an infected water.

The various recommendations, going the round of the daily and other papers, informing people that equal parts of wine and water form a fluid in which bacteria of disease do not long remain alive, are not altogether to be trusted; for a bacteriologist's skill is needed to interpret for each situation the results of the more or less reliable experiments on which these recommendations are founded. Some bacteria *do* perish speedily in wine. Yet the majority do not. Hence those persons who hail with satisfaction such a sound pretext for drinking wine would have a safer beverage if the water (to be mingled with their wine) were treated by boiling beforehand.

Boiled or distilled waters that have been aërified, by the use of bellows or by the more elaborate means employed by those who produce distilled water on a large scale, are both palatable and wholly safe to drink. Heating, even if only for a moment, destroys the harmful germs. . Aërifying restores the two per cent., more or less, of oxygen driven off by the heating, and the absence of which causes the insipid taste of some boiled water.

Bacteriological Examination of Water

The simplest bacteriological test is to take a definite small quantity, either a drop, a cubic centimeter or whatever amount of the water we choose to add, by means of a cool pipette, or other unvarying measure that has always been sterilized by heating it beforehand. This water is mixed with liquefied *nutrient gelatine* (spoken of later, in the chapter on Bacteria). This mixture of water and gelatine is then allowed to solidify on the side of the nearly horizontal, cotton-plugged tube, or preferably is poured into a small flat covered glass dish that has previously been exposed to a heat sufficient to have killed all possible germs, and then it is cooled to the room temperature.

If proper precautions are taken to exclude stray germs from the air and from other sources, we find that, from the second day onward, the thus cultivable germs of the original water manifest themselves by having developed into peculiar "colonies" (see chapter on Bacteria) which can be recognized and further studied by any one familiar with the work.

By this method and its modifications, cholera bacteria are recognized with much greater ease than are the typhoid bacteria. Yet even these latter have apparently been recognized a number of times by competent observers. Typhoid bacteria are often counterfeited by harmless varieties of water bacteria, and no process is sufficiently reliable for all the cases where we try to find these. They are further spoken of in the chapter on Infectious Diseases.

Bacteriological investigation of water has, accordingly, like the chemical methods, only a partial value in most cases. This is especially true when people who are not experts attempt such tests. In case of two or more waters to be compared, the one which yields the fewest varieties and the smallest number of bacteria, is generally the best. If a lake has more than 100 bacteria in one cubic centimeter (one-fourth drachm) of its water, or if a river has more than 1,000 bacteria in each cubic centimeter, the water must be regarded as inferior to the highest standard.

The best ground-water and mountain lakes have the lowest number of bacteria among ordinary sources. Some deep springs, however, are absolutely free of all bacteria or other forms of organic life that can be detected by the use of a microscope or by culture methods. Such natural water can be used with the absolute certainty that, in its fresh state, it carries no infection and is exceedingly wholesome.

Rivers in wild country usually have very few bacteria, when pure and under average conditions of rainfall. The same river, further down in its course and having in its valley large populations and industries, may contain many times the number of bacteria that were present in the purer water nearer the source.

Manured and cultivated soils cause large numbers of bacteria to be present in the rivers into which they drain. This is especially the case after rains that are so copious as to wash filth from the *surface* of the ground into the stream.

Chemical Examination of Water

Undue importance must not be attached to the chemical determination of the amount of organic matter present in any given sample of water. Like the biological examination, this has no absolute value in the majority of cases. A visit to the lake, well or other source, with a careful inspection of the ground that drains into these sources of supply, is of very much more value in enabling an expert to form an opinion as to the hygienic merits of a water supply.

It is true that, as a rule, the best water shows the best results even on a single analysis. Still, a contaminated water may reveal a relatively smaller amount of ammonias and other organic matter than the same water contains at a time when it is not contaminated. Furthermore, it is observed that chemists of good training, in testing samples taken at the same instant from a given source, differ at times considerably in determinations of the amount of organic matter present.

The mere *quantity* of organic matter contained in a water is not necessarily a guide to the degree of the danger. The harmful quality of the organic matter present can only be partially recognized by chemistry. Any danger of becoming infected with typhoidal, choleraic or other diseases by the use of an infected water depends solely (so far as the *water* is concerned) upon the living presence of the causative bacteria of the disease. Chemistry is quite unable to detect the presence of these in any case and may even be misleading in several ways. The main practical value of the chemical examination lies in the tests for the recognition of *mineral* substances that may be present.

To test water for lead, copper and zinc, evaporate a gallon or more of the water with the addition of nitric acid and solution of ammonium nitrate in a porcelain evaporating-dish till less than two ounces remain. Sulphuretted hydrogen gas introduced into this (in a glass) for several minutes causes a *black* precipitate if *lead* or *copper* is present. This is filtered, washed and then dissolved in hot dilute nitric acid. To the solution a few drops of sulphuric acid are added. *Lead*, if present, thereupon gives a *white* precipitate.

The solution is then filtered through filter-paper. On the addition to it of ferrocyanide of potash, a *red-brown* precipitate or discoloration results if *copper* be present. If either copper or lead be present, a water is to be considered unfit for drinking.

Zinc is tested for by heating the filtrate coming through the filter after we have added the sulphuretted hydrogen. When the gas is driven off from the solution so that no odor comes from it, an excess of caustic soda solution is added. This is filtered and then sulphuretted hydrogen is introduced into the solution. A *white* precipitate is due to the presence of zinc.

To determine *how much lead* is present (copper and tin being absent), a colorimetric test suffices. This consists of a comparison between a tube of the water being tested and several tubes each of which contains the same amount of acetate of lead solution (but which is of a different strength in each of these tubes). The standard is given by preparing the solution from a definite amount of lead, say one grain, dissolved in an excess of acetic acid.

This is diluted with one gallon of water. A carefully measured quantity (into each tube a different amount) of this standard solution is then added to each of the comparison tubes. These are next filled up to a uniform level with distilled water. All the separate solutions in the tubes then have one-fifth of their bulk of sulphuretted hydrogen water added. The same amount is added to the water being tested for lead, which water is beforehand acidulated with acetic acid. Of this acidulated water to be tested, the same amount is taken as of all the waters in the several test-glasses that serve as comparisons. Knowing the exact amount in these, the determination of the amount of lead in the water to be tested is easy.

Another (but a less exact) test for *lead* is to add a drop of ammonium sulphide to a suspected water in a tall tube. A blackish precipitate may be due to lead, copper or iron. If copper be the only metal present, the precipitate will dissolve upon the addition of a small amount of a strong solution of cyanide of potash. The addition of a little dilute hydrochloric acid causes the precipitate to disappear at once if iron be the only metal that caused it. This acid does not remove a precipitate due to lead. (For testing *utensils*, etc., for *lead*, see page 252.)

Iron is tested for by evaporating half a pint of water to dryness in a porcelain dish. Then the dried residue is dissolved in hot dilute nitric acid. A few drops of a solution of ferrocyanide of potash are added. Iron, if present, causes a blue color; or, if only a minute amount be present, a greenish color is seen.

Lime is best tested for if we first add hydrochloric acid to the water until an acid reaction is recognized by the use of test-paper. Thereupon the water is heated and ammonia is added to alkalinity. Then one per cent. of oxalate of ammonia in solution is added. A white precipitate is due to the presence of lime. Wilson states that 6 grains in the gallon cause a turbidity; 16 grains a distinct precipitate; 30 grains a large precipitate, soluble in nitric acid.

Magnesium is recognized by testing the filtrate from the above. A few drops of a solution of sodium phosphate are then added and well stirred in. A white crystalline precipitate of ammonio-magnesian phosphate forms within twenty-four hours.

Chlorine (as chlorides) is tested for by acidulating two ounces of water with a few drops of nitric acid. Then a little of a five per cent. silver nitrate solution is added. If chlorine be present, the white, fleecy silver chloride is formed. It is soluble in an excess of ammonia.

The **hardness** of a water can be roughly compared with that of a water of approved quality by seeing how much more of a one per cent. solution of soap in dilute alcohol is required by the one than by the other in order to cause a durable lather on shaking the waters in separate test-tubes or bottles. The term, *one degree of hardness* used by many chemists means that a water has one grain of carbonate of lime (or its equivalent) in one gallon. " Five degrees of hardness" means five grains in the gallon, and so on. It is preferable to express the quantity by parts in 100,000.

The method by soap solution can be more exactly used, than above indicated, if with a carefully adjusted soap solution we employ a graduated and exactly controllable dropping-tube (burette). This (Clark's) method is not sufficiently exact for complete accuracy and demands the resources of a laboratory as well as skill. Where the rough test or that indicated in the third and fourth paragraphs before this does not suffice, and extreme accuracy is required, it is best that an expert analyst be intrusted with the work, which involves time, skill and careful weighing and measuring.

The "**total solids**" in a water are found by evaporating a carefully measured quantity of water (one pint or less) in a platinum evaporating-dish that is perfectly clean and dry and has been carefully weighed by accurate, chemist's balance scales. The water is evaporated over a water-bath, then the residue is dried by a heat not to exceed 212° F. This drying should occupy a number of hours. After this, the dish and the residue from the evaporated water are weighed together. The increase over the weight of the empty platinum dish gives the result for the amount of water used.

For detecting **ammonia**, a colorless (large) test-tube is filled three-fourths full of the water. Then a fortieth or fiftieth as much of *Nessler's reagent* (mercurio-potassium-iodide solution) is added and shaken up with the water. A yellow or orange color (coming in a quarter of an hour) shows the presence of ammonia. Comparing the color with that of ammonia solutions of known strength, we can reach an approximate idea of the amount present. The potash hydrate of the reagent, when in excess, causes the lime and magnesia of the water to give a whitish (or grayish-yellow) precipitate. Free carbonic acid obstructs the test. Hence it is recommended that 3 parts of a sodium hydrate solution and 2 parts of a sodium carbonate solution be added to 200 parts of water; the whole is stirred and allowed to settle. One-fourth of this when clear is taken for the above-indicated test for ammonia.

For a chemical test, at least a gallon of the water is desirable. The demijohn or bottle used (preferably a new one) must be very clean. In any case it ought to be rinsed several times with the water from which a sample is to be taken. Then, this bottle or other receptacle is filled very carefully, and a little of the water is poured off so as to allow a slight air-space. A new cork that has been rinsed, steamed, and kept clean, is then put in above all. This may be tied in and covered with clean, boiled muslin or pure tin-foil. A seal is put on the neck of the bottle, if desired.

It is wrong to decide upon the absolute hygienic merits of a water from single specimens sent very far before examination. The water needs to be tested at different times of the year. In certain cases, it is important that not all the samples be obtained when the wind is blowing from the same direction. Various local conditions need especial consideration at times.

For a bacteriological test, it is best that the bottle, previously sterilized by heat, be managed with especial care to prevent contamination. In getting samples for any purpose it is always important to use great care and have the specimen an average one. Hence we ought to get water from a place some distance away from the shore, in a stream or lake. Surface water is not fit for an average test; neither is the first flow from a faucet or pump. We should have nothing (as a boat or clothing, for instance) between a current of water (or air) and the water-bottle when the sample is being taken. It is best to take the sample from water well below the surface.

The contrivance which is used for effecting this must be strictly clean in every respect. After being obtained, a sample of water ought to be tested as soon as possible. The bacteriological examination, to be reliable, must be begun on the spot, in most cases. A little ingenuity allows the plating to be done immediately. The plates, kept cool by suitable devices, can be transported and examined in a place hundreds of miles away if necessary, even in summer.

To interpret the results of quantitative analyses of waters, it is well to have some standard. The following table is based upon the results of the monumental work of Kubel-Tiemann-Gärtner, the late Professor Nichols, and other eminent authorities. The qualification is made—as already said—that no *absolute* and final hygienic importance must be attached to isolated chemical determinations, for they are only a partial guide except as regards "hardness" and the presence or absence of metals. The two standards are not given as being exactly convertible or identical. Either suffices for practical purposes.

A good water can have not to exceed:

OF	IN 100,000 PARTS.	IN U. S. GALLON.
Solids on evaporation	50 parts.	30 grains.
Lime and Magnesia salts . . .	20 parts.	$11\tfrac{2}{3}$ grains.
Chlorine (in chlorides)	2 parts.	$1\tfrac{1}{4}$ grains.
Sulphuric acid	10 parts.	6 grains.
Nitric acid	1.2 parts.	$\tfrac{2}{3}$ grain.
Nitrous acid	0 parts.	"trace."
Ammonia	0 parts.	"trace."

Ammonia may, however, be present in some natural waters without permitting the inference that the water is unwholesome. The ammonia is not of itself harmful. Most distilled water has much of this. Yet such distilled water is excellent and equal to the best as a pure drinking-water. It is not so much the quantity as the quality (and especially the *source*) of the organic matter that most needs to be considered. When a water from a public supply under ordinary chances of contamination has .015 parts of *albuminoid ammonia* in 100,000, and there is considerable *free ammonia* present also, it is at least suspicious from a chemical point of view. Further investigation then needs to be made. Yet harmless vegetable matter may be the cause of all this.

Chlorine may be present, in an amount that greatly exceeds that of the standard given above, in case that the water be from a salt district. Yet the amount given is set quite high. An increase over this maximum allows, under ordinary conditions, the suspicion of *sewer* or *privy* contamination. If a shallow well have, in its water, magnesia or *potash-phosphate* present to any extent, some contamination with manure or privy leakage may usually be suspected. Manufactory waste causes the presence of very varying products in the water, according to the nature of the industry.

When the water from a given region is tested, it is quite necessary to have examinations made of other (and standard) water from the same region, in order that fair comparisons may be made. Such comparisons, however, require one to examine and know all the features of the place. Not only must the situation of the lake, well or other source be studied with reference to its nearness to contaminations, but the geology of the region needs to be considered as well.

The judgment of the skilled hydrologist enables him to appreciate the factors that vitiate or count in favor of a given water. Not only are dangerous contaminations recognizable at one place and not present elsewhere, but also the rock formation may change along the course of a stream so as to make the water below a certain point much harder than is the water up-stream from that point. The "hardness" of water from limestone is liable to be from ten to sixty times as great as water from granite hills would give; and red sandstone or lias rocks might cause water derived from them to be nine times as hard as if coming from granite.

More difficult and more important, from a hygienic standpoint, is the judicial estimate of varying special factors that under unfavoring conditions are capable of furnishing a more or less serious source of infection, yet under the best conditions will probably be harmless. This brings up the question of whether water "purifies itself" of disease infection or chemical poisons after these have entered. Does a flowing stream, for instance, become a fit source for the supply of drinking-water, at a lower point in its course, if at a point higher up in its flow either the germs of disease or acids, lead, etc., have contaminated it so as to render the water, at that place, unsuited for drinking?

This important question was discussed at length in a monograph embodying original researches and published in the Transactions of the American Society of Civil Engineers, for February, 1891 (also in the American Journal of the Medical Sciences for December, 1890). The results of that and subsequent work go to show that all water tends to become pure after being contaminated. Daylight and the oxygen of the air especially contribute to the destruction of disease germs. Dilution and sedimentation also lessen these. The chemicals and metals such as lead, etc., are usually rendered harmless chiefly by extensive dilution of the original contaminated water into which they have entered.

These healthful improvements in the quality of polluted waters are, however, so slow and insignificant in many cases, that they in general deserve to be considered an uncertain reliance. The only wholly safe way is to keep all filth and waste out of the water which is to be used later by human beings or animals. Where lead, copper, arsenic or any other dangerous metal is regularly present in the water, this water should be distilled before being drunk. A very simple still suffices.

Disease germs, that enter the water used for a supply, remain alive there a varying number of days. Thus they may be the means of infecting many people with disease. Carelessness in allowing any portion of the bowel discharges from a single case of cholera or typhoid fever to get into a water supply may cause numerous deaths. It would require many books of the size of this to give a list of all the individuals, families and communities that have received the infection of typhoid fever, during the last thirty years, owing to such impurities having entered their drinking-water. Cholera comes nearly always from similar disregard of hygienic cleanliness.

Wells may be contaminated by substances flowing in over the surface of the ground. In such cases, walling the upper part in with water-tight cement down to the inflow level of the ground-water is a safeguard which is better when *this wall is carried up above the ground* and when provision is further made for the conducting off of all the water that reaches the surface by pumping. Water from a privy or barnyard can always pass down through the ground and so enter an adjoining well.

Ordinary soil usually prevents the passage of disease bacteria in this way. (See page 3.) When, however, a fissure or flaw exists in the ground, the passage of bacteria (with fluid filth) into a well is thereby facilitated. If a well has flawless, firm, natural soil between it and all barnyards or privies, and if it is tightly walled in as above indicated (so that no *surface filth* can enter its water), it may be considered comparatively safe. When thus protected by natural and artificial means, its water is not nearly so liable to be dangerous as it is under ordinary conditions. This is true even though the water contain much albuminoid ammonia and much oxidizable matter (as seen by the unusually great amount of permanganate of potash that it will decompose). *When a well-water has many bacteria,* in addition to ammonia, nitrous acid and chlorides, we must regard it as seriously contaminated.

Coloring matters are occasionally employed to color water in a given place and thus enable us to find out whether this water flows in a certain direction. Their value is not so great as that of the most delicate chemical means. The best way to determine absolutely whether a well receives any **contamination** from a suspected (neighboring or remote) privy or other deposit of filth (carried perhaps through a flaw in the ground or otherwise), is to add certain chemicals to the suspected privy or manure-heap, etc. If there be several possible sources of contamination, the chemical is added first to one of these. Then the water of the well is sampled before another possible source of contamination is tried in the same way. After the test-chemical has disappeared from the well-water, if any happened to enter the well from the first test, another privy or filth-pile receives the test-chemical, and the well-water is again sampled in the same way.

Lithium, in the form of a solution of lithium chloride (or carbonate), is the best chemical to use for this purpose. Even in very minute amounts, it is easily recognized by the *spectroscope*. It is not a common ingredient of well-waters. The solution of this trial chemical can be put upon the edge of the suspected source of infection, or may be poured upon it as in a privy vault. It can also be sunk into the ground through a clean iron tube driven in for the purpose.

After the well-water has probably received the lithium through the ground if there actually be any leak, a quart or more of the water is taken. To prepare it for the test, enough pure carbonate of sodium is added to precipitate any lime and magnesia. Then the water is evaporated to less than a tenth of its bulk. It is then filtered through thick paper and dilute hydrochloric acid added to the clear filtrate until it gives a slight acid reaction. Then it is evaporated to dryness. Hot alcohol will dissolve out the lithium chloride present, and—on this being evaporated—the lithium salt is ready for the simple *spectroscopic* test.

Selecting a Water Supply

Ground-water, when of the best quality, is the most desirable of natural waters. (See also pages 301 and 304.) Most artesian wells, therefore, yield excellent water. The supply source (however distant) must, in such wells, be pure and not contaminated from above. It should be deep down under *impermeable* layers. *Iron* may be present in these deep waters. This detracts from the value of the water.

The iron in such water, when exposed to the oxygen of the air (by the water rising to the surface), becomes an insoluble oxide of iron which settles as a slime and may require special treatment (as by means of careful filtration after aërifying it). Deep-well waters that contain iron usually show a marked tendency to develop *algæ;* and in such waters we expect to find the objectionable *crenothrix*, a sort of bacterial growth in minute threads which may form large masses that can obstruct pipes.

Wells should be zealously protected from the entrance of filth from above ground, and the *surface* contamination that may come in with rain-water (if the well be not tightly walled in) is always to be guarded against. When wellwater warrants suspicion, because of the nearness of privies or other possible source of defilement, boiling renders the water perfectly wholesome.

Nearly as good as the best ground-waters, or (under the best conditions) of about the same quality, is water from *upland lakes* with little or no population on the barren watershed, and where no filth whatsoever is allowed to drain into the water.

In the third rank may be classed good average *lakes* and *streams* that are neither navigated nor contaminated. Streams generally prove hygienically inferior to lakes that are fairly deep.

Rain-water, gathered from roofs and stored in cisterns, is often very unwholesome and at least should be boiled. It is very *soft* and desirable for washing, tea-making, cooking peas or beans, etc., and for manufacturing purposes where hard or " brackish " water is the only other kind to be had. Such water is, however, very far from being organically pure. Water from a good spring or well is much to be preferred.

After the first portion of a rain-storm has cleared away, from the atmosphere, some of the dust, ammonia, acids and other undesirable elements, present especially in city air, the water is purer than at the beginning of a rainfall. The roof surface accumulates dust and dirt of various sorts from birds, leaves, etc. Hence it is very well to manage that the first part of every rainfall shall have washed the air, the roof and the gutters before anything is allowed to enter the cisterns. This is not always done where such cleanly precautions are most needed. The automatic devices arranged to effect this often fail to do their work.

Cisterns, or other containers or pipes used for rain-water, must be wholly free from lead. This poisonous metal is more apt to be taken up by soft water than by that which is hard. Cisterns are very liable to become filthy and dangerously contaminated. Hence it is important to use extreme care not only in locating a cistern, but also in arranging the construction and in placing safeguards about it. In time of drought, the supply sinks very low. Then, too, the small amount of rain-water that falls is apt to be less cleanly. So, boiling is desirable before the water is drunk.

It may be estimated that on every 100 square feet of ground area occupied by the building properly roofed over in the usual manner, there can be collected a little more than 60 gallons of water for every inch of rainfall. This is for the regions where from 30 to 50 or more inches of rain (or its equivalent in snow) fall every year. Where the air is very dry, much moisture is lost through evaporation from the surface on which the rain falls.

In deciding whether a water is good or not, we rely somewhat upon the chemical examination as already explained. For determining " hardness " or metallic contamination, the chemical examination is of absolute value. The biological examination, including microscopical and culture tests, should also never be omitted ; but only experts can be relied upon. Yet the main reliance in almost all cases is *inspection of the source*. We may further say that, in order to be called good :

    (1) A water ought to have little or no color and no visible sediment or suspended matters. Yet tur-

bidity does not necessarily mean harmful contamination. Peaty waters may be quite fit for a supply and yet be as dark as beer. An illustration of this is afforded by the water coming from the "Dismal Swamp" of Virginia and North Carolina. The above rule is a good one, however.

(2) Warmed or not warmed it should be free from odor.

(3) It should be agreeable to the sense of taste. Yet an unpleasant taste or odor need not of itself mean dangerous contamination. Conversely, it may be said that some of the most limpid and delicious water may at times contain harmful germs which can cause disease and death among those using the water. This is particularly the case with wells in crowded towns and villages, and where suitable provision against surface washings and other contaminations is not made.

(4) The water should have a rather evenly cool and agreeable temperature throughout the year. Water that is warm in summer and cold in winter is apt to be of superficial origin or to have been through superficial conduits or shallow reservoirs on its way to the consumer.

It is recognized as a practical fact that the **rainfall** on a square mile of ground area is great in proportion as that is near the mouth of a river. It decreases as we go inland. Of the water falling, a considerable proportion is vaporized off. This loss may be one-third, more or less, of the total rainfall; yet evaporation necessarily varies greatly with the dryness of the air. The remainder either flows over the ground directly into the stream or sinks into the earth to flow through the ground gradually onward and downward as *ground-water* or "subsoil-water."

Ground-water makes thus an underground stream going toward some lake or river to which it is tributary, but flowing very slowly (usually at the rate of only a portion of a hundred feet per day) and showing slight oscillations of level. The condition and character of the soil as well as the local and other factors affect the ground-water, its flow, amount and level. From a valuable study of this subject embodied in the U. S. Weather Bureau Bulletin No. 5, of 1892. it appears that, at the Wisconsin agricultural experiment farm, the ground-water rises nearly five inches for every inch of rain falling on the surface. In general the ground-water level falls more rapidly during the daytime than at night.

Where this ground-water in any place does not flow on, but becomes stagnant, from being dammed up, by a rocky (or other impermeable) barrier, the water is undesirable and the site becomes unhealthful. Artificial drainage is then necessary.

If in twenty-four hours one inch of rain falls evenly over a given area, then every square mile will have received about 3,323,200 cubic feet. Taking the area of the entire water-shed and the average number of inches of rain (and its equivalent of snow) observed to fall in a year, it is easy to estimate how much water will probably be received upon the entire water-shed during one year.

Apart from the considerable percentage lost by evaporation from its large surface, a storage reservoir loses much water by leakage and by percolation through the soil. Allowance must also be made for waste by floods. The flood volume of a stream is inversely as the area of the basin. Allowing for evaporation at all times and also for the waste above indicated, as well as for occasional drought, one is enabled to avoid the usual error of providing too small a supply.

A city or a dwelling having a sewage system must receive daily at least enough water to allow 25 gallons or more for every individual of the population. Some cities wisely allow more than 100 gallons daily. Among those in this country that are thus liberal may be mentioned Memphis, Cincinnati, and Pittsburg. In the city of New York, between 90 and 100 gallons is the average amount used daily by each individual, 165,000,000 gallons per day being the estimated average amount supplied to that city during the year 1893. In summer and winter this average is exceeded. Experiments of attaching meters to the water-pipes supplying certain dwelling-house blocks there showed a consumption of 200 gallons per day for each resident. This means that some people use much more water than others. Other cities have a similar experience.

This large consumption is condemned by some as being wasteful. Yet that view is not a very wise one ; for the more water the people use, the cleaner is the city and the better is the sewage washed away. It would be better if water were so abundantly supplied that all people could use it freely and were encouraged to do so. Hydraulic motors, however, are not to be encouraged. In time of drought, special requests, if persistently repeated, cause some lessening in water waste.

Water-works ought to be under municipal control. Thereby both the supply and the maintenance of the entire water system are more satisfactory as well as cheaper, all things being considered, than when managed by private corporations. In New York City, the cost of water to those who pay for it by the quantity is only one dollar for 1,000 cubic feet (that being about 7,500 gallons). Some cities supply water at a price even lower than that.

For our country, it is not necessary to consider the use of rain-water stored in cisterns for general public use. Such water is undesirable, as already said. If cisterns be employed, they must at any rate be carefully guarded from contamination. In Constantinople, Aden and other oriental places, large communities are supplied from cisterns.

Those localities are in general to be regarded as illustrations of what not to do rather than as examples that we may with safety follow. Frankland tells us that the water in the "holy well" at Mecca reveals, on analysis, several times as much animal matter as is found in the same volume of London sewage ! It is not to be wondered at, that cholera and other filth-diseases perennially make fearful ravages among those who flock to such shrines.

Springs coming from uncultivated, unmanured ground, not liable to contamination, furnish excellent water, as has already been indicated. If carefully taken, such water can be utilized very satisfactorily for a considerable population.

Not all deep artesian wells are necessarily pure. Thus, underneath certain cities the various geological strata pitch almost directly downward. Accordingly, most of the artesian-well water there, even if from very deep layers, is open to suspicion. Very deep springs can occasionally carry impurities for miles.

On the other hand, water-bearing layers may dip under great bodies of ocean water, and yet when tapped many miles away may furnish very satisfactory water which, to both chemical and bacteriological analysis, is very pure. Such pure water from a distant source is got by boring deep on Long Island or on the tongue of sandy land in New Jersey outside of Barnegat Inlet. The same conditions exist in other places.

A supply of pure water, at a low cost for the plant, can be obtained by the tube gang-well system, which offers, for certain cities, more healthful water than any other available source of supply. Lowell, Mass., is one of the cities that have recently appropriated money for putting in a plant of this sort.

The application of the principle calls for the selection of a suitable surface of ground away from any chance of contamination and owned or wholly controlled by the town or city that is to use the water. Then tubes about two inches in diameter, and which are sharp at the ends and perforated above that, are driven suitably deep into the ground. In the Brooklyn gang-wells, some of the tubes are 90 feet deep; others are only half as far down in the ground. In one of the Lowell tests, water was obtainable at depths of from 15 to 55 feet. Going down to 28 feet, the yield of water gradually increased, being 25 gallons per minute at this depth. As the tube was driven in further, less water was got. At 33 feet, only 7 gallons a minute were obtained.

From that point, the water obtainable increased as the tube was sunk. At 45 feet, the yield per minute was 56 gallons.

Then, as the tube was driven farther on, the amount obtainable grew less and less. At 55 feet, no water could be got. Hence the tube was drawn up to a depth of 45 feet, and, after a day's test pumping, yielded more than in the beginning. These figures are given simply to show that each case must be judged by itself, the water-bearing ground layers of one locality being of course quite unlike those in another. It is furthermore not possible to determine the presence or amount of underground water by surface indications.

These tubes, sunk in two parallel rows, ten feet or more apart, are connected by cross pipes to a horizontal pipe running half-way between the parallel rows. All the joints must be air-tight, since the water is drawn out by pumps. At Frankfort as well as at Leipzig (in Germany) nearly the same amount of water is obtained by this method as is received at Brooklyn, N. Y., where over nine million gallons of water are delivered daily from such "driven wells."

Gang-well water has the merit of having been very well filtered by a very perfect filter—namely, the deep soil of porous ground. So, unless there be a flaw, such water will be found very pure as regards bacteria. It may, however, be quite "hard" in some soils. As already indicated, the ground selected for the purpose must be free from sources of contamination.

Whatever sort of pumps be used to raise such driven-well water (or any other), care must be taken that storage tanks or reservoirs are large enough to hold a supply for several days; since all machinery is liable to get out of order and considerable time is often needed for repairs.

Means for Improving Inferior Waters

A given locality cannot always command a wholly satisfactory water supply. The problem therefore arises, in such cases, of how a bad or badly appearing water can best be improved. Only a limited portion of the community can afford to buy bottled waters, even if the harmfulness of contaminated water be realized by the masses. Furthermore, it may here be asserted, as a result of many examinations, that bottled waters and various others which are freely advertised and widely sold are not always as good or genuine as persons who extol these claim them to be.

Distilled water, even if not aërified with air that has been filtered through cotton or other suitable substance, offers the best beverage where the ordinary supply is bad. Distilled water ought to be produced more extensively than it is. By means of large improved stills, it can be delivered to retail purchasers for less than five cents a gallon and yet return a very handsome profit to the producer.

Small stills are already in existence and others are being perfected which are adapted to producing pure water for domestic use. Some of these do not require the use of much (if any) water for condensing the steam. If they employ metallic surfaces for cooling (and thus condensing) the steam, care must be had to see that no lead (from the solder) gets into the water. Such devices are especially recommendable for rendering the "alkali water" of our great plains fit to drink. They are of course good for purifying any bad water. A simple still can produce good water. Aërifying makes the water more palatable. No matter how bad a water—even if it contain sewage and disease germs, salts or lead, acids or alkalies—the process of distillation insures that the water thus treated is perfectly wholesome. Boiling answers the same purpose as distillation, so far as removing infection is concerned. The germs of disease cannot survive the heat of either process.

Sterilization of water on a large scale has been projected by Yaryan, of Toledo. American cities and institutions, to some of which this principle seems peculiarly adapted (owing to local conditions), appear averse to putting the idea into practice. In France, Messrs. Rouart,

Geneste and Herscher have produced a practical apparatus which has been successfully used by a few cities, towns and institutions. It can be employed for completely sterilizing water by means of raising its temperature seventy degrees or more above the boiling point if so high a heat be desired.

This heating being done throughout under pressure, there is no distillation. Yet there is some loss of free oxygen, due to the fact that, while none can escape out of the heater, some is taken up by the contained organic matter. The amount of organic matter and gases present is considerably reduced by the process. Some of the carbonates of lime and magnesia are precipitated.

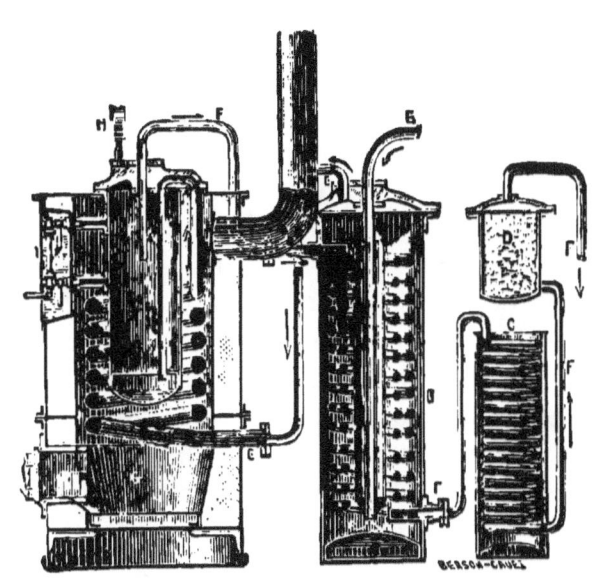

Fig. 43.

Fig. 43 illustrates the mechanism of a small portable apparatus yielding one hundred gallons per hour. The water, completely sterilized by the heat, flows out through the pipe F, on the right. The strainer D serves to clear the water which has passed from the heater through the coils in B and C. In these, it is surrounded by cold, inflowing water. The water is represented as coming in at E, on the upper part of the figure and to the right of the smoke-flue. The fire-box is at G. Into the arrangement above it, the water to be heated enters after having passed through the large coil. This very hot water stands at a level a little below the letter F, and is thence (by its expansion-pressure) driven out through the small coils of pipes to the right.

This principle, of causing the inflowing cold water to reduce the temperature of the outflowing hot water to nearly the original degree of coolness while the temperature of the inflowing water is thereby economically raised, makes the process very inexpensive compared with distillation. Yet it does not remove mineral poisons when they are present. It has been pronounced satisfactory by impartial critics. The future will determine the extent of its usefulness. The apparatus can be adapted so as to be moved about on wheels and serve for the use of several establishments. It is thus also valuable for an encampment where the water is very impure.

Turbid water is not necessarily dangerous; but it is liable to be so. People do not in any case like to drink water that is not clear and sweet. So attempts are often made to purify such waters. The various means used are alluded to on page 286. Of the chemicals there mentioned, *alum* is most commonly used in this country to cause sedimentation when added to water. Not more than one part should be used for five thousand parts of water. Often there is needed less than one-twentieth as much as that. Such a small amount of alum can fairly be regarded as harmless.

Settling-basins, used independently of chemicals or filters, may cause much of certain sediments to subside; yet the best system of that sort is at times very imperfect.

Filtration, on a large scale and well managed, is very much better. The ordinary domestic filters are of value only as *strainers* that remove visible dirt, eggs of worms and coarse parasites. Flannel bags that are kept clean are about as good for that purpose. To destroy all parasites and possible germs of disease, infected water that has passed through such strainers requires to be boiled *afterward*. Then it is harmless.

To exclude bacteria, even for a few hours or days, a filter must be composed of very close, dense, porous substance in which no flaw exists. Porous porcelain is probably the best of all such materials. Yet it is fragile, slow and, as recently shown, changes the water somewhat. It needs also to be cleansed every few days and at the same time to be sterilized by hot water or steam. Hence it is hardly to be universally recommended, even if flawless. At time of epidemic, such things are to be absolutely relied upon only in laboratories or in other places where they can often be tested.

All slow filters, attached to the faucet of an ordinary lead pipe, keep the drinking-water, that goes through them, for a long time in contact with the lead pipes. Thereby, *lead-poisoning* is rendered more possible than it is when the water is drawn rapidly through such pipes.

When the water used for drinking is undoubtedly infected, **boiling** is the only ordinary means that housekeepers should employ for rendering bad hydrant- or well-water fit to drink.

Large filters are a valuable means of rendering impure water purer and freer from bacteria. Yet disease germs pass through these at times. To prevent this as much as possible, and to secure the best results in general, constant and vigilant effort is necessary. The rapid sand filters, which various makers produce, are very much alike in quality. They are used by numbers of towns and small cities, and generally cause unsatisfactory river water to become much better than it is when unfiltered.

On a very large scale, filter beds, as used in Berlin, greatly improve a bad water. Those of that city are mentioned because of their excellent construction and because they have been very thoroughly tested for ten years.

In such very large filters, rocks and stones are covered by gravel over which is a thick layer of coarse sand. Above this is very fine sand making the entire filter bed a little more than six feet thick. The top is scraped off slightly in the weekly cleaning. This sand alone would not hold back any considerable number of bacteria. To form a more perfect surface for the top of the filter after each weekly emptying and cleaning, water is allowed to flow gently into the large filter bed till the basin is filled to the level of three feet above the sand. Then it stands for a day or more.

By the settling of the minute vegetable growths and various organic and inorganic particles present in that water, a very close, fine film is formed which, by its mechanical action, serves to hold back almost all of the bacteria in the impure water afterward let in for filtration. This water passes through under a pressure of only six feet (of overlying water) and preferably at the rate of not much more than ten feet a day. This flow through the filter must be not only *slow*, but also perfectly *steady*.

The cost of providing such filter beds as are used for purifying water supplied to London, Berlin, Hamburg (since 1892) and other European cities, averages less than fifteen dollars per square yard for those beds that are roofed in. The open beds are less expensive. The only usual advantage of covering these is that the water is thereby kept cooler and that in winter they are more easily cleaned and thus work faster in cold weather. When the temperature of the air is much below the freezing point, open filter beds are very difficult to clean. The healthful action of the air and light is of course more operative when the roof is absent. Roofs are effective in restricting the growth of *algæ*.

From every acre of such filter beds, under skilful management, nearly two million gallons of purified water can be produced in a day.

While, in intermittent filtration of sewage, it is shown by repeated experiments (including the latest reported results from Lawrence, Mass.) that it is better to break up the scum on the surface, it is in this continuous, practically economical filtration of water for city use considered better to utilize the sedimental film. By its presence, the uninterruptedly continuous film holds back bacteria and suspended particles which otherwise would pass through.

The practical filtration of river water for city use by means of the mechanical film is in the main a very different process from the intermittent purification of sewage which is passed through sand beds. In the latter instance, the process is to be regarded as a chemical one effected by the active vital processes of bacteria in the presence of oxygen and requiring time for the chemical action. Moreover, in this latter (sewage-purifying) process the sand should not be very fine. (See following chapter, page 329.)

To illustrate the value of such filtration in holding back the germs of disease and thus rendering bad water less harmful, the comparative experiences of Altona and Hamburg in 1892 may be cited. These two cities are on the same northerly side of the river Elbe. The former is practically a suburb of the latter, being situated immediately adjoining it down-stream.

Altona used the Elbe water only after it had been passed through the efficient public filter. Hamburg took its supply of water from the same river, but without any filtration. In that city thirteen persons out of every thousand of the population died from cholera; while its neighbor had less than one-sixth of that proportion of deaths. In a street which crosses from one of these two cities into the other, numerous cases occurred on the Hamburg side of the boundary; but on the Altona side, using the *filtered* Elbe water, there were almost no cases.

Cold weather does not prevent the Berlin filter beds from working well, although it slows them somewhat. A weighty objection to implicit reliance upon such purifying means in the presence of an epidemic comes from the fact that some disease germs may get through at the time of the regular (necessary) cleaning of the surface of the beds. Yet public warning could always be given whenever the water merited suspicion. By far the safest means of averting possible disease at such times lies in insisting that people then drink water only after it has been heated, for a minute at least, to the boiling point or nearly that.

With regard to **hydrant** pipes, it may be said that the most careful fitting and adjustment is required. Otherwise, water is wasted by leakage from the mains. The pressure of the water within makes it improbable that filth enters a perfect water-main through which water is going in a stream that fills the entire bore and is under pressure besides. When, however, aqueducts or imperfectly jointed pipes, that are only partially filled, pass through ground abounding in organic filth, there is danger that some of this filth be drawn into the water. Such possible contaminations ought to be guarded against.

Water-mains should be laid deep enough to escape the danger of freezing. Corners and "dead ends" that are not constantly in contact with the moving current of the water are to be carefully avoided in hydrants.

Large main pipes, with frequent outlets to which *several* fire-engines can connect, afford better provision against danger from conflagration than when only small hydrants exist. The pipes should not be larger than sufficient for all possible needs. They must, however, not be insufficient in size. In one of our largest cities, where this is the case, people have had to resume the use of condemned wells for supplying their domestic wants, with the result that numerous cases of typhoid fever and other diseases have been traced to that cause in the last few years.

All reservoirs should be open, but so situated that they will not receive any surface filth or other contamination. The less city dust they receive, the better. They need to be well fenced in and carefully policed. On the inside, reservoirs should be water-tight. Their construction and that of stand-pipes must be so strong as to prevent the possibility of their giving way.

For piping water, from a supply, into and through a house, lead pipe is commonly used. Yet it often causes *lead-poisoning* because of the metal being acted upon by well-oxygenized water and by that which has free carbonic acid. New pipes are especially liable to be affected. The softer a water is, the more liable it is as a rule to take up lead; and the more silica or lime it has, the less is it apt to take up the poisonous metal. When hardness is due to sulphates, it is more probable that the water will take up lead than when carbonates cause the hardness. To determine whether or not house pipes give off lead to the water that they conduct, draw off a gallon or more of the water after it has stood in them over night (or for days if possible). This water is then tested as explained on pages 253 and 290. Water that has been standing should flow out a long time from pipes before any is taken for drinking or cooking.

Lead-encased, block-tin-lined pipes are somewhat used. They should be of good quality. A flaw by which the lead coating becomes exposed to contact with the water may cause lead to enter by galvanic action of the two metals. These pipes have hardly proved a success. Those who can afford the expense, use brass pipes coated with tin. Water that has stood in these ought to be allowed to flow off before any is taken for drinking or preparing food. Galvanized iron is very good for pipes. Yet even these are slowly but continuously affected by the water, and zinc is dissolved from the coating of the pipe. The symptoms coming from the presence of *zinc* in the water are said to be constipation and in any case are *much less serious* than the effects of lead.

Pipes must be put where they are protected from the extreme cold of freezing weather. Thick felt covering the pipe guards it somewhat from freezing if exposed to severe cold. By reason of the growing abundance of electric currents carried through insufficiently insulated wires, underground water-pipes (and gas-pipes) are at times eaten away by electrolytic action. This is especially the case when *lead* is used for pipes, although iron may also be attacked. As before said, storage tanks should not be of lead or soldered metals. Wood is preferable to lead, although not durable or cleanly. Iron or slate (or stone) serves better.

Ice should come from a pure lake or river. Otherwise bacteria, possibly harmful, freeze into the mass of the ice and there remain alive for weeks or months. Hence, all ice from a river or lake that receives sewage must be regarded as hygienically inferior. In no case ought such impure ice to be swallowed or put into water or allowed to come into contact with food. Water is most healthful if drunk without icing. (See page 259.) The bottle, or other container of the water, can be put near ice or can be surrounded by ice if great cold be desired. Cooling-coils, which are frequently employed to carry water through ice for the purpose of cooling the water without bringing it into contact with the ice, ought not to be of lead.

Since freezing does not kill the bacteria of water, and since very many supplies are suspicious, it is safest to use only ice that is made artificially of water that is carefully distilled. Yet some distilled water produces ice that has a taste like boiled water. This defect can be remedied somewhat by care and is not a very serious one. Artificial-ice making is practicable, cheap, and certain of insuring a sufficient supply. The most recent improvements in water stills and in anhydrous ammonia ice-machines enable such wholesome ice to be made at a cost so low that it can be sold at a profit in New York or Philadelphia, for instance, for less than the price that dealers charge for natural ice.

DISPOSAL OF FLUID WASTE. SEWERS

Refuse matters are produced in great quantities by the processes of daily life and in various industries. As much as is easily possible, these waste products ought to be taken away at once, especially if they tend to interfere with health or the comfort and usual pursuits of those who may be affected by such refuse.

Ashes, garbage (and offal) as well as street sweepings are, in towns and cities, usually removed by the municipality. This refuse is in some cases disposed of at immediate private expense. So also is stable manure. In whatever way this is managed, careful control is needed to see that it is effectively done and that the means employed allow nothing to escape into the streets or be deposited in places where such refuse can be or become in any way unhealthful.

Besides these coarser matters, very important waste products constantly come from our bodies, as well as from households, stables and various establishments. Much important waste comes from city street washings. When, as is usual in cities of any size, these matters are conducted off in water holding them dissolved and in suspension, we class the fluid as **sewage.** This contains much organic matter and also innumerable putrefactive microörganisms that multiply rapidly upon this matter, since they find it very nutritious.

By the vital activity of these low forms of life, the organic substances are decomposed and gases are produced. Some of these gases are not detectable by their odor, while others are very offensive even though presumably not in themselves harmful in the amounts in which they reach us.

Without these microörganisms, there can be no decomposition. As, however, these are invariably present, it is important to remove such filth before the destructive processes have gone very far. With all these decomposable waste matters, it is essential to utilize the inevitable bacteria present. We must cause the microörganisms there to aid us as scavengers rather than permit them to trouble us by their offensive and dangerous activity.

Harmful bacteria, that are the presumable cause of serious diseases, are always to be suspected in sewage, notably when that comes from hospitals, from dwellings where infectious diseases exist, from certain streets, and at times from other sources. Fortunately, most of these disease-producing bacteria are much less hardy than the ordinary microörganisms of sewage and are apt to be speedily killed by reason of the natural antagonism and strife occurring among these low forms of life. Yet it is not well to depend upon so uncertain a factor of such indefinite force; for the disease-producing bacteria can occasionally live for a considerable time in sewage. If this then become dried in a fresh state and allowed to be diffused about as dust, these harmful germs can cause infectious disease.

Sewage and other refuse, having in it the discharges of cholera, typhoid fever and other diseases, must not be allowed to pollute the water which we drink. The peril from this source is very great. If fresh sewage be allowed to flow into streams or other sources of water supplies, it must not enter except down-stream below any neighboring water intakes and as *many miles* as possible from the place whence any other community is obliged to derive its water.

In flowing streams, the beneficent action of sunlight, the oxygen of fresh air, and other factors, among which may be mentioned the antagonism of various microörganisms present in river-water, tend to destroy after a while all of the harmful bacteria that come with sewage or by other means into the current of a river. Dilution in the great and constantly enlarging volume of flowing water is also operative to an immense extent in lessening the danger that comes from contamination of rivers.

Sewage, therefore, can as a rule be allowed to flow into most of our large rivers if this be done advisedly and with due regard for the health of all. Where the rivers are small and the volume of sewage is large, as in thickly populated valleys, it is usually safer to seek some other and more hygienic disposal of the sewage than allowing it to flow into a river to endanger the health of those using the water of such a stream.

The harmfulness of sewage is lessened if all discharges from persons having infectious diseases (as also all infected matters) are always promptly and properly disinfected by the liberal use of fresh milk of lime or by the other means indicated later in the pages treating of Disinfection.

Sewers are underground pipes which form an indispensable part of the public works of a civilized city that has a supply of water. The removal of the human excreta, that in some towns are received in privies and substitutes for water-closets, is only a very small though yet an important part of the service rendered by sewers in promptly disposing of the fluid waste of a community.

Sewers (and the gravel that ought to be laid along them) insure a varying amount of drainage of the soil with the consequent removal of such uncleanliness as the water thus carried off may have received from the surface of the ground.

Rain-water from streets and houses usually flows into sewers. They also receive the drainage from the interior of dwellings, manufactories, stables and other buildings. The connection between these and the sewer is through carefully joined pipes, preferably not more than six inches in size. Toward the sewer, these house-junction pipes may be of sound, glazed earthenware, very carefully selected and evenly laid. Near the building, this pipe must be of iron, for that is much less fragile than even the best vitrified earthenware. The cast-iron pipe known as "extra heavy" is to be preferred. Lead is not only too expensive but also unsuitable. Rats can gnaw through it. A "relieving arch" or large iron pipe should be in a wall at the place where a drainage-pipe passes under or through that wall.

Between the common sewer and the house plumbing, there should be a *trap* holding water of a depth sufficient to prevent any inflow of bacteria or air from the sewer. [Traps are spoken of in the following chapter. See page 333.]

This trap must be where it can be readily got at for the purpose of inspection. The location shown by the downward bend of the pipe (*running trap*) just inside of the wall in Fig. 47 is a good one. Some intelligent people contend that such a trap is undesirable because it does not allow the public sewer to be ventilated through the house plumbing!

For sewers that are properly constructed and well managed, ventilation through house drainage systems is not necessary. If no matters that enter are allowed to be retained in sewers, and if all sewage is kept in constant motion from the time it enters the smallest pipes till after it flows out of the largest sewers through which it has to go, sewers can ventilate themselves through the usual openings.

The best safeguard is to have the sewers so copiously flushed by free use of water that no organic matter lingers in them to decompose and produce gas or to favor the existence and activity of bacteria which need to be feared vastly more than any ordinary sewer-gas. The circulation of air that is needed in sewers ought to be provided for by occasional ventilating openings from the street. Perforated manhole covers answer the purpose. If sewers are so defectively made and cared for that matters remain in them and decompose, or if illuminating gas leaks into them, they ought certainly not to be ventilated through any house.

It is unwise to construct our house drainage systems so as to draw air up from a sewer and into and through our buildings. If the germs of diphtheria or other infectious disease be present because of the unclean sewer having received disease discharges, these germs may become dried and then be carried into or through the house by such an upward current of air from the sewer as results when no trap intervenes between the sewer and the house. If then the plumbing be defective, these bacteria of disease may thereby effect lodgment in a house. It is claimed by recent medical observers that they do so under such circumstances.

By the use of a trap as shown in Fig. 47, the private house-drain contains no filth except such as comes from within the house. By liberal use of water there, all matters are driven out into the sewer. Once in the sewer, such matters ought to be carried off so quickly by the abundant flow of water that they neither dry and become dust nor decompose to give off gases.

Sewers vary in size between six inches and twenty feet. An eight-inch sewer-pipe is much less liable to become obstructed than a six-inch one. In Paris some are larger than fifteen feet. New York City, with more than 440 miles of sewers, has only one (on Canal Street) that is nearly as large as that. Ten feet is the largest size as a rule, and that is very large. The usual error is to make sewers too large, even with all due allowances for prospective growth of a city. The smallest and largest are round: the medium-sized ones are of a shape resembling an inverted oval, as shown in Fig. 44.

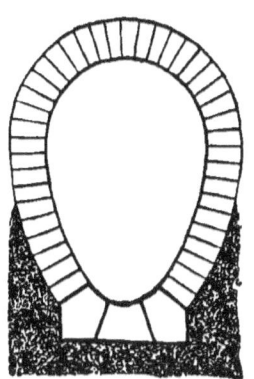

FIG. 44.

This form is stronger, cleaner and better washed by a small flow of water. Yet a large volume can also flow through a sewer of such a shape. The hollow base, shown at the bottom of the sewer in the figure, is not commonly used, brick being usually employed for the entire sewer when thirty inches or more in diameter. Yet such a hollow base, made heavier and stronger than shown in the illustration, is considered as of value in a soil that will not wash in and undermine; for it serves to carry off much drainage water from the soil. The smallest, up to fifteen inches, are of round salt-glazed pipe, jointed with cement and laid in concrete. Larger ones are of brick.

A city of 25,000 inhabitants may get along well with main sewers no larger than two feet, and a few of our cities have much smaller sewers. Yet it is regarded by superintendents of sewers, and others who are personally familiar with sewer cleaning, that obstructions cause much more trouble in the smallest pipes than in large ones. There is a limit to the availability of small sewers for large cities. The experience of Omaha illustrates this. The small sewer system introduced there has been almost entirely reconstructed.

Sewers must be very smooth within. They ought to be water-tight. Otherwise, water with organic matter and bacteria can go out through the walls. With good sewers, very little contamination of surrounding ground occurs. The bricks used need to be firm and impervious. Glazing on the exposed surface of such bricks is an advantage. To prevent matters from accumulating, frequent flushing with large amounts of water is necessary. Wherever such undesirable things as "dead ends" or long, irregularly used branch pipes are permitted to exist, flush-tanks are required in order to drive large volumes of water through the pipes at times.

If, during the construction, a crossing stream of water is met at the sewer level, this is either run into the sewer or else the sewer is made to deflect its course downward. It thereby describes a curve under the stream and, after passing that, is caused to rise so as to return to its former level. A suitable narrowing of the sewer at such a depression, renders the stream swifter and thus prevents lodgment of particles of sewage.

When one line of pipe makes a junction with another, the smaller should be at least a little above the larger. This junction is not to be at right angles, but must always be at an oblique angle as shown by the Y-shaped joint piece in Fig. 45. In this way, obstructions in the pipe are prevented. The figure is introduced to illustrate the readiness with which serious leaks in drain-pipes occur unless great care is taken to have the pipes properly matched and accurately set in place with perfect joints.

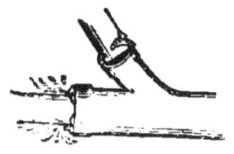

FIG. 45.

Especially necessary is it to have, throughout the entire length, a **continuous fall** adjusted so as to equalize the velocities of the current. This calls for good engineering. The velocity ought to exceed two feet per second. Sewers of ordinary brick cannot stand a permanent velocity of more than eight feet per second. The downward slope is to be at least 1 in 1,500 for large sewers; 1 in 400 to 700 for medium sized; 1 in 200 for the smallest. Inside of the house, the rate of incline of the drainage-pipe must never be less than 1 in 48. All curves must be gentle.

All portions of sewers are to be at least three feet beneath the surface of the ground, and in any case below the level of freezing. If the ground in which the pipes are to rest be found defective in any place, it requires to be carefully prepared and packed down. To support the smaller pipes (while they are being laid) at the proper level in the trench dug for them, Waring suggests "saddle-piles" made of inch boards, pointed at the bottom and sawed out at the top so that the pipe rests in and upon these.

Coarse gravel is the best filling under these pipes and

sewers; for it serves as a drain to allow the ground-water to run off. Until after the earth is thrown in around the pipe and carefully filled in for two feet, no one should step upon the filling or throw rocks or dump earth upon the pipe, since bad cracks may thereby be caused.

From the surface of the street, *manholes* with perforated covers go down to the sewer at intervals. These are introduced for ventilation and to allow inspection and cleaning. There ought to be more than a dozen of these for every mile of sewer. If the pipe between two manholes is straight, the recognition of obstructions is very easy. In some cities, small "lamp-holes" are introduced at intervals of not more than two hundred feet. If a lighted lamp be lowered down one of these and a good mirror (at an angle of forty-five degrees) be at the bottom of the next opening, the intervening space can be seen, provided that the sewer is straight.

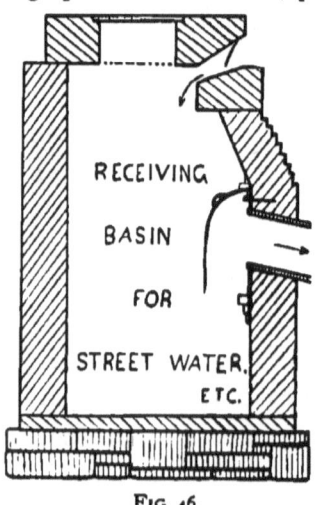

FIG. 46.

Men are constantly patrolling the larger sewers. For cleaning the very smallest, a float and an oiled cord (drawn by it) are passed through by the agency of the current. Then a brush attached to a stronger cord is pulled through the small sewer-pipe. To clean large sewers, a temporary damming up of the flow is often employed. Gates may be used for the purpose. The brisk rush of the volume of retained water has a scouring effect.

To prevent very large objects from entering and obstructing the sewers, gratings are placed at the opening from the street into the sewer. It is in some places necessary to have cylindrical catch-basins (see Fig. 46). These gratings and basins, or such devices as "hanging traps," serve to intercept all sorts of things that are thrown into them. They require to be cleaned often. They especially need cleaning after a heavy rain. In such catch-basins, the sewer inspectors discover at times very large planks as well as even much more bulky objects which enter in some unexplainable way and occasionally get into sewers. Small sewers become thereby stopped up. Traps to sewer inlets restrict somewhat the ventilation of sewers.

Where gutters empty directly into sewers, there may be a slight depression on the bottom of the sewer in order to catch sand and other particles that pass the usual grating. As already said, flush-tanks are needed for cleaning out small sewers, particularly if these pipes have dead ends. The more pure water we cause to go through any sewer, the cleaner the sewer will be. Turbid water is not desirable for this purpose, since it tends to deposit silt, and forms a film on the walls of the sewer. All breaks in sewers need to be promptly repaired, for through these much leakage of filth into the soil may occur. Steam is to be kept out of sewers and drain-pipes.

Sewer-air, when analyzed, proves to be less impure than it is generally considered by people unfamiliar with the exact facts. Although the filth of streets as well as of houses and other buildings flows into the sewers, these receptacles have very few bacteria in their air, and those bacteria are of harmless varieties. This is perhaps because of the usually good ventilation of our sewers and owing to the moisture of the walls which arrests the germs of the air.

Sewer-air seems less dangerous to breathe than the dusty air of our worst city streets and certainly less so than the air of many ill-ventilated public rooms where the air is bad and where dry bacteria are floating about with the dust of the air. The general high average of good health among men who work regularly inside of sewers is noted by scientific observers in this country as well as in Europe. No infectious diseases, that possibly could be derived from a sewer, are carried by them to their families, so far as can be learned by inquiry. Yet these men are originally neither conspicuously strong nor very careful about their habits.

"**Sewer-gas,**" therefore, in the sense in which the term is still employed by a few and in which it some years ago was very widely used to mask ignorance, is presumably very much of a *myth*. Gases can of course exist in sewers. They occur anywhere that bacteria cause organic matters to decompose. The gases are naturally most offensive where the defective construction and insufficient flushing of the sewers allow the moist filth to stand and then necessarily to decompose. Yet with fair ventilation of proper sewers, and certainly with suitable flushing by abundant water, these gases need not be considered a menace to the health of the average person, especially when neither the men who work in the sewers nor their families appear to have any notable degree of general or special illness.

The one gas that is conspicuously dangerous in sewers, as also whenever it leaks in any way into rooms where people live, is *illuminating gas* as supplied through pipes laid in the streets and into houses. The danger of this is especially spoken of on page 132.

The author, on inquiring at the New York City sewer department, found that, in the only genuine cases where distinct symptoms of any kind had been traced to "sewer-gas," it was always illuminating gas that acted as the noxious agent. That there was no error on the part of the informants is seen from the fact that the worst cases, with alarming unconsciousness and the other familiar symptoms of illuminating-gas poisoning, were observed in wholly *new sewers into which gas had leaked* from the neighboring mains. No sewage had ever been near these sewers.

. Any odor from a sewer indicates either that illuminating gas is leaking into it or that it is insufficiently cleaned.

Wherever sewers are introduced, they must not only be carefully planned and well constructed, but in all cases an abundant supply of pure water is needed as well. Thereby the sewers can be properly flushed out and kept clean. Those who are not familiar with public works, need then never realize that such things as sewers exist. Proper sewers neither offend the senses nor endanger the health.

Sewage contains phosphates and other salts as well as a considerable amount of nitrogenous matter. These are dissolved or suspended in a large volume of water. Sewage is accordingly a valuable though a very dilute fertilizer for cultivated ground. When the sewage of a city is discharged into a river or otherwise thrown away into the most convenient body of water, there is wasted an estimated manure value of five times as many dollars as the city contains inhabitants.

The human excrement yields daily only two-fifths as large an amount of solids as are contained in the urine. The entire amount from both of these contained in the sewage makes only a very small fraction of the total solids contributed to sewage by various industries, kitchen and other house washings, street water, stable rinsings and from other possible sources. In analyses of sewage from various English towns, in some of which (by reason of their having water-closets) solid excrement was regularly added to the sewage, while in others the excrement was disposed of by being received in privies and otherwise kept out of the sewers, the difference in organic contents between the one sort of sewage and the other was very slight or almost none at all. Sewage varies greatly in its character according to the time of day at which a sample is taken. The amount of organic matter in sewage averages between 25 and 30 grains per gallon.

That the comparatively insignificant proportion of organic matter which comes from the healthy human body can have much effect upon the water of the rivers into which it is carried with the sewage, seems therefore out of the question. *It is when disease germs enter sewage that danger of infection is present.* The proper place for the disinfection of disease discharges is in the sick-room, and the best time for disinfecting is before these discharges enter the sewer. Yet only a small portion of cases are properly attended to in this respect. Hence the hygienic importance of considering in how far the various processes for the treatment of sewage are of value to the health of the communities using the water of rivers or lakes into which sewage has entered.

Processes for the treatment of sewage always add considerably to the expense of disposing of it. When, owing to the peculiar situation of a city or because of legislative or other restriction these processes have to be undertaken, recourse is had usually to mechanical and chemical means or to irrigation fields. Electric processes are effective, yet are exceedingly expensive.

Chemical means have been very carefully and instructively employed in England and on the continent of Europe. Especial study of the processes at Frankfort, Wiesbaden and Essen should be made by those who are interested in investigating these in the places where they have been most scientifically managed. Mr. Crimp, whose experience and observation at the works in Wimbledon, London, and elsewhere in England, make him an authority, states that the settling tanks at Dortmund, in Germany, are much better than the English ones. They are shaped, at the bottom, like an inverted cone and are deeper than those of the Röckner-Rothe system at Essen. They also allow a continuous flow. This appears to be superior to the intermittent system.

A preliminary straining removes paper, twigs and other floating substances. Sand ought to be allowed to settle under a slowed current. Then, to the clear sewage in tanks, milk of lime is added. This is made of thoroughly slaked lime with about ten times its weight of water. This milk of lime is mixed with the strained sewage so that five grains of lime are used for every gallon of sewage. Occasionally, three times as much as this is used; but any excess is by some considered undesirable as favoring subsequent decomposition because of its alkalinity.

The lime takes up carbonic acid that is in the sewage and thus causes the lime that is already present as a bicarbonate to be precipitated as insoluble lime carbonate. This carries down much of the suspended matter called *sludge*. That is later burned or otherwise disposed of. Sometimes it is used extensively for fertilizing, as at Birmingham, in England. Usually, however, this sludge is not popular for agricultural purposes. Still it has been demonstrated to be of value as a fertilizer. Near Worcester, Mass., three or more tons of Hungarian grass to the acre are raised on gravelly soil by aid of such sludge.

Other chemicals are at times used with (or without) lime. The chief of these are *alum sulphate* (common alum) and *protosulphate of iron*. The latter is used in London, and is greatly valued. All of these processes, when well carried out, can cause the water (called the *effluent*) which flows off from the sewage to be rendered clear and inoffensive.

It is found by most observers that if a thousand parts of sewage water, containing the bacilli of cholera and typhoid fever, stand for a few hours with one part of quick-lime present, all of these harmful bacteria will have been destroyed. Klein has reported that the water is satisfactorily sterilized when lime is used in somewhat lesser ratio than this, or, say, a little more than forty-seven grains to the imperial gallon (that is, three tons of lime to a million gallons of sewage). This is a much larger proportion of lime than is commonly used.

The opponents of the system state that, in the ordinary

cases, many bacteria remain alive. Pfeiffer, of Wiesbaden, asserts this. From what we know by laboratory researches it seems probable that very much more than ten grains per gallon ought to be used in order to insure destruction of the harmful bacteria present in sewage. The processes which (like the Röckner-Rothe, at Essen) use the sludge mass settled by the lime to filter out the bacteria, are the most satisfactory.

Use of Soil for Purifying Sewage

Sewage poured upon light porous soil will **filter** through. The "nitrifying" bacteria present in the upper few feet of such a soil will, in the presence of oxygen, have converted the ammonia and various other organic matters of the sewage more or less perfectly into carbonates, nitrites and nitrates. When working at their best, such soil filters can—according to the reports of the valuable experiments of the Massachusetts Board of Health—remove nearly all bacteria from sewage and yet treat over 100,000 gallons per day on an acre of filtering soil. These results are superior to those that any other part of the world has ever achieved. In some places, only twenty thousand gallons are treated on an acre of soil in a day.

Intermittency in the pouring on of the sewage is generally regarded as desirable in practice for the reason that otherwise the air which supplies the oxygen needed does not always penetrate deep enough beneath the surface to enable the bacteria to do their salutary work. If continuous filtration be attempted, care is needed to keep the upper layers permeable to air, and the rate of filtration must be slow.

Sand, used for such filters, soon acquires the necessary bacteria upon the surfaces of its grains, and then works very effectively for years of sewage filtration if not too much be poured upon it at a time. Contrary to what holds good regarding the surface portions of the filters used for purifying drinking-water (see page 309), it is found that these sewage filters are best when the sand grains are of mixed sizes, no considerable quantity of the grains being finer than one one-hundredth of an inch; gravel coarser than one-fourth of an inch should not abound.

Some alkali, as lime, soda or potash, must be present in the filter in order to combine with the nitric acid produced by the bacteria, especially when the sewage to be filtered is acid. The mixing of a little limestone with the upper layers of the filter serves this purpose. Deep filters are better than shallow ones. They should not be less than six feet deep. In cold weather the process is less perfect than when the filter beds are warm. As the upper layers of the soil are found to be the most effective for sewage destruction, *subsoil irrigation* is theoretically unsatisfactory. Practically it is not to be recommended by hygienists.

Surface irrigation is a similar use of cultivable soil to produce the same results more satisfactorily by employing a much larger surface of ground. The natural process is greatly aided by growing crops, especially such as rye-grass and vegetables, upon the soil to which the sewage is judiciously supplied in an intermittent manner. The average allowance of ground surface is one acre for every hundred people of the population whose sewage is to be used for irrigation. Waring states that under the most favorable conditions and management one acre may suffice for the purification of the sewage of one thousand persons by irrigation. It is well to be very liberal with soil surface in such work. No less than 250 square feet of dry soil should be allotted for the sewage of each individual if the method be carried out in a limited way, as for a country house. It is better to allow more than twice this amount of land.

Various communities have made costly experiments with the method. These show that *intermittent* deposit of the sewage upon the soil is the most satisfactory. The fields must be carefully selected and graded nearly level after providing porous sub-soil drain-pipes two inches or more in size. These drain-pipes are at a depth of from four to six feet, and are to be arranged in parallel lines that are from twenty to one hundred feet apart. They connect with larger drains if such be needed to empty them.

The best soil for sewage irrigation is a light, porous loam. Rich moulds are found good for the purpose. Clayey soils are unsatisfactory because not sufficiently porous. If there be a subsoil of gravel, this is an advantage. By means of ridges a few inches high, the large surfaces are divided into smaller fields not more than ten acres large. They are usually three or five times as long as broad.

The whole surface has to be slightly sloping in one general direction at the rate of at least one foot in one thousand. Some prefer a greater slope than this. *Across* the fields, the slope is double that which it is lengthwise. There should be no places where water can lodge. To carry the sewage from the upper corner where the supply flows in, ditches run along the upper edge of the longer sides. Cross-ditches run from these every hundred feet or so. The inflowing sewage can be directed to any part as desired by using boards or other means of temporarily cutting off the flow from other parts. The proper grading of the surface insures an even distribution of the sewage over the field.

Within four hours after sewage is poured on, some water will have passed through from the surface of the irrigation bed to the drainage-pipes beneath.

At the very first, this water is less pure than when sewage has been running through for a while. The flow soon becomes quite pure; for the ground holds back all of the suspended matter, all or nearly all of the bacteria of the sewage, and three-fourths of its dissolved organic matter.

Sewage is conducted to the irrigation fields in pipes or other conduits which permit it to flow by gravity to the highest part of the irrigation ground. The cost of pumping should be avoided. For a country house, the use of tanks for receiving the sewage is found practical. Sometimes these tanks are adapted so as to be moved about on wheels.

It is well to allow sand and other heavy matter to subside in the sewage before that is poured over the ground. Floating particles are held back by a screen and removed from time to time. Sewage can be applied to the soil in winter, provided that the pipes be guarded against great cold and if an excess of ice do not form over the field. Even where the thermometer remains below zero (Fahr.) for days at a time, it is found that sewage (being warmer than the air) keeps the ground from freezing. When the crops raised on these fields are being harvested, the constantly flowing sewage may be received and stored for a while in a tank.

Besides being a valuable hygienic means of restoring waste organic matter to its place in nature without allowing it to undergo any offensive or unhealthful changes, such irrigation farms can yield a financial profit at times. This is notably so on a light, dry and porous soil, such as is especially adapted to the purpose, and which without sewage would yield very poor crops. Thus, the director of the Berlin irrigation fields reports that some of the fields there yield a net return of two and one-half per cent. upon the capital invested and above the fixed charges.

Adverse criticisms are occasionally made upon this highly healthful means of rendering filth both useful and harmless which otherwise might become a dangerous nuisance. Such criticisms are said by the especial champions of sewage farming to be due either to ignorance, and possibly the observation of unintelligently managed irrigation fields, or else those who condemn the method are said to be actuated by pecuniary motives which are hostile to the success of any sewage irrigation.

The most valid hygienic objection made by such critics

appears to be that vegetables raised upon a sewage farm may have unclean and unwholesome matter adherent to them. This is very true of vegetables from any farm where manure from the usual sources is employed as a fertilizer. Whether during epidemics or at any other time, sewage-farm products, as also *all vegetables wherever raised, ought to be cooked* before being eaten by human beings. The ordinary cook is not apt to cleanse lettuce and other vegetables properly. Whoever eats such food uncooked, runs a risk which may be very slight or, on the other hand, may prove to be extremely serious.

[This refers to the possible presence of disease germs. The frequent use of "Paris green" or other poison, for the purpose of destroying insects upon growing plants, also makes it desirable that *all* vegetables be well rinsed if of common origin.]

Prolonged observations show that properly conducted sewage-irrigation farms are not in any demonstrable way dangerous to the neighborhood in which they are. Laborers on such farms are reported to be more healthy than the average of their class, and their families, when residing there, share the same good health. Animals working on the fields, or fed with the products, show no special liability to parasitic or other diseases. Trout and other delicate fish thrive well in the clear drainage water from such farms. Yet the original sewage water is fatal to these fish. Gourmets and fish experts pronounce the color and taste of the flesh of trout that have grown in such purified water to be exquisite.

HOUSE DRAINAGE. PLUMBING

WHEN a house or other structure designed for ordinary use is so situated that it can readily be connected with a system of properly constructed and well-managed sewers, it is desirable that within the building there be provided certain suitable fixtures for receiving the excreta and fluid waste resulting from the occupancy. Each of these fixtures must be skilfully connected, with the utmost mechanical exactness, to a. properly arranged *waste-pipe* connecting with an *iron drain-pipe*. These, by the liberal use of water, insure the prompt removal of all domestic or other waste that enters the sinks or water-closets under proper conditions.

This complete system of fixtures and pipes constitutes the **house drainage.** (See page 334.) It connects with the public sewer as explained on pages 317 and 318. It is there recommended as being upon the whole best that, between the house-drainage pipes and the sewer, a carefully adjusted downward bend called a *running trap* (represented just inside the wall in Fig. 47, and shown also among the traps in Fig. 49) be introduced into the soil-pipe so as to offer a *water-seal* against the upward and backward passage of sewer air and germs of disease.

For the same reason, traps shaped more or less like the letter S (∽, see Fig. 48, representing a vertical section through such a trap) must invariably exist as a part of each waste-pipe that carries waste water and other matters from any one of the fixtures (such as sinks, water-closets, tubs, etc.) to the soil- or drain-pipe into which they all empty

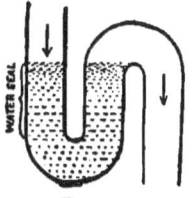

FIG. 48.

334 HOUSE DRAINAGE. PLUMBING

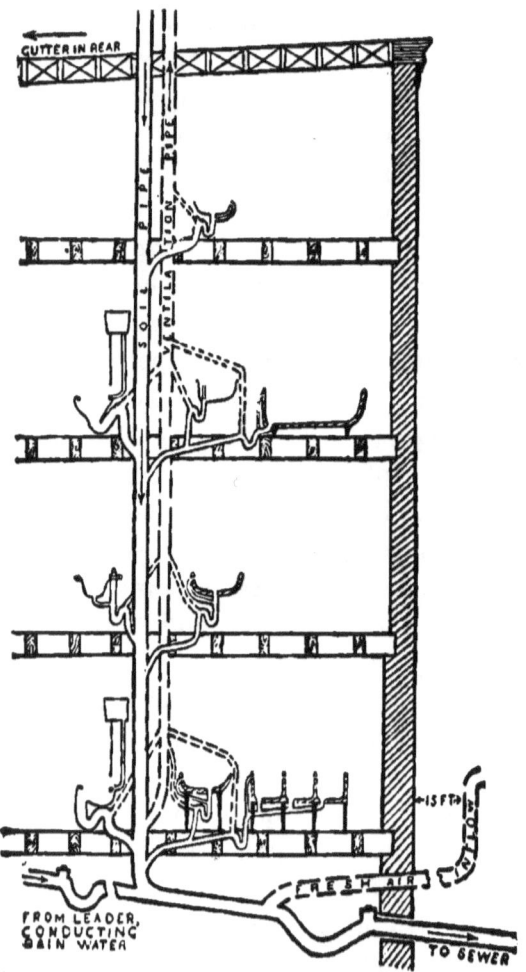

FIG. 47.

HOUSE DRAINAGE.

The running trap at the house wall is often deeper and more rounded.
It is common not to have overflow pipes on the lower floor.
The traps ought to be as near as practicable to their fixtures.
The dotted lines indicate the *continuous* walls of pipes that convey *only air* for ventilating purposes.

through the separate waste-pipes. Fig. 49 shows some of the different shapes which such traps may take.

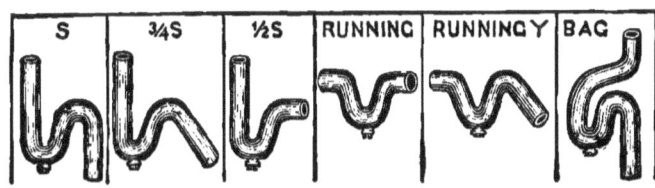

FIG. 49.

A trap must invariably be as near as possible to the fixture which it protects. When water stands in traps of suitable shape, it wholly prevents any possible gas, air and accompanying bacteria from passing *backward* through the pipe.

This water constitutes what is called a **water-seal**, an element of paramount importance in all house drainage. In Figs. 48 and 52, the *depth* of the water-seal is indicated by the space beside which the words " water-seal " and the brace (}) stand. When all of the water that constitutes the seal flows out or is drawn out or driven out (as explained later), and also when it evaporates, the seal is " lost."

This is especially liable to occur when the trap is very shallow. If the trap be defectively constructed (as illustrated in the bend of the pipe shown in Fig. 50, and which does not deserve to be called a trap), it is of course a false reliance and a danger to health ; for it does not prevent the flow of soil-pipe air and possibly bacteria back into the room where the fixture is located which it ought to guard by an efficient water-seal.

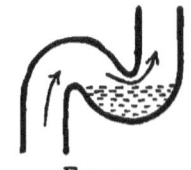

FIG. 50.

In Fig. 47, the traps are arranged so as to insure proper water-seals. The running trap at the house wall is there made rather shallow so as not to obstruct the outflow of all household waste when water is driven through for the purpose of flushing out the soil-pipe. When such a trap is present in that place, there should be a *fresh-air inlet* pipe to the lower part of the house drain as indicated in that figure.

Even in the absence of any gross defect, it is found that the water-seal is not constantly preserved under ordinary conditions. One reason for this is that very deep traps are not commonly employed; for, although deep seals are preserved better than shallow ones, it is nevertheless regarded as best that traps should not be made so as to have a very deep water-seal. This is because filth is especially liable to be retained in deep traps, and finally much may accumulate. The seal ought, however, to be at least an inch and a half or two inches deep.

A common cause of the loss of a water-seal from a trap is *siphonage*. A less frequent, although not unimportant cause, is *capillary attraction* resulting from the presence of rags, threads or hairs in it and on the outflow edge. The water can thus be drawn out of the trap, and the water-seal may thereby be lost. This capillary action may take place in any trap, but is probably not of very common occurrence. To prevent it, the traps and pipes must be very smooth within, and of the same even size throughout. They require also to be flushed often and well. Much water must flow through to keep them clean.

In order to facilitate cleaning out these traps or their modifications, openings that close tightly by perfectly fitting screw-plugs can be introduced at the bottom of the trap (as shown by Fig. 51 and several of the previous figures). A screw arrangement for the same purpose ought to exist at the opening for the vent-pipe at the top as well. (See Fig. 51.)

FIG. 51.

All traps are liable to lose a part of the water which they hold and which constitutes the water-seal. This danger must be apprehended even with the most perfect mechanical work and even though the traps have "back-vent pipes" or other devices to be spoken of shortly, as more or less satisfactory means of maintaining the water-seal or at least the greater part of it.

Whenever a change of pressure and consequent movement of air occurs in the soil-pipe with which a trap is connected through the waste-pipe, this change of air-pressure causes the water-seal to be either pushed back or drawn out according as the pressure is increased or diminished.

A constantly recurring condition of ordinary usage is given when, from a water-closet or other fixture, especially from one high up in the house, a considerable body of water (together with paper and other more or less solid matters) enters a soil-pipe that is not open at the top. The downward flow of such a mass of water (and the somewhat solid substances with it) acts as a "plunger" which is apt to cause a momentary and partial vacuum in various parts of the drainage system. This tends to suck out more or less water from water-seals in the traps of branch waste-pipes emptying into this soil-pipe.

Similarly, in a long and steep waste-pipe, especially if it be curved, the momentum of water going swiftly down the pipe may cause so much water to be drawn out of the trap back of it that not enough remains there to form a seal against the backward flow of air through the trap (unless proper provision against this be made as will shortly be explained.)

Traps lose their water-seals under various modifications of these conditions. The practically important fact to be remembered is that in "plumbing" there is usually a liability of the water-seals of traps to be drawn out. It is accordingly necessary here to consider the means employed to prevent this.

A vent (in the shape of a large hole) is made experimentally in a given case, let it be assumed, at the highest part of the trap (on the discharge side of the water-seal) or a little further along down the pipe. The effect of introducing such an air-outlet is thereupon seen to be that the air can rush freely in or out through that ventilating opening whenever for any reason the pressure of the air within the pipe suddenly diminishes or increases. In such a case, the water-seal in the trap is not appreciably affected by the variations of air-pressure in the pipe, and hence cannot thereby lose any of its water.

Such an expedient, however, as is indicated in the above paragraph, is impracticable (at least in the simple form there given) because the air from the waste-pipes can flow out *into the room* through such an opening in the pipe. In order to prevent this objectionable air escaping inside the house, while yet at the same time the advantages of the ventilation opening were retained, the custom arose many years ago of securely attaching a long, continuous pipe to the hole made on the top of the trap.

In Fig. 52, the word *vent* indicates the usual location of this connection between the trap and such a *ventilating pipe*. This air-pipe needs to be two inches large, or as large as the trap, if that be smaller than two inches. Such a trap "vent-pipe" can be made to communicate directly with the air upon the outer wall of the building, and a few intelligent engineers sanction such a contrivance. But any makeshift of that sort is not to be commended. The usual method, shown in Fig. 47, is very much better.

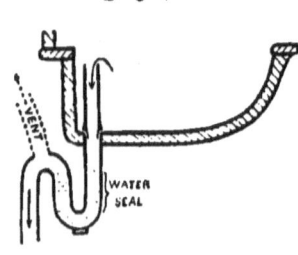

FIG. 52.

Back ventilation, or "back venting," is the name given to the use of perfectly tight pipes that rise from each trap for the purpose of allowing the air of the waste-pipe to flow in and out and thus be the means of preserving the water-seal. In all properly arranged plumbing, where this system of back ventilation is carried out, the several ventilating pipes, one from each trap in the house, rise gradually to enter a larger main ventilating pipe, which rises vertically through the building to an opening above the roof. (See pipes with dotted outlines in Fig. 47.)

Back-ventilating pipes necessarily offer much *frictional resistance* to the air that is drawn or driven through them. It is essential, therefore: (1) That these pipes be not exceedingly long. (2) They must be large enough (as explained later). (3) They require to be straight or to have, at any rate, only very few and very gentle curves. Such pipes as conform to these requirements serve to prevent the water-seals of the traps from being entirely lost under ordinary conditions of varying pressures occurring in house-drainage systems.

If all the rest of the plumbing be good and kept in perfect order, back ventilation, carried out in the most intelligent and conscientious manner, is a very satisfactory means of protecting the water-seal in a trap. Some work is at times, however, very defectively done. There are details which an inferior mechanic is liable to slight or wholly neglect. All plumbing needs also to be inspected occasionally in order to insure the absence of obstructions in these ventilating pipes, especially where they join the traps. Accordingly, this method cannot be regarded as reliable unless it is well planned, carefully executed and kept in good order. Yet, as has just been said, it is excellent when at its best.

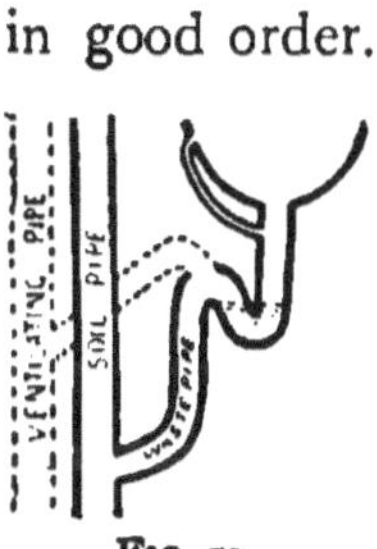

A ventilating pipe must always rise constantly from the crown of the trap. (See Fig. 47.) In no case should any part of this ventilating pipe sink below the level of the fixture which it serves. If this rule be violated as indicated by the dotted lines in Fig. 53, the fault is a grave one. This is of altogether too frequent occur-

FIG. 53.

rence, particularly in connection with pantry sinks and others that are isolated because of the necessities of the construction. Such a defect can wholly defeat the purpose of the ventilating pipe, because it renders that *dry-air* pipe liable to become filled with filth from the overflow in case of any stoppage of the waste-pipe.

Ventilating pipes, according to most practical men, also tend to become stopped up by substances falling into them. When iron that is not galvanized is used for such pipes, it is apt to rust and cause at least partial obstruction of the pipe. Stoppage also occurs because of filth being dashed up into the vent-pipes and there drying so as to form an obstruction. This happens especially at their origins,—that is, at the places where these pipes (see *vent*, Fig. 52) begin to rise from the trap. Most ventilating pipes probably allow somewhat less free passage of air than they are supposed to.

The waste-pipes are dryest within when back ventilation is carried out in the best manner. More air flows through them when they are ventilated, and more oxidation of the filth upon the inside of the pipe then takes place. This drying is not found necessary when abundant water is made to flow through a pipe so as to keep it perfectly clean. Under ordinary conditions, however, people do not flush the pipes sufficiently. Then the dryness and circulation of air within the pipes may be considered an advantage for the reason just given.

Interior dryness, however, becomes a defect when the pipes are left long unused; for it is considered that the water-seal of a ventilated trap dries out at least three or four times as quickly as when there is no ventilation. This evaporation of water from a trap is highly objectionable since it may cause the water-seal of the trap to be lost. Then it permits bad air and germs to come out of the waste-pipe and into the apartment.

All houses that have long been unoccupied require that

their pipes be well flushed. The rooms and the entire inside of the building must be thoroughly aired before being occupied again. If there exist a slight leakage of water from a faucet, this will keep sufficient water in any traps below it; yet it is a wasteful means.

There are "safety traps" made which, by means of a "turn valve," obviate or lessen this evaporation, because they shut tightly. They can prevent any backward flow of air from either the waste-pipe or ventilating pipe, whether there be any water present in the trap or not. They must be from the best makers if used at all, and are not to be recommended for ordinary cases. As they entirely close the pipe, a leaky faucet of the basin above (if not provided with special stops) may cause overflows when such traps are used. At the best, they call for an effort of the memory to see that they are properly turned off or on as the situation calls for.

If the connection of the back-ventilating pipe with a trap be by a *screw-joint* coupling as already mentioned (see Fig. 51), made air-tight, this joint can then be opened from time to time and inspected and cleaned more effectually than when attached by soldered joints in the usual manner. If traps or pipes used for plumbing fixtures could be durably made of glass and *kept clean*, that would afford a valuable safeguard, since it could permit the recognition of stoppages and defects in working. Practically, no extensive use of such an aid is found to be feasible.

Back ventilation is, as has above been indicated, the most approved expedient for preventing the loss of water-seals from traps. Yet there is always a chance that the work may be poorly planned or badly done. This is particularly the case when much is entrusted to unreliable workmen and when the simplest principles are deviated from. Intricacy, as illustrated by some very pretentious work, is often dangerous. Every extra joint involves additional chance for insecurity.

Recognizing these possibilities and with a view also of lessening somewhat the considerable expense of back ventilating, numerous inventors have brought out various more or less complicated traps and other patented devices to take the place of that. These all have the attractive merit of reducing the cost of plumbing work, while all back ventilating (as above outlined) considerably increases the expense, since it calls for more piping and more work.

On trial, most of these work very well and ordinarily preserve the water-seal until their more or less complicated mechanism gets clogged with the usual filth or becomes obstructed by something else that chances to enter. If these are used without back ventilation, the waste-pipes are apt to be more slimy within than when perfectly working back ventilation exists. This tendency is lessened when the pipes are flushed often and with sufficient water to cleanse out all filth. If copious flushing be neglected, dry pipes are much to be preferred for the reason that, as above stated, there is less likelihood of decomposition of matters there.

There are many of these traps. Fig. 54 illustrates the flow of water through one of the best of them,—the Putnam trap. It is a considerable departure from the simple S-trap; yet, in special tests, even when not ventilated, it appears to keep its water-seal better than the ordinary S-trap does, although that be provided with the average back ventilation. If, however, such a trap is allowed to become clogged with filth, it has no advantage over the common S-trap. Whenever any of these "non-siphoning traps" is employed, it is well to choose one of the simplest. They all have the defect of an uneven calibre and irregular surface in parts.

FIG. 54.

An ingenious device that allows the use of a simple S-trap, and yet preserves the water-seal under ordinary conditions without employing any other back ventilation, is the "Mc-

Clellan vent." This consists of a light (aluminum) inverted cup (B, Fig. 55) the lips of which rest in mercury (L, Fig. 55), unless, as represented in the figure, air is being drawn into the waste-pipe below the trap. When there is no pressure in either direction, and also when the air for any reason is pressed backward and upward out of the waste-pipe, the cup (B) rests closely in the mercury seal (L).

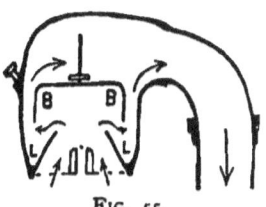

FIG. 55.

As this vent then forms a tight closure, no air can flow backward in a direction contrary to that of the arrows in Fig. 55. In this backward direction, strong currents of air are not much to be apprehended. Violent back currents of waste-pipe air occur only in wholly exceptional cases of defective house-drainage. They may be expected in case of the accidental stopping up of the lower part of a soil-pipe. In that event, the non-yielding of such vents would tend to cause a desirable warning to be given by the backward gush (into or toward the sink) of the contents of the trap; for, unlike back ventilation, this device and the various "non-siphoning traps" do not provide for such backward flow of air.

FIG. 56.

Under the ordinary conditions, where air is sucked out of the waste-pipe, this "vent"—connecting as it does with the crown of the trap (see Fig. 56) by a short pipe—allows the entrance of air. The only resistance is that which is offered by the light aluminum cup. That resistance is considerably less than is afforded by the water-seal of the trap. Consequently this device enables the water-seal to remain unbroken under ordinary conditions of usage. The vent must be above the level of the fixtures which it serves.

With fixtures, then, not far from a soil-pipe, this "vent" (like the best of the various "combination" or non-siphoning traps above spoken of) allows the desired water-seal to remain practically undisturbed. These accordingly fulfil the desired object (of maintaining a water-seal in the fixture trap) better than defective back ventilation. Yet *when the back ventilation is perfect* in all of the essentials indicated in these pages, it is generally considered preferable to these devices. It does not maintain the water-seal any better, the plumbing below being clear and perfect in both cases. Yet, as already explained, it allows more free passage of air upward as well as downward through the waste-pipes. That is usually an advantage.

Ventilating pipes, as used ordinarily in good "plumbing," must be as large as the pipe that forms the trap, unless the size of the trap exceed two inches. The size of ventilating pipes requires to be gradually enlarged as the distance from the trap increases. The large pipe either rises independently through the roof (see Fig. 47), or it may open into the upper part of the soil-pipe above all fixtures. All of these pipes are to be as short as possible, and should have only gentle curves if any.

Sharp bends (as shown by Fig. 57) are to be avoided. Every bend or obstruction increases the frictional resistance to free movement of air, and thereby tends to defeat the purpose of the device. Hence many prefer that all of these rising pipes be left open on the top (above the roof) and not even curved over

FIG. 57. to keep rain, snow, leaves and other things from entering. A very light open wire basket may be used over the top to keep out animals, leaves, etc. Ice-guards are usually complex and a hindrance to the free movement of air. Galvanized iron is preferable to ordinary iron piping for "vent-pipe" risers. In no case should the openings of soil-pipes or ventilating pipes be near a window, ventilating flue or chimney.

In Fig. 47, the various fixtures are represented as being quite near to the soil-pipe. That is the best way to have them arranged. Unlike the English usage, it is in our country as a rule preferred to have the waste-pipes, from sink, water-closets and tubs, empty as directly as possible into the soil-pipe. Rather than have long horizontal waste-pipes, it is better to have separate vertical ones where plumbing fixtures are situated in a somewhat distant part of a house. That is, it is better to duplicate the simple system shown in Fig. 47 rather than to have a number of long pipes nearly level run between the floors to empty into a remote soil-pipe.

All pipes ought to be put in place in such a way that they are exposed to view as much as possible. Whenever they are covered in, as under a floor or elsewhere, they should have especially arranged and easily removable boards as flooring or wood-casing over the place where they run.

As a luxurious safeguard against leakage, little water-tight troughs may be under waste-pipes and plumbing fixtures. These *catch-troughs* have independent pipes carrying off leakage water to the basement. Yet they ought not to be needed. Such things add greatly to the cost, and they fail to give the hygienic security that comes with simple, uncovered plumbing limited to the absolute needs of the occupants.

Complexity of detail and bad joints in plumbing are productive of much disease in our houses. Through defective joints, harmful filth can escape. With complexity, more opportunity for errors and for mechanical defects is introduced.

Even though in the beginning the pipes appear acceptably well put in, and stand the usual test pressure of ten pounds to the square inch with only a very slight leakage or even none at all, the quality of the material may be quite imperfect. The custom of doing much elaborate plumbing by contract, the lowest bidder being usually the successful one, causes work to be slighted. Too often, defective material is used which, although seemingly corresponding to the precise and adequate specifications, is yet liable to give very early and unhealthful evidence of its inferiority.

Soil-pipes rarely need to have an inside diameter exceeding four inches. This diameter should never be greater than six inches. It is desirable that the inside surface be perfectly smooth throughout. So also must the inside of all the waste-pipes emptying into them. These latter, which serve to empty the watery contents of sinks, tubs, etc., into the main soil-pipe, ought never to exceed a diameter of two inches inside (except when from water-closets or special apparatus). An inch-and-a-half size is preferable for most fixtures. It will suffice for an ordinary wash-stand sink. The trap and all other parts between a given sink (or other fixture) and the soil-pipe must be of the same unvarying size throughout. These essential requisites to good house drainage are emphasized because of the extreme importance of attending to them. If properly adjusted, the pipes will constantly be kept clean in all parts by the flushing force of the water that flows freely through, and thus will allow no chance for filth to accumulate.

"**Extra heavy**" **pipe** ought to be required in all specifications for good plumbing, especially when *cast-iron* is to be used. This material, three-eighths of an inch in thickness, seems, in the long run, to be about as good as any other. The lengths of such pipe are usually not much more than five feet from joint to joint. At curves and branches the joints are necessarily much nearer. When these joints are imperfect, they afford great opportunity for filth to lodge to a dangerous extent and make its way out (through such faults) into the air of apartments.

The most intelligent and experienced observers are disposed to regard that the germs of diphtheria and various other infectious diseases frequently get into rooms by having passed out of the house drains through these plumbing defects, and thus cause many cases of disease. Even such gross faults as are indicated in Fig. 45 are far from being of the worst that are encountered among very many cases of bad plumbing.

Not only these, but also slight defects in the oakum-and-hammered-lead joints, that have to be used for connecting these cast-iron pipes, may allow disease germs to get out from the pipes. Hence the importance of having no more pipes and plumbing fixtures in a house than are actually needed. Hence, too, the necessity of having the materials and workmanship of the very best and always kept in order.

All of these require, as already mentioned, to be so placed that they are always visible and not cased in with woodwork. White paint, having much white lead in it, ought to be applied over all of these joints as, in case of leakage, sulphur gases escaping with other products of decomposition, would tend to darken the white lead and thus betray the leak to any careful observer.

Glazed earthenware pipes do not corrode; but they are not to be recommended for use within doors, because of their great liability to breakage. Cast-iron pipes, even, sometimes suffer injury from the necessary hammering in of the several pounds of lead used to make the joint. These flaws are not always noticed, and may later increase in size and become dangerous passages that allow filth to exude. Furthermore, joints made in this way tend to leak when deteriorated by the expansive and contractive influence of extremes of heat and cold. Hence soil-pipes of wrought-iron or other metal are more and more being introduced with screw joints as used in steam-piping. Joints of this kind can be made very tight, and therefore **seem preferable to the ordinary (hammered lead) joint.**

Brass is very rarely used for soil-pipes. It does not seem durable for such purposes. Criticism is also made upon the durability of galvanized-iron soil-pipes, such as are called for by the very thorough (1893) plumbing regulations of the District of Columbia. Practically, these two metals have not been used sufficiently to determine their fitness for soil-pipes. They are, however, excellent for back-ventilation pipes. So, too, is lead. It is very durable if kept dry. Gnawing by rats is not to be feared with dry and exposed pipes.

It must be remembered that the cutting of threads for screw joints takes away a considerable portion of the material. Hence the metal must be sufficiently thick to permit without danger this loss of substance. Some recent contract plumbing work, that is very elaborate and very costly, appears to be sadly remiss in this respect.

Soil-pipes must not be level in any place. They must always have a distinct downward slope, say of at least 1 in 48. The regulations, above alluded to, require a slope of 1 in 40. Then, with the use of abundant water for flushing them out, nothing will remain lodged in these pipes if unsuitable substances are kept out. They ought to be visible and painted white in the basement as well as in all other parts of a building.

It is preferable that no water-closet or other plumbing fixtures be in the basement. If as is usual such fixtures be located there, they must in every case be so situated that their outflow is distinctly downward toward a soil-pipe which flows directly into a sewer. In no case should they be allowed to remain if they necessitate the presence of a cesspool.

It is well that, near the lower part of a vertical soil-pipe, a readily accessible brass trap-screw exist in order to facilitate cleaning out of the main drainage pipes of the building. There should also be such a screw for cleaning purposes on the further side of the trap at the wall of the house. (See Fig. 47.) Some traps have these on both sides.

Water-closets, when properly made, of suitable form and perfectly connected with the soil-pipe, are no more unhealthful or objectionable than any other plumbing fixtures. The average bedroom sinks and kitchen sinks are presumably more often instrumental in propagating and disseminating infection than any really good water-closet.

The worst water-closets in common use are *pan closets.* (See Fig. 58.)

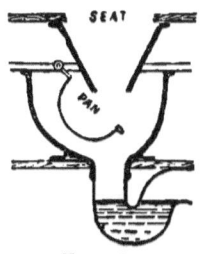

FIG. 58.

This inferiority is chiefly due to the fact that they have a wide enlargement around and beneath the "pan." When the contents of the pan are splashed down, as they have to be in order to empty the closet after use, part of this filth may be thrown upon the walls of this very undesirable space and remain there. The low price of such closets explains their extensive use. By paying five dollars more than the cost of this, a hygienically correct *hopper* or *washout* style of water-closet can be bought, even though it be not of the highest quality of material and wholly lacking in superfluous elegancies.

Hopper closets are much better than pan closets. Being both inexpensive and strong, owing to the customary exclusive use of iron for their construction, they are often employed for institutions and public places. In Fig. 59, the hopper is the funnel-shaped part above the trap and its visible water-seal. Those water-closets are best where both trap and hopper are in one continuous piece without any joint between, and where the sides are flushed clean by jets of water coming from all around the rim at the upper part. It is best also to have the *trap above the floor,* but this is not usually possible with very

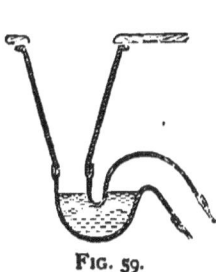

FIG. 59.

long hoppers. The particular closet, represented by Fig. 59, is of the *long hopper* variety. It is without back ventilation.

When the hopper is short, so that the trap is above the floor, the result is a more satisfactory kind called a *short hopper* water-closet. If, in such a pattern, the rim be provided with a flushing arrangement through which several gallons of water flow whenever the closet is used, this bowl can be kept clean. In public places it is found well to have an automatic arrangement for effecting this regular and thorough flushing. Such a device must be certain in its action. In any case, extra cleansing, as by a brush, is occasionally needed for this or any other water-closet. Even the average hydrant water leaves a certain amount of sediment on the walls of any bowl.

The "plunger" and "valve" water-closets are not to be recommended; and, as they are not often introduced into new work here and comparatively seldom found at all, they are mentioned simply to state that these have some of the objectionable points of the pan closet and are inferior to the hopper closets or those next to be described.

Siphon and particularly the **siphon-jet water-closets**

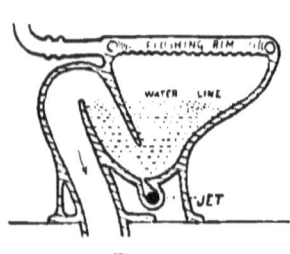

FIG. 60.

(see Fig. 60), when of the best makes, are to be considered as equal to the best "washout" patterns. Many consider them much better than any washout closets. All of these are good when simple and when offering no recesses or roughnesses that allow matters to lodge or cling. They are made so as to form a solid piece of glazed earthenware, in which the trap is enclosed. In practice, they are found to work better when the outflow pipe is contracted or bent at or below the place where the arrow is in Fig. 60.

Siphon water-closets may be considered as improved hopper closets having a deep trap above the floor and a bowl that is shorter and of a better form than in the ordinary hopper closet. In this bowl is a considerable amount of water which makes a water-seal so deep and lasting that no second trap is needed. Especially to be guarded against is the presence of roughnesses and unflushed recesses on the inside surfaces of the siphon back of the bowl. Some closets of this pattern make very little noise when used. That is a minor consideration. Intricacy and elaborations are in general to be avoided. The most costly water-closets are not necessarily the best.

Washout water-closets, when allowed several gallons of water at each using, and when thoroughly flushing all parts of the bowl with this water, deserve to be classed among the very best of all. Those which have the outlet to the rear of and under the seat (see Fig. 61) are not quite so good as those which have the outlet toward the front (as shown by Figs. 62 and 63).

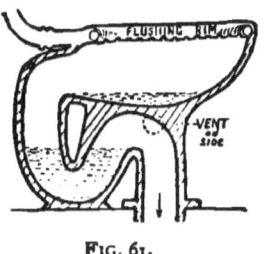

FIG. 61.

The hygienically preferable form of these is indicated by Fig. 62. The superiority lies in the fact that the water-seal within the trap is wholly visible, and that all parts above the seal are open to easy inspection. Thus the retention of any filth is at once recognized

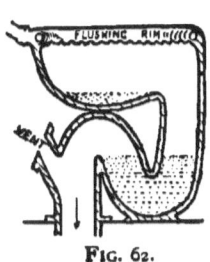

FIG. 62.

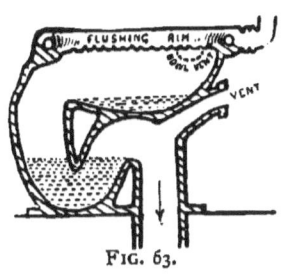

FIG. 63.

and the bowl and outlet tube are kept clean. Some find that, *when the bowl is deep*, there may be some splashing of the water on the front part.

Accordingly, a bulging front is introduced into some

closets of the front-washout pattern. This is shown by Fig. 63. Comparing that with Fig. 62, the difference is evident. While a slight projection is permissible, the one shown in Fig. 63 is too great.

Such a protrusion is in the way of those who use the bowl. The hygienic criticism to be made upon that shape is that it may allow unclean substances to remain, and does not permit the recognition of any retained filth so readily as does the better shape, shown in Fig. 62. Besides being hygienically good, a washout closet can be purchased at a very much lower price than any good siphon closet. This is a point of great importance to most people.

Whichever of these better varieties be selected, *sufficient water must be used* for flushing from the rim and washing out all parts of the bowl. The supply must never come from direct communication with the water supply of the house. It must always be from a tank especially introduced and arranged for water-closet use and for no other purpose.

It is usual to have this tank about seven feet above the floor so as to insure sufficient head of water for flushing the bowl and washing out everything. Several ingenious contrivances provide for a secondary flushing. A continuous flow, of which the *first portion is brisk* enough to wash out everything from the bowl, answers equally well.

The important thing to provide in any case is *plenty of water*, and that must come promptly and with certainty when needed. Three gallons ought to be allowed for each using. In Philadelphia, more than twice this amount is called for. That extra consumption of water is of hygienic advantage; for the more water a water-closet and the pipes below it in its drainage system receive, the better are they cleaned out.

A ventilating pipe (or its substitute) should be connected with the trap beneath the bowl of a water-closet (at the place indicated by the word *vent* in Figs. 61, 62, 63) in order that the trap shall not siphon out. Yet, as above said, the best siphon closets (see Fig. 60) do not usually need this. The size of this ventilating pipe must in no case be less than two inches.

It is becoming more common than formerly to introduce "local" ventilating pipes upon the water-closet bowls (above the water-seal) in order to draw off the odor that comes from the excrement when the fixture is being used. (See the words "bowl vent" below the seat in Fig. 63.) It is eminently desirable that rooms which contain water-closets be ventilated by exhaust shafts, especially if proper ventilating windows are absent. Yet it can hardly be recommended that these ventilating pipes originate at water-closet *seats*.

It seems better to have their openings begin further away, where (if efficient) they would purify the air and yet not rapidly dry up matters that may be allowed to remain upon seats owing to neglect of the first essentials of cleanliness. To be of value, the principle of bowl ventilation must be carried out very perfectly, with large, straight, independent "risers." That adds to the expense and increases the complexity. As a rule, bowl ventilating is badly done. So, it seems quite improper to compel *all* people to introduce "bowl vents," as some boards of health appear to require. These bowl vents are to be regarded as a *luxury*. Those who can afford to have such work done in a proper manner will probably attend also to the requisite cleanliness. If not maintained in good working order, seat ventilation is undesirable.

Enough has been said elsewhere in this book about the hygienic significance of disagreeable smells. However unpleasant they may be, it must be said that all odors that are produced in a water-closet are hygienically insignificant compared with the danger from *dirt* and *dust* that result from the drying of disease discharges. While it is very desirable that we prevent offensive odors from annoying our senses, that must be effected in a way which cannot create a positive danger. It deserves to be emphasized that a sink or wash-basin is usually a more dangerous fixture than a good water-closet that is kept clean.

In the presence of cases of cholera, typhoid or other intestinal disorder, it is exceedingly important that the discharges, especially if not disinfected, be washed down the water-closet very promptly and with liberal use of water. *They must be kept moist* until after they are washed away. A "local vent" tends to dry (and convert into dust) such discharges as may cling to the seat or upper part of the bowl. The upward current (if the device be actually efficient) can cause the germs of disease to be drawn up the ventilating pipe or flue. When they have entered, they are not necessarily carried off, but may linger within the pipe and be returned to the house air by back currents through the usual ill-adapted and neglected flues.

Water-closet bowls, the tanks used with them and also sinks or other fixtures ought to be without wood-casings. They must have all external parts quite open to inspection and to the healthful influence of light and fresh air. Covers of any kind are undesirable. It is better that the water-closet bowl be opposite or very near a window rather than in a dark location.

A window communicating directly with the open air is required in every room that contains a water-closet. If such natural ventilation be lacking, an independent ventilating flue, having a sectional area of more than forty inches, ought to be provided on the wall. (See chapter on Ventilation.) Through that, by means of a large lamp or a gas-burner that uses at least four feet of gas every hour, an upward draught can be produced to draw offensive odors out of the room. Such ventilating flues are less efficient than windows. This is partly because of the usual bad arrangement and partly owing to neglect. Constant warmth is required in order to maintain the upward current. If back currents are permitted, such flues are hygienically worse than useless.

In no case ought draughts of air to flow out of the water-closet room into other parts of the house even if the door be left open. The arrangement and management of the ventilating facilities should be such that currents of air invariably flow in the opposite direction, that is, out of the house through the water-closet room. If cigar smoke, or any odor produced in the room, be recognized in any neighboring part of the house, it is proper to infer that at least the ventilation needs to be improved.

In an elaborately arranged house, as also in hotels and institutions, the water-closets may be in special and separate rooms. Yet, in average houses the ventilation is, as a rule, more satisfactory when a single room contains all the usual necessary fixtures (including a water-closet) in addition to the bath-tub.

In a small house, the water-closet bowl serves quite well as a slop-sink although allowing matches and coarser articles to enter the soil-pipe and possibly cause obstructions. That is the only hygienic objection to be offered against such an arrangement. The advantages of simplicity (and of the avoidance of any more fixtures than are actually needed) are so great, that a slop-sink is to be omitted if not especially desired.

Slop-sinks ought to be readily cleanable and have their rims provided with flushing arrangements. They should receive water from separate cisterns. On sinks, as on water-closets, covers are not an aid to health. Such things ought to be kept scrupulously clean. If dirt be present, it must not be covered up. If odors exist, the cause should be sought out and removed.

The fewer special urinals that are introduced beyond what are absolutely needed, the better. It is not well to use ice in these, nor should reliance be put upon camphor or any strongly smelling substance. Water must be used freely with these fixtures. Nothing can supply its place.

Wash-bowls, called "lavatories" by the plumbing trade, should be very simple and of a kind that can easily be kept clean. The overflow pipe is usually made too small and too sharply curved. In it, much filth then lodges, and scientific observers find that it often serves as a culture-field for germs of diphtheria and other diseases. An overflow pipe ought to be as straight as possible and large enough to be seen into with a light.

The most hygienic style of all is the very old-fashioned kind known as a "standing overflow" and indicated by Fig. 52 (on page 338). It is simply a tube (smooth inside and outside) which serves as both plug and overflow. This calls for the peculiar shape of the wash-bowl shown in Fig. 52. Such an overflow cannot well be in the centre of the bowl. The same simple device can be used for bath-tubs. Several manufacturers produce suitable contrivances (which, however, are not necessary) for raising this "standing overflow" out of the outlet where it serves as a basin plug.

There is a showy and convenient overflow contrivance operating in a tube back of the bowl as indicated by Fig. 64. It serves either to plug or to open the pipe (which provides for the overflow from the bowl) by the action of lowering or raising the knob (at the upper part of Fig. 64). This attractive but usually complicated overflow arrangement has been extensively used in recent work. It seems, however, decidedly inferior in hygienic merit to the simpler kinds.

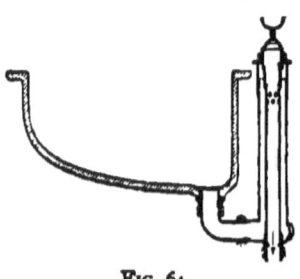
Fig. 64.

The waste-pipe, that carries water off from a wash-bowl or other sink, should be uniform in size throughout, and, like the trap, this pipe usually has a diameter of one and one-half inches. The trap must be just as near to the bowl as is practicable. Thereby, the pipe can be inspected and easily cleaned as far down as the water-seal of the trap.

Water-pipes and sewage-pipes should (owing to the severity of our winter weather) be within and on a warm side of a house, and properly protected against freezing. It is, however, not desirable to have soil-pipes hot.

For **water-pipes,** galvanized iron, although even that is slightly affected by water, is hygienically preferable to lead or brass even if the latter metal be tin-lined. The simplest "ground-key" faucets are the best if not exposed to freezing cold and if made only of good material and guaranteed. Wood-work, or any casing, is undesirable around sinks or other plumbing fixtures. This holds with regard to bath-tubs, which are spoken of on page 61.

Kitchen sinks, pantry sinks and other plumbing fixtures that are used largely by servants need to be of good construction, and as well trapped and carefully attended to as any others. The average kitchen sink may fairly be considered as having more dangerous filth enter it and remain near it than the ordinary water-closet does. The wash-water from vegetables and from various work may introduce many germs of disease into the lower part of the house. Sinks, therefore, should be smooth and free from wood-casing. They ought to be entirely without deep depressions and places, however minute, where filth of any kind can lodge. Earthenware, copper or iron (not galvanized iron) is always to be preferred to wood for sink surfaces. If rubber be used for a mat to cover a marble or other hard draining-board, care must be had to see that this rubber is clean and smooth.

Refrigerators must not be connected directly with drains. If any such connection is to be made, it ought to be entrusted to skilled and reputable workmen who will commit no grave fault in their work. Cess-pools should be banished from all houses. Grease-traps are usually not needed. If traps clog because of the entrance of grease, very strong and hot solutions of crude potash may be poured into the pipe after that has been warmed by boiling water. This strong alkali affords an excellent means of cleansing and, at the same time, it disinfects the trap and fixtures. Other disinfection of house-drainage fixtures is spoken of later, on pages 450 and 451 (in the chapter on Disinfection).

Steam is occasionally applied with great success for disinfecting drainage pipes. It, however, requires especial care in its use, and is not to be employed promiscuously. It acts unfavorably upon the joints of ordinary pipes. Hot water, to be an effective disinfectant, must be *very* hot, as explained in the chapter on Disinfection. Waste-pipes are at times fitted with stop-valves to permit the disinfecting use of steam for a drainage system. Such things add an undesirable complexity. Steam must not be allowed to escape into drainage pipes or sewers.

Plumbing may last for a dozen years without requiring any repairs. Yet it is well as a rule to have the house drainage examined by skilled workmen at least once a year. If they introduce such a strong-smelling substance as peppermint essence into the pipes, or if they force pungent smoke (see page 212) into the closed pipes, any leaks allow these betraying odors to come into the air of the house, and thus defects are recognized. The best time to have plumbing attended to is before the re-occupancy of a house or other vacated building. Rooms should be well cleaned and aired after such work has been done in them.

OTHER DISPOSAL OF HUMAN EXCRETA

"Dry closets" have been extensively used in the schools of some districts, and attempts have been made to introduce the principle elsewhere. The method consists in drawing a current of air up a heated flue and causing this air, before it enters the flue, to have passed over the bowel discharges lying upon a carefully arranged brick floor. This brick floor forms the bottom of a vault for receiving the bowel discharges (and urine) entering through seats above that are arranged very much like the usual privy seats. Air is drawn downward, from the rooms, into this vault when the draught is upward in the chimney. Thus odors are removed and whatever excrement enters the vault is apt to become dried. The parts about being of fire-proof material, petroleum or other inflammable substance can be poured upon the contents of the vault and burned whenever that purifying process be desired.

Such "dry closets" must be considered as decidedly inferior to good water-closets under all circumstances. This was stated on page 99. When back draughts occur, as they appear to do contrary to the design of the construction, *filth may be carried back* into the rooms of the building. This is especially the case in any system which makes use of the foul air (drawn down out of the rooms through *intricate* ventilating flues under the floors) in order to employ it economically for drying the contents of the vaults. Facts seem to show that infectious diseases are caused and spread by reason of the use of such unsanitary devices as the more complicated kinds of "dry closets."

Privy vaults are very commonly used in country districts and even in towns of considerable size. Unless properly constructed and cared for, they may be very offensive. This is because the organic matter, which they receive, decomposes extensively. Accordingly, a single foul privy may develop many cubic feet of gases in a day. Carbonic acid gas is given off in considerable quantities from the contents of privy vaults; yet it is not odorous. The volatile fatty acids, the carburetted hydrogen and certain allied gases produced there in large quantities are extremely offensive, as is also the less abundant sulphuretted hydrogen. Ammonia is usually present in sufficient quantity to be quite evident to the nostrils.

The average privy-vault gases are unhealthful when strong. Hence privies, unless exceptionally well constructed and attended to, should always be twenty feet or more away from any house, and several times as far away if the vault be leaky or open on the sides. They also need some arrangement by which they can be ventilated at the top. A well-arranged flue, from the vault and rising into the air above the roof, will carry off much of the gases of decomposition. Heat, *constantly* maintained by means of a suitably large lamp (or gas flame) safely placed inside this flue, aids ventilation through producing an upward draught. Around the lamp, metal or earthen pipe guards against fire. It is usually not desirable to have this ventilation effected by a flue warmed by the house fires. Privies need to be kept light and well aired.

Privy vaults ought to be made *water-tight*. It is well that—as directed in the very explicit model Bye-laws of the English Local Government Board—their capacity does not exceed eight cubic feet. With us, the great majority of privy vaults are very liable to be leaky, and in many cases are not walled in at all. Hence, they should be down-hill from the house, if possible, and they ought invariably to be so situated that the underground water, which supplies any wells, always flows downward toward the privy and never from any privy toward a well or water supply used for human beings or animals. This all-important rule is very commonly violated in all parts of the country. In prairies or other level regions a privy requires to be one hundred feet or more away from a well. Even at that distance it may be unsafe, especially if the well be not walled in as explained on page 297.

Ignorance and indifference as to these essential points are to blame for the occurrence of most cases of typhoid fever and choleraic and other diarrhœal diseases met in country and town practice. The ordinary contents of privies are, however, not to be regarded as very poisonous. Their presence does not of necessity provoke illness unless germs of harmful disease are diffused from them. So long as the contents are moist, no bacteria escape thence into the air, although, through any existing fault in the ground, they can get into wells. A well-kept privy, if properly located, rarely endangers health in any way.

In the ordinary course of things, the bacteria of typhoid, cholera and other diseases get no further than the vault if they fall in there. After a few days or weeks, the action of ammonia or other chemical substances (especially if acid) that are formed there or may otherwise be present, aided by the potent antagonism of other bacteria present, suffices to destroy the germs of disease. The oxidation caused when large amounts of ashes and other dry porous substances are added, works somewhat toward the same end. Yet abundant fresh air is then needed as well. Since *time* is requisite for these healthful natural agencies to operate, it is obvious that the removal of disease discharges is usually more harmful when these are *fresh* than when they have been standing for some time with the contents of the vault.

When, however, any of the more serious diarrhœal diseases is recognized, or even suspected, and infectious discharges have entered the vault without having undergone complete disinfection, it is desirable to *sterilize* the contents of the vault. For this purpose, two per cent. of crude hydrochloric acid or one per cent. of freshly slaked quicklime should be mixed thoroughly into the contents of the vault. Small amounts sprinkled over the foul matters are probably useless. (See also page 451.)

To *deodorize* (which does not mean that harmful bacteria are necessarily destroyed), sulphate of iron is used. If ammonia be unpleasantly evident in a vault, gypsum may be added to lessen this odor. Where the odor of fatty acids predominates, quicklime effects a deodorization through chemical union. Crude permanganate of potash is an excellent deodorizer, but rather expensive. Chloride of lime is cheaper, and better if fresh. If not much water be allowed to enter a vault, the familiar use of ashes, dry loam or other fine dry porous earth sprinkled liberally over the contents, restricts or removes unpleasant odors, with the occasional exception of the ammonia smell. Dry earth, however, does not destroy bacteria. Carbolic acid does not remove the odor of a vault.

Privy vaults must not be allowed to become overfull, for then disease discharges that enter are found to be more liable to diffuse infection. In thickly settled neighborhoods, the removal of privy contents often causes very unpleasant odors for those near, although such odors in themselves do not necessarily involve any menace to health other than the discomfort of nervous and sensitive people. As already said, the filth removed does not contain the germs of disease, unless *infected* matters have entered. The pneumatic methods of removal and transportation in air-tight wagon-bodies or specially made tuns are an improvement upon the usual primitive methods. The fire of such improved apparatus used for pumping out the contents can be utilized for the consumption of the foul gases.

To test whether privies, cess-pools, etc., connect with wells and are liable to contaminate the water of these, one ounce of the chloride of *lithium* is dissolved in a quart or more of water, and this is poured into the vault or other questionable source of contamination. (See page 298.)

Saprol, a coal-tar product, is used similarly for a more simple, ready test. Its strong odor and taste (like naphthaline or illuminating gas) cause it to be recognized by its smell, and more readily by its taste, even if only one part be present in a million parts of water.

Modifications of the privy system are employed with the idea of utilizing the manure yielded by human excreta. In some large towns and cities, especially in Great Britain, metal boxes on wheels, or petroleum casks sawed in two and tarred within, or pails of tarred oak with tightly closing, rubber-edged covers (see Fig. 65) are used in place of privy vaults. These (with the cover removed) are kept under the seats. In some places they also receive all the dry refuse from a house.

Fig. 65.

This system is managed in a model manner in Greifswald (Germany). There it is found that the use of mingled streaming water and steam (at a temperature of 235° F.), driven into an empty, inverted pail for two minutes, effectually sterilizes it. A pail that is new and smooth requires less than half that time.

It is necessary to remove the receptacles and their accumulations at frequent intervals. At the same time, empty receptacles are substituted. Various complications are introduced into these systems. They are not inexpensive; while, too, they offer a ready means for the dissemination of infection, unless most carefully managed.

Therein lies a very important defect. Privies would be preferable but for the usual defects of their construction and their consequent greater liability to cause contamination of wells. When offal, garbage, coarse ashes and other household refuse are thrown in, the manure produced is not of much value. Voelcker, who studied the manure question very thoroughly, stated that the theoretical value of night-soil manure at its best is never more than five dollars a ton unless superphosphates or other fertilizer be added.

All these methods are inferior to good sewer systems and are more liable to endanger health. It is doubtful whether the manure therefrom obtained ever pays for the cost of securing it. Like privies, these devices all fail to provide for house-water, slops, manufactory washings and other fluid nitrogenous waste. This is a great hygienic defect.

There are various methods of treating human excreta by adding chemicals. As an instance, the "alum-blood-clay" process used at Leeds in England may be mentioned. This, like the use of combinations of quicklime and other chemicals in various cities, deserves no further consideration here. All of these are without distinctive merit. They are more adapted for special foreign conditions than for American cities. The Liernur system, used in some parts of the Low Countries of Europe, cannot be recommended for any part of America. A sewage system, even if the location necessitate pumping facilities, is in every way preferable where a sufficient water supply exists.

Earth-closets furnish a very satisfactory means for disposing of excrement under certain conditions, and that without odors arising, if sufficient dry earth be used. Owing to the fact that a sufficient supply of suitable soil cannot usually be furnished cheaply for a large population, the cost is considerable if the system be adopted for cities. If ashes or sand are substituted, the results are less satisfactory. This method does not permit the entrance of watery refuse.

Hence it provides for only a fraction of the waste matters of a community. It is better adapted for a dry region where there is a scanty water supply than for a wet one. It is excellent for camps where all disease discharges are promptly disinfected. The original cost of the earth-closet is small.

The manure value of the compost produced is rather overestimated by the extreme advocates of the earth-closet system. Yet this compost, when no disease discharges are present in it, is excellent for garden use. The danger of the spread of infection is apt to be greater in case of disease germs entering an earth-closet than when well-located and water-tight privy vaults are used, no special means for the disinfection of disease discharges being adopted in either case. When dried, bacteria are not at once destroyed; but are thereby rendered more liable to remain alive and to be diffused than when they are kept moist in contact with other, hardier bacteria as is the case in the ordinary privy vault.

Earth-closets can be very near or even within a house without any objectionable odors existing. It is not advisable that they remain inside of a house. So effective a deodorizer and absorbent is suitable dry loam, that it makes an excellent material for strewing in bed-pans. Yet discharges, that enter these, always need subsequent sterilization if the disease be infectious. If the used soil of an earth-closet be suspected of having received disease discharges, it ought to be treated with great caution and in no case to be employed again. Ordinarily, when it has received only the discharges of healthy people, the dry earth can be used over and over again; for after a number of months the matters removed from the receptacles are found to have become converted into garden mould appearing quite like the original earth used.

Earth-closets require, for each individual using them, a daily allowance of from two to five pounds of dried loam or heavier, clayey soil without much sand in it. Peaty soil will suffice for the purpose. Vegetable moulds are in general excellent as absorbents in these closets. A special stove or other means of thoroughly drying the earth is needed, and the earth must be kept dry in the closets before use. The coarser particles, stones and twigs must be removed by screening so that only fine earth is used for sprinkling over the excrement deposited in the closets.

Earth-closets can be efficient and yet very inexpensive to construct. The essential parts in their construction are: (1) A supported seat under which is (2) the removable receptacle for excrement. (3) A holder is needed for fine dry earth, which is to be sprinkled liberally upon the paper and discharges that are thrown in. This holder may be merely a box with a scoop, or it may be a "hopper" with a more or less elaborate arrangement for sprinkling the earth over anything that enters the removable receptacle beneath the seat. Moisture does not as a rule reach the walls of the box used for this latter purpose if proper care be taken to use enough dry earth and if two inches or more of such dry earth are in the bottom of this box when it is put into place for use. Yet it is well that the receptacles for excreta, when of wood, be coated two or three times with asphalt varnish.

All the systems of keeping the discharges with a view of utilizing them for manure are less economical than they seem. The production of salable manure by the conversion of the contents of privy vaults and similar receptacles, even in the systematic and scientific way that this is done in Paris (at La Villette), causes more or less of a nuisance, and is rather expensive. If ashes have been added, the manure value of the product is slight.

Wherever earth-closets, or receptacles of any sort, are used for the solid waste, care must be taken that the house water and other liquid waste is not disregarded and carelessly allowed to soak into the ground near the house.

Cesspools or other vaults must be made perfectly tight. Wherever these are used, especial attention must be given to preventing all contamination of the water supply.

A good system of sewers with an abundant water supply is hygienically preferable to any other method, when it is a question of caring for the wastes of a large community. For smaller settlements, the same is true if the construction and maintenance of the sewers are of the very best. Figures recently given by some of our cities appear to show that, when good sewers are once introduced, they provide for the removal of waste matters at a cost much lower than where scavenger fees are made necessary because of the employment of privies and other inferior substitutes for good drainage systems.

A liberal supply of pure water ought to be assured before sewers are introduced. The imposition of restrictions and penalties upon those who use water freely in order to keep their house-drainage pipes and fixtures constantly clean is usually a detriment to health. A community should strive to secure a pure water supply so ample that a lavish use of it is permissible.

DISPOSAL OF GARBAGE AND OTHER SOLID REFUSE

It has been clearly demonstrated that germs of disease are at times abundant in the dirt of our streets. The more this dirt is allowed to increase, the less easy it is for the healthful activity of the sunlight and fresh air to be operative and destroy the germs of disease. Decomposition also takes place in street filth unless that remain very cold and dry. Accordingly, the streets need to be kept very clean. (See page 159.) All decomposable (organic) refuse must be removed from streets and dwellings. Otherwise, diseases of various kinds are more apt to abound and be serious.

All house refuse and manufacturing waste, that will not readily flow off in the drainage systems connecting with the sewers, must also be disposed of very promptly and in a way that will effectually prevent any danger or annoyance. The problem of how to do this most satisfactorily and at the same time economically is often a difficult one. The solution of the question always depends upon the locality.

Use of the ocean, in parts several miles away from shore, for receiving refuse, has been extensively made by the cities of Liverpool, Dublin and New York. In the case of the latter city, about half of the yearly total of somewhat less than two million cartloads of material there deposited in the "dumps" by the street-cleaning and refuse-removing department has, up to the present time, been emptied far out in the open sea. This refuse is towed out in scows.

At time of very unfavorable weather, these scows (especially if of the old, flat style) cannot get out to sea. The matters then accumulate to the annoyance and ill health of all. In any case, the refuse is liable to block up channels and defile distant shores. In the long run, the use of the ocean for receiving this waste is unsatisfactory.

The refuse collected in New York City consists of :—

Ashes,	62 per cent.
Garbage,	12 " "
Street sweepings,	24 " "
Ice and snow,	2 " "

The greater part of these substances could be used for filling in submerged lands which it is desired to reclaim. For the coming seven or eight years at least, the refuse of that city will be utilized for thus making new land.

More than one-third of the average housekeeping refuse is of a sort that will decompose with offensive odors. Burying this is usually an unsatisfactory means of disposing of any very large amount of such putrescent waste. Burning it by specially constructed furnaces is the most satisfactory way to get rid of garbage. Kitchen ranges can be made to accomplish this in a small way. It is cheaper and more convenient, however, to have garbage and street sweepings consumed in large *crematories* or "destroying furnaces" built for this particular purpose.

Garbage-destroying furnaces have been much used in England during the last seventeen years. The continued and increasing employment of these appears there to give highly satisfactory results. In this country, only a limited number of those experimented with are considered successful. Local conditions are important in determining the economic value of such appliances. It is stated that a furnace, costing originally $5,700, disposes of thirty tons of garbage per day and is operated at the cost of only $150 per month. Yet in Buffalo and other cities, this healthful method is reported to have failed for various reasons.

The fact that most of the furnaces used with us are defective has had much to do with the failure to adopt this sanitary method of destroying garbage and other harmful waste. The ordinary furnace is objectionable because, even though otherwise satisfactory, it does not provide for consuming offensive gases. This can constitute a serious defect and may even cause the apparatus to become a nuisance.

Municipalities contemplating the adoption of **crematories** for destroying garbage and street sweepings would do well to consider the healthful results and low cost of the best English garbage furnaces, the cost there being given as even less than from seven to fourteen cents per ton. The economical management of the garbage destroyers at Southampton and at Chelsea (London) is worthy of study, together with the results from others of the forty or more English cities using such admirable methods.

The various British furnaces are to be divided into three classes:—(1) Those burning up only street sweepings and house waste. These can exist in the midst of cities without causing nuisances. (2) Others are used to burn up sewage sludge also. (3) Some places employ furnaces to dispose of all the above and of "night-soil" as well. A chimney 175 feet high is needed for each crematory. Arrangements should be provided at the base of the chimney for burning up the unpleasant smoke, as is done at Ealing (near London), at Bradford and elsewhere.

The **collection** of household waste must be systematic and cleanly, whether done by private agents (as in New Haven, for instance) or by the city authorities. It is best that people keep garbage separate from ashes in the household, as also in the process of collection. In any case, the carts used with the prevalent methods should have covers. A satisfactory way, for a small community at least, is to use closed, galvanized-iron receptacles to be taken away filled and unopened and to be returned after emptying. This adds to the cost. If households do not regularly receive the same receptacles, they must not get any container that has received infected matters without having undergone subsequent disinfection (preferably by steam).

Carcasses of animals must always be under the control of health officers. A penalty should be inflicted upon establishments which do not reveal the fact at once whenever they receive carcasses that have the signs of infectious disease. Carcasses of animals that have had these diseases, notably glanders and splenic fever, are to be handled with great care, owing to danger of infection being communicated from them to human beings as well as to animals. Such carcasses ought to be destroyed at once either by fire, by steaming, or by burying with abundant quicklime. The burying must be very deep and far from any buildings.

When once in the steaming caldron of the rendering establishment, the germs of disease need no longer be feared. By using suitable appliances, which do not much increase the cost of working, the business of utilizing such things is rendered much less of a nuisance than it usually is. Extreme cleanliness should be enforced upon those who manage such things. The closed wagons used for conveying the carcasses of horses and other animals that have died from disease should be especially adapted for the purpose, with large and tight boxes so that no blood or other matters escape during transportation. All manure from such animals must be burned. The use of the apparatus that is shown in Fig. 85 is valuable for disinfecting wagons. (See page 443.)

DISPOSAL OF THE DEAD

When death has resulted from an infectious disease, extreme care ought to be taken to prevent extension of the infection through thoughtless contact of mourners or others with the body or shroud. A few diseases are conspicuously liable at times to be disseminated by such means.

Diphtheria is one of these. It is too often caused by kissing the face of one who has died from that disease. This also, like other diseases of childhood, may be carried from the death-chamber to children and others who have not been near the house. The burial should take place as soon after death as is possible consistent with decency.

The management of funerals seems most satisfactory and capable of being most hygienically conducted when in the charge of large concerns, as is the custom in some cities of continental Europe. These concerns have specially skilled employees. Such people can have had the proper training in the exact steps to take for preventing the spread of infection. They may accordingly be a valuable aid to the restriction of communicable diseases. The suitable measures to be taken with corpses from infectious diseases are explained in the chapter on Disinfection.

The final services are best held in chapels near a cemetery or crematory, where rooms may be arranged for the bodies to lie. In these special rooms, various electrical devices, of extreme sensitiveness, can be adjusted to the body so as to reveal (by bells and indicators) any movement or sign of life whatsoever. These appliances give great relief, at times, to apprehensive friends who consider that sometimes people are buried while life yet remains in the body.

Under ordinary circumstances, the dead body begins speedily to decompose, owing to the presence of bacteria. These multiply rapidly in the organic matters of the body. The conditions there existing after death, favor such microorganic growth. In the beginning, the decomposition bacteria come chiefly from the bowels. Then others enter the body. They develop greatly after the skin has been caused to burst owing to the considerable production of hydrogen, carbonic acid and other gases resulting from the action of the bacteria. After a while, the larvæ of flies and earthworms develop and take a part in the process of organic destruction. Toward the end, the bacteria lessen. The dryer, loamy substance remaining has perhaps chiefly moulds present for a time. This healthful natural process of destruction is obstructed by impervious coffins, which therefore are not to be approved of. The porous and quickly destructible coffins advocated by Mr. Seymour Haden are much to be preferred.

The germs of most infectious diseases almost always have lost their virulence or are dead within a few months of ordinary interment. The few exceptions are mentioned on page 376. The organic matters of the body are usually destroyed within from four to ten years of interment, according to the size of the body and the character of the soil. Other factors, as warmth, dryness and access of air, hasten the process. Yet, for a while, corpses decompose several times as fast if floating in water or if, when buried, they be covered by the water of the ground.

When the decomposition of a body in water has advanced somewhat, it is liable to be arrested or, in rare cases, the tissues change, especially in the skin, into *adipocere*. This is a grayish, odorless, crumbly substance looking like fat or hard wax. Its origin is not well explained. If a corpse that has been kept wet be left to decompose in dry ground, the process then goes on very rapidly.

Great dryness, as prevailing for instance in high altitudes, prevents decomposition. So, too, does very low temperature. Uniform cold, such as that of ice with colder air about it, keeps the tissues largely unchanged even for centuries. Dry warm air, and also cold winds when not damp cause the moisture to leave the body so that bacteria cannot act. Then the corpse becomes dry and crumbly like a mummy. This drying does not necessarily destroy the bacteria as quickly as the usual processes in interment.

Corpses are also to a varying extent preserved from decomposition when death has come from poisoning by sulphuric acid, alcohol, phosphorus and especially when arsenic or corrosive sublimate of mercury has been the means of death. Hence the use of the latter two chemicals for embalming purposes. The process of *embalming* must not be employed except when unquestionably necessary. At times it may be used to disguise a crime.

Cemetery sites should be free from residences. An elevated, dry, porous and quite level plain is excellent for the purpose. There ought to be considerably more than six feet of soil. A sandy loam is best. An admixture of limy soil with it is good. Clay is an objectionable element in the ground above the subsoil.

It ought to be carefully determined how high the ground-water rises. The upper level of this must always be considerably below the six feet or more of earth into which the grave is to be sunk. Subsoil drainage is necessary if the ground-water level seem liable to rise near to the bottom of the graves. Vegetation should be encouraged, both for its beauty and because it disposes of the products of decomposition. There should not be an excess of trees. Those which do not shed their leaves are best. **Ivy for** graves and walls is to be recommended.

Habitations are usually required to be fifty feet or more away from graves. It is not thought proper to have a well within two hundred feet of a grave if the ground-water flows from the grave toward the well. The usual efficacy of the soil in arresting the passage of bacteria is as a rule very great, as indicated on page 3 and elsewhere. Owing to the possible occurrence of flaws in the ground, the above distance is given in order to err on the side of safety.

Tombs and vaults ought not to be used for any but exceptional cases, and never for corpses from infectious diseases. If several bodies are buried at the same time, each should be allowed an area of not much less than fifty square feet of ground surface. Corpses from infectious diseases should have been enveloped in cloths wet with solutions of carbolic acid (1 to 25) or corrosive sublimate (1 to 1,000), to which glycerine has been added.

The question as to the harmfulness of interring a body in the soil of a burying-ground has caused much discussion among thoughtful people. Some allege that air, in the neighborhood of graves, is apt to be contaminated, that the water is there injuriously affected and that the soil is rendered permanently unhealthful. If the precautions above indicated have been observed, these apprehensions are found not to be substantiated. Careful scientific investigations have proved that the dangers of graveyards are in general much exaggerated.

The five feet of dry, loamy soil above the corpse absorbs and beneficially converts most of the gases produced. Their existence is not recognizable or harmful if ordinary care in burial be taken. If the body be disturbed before the above described natural processes, of destroying the organic matter of the body, have run their course, odors may arise and bacteria be scattered abroad.

It is found that the water is not affected for more than a very few feet away from the grave, if the burial be in proper, porous ground. In this country, as in Europe, the water of wells and springs in burying-grounds is usually found, on careful analysis, to be in every respect purer than the average drinking-water that people use with safety. From an average tenement or boarding-house, contamination of water near it is much more liable to result than from any properly managed and suitably located graveyards.

The soil appears to receive the infection in only a very limited way. The activity of various bacteria of decomposition and the presence of gases or the deficiency of oxygen are operative to cause the destruction of the germs of disease. Hence it is found that harmful bacteria die out generally within a few weeks or months after the interment in proper ground. As an exception to this rule, it may be mentioned that the bacilli and spores of the rare disease anthrax (*splenic fever*) can survive at times for even five years. Pasteur has shown this and has explained, too, that earthworms can at times carry the germs of this disease up to the surface of the ground. Hence such cases ought to be buried very deep, and are proper subjects for cremation.

Cases are also reported on good authority where the germs of disease in buried corpses apparently retained their virulence for several years. Schottelius has found that portions of a tuberculous lung were infectious for thirty months after burial. Scholl also relates that cholera bacilli are at times very long-lived when interred. In bones, the dangerous bacteria live much longer than in the softer organs. So, it appears that the bodies of those who have died from infectious diseases ought to be buried deep and with great care, following the precautions indicated here as to choice of proper ground. Such graves must not be opened within *five* years after the interments. Thereby, safety is secured.

It is not generally realized that the domestic and general waste of an average population causes one hundred times as much organic matter to be given into streets, sewers and garbage in a given time as is contained in the bodies of those dying in that period. Mild cases of disease, even, may be highly infectious, and a careless patient having consumption or diphtheria, small-pox, typhoid, cholera or other disease of an infectious nature can be vastly more dangerous than a corpse, especially if proper precautions be taken to prevent disease germs escaping from the body whether to be cremated or buried. When once in the ground, the body can cause no harm if the interment have been rightly managed.

Cremation is much advocated for disposal of the dead. It is very valuable for infectious diseases, especially when they are epidemic and where insufficient burial accommodation exists. On the high seas, corpses from such diseases should be heavily weighted and sunk in deep water at once if they cannot be burned in the vessel's furnace.

Fire is an ideal and æsthetically pure means of quickly destroying all infection and bringing matter back to its original elements. Yet cremation offends the religious and sentimental feelings of some people, and it may furthermore be employed to destroy all evidence of crime in cases of murder (whether by violence or by poisoning). Hence, any suspicion of homicide ought to prevent cremation.

Thus far, cremation is too expensive for adoption by the multitude. Thirty-five dollars is the customary charge in New York State for the mere conversion of the body to ashes. There are other unavoidable expenses to be added.

BACTERIA AND DISEASE

From the invaluable results of scientific observations made during the last fifteen years, we have come to regard that certain minute living organisms possess an extreme importance as causes of various infectious diseases. These disease-producing microörganisms (or microbes) are visible only by means of high powers of the microscope, and nearly all of them are to be classed as *bacteria*. The word "germs" is often specifically used to indicate bacteria.

Bacteria belong in the botanical class called *schizomycetes*. This Greek term signifies that they multiply by *division* of the cell (that each one consists of) into new cells. For this division, the minute protoplasmic cell increases slightly in size. Then it divides into two independent cells which are like the original (parent) cell. This process requires from a few minutes to several hours for its completion. Multiplying thus rapidly, a single individual bacterium can in one day increase to several millions of bacteria if the conditions be favorable.

Good microscopes with strong "dry" objective lenses suffice for recognizing many of these bacteria. To distinguish definitely the smaller and less distinct forms, *oil-immersion* objectives magnifying a thousand times or more are necessary, and the stage of the microscope requires to be provided with an Abbé condenser.

Using hanging drops (of heat-sterilized water or beef-tea as illustrated on the next page) we observe that bacteria differ greatly in their mobility. The bacillus of typhoid, for example, moves about very vigorously. Others may even show no motion at all.

To study this movement and also the developmental activity of bacteria, we commonly use a microscope slide having in the middle a slight hollow. (See Fig. 66 ; *A*, face view ; *B*, side view.) On the under side of a thin film

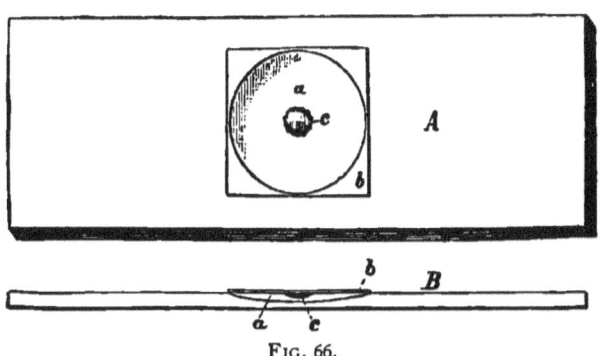

Fig. 66.

of "covering glass" (*b*), which rests over this hollow (*a*) in the slide, is a *hanging drop* (*c*) of sterilized beef-tea or water. Into this liquid, a few bacteria are introduced by the tip of a previously sterilized platinum wire that is fixed in a glass rod. (See page 381.)

In order to measure the size of bacteria, we employ an accurately marked and tested glass plate in a special one of the eye-pieces of the microscope. By a delicate machine, the markings on the glass plate are exactly ruled so that each corresponds to a definite distance on the field where the object is seen. As a standard of measurement for these microörganisms, we commonly take the thousandth part of a millimeter. This is called a micromillimeter or *mikron*. In scientific works it is usually indicated by the Greek letter μ. It is nearly equivalent to $\frac{1}{25000}$ inch (or one-eighth of the size of a red blood corpuscle), since 25.4 millimeters make one inch.

ERY-SIPELAS × 650. FIG. 67.

A *mikron* (μ), then, is the standard for measuring the size of the smaller forms of microörganisms. Some bacteria, among others

PUS-COCCI × 1400. FIG. 68.

the round ones that cause erysipelas (see Fig. 67) and also several of the kinds that cause suppuration (see Fig. 68), are less than one mikron in size. Others, like the bacilli of typhoid fever (see Fig. 74), are perhaps two or three mikrons long and about one-third as broad. The bacilli of tuberculosis are slender and vary from 1½ to 4½ mikrons in length. They may at times be longer, but are always slender. (See Fig. 80, where some of them are represented as unusually thick.)

The forms of bacteria may change somewhat under various influences. But the shapes are typical, as a rule. For purposes of description, we speak of them as :—

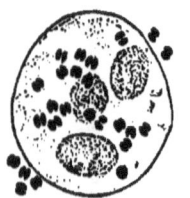

GONOCOCCI AND PUS-CELL
× 1400.
FIG. 69.

(1) *Bacteria* (a general term not indicating size or shape).

(2) *Micrococci.* These are round (or roundish) bacteria. They may occur singly and isolated, or may be in pairs (*diplococci*, Figs. 69, 70); in fours (*sarcina*); in chains (*streptococci*, Figs. 67, 68, *D*); in bunches (*staphylococci*, Fig. 68, *C*); in masses (*zoöglea*), etc.

(3) *Bacilli.* A single one is called a bacillus. These are *rod-shaped* bacteria, their length being greater than their breadth. (See Figs. 71, 74, 75, 78, 79, 80.) Some varieties are only slightly longer than broad, thus seeming almost like those of class 2. In general, the older they are, the longer they become. Very many are several times as long as they are broad. It is important to notice whether their ends are rounded or square. Some show fine, hair-like processes on their outside. Some have bulging ends. (See Fig. 78.) Most bacteria are straight. A few are curved. Conspicuous among these are the characteristic "comma bacilli" of Asiatic cholera. (See Fig. 75, *B*.)

(4) *Spirilla*, or spiral-shaped bacteria. [To designate an individual, the word "spirillum" is used.] This is the shape produced when a number of the curved comma bacilli of *cholera* (see Fig. 75, *A*, page 411) are joined together end to end, as occurs under certain conditions of their culture. There are several varieties of spiral forms; but, by their microscopic appearances and by culture methods, the others can be distinguished from the harmful kind that is associated with Asiatic cholera.

(5) *Spores* occur in many kinds of bacilli as round or oval appearances (see the dots in Fig. 71), often with enlargement. Spores appear to have a relatively resistant membrane about them; for they stain much less readily than the simple bacterial forms, when the usual aniline pigments are employed for coloring

them. Spores refract light strongly and are recognized under the microscope as rather brightly shimmering round or oval dots inside of the bacilli. At times, also, they can be seen in quantities by themselves when the bacillus that has held them is dead and wasted.

Spores are capable of developing into bacteria like those from which they originated. The importance of these, or rather of the forms that exist within bacilli (*endospores*), is due to the fact that the spore-bearing forms of bacteria are more resistant (than ordinary kinds) to various disinfectant agents.

Bacteria thrive best in organic fluids, notably in beef broth, in prepared blood serum and in milk. They also grow luxuriantly upon the surfaces of meat and various animal and vegetable substances.

Potato surfaces are a very important means of cultivating most kinds of bacteria. After a bit of potato is cleaned, it is put into a broad test-tube (with cotton at the bottom to hold moisture). Then the top is plugged with cotton. (See Fig. 72. from Emmerich and Trillich.)

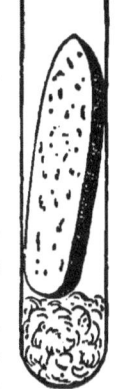

Fig. 72.

This tube is then steamed for *more than an hour* to kill the hardy bacteria of the soil that are with all potatoes. It is usually necessary to steam the tube again within the next day. All the germs of any kind that may be there are thus killed. The cotton plug permits air to pass, but allows no microörganisms to get through into the tube, at least till after several weeks, if it be kept quite dry.

If we then carefully touch the potato surface with only one kind of bacteria, that kind alone will grow there. For the purpose of introducing only the desired kind, we use a piece of platinum wire less than two inches long, and fixed in a glass rod seven inches long. This wire must have just been passed through a flame (and allowed to cool). The flame destroys all life that may have been on the wire. The above-described potato cultures (especially if slightly *acid*) will even grow the tubercle bacilli.

If we solidify beef broth by the addition of about one-tenth its weight of gelatine or considerably less of other cohesive substance (such as *agar* or Iceland moss) we secure thereby an excellent solid substance (*nutrient gelatine*) for the growing of bacteria. The combination of beef-tea and gelatine, made neutral, filtered clear and sterilized by steaming, affords the most useful of all means for *isolating* various kinds of ordinary bacteria. The bacilli of tuberculosis and some others will not grow on this. For such kinds, stiffened blood serum or agar jelly with glycerine usually suffices. Some kinds grow best when air is excluded. (See next page.)

Into a test-tube of sterilized *nutrient gelatine* (when softened) we introduce, by a sterilized platinum wire or otherwise, a minute drop or particle of whatever we wish to test. A drop of this softened gelatine may be still further diluted by adding it to another tube of gelatine and then even still further diluted if desired. The gelatine is next poured upon cool plates or shallow dishes of glass that have previously been sterilized by heat. This fluid gelatine, with whatever bacteria we have introduced, is there allowed to cool and thus to become solidified. All care is taken to prevent the entrance of germs of any kind from the air.

Each of the single bacteria is thus more or less *isolated* in the gelatine. This " culture medium " proves very nutritious for bacteria (because of the beef-juice and other organic matters present). Hence it enables the microscopic individual germ to multiply (within two or more days) so as to make distinguishable dots, spots, etc., of various peculiar appearances and colors and containing perhaps millions of single bacteria. These are called *colonies*. Those characteristic of cholera are represented in Figs. 76 and 76a on page 411.

From a separate (*isolated*) one of these colonies, we get a *pure culture* by carefully touching our sterilized platinum wire to it and then touching that to a protected potato surface as shown in Fig. 72. If we similarly run the needle (with a few of the bacteria on it as *seed*, so to speak) into some of our stiffened (sterile) nutrient gelatine that is in the lower part of a test-tube as shown by

FIG. 73.

the dark lines in the middle of the lower half of Fig. 73 (from Hueppe), the bacteria introduced multiply there. In that figure, the gelatine in the right-hand tube is represented as liquefied by the vital activity of the bacteria introduced. In the left-hand tube, the gelatine is not at all liquefied. The appearances differ according to the variety of bacteria and afford an important means of recognizing different kinds. Those characteristic of cholera are given in Fig. 77, page 411.

The harmful bacteria are usually by far the most delicate as regards their necessary food and other conditions of subsistence. Many of the harmless varieties can increase and thrive upon a very scanty food supply. Being hardier, as a rule, the ordinary bacteria that produce decomposition live where many of the disease-producing kinds perish from lack of food or of other favoring conditions.

There is also more or less *strife* among bacteria. It is found that certain very harmful varieties, such as for instance the germs of typhoid and probably those of cholera, do not long survive when they have entered a foul sewer or cesspool or when they are diffused through water abounding in bacteria of various kinds. When in pure water or otherwise free from any special destructive influence, these pernicious varieties can live longer than when antagonistic bacteria (or suppressive chemical or physical agencies) are acting upon them.

Some bacteria grow either with or without air being present. A number thrive only when little or no oxygen is present. They are called *anaërobic* bacteria. Some of these cause fermentative processes (somewhat as yeasts do). All varieties that live without air, seem to need (as nutriment) grape-sugar or other food substances that yield up a little **oxygen.** Numerous bacteria partake of part of the characteristics of the above. The great majority of bacteria are classed as *aërobic*—which means that they cannot develop except in the presence of the ordinary, oxygen-bearing air.

Bacteria thrive best in darkness or in the absence of

strong daylight. Light restricts or destroys, after a while, most all of the disease-producing varieties if abundant fresh air also be present. Direct sunlight acting upon bacteria exposed to fresh air, destroys them (or at least the common disease-producing ones) in a few hours or days. Its healthful influence is therefore to be employed in houses, on clothing and especially upon all objects and places where infection may have entered. The great hygienic value of sunlight and fresh air merits repeated emphasis.

When **moisture** is absent, bacteria do not multiply and cause decomposition or disease. Some bacteria perish upon drying. The cholera bacilli, for instance, are very sensitive to dryness. Yet they are less so than Koch at first stated.

Very many bacteria can remain alive in our severest **cold** weather. The ice and snow of our dirty streets abound at times in living bacteria. The freezing temperature keeps them from increasing; accordingly, if that degree of cold (or nearly that) be continued without intermission, it prevents decomposition and the other effects of microörganic life. When such cold lessens, the vitality of the bacteria may become renewed. Certain varieties appear to thrive at a temperature only a few degrees above the freezing point. As a rule, bacteria flourish best at or near the normal temperature of the human body ($98.6°$ F.).

When the temperature is raised somewhat, certain bacteria succumb. Mild heat weakens them in many cases and reduces their virulence. A temperature above $140°$ F., if maintained for an hour or more, destroys many, but not all, of the harmful varieties. In order to be certain that all are killed, a higher heat is necessary, as will be explained later. **Moist** heat, as of hot water or steam, is more destructive of microörganic life than is dry heat, both kinds being of the same given temperature.

Disease-producing bacteria cannot remain alive in water

kept at the boiling temperature for ten minutes. This statement comprehends all varieties, even the spore-bearing forms of splenic fever (anthrax) bacilli. The majority will perish long before the water, in which they chance to be heated, has reached the boiling temperature. Momentary heating in water or milk at the boiling point kills the bacilli of tuberculosis.

Yersin has shown that a temperature of from 160° to 175° F. quite surely kills the germs of tuberculosis if the heat be kept up for ten minutes. Forster has recently demonstrated that moist heat at 140° F., if maintained for one hour, destroys all tuberculosis germs that may be in expectorations or in milk treated by this degree of heat. The bacilli of cholera and typhoid are still more sensitive to heat. These facts are mentioned as being of importance in explaining the great practical value of *Pasteurization*.

Pasteurization consists in the partial or complete sterilization of a liquid by means of heating it to a temperature considerably below that of boiling water. A temperature of from 158° to 176° F. is usually employed. After this heating, the fluid is rapidly cooled to 54° F. or still lower. This cooling is to insure that no considerable increase, if any, can take place among the hardier decomposition bacteria that may have withstood this heating. The heat, however, can be relied upon to have killed such disease germs as might otherwise be present.

Milk of doubtful origin, for instance, is by this process rendered fit for immediate use, and yet does not suffer the coagulative, disintegrative and other undesirable changes that occur when it is heated to a higher temperature. It is well, however, for those who are not especially skilled, to beware of using too low a heat for the purpose of destroying disease germs.

Heat, therefore, especially when *moist*, is a most valuable means of destroying all microörganic life. Yet in utilizing this fact for annihilating the germs of infectious disease by employing this agent in order to *disinfect* them, the number of minutes allowed for effectual action of the heat is to be counted only from the time when a suitable degree of high heat shall have penetrated to even the remotest parts of the garment or other infected object.

Steam-heat used in a disinfecting apparatus, as explained in the pages treating of Disinfection, must accordingly be maintained for from ten to thirty minutes. Yet infected cloth that is kept in boiling (or even hot) water for a much shorter time will probably be found to have no living disease germs upon it. The same principle, that adequate heat must penetrate to the remotest and *innermost parts* in order to be effective, has been emphasized in speaking of cooking food. (See pages 221 and 254.)

Chemical agents are, to a very varying extent, effective in destroying or influencing the activity of bacteria. Unlike moulds, bacteria and amœbæ do not thrive when weak acid is present. Strong acids destroy all life. *Sulphuric* acid is considerably more potent than *hydrochloric* acid in this respect. Yet either of them, if present in the strength of 1 part to 400 parts of water, will restrict the activity of any of the germs of serious disease.

To effect rapid destruction of bacteria, the acids must be quite strong. Thus, either sulphuric acid or hydrochloric acid kills the germs of suppuration, of wound infection or of erysipelas in five minutes if those microörganisms be for that time exposed to contact with either of these acids of the strength of 1 part in 10 parts of water. One-tenth of that strength suffices to kill the bacilli of cholera, typhoid fever and splenic fever in the same time.

Other acids differ greatly in their efficacy as destroyers of bacteria. *Carbolic acid* is frequently used; for it does not corrode steel and other metals to any extent, and its odor and taste tend somewhat to prevent accidental poisoning from its use. If a solution of this be added to an equal bulk of typhoid discharges, it must have a strength of five per cent. A strength of at least two per cent. is required in order to destroy the bacilli of typhoid fever in five minutes. Cholera germs are found to be four times as sensitive as this. Typhoid bacilli seem comparatively sensitive to ammonia.

For the various round bacteria (*cocci*) of septic and infective nature (causing surgical and other wound complications) carbolic acid solutions need to have a strength not much, if any, less than two per cent. When this acid is of inferior quality, the strength must be greater. Loeffler's experiments on diphtheria showed that a two per cent. solution of carbolic acid in water was not sure to kill the characteristic bacilli of diphtheria instantly. When, however, one-third of the water of such a solution is replaced by alcohol, a two per cent. solution is quite capable of serving for this purpose.

Salicylic acid is another efficient disinfectant acid. A solution of 1 part of this in 1,000 parts of water kills the bacteria of suppuration and of disease processes in general within five minutes. Although quite valuable against various other bacteria, it is not so against all. *Boric* acid is less powerful as a complete strong disinfectant. Yet in one per cent. solution, it prevents the development of bacteria. For soaking the nipples of nursing bottles, a three per cent. solution is used. *Borax* is only one-third as strong. *Creosote* is an efficient, though costly, disinfectant. If a solution of this have a strength of 1 to 500, it will destroy, in five minutes, the germs of cholera, typhoid and some other diseases when they are exposed to it. *Chloride of lime* and *quicklime* are also very useful as disinfectants and will be spoken of in treating of Disinfection. Ammonia is a weak disinfectant.

Mercury, in the form of its soluble salts, deserves especial mention more than any of the numerous other chemicals used. It combines cheapness and great potency. Whenever such salts as either *corrosive sublimate* or *cyanide of mercury* be used, the label "*Poison*" must invariably be affixed; for these valuable disinfectants are dangerous if carelessly handled.

To have their fullest disinfectant effects, these mercury salts should be used in the strength of one-tenth of one per cent. (one-half grain to one ounce). If they be much diluted, as for eye-washes, the danger of poisoning may be absent. Thus, when corrosive sublimate is used in the strength of 1 to 20,000, an eight-ounce bottle of the solution contains about one-fifth grain of the salt, or less than a poisonous dose. It is well, however, to add a little harmless coloring matter to all such solutions and to label them carefully in order that they be not mistaken for water.

Cotton-wool and various dense, fine fabrics, when no moisture is present, can for a varying length of time hold back bacteria. Yet air can pass through. This property is often utilized (in addition to the laboratory use mentioned on page 381) for purifying air by mechanically filtering out its fine dust and germs. If considerable pressure be used, bacteria may readily be driven through this cotton. Screens used for filtering air in this way work more effectively when water flows over them as indicated on page 205, or when sprays are skilfully used, since bacteria do not fly off from surfaces that are thoroughly moist.

Any very fine substance can mechanically restrict bacteria. Thus, porous soil, porous baked clay, infusorial earth, asbestos and various membranes, while allowing the passage of air or water and other fluids, will more or less completely hold back bacteria, for a time at least. Impermeable layers of any substance will not allow them to pass. Fat or oil obstructs their passage.

Bacteria occur almost everywhere. Innumerable millions of bacteria are in the upper layers of the ground, also in rivers and other waters. They abound in the air, especially when it contains much unclean dust. Nearly every ordinary object has them upon it and at times in its substance. The character of those present in any case depends to a varying extent upon the nature of the object considered and what it has last been in contact with.

Of all bacteria that are of hygienic interest, the great majority tend to produce either *oxidation* or *nitrification*. It has been indicated, in speaking of sewage, that, when rightly managed, bacteria are invaluable scavengers and the natural agents for the resolution of waste organic matters into their elements. Without microörganisms, decomposition of such substances cannot take place. Any substance that is wholly without bacteria (or related microörganisms, such as yeasts and moulds) cannot putrefy or ferment. In some cases, several varieties of microörganisms work together to effect these processes.

Only very few kinds of bacteria are known to act upon starch. Yet many varieties can cause milk to "change," organic acids and carbonic acid being produced from the sugar of the milk. Various bacteria, that destroy albuminous substances and produce lower chemical compounds by the more or less complex process of decay, give off unpleasant gases in this process. This explains the odor noticed when the organic matter of the teeth or of any other part of the body is undergoing decomposition. Without bacteria, this decay does not take place.

The manifestation of bacterial activity with the usual production of unpleasant odors may be upon the outer surface of the body and especially in the folds of the skin, or it may take place within the body. If food be decomposing or fermenting in the intestine, gases are then given off, manifesting themselves usually as flatulency.

Because most bacteria are apparently harmless, it is not wise to reason that their presence in the digestive tract is desirable. The fewer living bacteria our food and drink contain, the better for us. The digestive potency of bacteria is very trivial compared with that of the healthy digestive juices. These microörganisms produce *indol*, *skatol*, fat acids and other undesirable and absorbable gaseous products which can cause disturbance when indigestible foods linger to ferment in the digestive tract.

Ptomaïnes, leucomaïnes, toxines, etc., are organic chemical (alkaloidal) bases produced by the action of some bacteria acting upon and in various albuminous matters. Occasional cases of serious poisoning occur when these highly poisonous substances chance to have developed in milk that is used in its raw state or employed for making ice-cream. With cheese, meat and sausages, such poisons may also enter the system and cause poisoning as manifested by vomiting and purging with irritation of the stomach and bowels and also by various intoxication symptoms.

Most bacteria are harmless. The immense majority of all microörganisms that are upon and about us are presumably not harmful so far as their capacity for distinct injury to the health of human beings is concerned. Most of them thrive only upon dead organic matter. These are called putrefactive (or *saprophytic*) bacteria. Some varieties of disease bacteria thrive only in living animals and are called *parasitic*. A few seem to flourish only in human beings, just as other kinds are limited to the tissues of certain species of lower animals. Many of the varieties of bacteria that produce disease can thrive both in living tissues and also upon dead organic matter. Such bacteria are classed as *optional parasites*.

The bacteria that can cause disease, when in their parasitic activity they have entered into the system of a human being or a lower animal, must usually be present in considerable numbers in order to cause appreciable symptoms. If a small number of the bacilli of typhoid, of tuberculosis, of cholera, etc., enter with water, milk or otherwise into the average healthy human stomach, for instance, they are presumably destroyed there. This is because bacteria do not thrive in the presence of any considerable amount of acid such as is contained in the normal stomach juice. They usually require neutral or mildly alkaline substances for maintaining their vitality and for growing.

If, however, there be a slight catarrh or other injury of the mucous membrane of the stomach and intestines, or if a similar unhealthy condition exist upon the breathing surface of the lungs, such a condition may allow harmful bacteria to enter the system. They can also enter readily by wounds upon the skin or upon other surfaces. It is not probable that they enter through sound surfaces to any notable extent.

When only a few bacteria get into the system, they are probably destroyed by the serum of the blood and by other body elements. If, on the other hand, very many enter, they are liable to increase and cause disease, especially when the system is "run down" or in an enfeebled condition. In case the person invaded is exceedingly susceptible and there are very many harmful bacteria present, they overwhelm and conquer the body forces.

Death can then result if the microörganisms be virulent and of a fatal kind, while at the same time the system invaded is unable to resist. The fatal issue is preceded by symptoms more or less characteristic of the disease to which the particular microörganisms are peculiar. In most cases, the invading bacteria produce illness of varying seriousness, but not fatal. Deteriorated general health, as above said, renders the system less capable of resisting these parasitic germs of disease. The especial importance of sound health, when one is exposed to infection, is therefore obvious.

It is not the mere presence of even very large numbers of bacteria that causes the severe symptoms which result in case an infectious disease has invaded the system. The cause of the symptoms lies rather in the noxious influence of various **organic poisons** *that these harmful bacteria produce* when they are living in and upon the body tissues. In diphtheria, for instance, the peculiar bacilli that cause the disease are localized usually in the outer layers of the tissues of the throat and are not often found at all in the blood. Yet the poison, that these microörganisms there produce, enters the system and causes very serious general and special symptoms, including the unique paralysis of diphtheria.

These poisons can be isolated chemically from cultures of some kinds of bacteria. They can then produce the symptoms peculiar to the bacteria from which they were derived. If preserved in glycerine, oil or in other suitable way, they can retain their full virulence for years.

The exact character of the peculiar poisons produced by disease bacteria in a susceptible, infected subject is as yet only partially known. They appear to vary somewhat with the degree of vitality of the bacteria and with the nature of the "soil" in which they grow—that is, in which of the organs of the body the harmful bacteria are located. It is assumed that the varying severity of different cases of the same disease is largely dependent upon the fluctuating intensity of virulent capacity on the part of the causative germs.

Bacteria become weakened or "attenuated" at times, but can renew their vigor under favorable conditions. Thus, cholera bacilli are often found to attack the first case or cases, occurring in an epidemic, with less severity than subsequent ones manifest. Yet the bacilli from one of the milder cases (called *cholerine*) are capable of inducing the most malignant form of cholera in another person. In diphtheria and other diseases the most virulent attack can at times result upon infection from a mild case.

Animals and also human beings differ greatly in their **susceptibility** to the influence of disease germs. Cholera, typhoid fever and a few other diseases are very dangerous for human beings, yet they are not so for any animals. On the other hand, some diseases attack only certain animals and not mankind at all. *Tuberculosis*, which kills a large percentage of the human race, is also exceedingly fatal to cattle and considerably so to swine. The latest researches tend to establish the fact that the tuberculosis of poultry is due to the same cause as in human beings. Sheep are not very susceptible to this disease, and goats almost never have it. Hence mutton and goat's milk (and flesh) are not so liable, as pork, beef and cow's milk, to convey the infection of tuberculosis.

Negroes are comparatively insusceptible to yellow fever. Malaria affects them much less than it does white people. Syphilis is also a less severe disease among negroes. On the other hand, they are more liable to die if attacked by pneumonia or other infectious lung diseases. Various races and individuals among human beings and lower animals are less liable to become infected than are others.

The cause of the more or less complete **immunity** noticed in different races and individuals has been discussed and disputed over in very many and very voluminous monographs. But no general agreement has yet been reached. To sum up that which is most probable out of all the divergent theories, it may be said that the recognized immunity appears to depend chiefly upon some *chemical* condition of the system, which condition in some cases is constant and permanent, while in others it is changeable and fluctuating. The quality of the blood serum seems of great importance in controlling the immunity. Some few regard the white blood-cells as very powerful agents in annihilating disease germs that may enter the system (*phagocyte theory*). Such may be the case in a limited way. Yet certain kinds of disease germs can multiply even within the white blood-cells.

Susceptibility to infectious diseases is lessened by some conditions and increased by others. Perfect health is a valuable means of strengthening the system against the invasion of disease. Hunger and fatigue make one generally more liable to receive an infection. Various chemical substances, usual or unusual, that may be present in the blood influence the susceptibility to infection. For instance, the presence, in the system, of a sufficient amount of quinine, or of certain substitutes for this potent drug, is a very reliable preventive of the various symptoms of malaria.

With a large number of the infectious disorders, it is found that among those who are susceptible to a certain disease, and hence acquire it when exposed to the infection, *a second attack is very rare.* The system, in the case of those who have had the disease, has somehow lost its liability to receive the infection.

Small-pox is one of these diseases which a person very rarely has a second time. With this particular disease, it has for many hundred years been recognized in the Orient that local inoculation with matters from one of the fresh pustules of small-pox produces a very mild case of the disease which causes the person thus inoculated to be freed from all danger of a subsequent attack.

Vaccination, however, is a great improvement over this means of averting very serious attacks of small-pox. Nearly a century ago, it was discovered that inoculation of a cow with human small-pox virus produced, on the animal, a very mild pustular disease, said also to have occurred independently in cattle and horses, and called *vaccinia* or cow-pox. Taking matter from one of these fresh cow-pox pustules and inoculating human beings with it, it was found by Jenner that people thus "vaccinated" secured immunity from danger of small-pox.

In nearly all cases, this immunity continues for a period

of at least twelve years after the inoculation. (See page 423.)

Impressed by the results of vaccination against small-pox, numerous investigators have sought similarly to find equally efficacious preventives of other infectious diseases. Pasteur's genius enabled him first to find means of attenuating the infectious elements of various diseases such as e. g. *rabies* (canine madness, hydrophobia) the mortality from this being reduced fifty times or more by use of the " attenuated virus " derived from a series of inoculations in rabbits. Against plague, cholera and certain other diseases the method has been skilfully elaborated by Haffkine and others, so that wholly impartial judges acknowledge the merits of the methods. Among domestic animals an immense saving of life has been effected by Pasteur's specific inoculations against splenic fever and other devastating infections.

Antitoxine treatment has been developed more or less successfully for the prevention of nearly all infectious diseases, including yellow fever and suppurations. It is akin to the Pasteur method; but instead of employing like that an attenuated bacterial poison directly or a local infection mitigated by preliminary inoculations, it uses antidotal products evolved by the cells of an animal especially inoculated with the bacterial products of a given disease. It was early recognized that the harmful influence of disease bacteria depended on *toxines*, the poisonous substances produced by bacteria in their growth; and when this occurred in the body the result was the fever, weakness and peculiar symptoms due to the specific bacteria. Later it was recognized that, in the blood of those who withstood a poisoning by bacteria antidotes occur in the form of the so-called *antitoxines*. It was shown that the organism immune against certain diseases, e. g. cholera or typhoid, contains antidotal substances capable of destroying and dissolving up the bacteria of these diseases. Diphtheria is, among us, the most notable of the diseases alleviated by such *isopathic* treatment (to use Behring's term). Accordingly the preparation of the specific remedy may be explained briefly, since other curative serums are prepared in a similar way.

Antidiphtherin. This remedy is derived from the blood serum of strong, healthy horses. In a hygienically clean stable, under expert inspection, each horse receives an injection of abou 1 c.c. of a filtered, strong, alkaline bouillon culture (toxine) of pure diphtheria bacilli, its strength being determined from its virulency upon guinea-pigs. Every week or so a larger amount is carefully injected. After about twelve weeks, a large amount of the remedial serum is obtained by bleeding antiseptically. A preservative may be added. Guinea-pigs serve for testing the potency of the serum. Its strength is expressed in " units," one unit being defined as ten times the quantity of serum needed for immunizing a 250 gramme guinea-pig that has received subcutaneously ten times as much of the *toxine* as would kill it if not immunized. The stronger and purer the serum the better. It is usually dispensed in small phials. Each c.c. ought to represent from 100 to 500 units. It is administered subcutaneously in doses of from 1000 to 3000 (or more) units, according to the case. The more promptly it is given, the more effective it is. One-tenth the curative dose suffices to protect for from three to eight weeks against the infection.

Most physicians regard this treatment as of great value both for curing and preventing diphtheria. Yet a few skilled observers of large experience discredit it and even claim that it does more harm than good, irrespective of the rashes and other effects ascribable to the use of serum from the horse, alleging that the decreased mortality and milder symptoms generally reported by those using antidiphtherin are owing to the fact that the disease has in the last decade been of a less severe type than formerly. Yet statistics are strongly in favor of the prompt use of this preventive serum

INFECTIOUS DISEASES

INFECTIOUS diseases unquestionably cause more than a third of all deaths. A much larger proportion than a third of all cases of more or less serious illness would be averted if ideal hygienic precautions were everywhere adopted. Practically, the carrying out of adequate measures to prevent the extension of communicable diseases is not always possible. This is especially because of the fact that a long period of teaching is necessary before the immense value of such healthful measures is realized.

The progress of popular education in the all-important truths of sanitary science is slow; but it must in the end effect most gratifying benefits. Without receptivity on the part of those whom they should guide in matters of health, any labors of physicians and other scientific teachers and workers can achieve only very limited practical results. Happily, every decade shows great improvement in these respects.

At times we are met with assertions by sciolists who claim that, by restricting disease and prolonging life as well as making it more comfortable and secure, we of necessity interfere with natural processes and perpetuate the weakly and degenerate. To the trained scientific observer, the fallacy of such arguments is very obvious in the light of statistics as well as of the facts of history. These demonstrate the unquestionable supremacy of precisely those races and nations that, if not especially favored by nature, pay most attention to preventing disease and improving in every way the welfare of their people.

Attention must also be directed to the fact that infectious

diseases do not attack those alone whom we by any usual standard can class as weakly. Small-pox, typhoid and yellow fever, for instance, do not inevitably single out for their invasion the races and individuals that are least worthy of a high place in the records of physical prowess or mental achievement.

Even such filth diseases as typhus and cholera have during the past year killed people of the highest social and intellectual rank. It is unwise to tolerate the diseases of degraded people. These diseases can escape from their usual barriers and become diffused everywhere unless a proper guard and constant warfare be maintained against them.

Like tubercular consumption, nearly all other infectious diseases may invade any abode from that of the greatest ruler to that of the lowliest, bringing death or lasting enfeeblement.

Death is not all that is to be feared from these preventable diseases. Even if recovery take place, it may be only partial: the impaired health that follows may at times be worse than death.

Furthermore, the time wasted in disease means an enormous economic loss to the commonwealth when disease interferes with the activity of any of the productive classes of the population. This material detriment, to the community that does not do its utmost to restrict and suppress preventable diseases, can be excessive.

Comprehensive and accurate statistics make it appear that nearly three weeks (or, say, twenty days) is the duration of the average serious illness, not to consider any subsequent feebleness and lessened capacity for the best work and usefulness. German authorities infer from careful study that thirty-four cases of more or less serious illness occur for every death registered. In America, the number is probably greater than this. Statistics show that the fever death-rate in England is at present not much more than one-third of what it was there twenty years ago, before the introduction of modern methods of scientific cleanliness and hygienic precaution.

Not to take advantage of such overwhelmingly significant figures, let it be supposed that in the case of a given population, ordinary efforts toward the restriction of communicable diseases bring about only a limited improvement. Say that, for instance, to borrow the illustration of Prausnitz, in a laboring population of 100,000, the number of deaths from all such diseases is lessened by only one per thousand of the population. This means that 100 fewer deaths occur among these producers in one year.

Accepting the above postulates, it is clear that even the small improvement indicated means a direct, positive gain to the state of 68,000 days of productive labor. Allowing only $1.50 per day as the value of this labor at its best, and omitting all consideration of the avoidance of outlay for attendance and supplies which would have been necessary for these people in case their illness had not been averted, we have the not inconsiderable saving of $102,000 per year in that population (of 100,000 workers).

Besides the immediate, economic advantages, there must also be considered the increase of welfare and happiness among those dependent upon and devoted to the workers whose liability to suffering or death is lessened by the most intelligent scientific sanitation.

The study of various civilizations, and of peoples who never emerged from barbarism, proves that the lack of intelligent means of averting preventable diseases has always caused incalculable suffering and losses. A disregard of measures for arresting and removing avoidable dangers to health seems always to have impeded the pastoral, mercantile and industrial advancements which are the precursors of all civilized progress.

In any community, a valuable feeling of confidence is secured when all are assured of protection by adequate scientific safeguards against the invasion of infectious diseases. The dread of impending epidemics creates a disastrous stagnation of commercial activity: the panic resulting from even a few cases of a dreaded disease may, for the time being, unnerve or at least disturb nearly everybody.

General Considerations

Infectious diseases (often called *zymotic diseases*) are explained, in the preceding pages, as being attributable to peculiar poisonous influences that have entered the systems of those affected. A great many of these poisons have been demonstrated to be due to vegetable microörganisms, usually *bacteria*. A number of the infectious diseases, such as small-pox, dengue fever, scarlet fever and syphilis, have not yet been shown to be due to a distinct microörganic cause. Yet they are so much like the other infectious diseases in their general character, that they are classed with these. It is expected that definite (but now unknown or very imperfectly understood) microörganisms will eventually be shown to be necessary elements in the causation of each of these diseases.

When parasites of a purely animal quality, such as for example either the *itch-insect* or the *trichina* (see page 223), cause diseases, some authorities choose to class these arbitrarily as *invasion diseases* as distinguished from the infectious diseases above spoken of as due to vegetable parasites. *Malaria* and some forms of *dysentery* are now classed among infectious diseases. They are presumably due to *protozoa* or *amœbæ*. These are low forms of (single-cellular) organisms that are upon the border-line between animal and vegetable life.

It is considered that a disease is due to the influence of a definite, characteristic microörganism if this parasite be constantly present in all cases of the disease in question, and no other microörganism be regularly found there. The certainty is strengthened in case we can demonstrate with a given kind of bacteria, for instance, that the same disease regularly results in animals that have been inoculated with these microörganisms, and that they abound in the tissues of the infected animal.

Miasm is an ancient term which, in view of the increased accuracy of the present time, means less than formerly. It served to indicate a vague, gaseous influence pervading the air, and which was assumed to be very potent in causing disease, but of whose nature nothing definite was known. Now that we realize the great importance of microörganisms as causes of disease and feel certain that these in some form are probably operative even in the infectious diseases of whose exact causation we thus far know little or nothing, the word "miasm" is of less precise significance. Some of the diseases formerly classed as miasmatic (for instance, malaria and typhoid fever) are now definitely known to be due to microörganisms. In so far as *gases* vitiate the air and are liable to *intoxicate* the system, they are to be regarded as very objectionable. They are spoken of in the chapters on Sewers, Lighting and Occupation.

Contagious diseases are those infectious diseases which are conveyed to one individual from another who has the disease or is recovering from it. In some cases, such as hydrophobia and the venereal diseases, there must presumably be immediate contact or the infective matters must be quite fresh. In others, the clothing or other objects that have received the infection may retain the contagion in full potency for a considerable length of time. Diphtheria is one of such contagious disorders. Certain contagious diseases, like small-pox and typhus fever, seem much more communicable than others. Yet the prevalent views of their extreme contagiousness are probably exaggerated, if we can judge by careful studies recently made.

Incubation is a term constantly used (in speaking of infectious diseases) to indicate the development (in the body) of the invading bacteria (or other cause of infection) together with the accumulation of the poisonous products of these. It covers the interval beginning with the entry of these causative elements into the body and ceasing when their harmful power has become manifested by producing some of the symptoms of the special infection. The time required, or *period of incubation*, varies greatly according to the nature of the disorder.

In some diseases, only a few hours are required, as with influenza or cholera at times. Usually, these two diseases are from one to three days in developing. Scarlet fever requires less than a week, as a rule. In diphtheria, the limit is usually a week; while in measles, typhoid fever and small-pox the development of the infection takes nearly two weeks, and sometimes longer. Hydrophobia may require many weeks and probably never manifests itself within twelve days after the infecting dog-bite.

As for the **season** of the year when microörganisms of disease most thrive, it may be said that as a rule the *warmer* periods, provided that the heat is not dry and excessive, are most favorable to these. Flies and other insects then abound and tend also to carry disease germs about. Numerous observations made by various scientists during the last decade demonstrate this. Furthermore, it has been shown by Simmonds and others at the time of the epidemic of 1892 that flies carry the infectious germs of cholera from discharges that have not been promptly disinfected. It is probable that the cholera bacilli can remain alive and dangerous for more than an hour when upon a fly moving about. Other bacteria may live still longer under such circumstances.

In summer, more microörganisms are present in the air and upon food than is generally the case in winter. This fact, together with the debilitating effects of prolonged constant heat, explains the great prevalence of diarrhœal diseases in very warm weather. Other non-contagious, infectious diseases also are then relatively more abundant. In summer, the healthful influence of more abundant out-door air is of value as lessening the exposure to disease germs that abound in warmed and over-peopled houses in winter.

INFECTIOUS DISEASES 403

In winter, tropical diseases, such as yellow fever and usually cholera, tend to be lessened to a very great extent or to die out entirely. Cold alone cannot be absolutely relied upon to destroy even these infections. In winter, ordinary disease germs are much less active out-of-doors. Yet warm, close dwellings, especially when thickly tenanted by unclean people, are liable to harbor and be the means of spreading small-pox, scarlet fever, measles, tuberculosis and other infectious diseases that withstand the weather.

"*Colds*" are most frequent in winter, and attack particularly the lung surfaces. Bronchitis is then a very common occurrence. Such disorders facilitate the entrance of the infection of pneumonia and of other lung diseases. These influences affect notably the poorer classes and others who for any reason do not have proper food, fresh air and hygienic guidance. Cleanliness and dryness of the ground and good drainage are, as elsewhere explained, of great importance in restricting the effects of disease germs. Abundant pure air and general cleanliness are invaluable preventives of infection.

Specific Infectious Diseases

Malaria is accompanied by the presence, in the blood, of minute, rounded, crescent-shaped or rosette-like bodies usually inside or outside of the red blood-cells. These are most common at the time of the fever attack. They change their forms and interior appearances under varying conditions of growth and with the variety of malarial attack. After the early stages, they regularly acquire pigment. This one-celled microörganism (discovered in 1880 by Laveran) is called the *plasmodium of malaria*, and is classed among the *parasitic protozoa*. The size is usually from one to two *mikrons* (see page 379) but may be more than four times that. Dock (in Texas), like Italian and other observers, found the smaller forms most common in severe cases. In some mild cases, the microörganisms may be even larger than a red blood-cell. They cannot be cultivated artificially like ordinary bacteria. Hence our knowledge of them is as yet limited. Yet these are to-day regarded as the cause of the symptoms.

Malarial manifestations are very varied. The most common is a more or less severe chilly sensation followed by *fever regularly recurring* every one, two or three days (intermittent fever). These symptoms are preceded by pains and lassitude. After the fever, comes sweating. This series of symptoms may occupy six hours or more. Between the attacks comes an interval of hours or days. Other forms of fever, not yielding to quinine or to the other usually potent remedies, may be malarial. If an intermitting fever or neuralgia, anæmia, etc., yield to a few large doses of quinine, the hygienic indication is that a malarial influence is present and that it calls for some remedial measures besides the persistent use of drugs.

Malarial manifestations are considered due to the presence of the above-mentioned microörganisms in air that has been directly in contact with certain soils, usually *marshy*. Yet the term "marsh-fever," used to designate these disorders, does not always indicate enough; for we find malaria over great districts that are not marshy. It may even occur in deserts. As a rule, it is most prominent in low, moist, warm regions where the water-level fluctuates considerably at times and thus favors vegetable decomposition. The breaking up of some fallow fields and other soils causes malarial attacks, especially where underground water remains stagnant instead of being drained off.

Malaria tends to be carried by gentle winds along valleys and level tracts in warm or mild weather. It is much less to be apprehended during the sunshine hours of the day than toward night. Although it is reported to rise at times hundreds or even thousands of feet up into the air after leaving its place of origin, the rule is that the subtle influence of malaria remains usually within a few feet of the soil. So, the nearer one is to the soil, the greater the liability to the disease. Accordingly, it is safer to have the sleeping-room situated more than twelve feet above the surface of the ground, especially if the earth is being dug up. It is best in "ague districts" not to breathe the air near the ground either very early or late in the day. Fires at night and moderately warm clothing are of service against the infection.

Forests tend to intercept this strange poison. Tropical regions covered by dense forests are said to be generally very free from malaria. It does not appear to cross bodies of water of any size. Hence one is much better protected against this infection when on a boat out upon the surface of a considerable sheet of water than when one is upon or near a marshy, ill-drained shore. Moisture and warmth favor malaria. Where the average temperature of the air is not above 60° F. in the warmest weeks of the year, the infection is not to be feared. The winter season is least dangerous for visits to malarial districts.

To escape malaria, one must avoid locating on undrained soils. Even if they be sand or gravel, but yet have sub-soils of clay or other impermeable substance, sites are liable to be insufficiently drained. Then they are to be considered unhealthful. So, too, are rock formations that allow underground water to stand. Ballast from malarial soil may carry the infection. Better for such a purpose are rocks that have long been deep under water. Irrigation water from malarial soil may, like such soil when used on gardens, convey the disease. Food and water should therefore in doubtful cases invariably be cooked before being taken into the system. It is presumable that mosquitoes and other insects are a means of diffusing this disease. Hence mosquito-nettings are to be recommended. (See page 414.) Cleanliness of the person and of all surroundings is important. The general health should be well maintained. Excesses are especially to be avoided.

Malarial marshes, that cannot well be drained, are rendered less harmful when water is backed over them so that they are covered. It is found that when dry earth or sand from a non-malarial place is spread over a malarial soil, the infectiveness is thereby lessened. Close pavements tend to prevent direct infection from the soil. The cellars of houses should, as is elsewhere explained in this book, be so tight that no water can rise into them from below.

The cautious administration of arsenic and the liberal use of decoctions of sliced lemons, together with the drinking of only such water as has been boiled, are well-tested and approved general preventives of infection in malarial regions.

Dysentery is in many cases probably caused by amœboid microörganisms similar to those of malaria. Because of these and the various forms of bacteria that cause diarrhœal disorders (especially among the very young) in summer, it may again be emphasized that all food and drink then swallowed ought to have been recently cooked.

Artificial feeding of infants causes a formidably large number of deaths from the diarrhœa of warm weather (*cholera infantum*) where proper care is not taken to have pure and fresh milk. Crowding in filthy tenements aggravates this. Sterilizing bad milk, by boiling it, renders such inferior milk safer; although perfectly pure and fresh milk is preferable as a food. The bowel discharges of patients with diarrhœal and dysenteric diseases ought always to be disinfected.

Typhoid fever (*enteric fever*) is regarded as due to large, very mobile bacilli which are seen, under a good compound microscope, to be thick, three times as long as broad and having rounded ends. (See Fig. 74.) Excepting Elsner's iodide of potash and potato jelly culture test, it is at present regarded as doubtful whether any of the various lauded methods of recognizing these bacilli in suspected water be actually reliable. The peculiar growth (or apparent lack of growth) on acid potato culture-surfaces (see page 381) seems distinctive, if used with other tests at the same time. The typhoid germs grow in sterilized milk *without coagulating* it. Growing *in beef broth, they develop no gas.* Various harmless bacteria resemble these very closely.

FIG. 74.

In milk and on other foods the germs of typhoid can increase very rapidly. Hence milk, like solid food, is at times an important means of carrying the infection. The adulteration of milk with water from a contaminated well, or the use of such water (when unboiled) for the purpose of rinsing out milk cans or bottles, can unquestionably cause this disease. The period of incubation is usually twelve days, but may be longer.

Typhoid fever is most commonly caused by the use of water into which the harmful bacilli have entered from the bowel discharges coming from a person who has the disease. These discharges contain immense numbers of the dangerous germs. Hence a single patient can, through carelessness, be the source of infecting more than a thousand people. When a distinct case of typhoid occurs, the possibility that the water is infected must always present itself. Defective privies and drains, or the careless throwing out of discharges that are not disinfected, usually explain the origin of the disease.

Typhoid fever often appears in milder forms which are mistaken for other (less serious) diseases. Vague headache and indisposition with slowly developing fever in which the temperature increases for days gradually and regularly (oscillating slightly downward in the morning), allow the case to be considered as typhoidal even if there be no diarrhœa. If the spleen is enlarged, this diagnosis is a very safe one where the disease cannot be classed as anything else. This point is of considerable hygienic importance. *In case of doubt*, the health of others demands that the patient be carefully nursed and *the discharges disinfected*.

The matters which come from the patient are in no case to be allowed to remain where they can possibly be washed into a well or water-course. Even when typhoid fever (or *mountain fever*, as it is sometimes called) arises in wild regions, it can usually be traced to neglect of the above-indicated precautions to keep the food and water clean. The germs of the disease can be carried alive many miles down a stream or diffused far through water. The recent experience of Newburyport, Lawrence and Lowell (on the Merrimac), as well as of Chicago, St. Louis and very many other communities, proves this.

Typhoid fever is preventable. It does not arise or spread where proper precautions are taken to disinfect discharges, to cultivate true cleanliness and to use only cooked food and water whenever they are not wholly above suspicion. This disease destroys many thousands of lives every year. Even in India it deserves to be dreaded more than the cholera. Typhoid fever invades all classes of people. It is most common in the years between puberty and middle age. Those who have once had this disease are very rarely attacked by it a second time.

To prevent typhoid fever, general and special *cleanliness* are demanded. The discharges of real or suspected cases of typhoid must not be allowed to become a source of infection. They need to be *disinfected* (as explained in the following chapter) by milk of lime or other means. The clothing, soiled linen, all objects that have been near the patient and also the hands of attendants require disinfection. When travelling or when suspicious cases of fever are known to be in the neighborhood, water, milk and other food should be cooked before being used. In this, as in other diseases, a weakened or diseased condition of the system predisposes to infection.

The plague (*Bubonic plague, Black death*) is the same disease that ravaged Europe during the fourteenth century. Since then it has occasionally been introduced there from its lurking places in oriental lands where filth and other unhygienic conditions induce irregular outbreaks of varying severity. Cleanly people do not acquire it unless exceptionally exposed to the infection. Domestic animals are susceptible to it and epidemics of plague are preceded by a great mortality among rats and mice, which afford a common cause of disseminating the infectious bacilli. These are short and thick, resembling those shown on page 407, but are smaller. Since the period of infection is always less than a week, we can easily quarantine against cases among trans-ocean passengers. There seems to be more danger in the entrance of infected goods from China, India and other eastern lands. There it caused many thousands of deaths between 1894 and 1898. Carried presumably in a ship from Hong Kong to Bombay in July, 1890, the resultant mortality was enormous. Even as late as March 17, 1898, there were reported 265 deaths daily from plague.

Yersin, in 1894 and 1895, demonstrated the curative and preventive value of the antitoxine from the unfiltered but sterilized cultures of the plague bacillus. Yet Haffkine's double inoculation method superseded it for preventing the disease, as tested in many thousand cases. Lustig's serum method is said by the Lancet to be curative.

Cholera (*Asiatic* or *Indian* cholera) always exists in the warm, moist, alluvial ground of the Ganges delta and in Bengal. Thence it is carried, chiefly by pilgrims, toward Mecca in Arabia and to Hurdwar where the Ganges river breaks out of the mountains. Fostered by the filthy habits of the masses that resort to these shrines or market-places, the infection is at times gradually diffused to many remote regions, usually by overland routes. Yet the germs of cholera can survive an ocean voyage of weeks, and then cause infection. The rapidity and extent of the wanderings of the disease from its filthy East Indian home and from other haunts of the infection have increased with the swift railway and steamship facilities of the last half-century.

Cholera reached this country first by way of Canada through Ireland during the epidemic of 1827 to 1837. In 1849, from another epidemic, cases crossed the Atlantic, and again in 1866 the disease was brought here. In 1873 it entered through New Orleans and extended considerably. The epidemic of 1883 was kept out by our quarantines, but reached South America. It was very severe in Japan and part of Asia, and caused many deaths in southern Europe, especially in Naples. The sixth of the great epidemics became serious in 1892, causing thousands of deaths in Asia and eastern Europe, notably in Russia, where, as also in Galicia and Turkey, it lasted till February, 1896. It lingered still longer in Egypt. In 1898 this epidemic had ceased, even in India. Hamburg was sorely visited for weeks after August 15th, between 8 and 9,000 deaths resulting from the infection which was clearly shown to have come solely from polluted drinking water. [See pages 310 and 311]. Thence several cases were brought to New York, chiefly by Russian exiles. Almost all of these were kept out by quarantine measures. The few that entered were isolated. No cases have occurred here since then. A few got into South America and Hawaii.

This epidemic not only demonstrated the value of pure water supplies, but also enabled valuable contributions to be made to a scientific understanding of the disease. It showed the great preventive value of Pasteur's inoculation method as worked out by Haffkine and practised in India with great saving of life.

CHOLERA

Cholera is generally regarded as due to the entrance into the digestive system, and the presence there in and on the walls of the intestine, of the peculiar curved or *comma*-

Fig. 75.

shaped (see Fig. 75, *B*) bacilli discovered by Koch in 1883. These are usually considerably less than $\frac{1}{12000}$ inch (0.8 to 2 *mikrons*) in length.

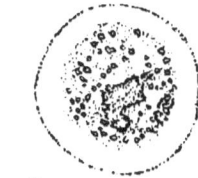

Fig. 76.

They are seen to be actively mobile when examined in a hanging drop, as explained on page 379. When a number

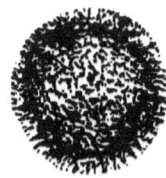

Fig. 76a.

of these *comma bacilli* are joined, end-to-end, there results a spiral appearance (*spirillum*. See Fig. 75, *A*). The peculiar appearance of (two-day-old) "colonies" of the comma bacilli upon gelatine plates (see page 382) is shown in Fig. 76 (from Dr. Shakespeare's book) and Fig. 76a. They are there represented as enlarged nearly fifty times. Fig. 77 is a half-size representation of gelatine tube cultures (see page 382) of the cholera bacillus. The tube on the left shows the appearance at the end of the second day after introduction of the culture. In the right-hand tube, the culture is twice as old.

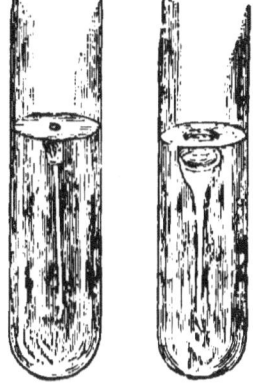

Fig. 77.

Although more than six other kinds of spiral bacteria have been reported, they need not be mistaken for the germs of Asiatic cholera by any one skilled in practical bacteriological work. This fact aids the definite recognition of the disease whenever a *mild case*, in the guise of severe diarrhœa or *cholerine*, occurs as the forerunner of an epidemic. More than thirty-six hours are needed to determine accurately whether the bacteria coming from a given doubtful case are genuine cholera bacilli. Hence one must not wait for a laboratory decision before taking decisive measures to isolate a suspected case and to disinfect the discharges and all else that has come from or been near the patient.

These precautions must be taken, if possible, even before the appearance of all of the characteristic signs. The severe symptoms are cramps, violent vomiting and purging, with copious watery discharges from the bowels, drying up of the body, collapse, etc. At times when cholera is known to prevail or be impending, any case of diarrhœa should be treated with more care than usual as regards disinfection of the discharges. Several times since the experience of Canada at Grosse Isle, in 1834, the importance of not ignoring mild diarrhœal cases, where the possibility of cholera infection exists, has been made painfully evident. The experience of the Hamburg physicians shows the undesirableness of using much opium in such cases. Cholera usually manifests itself within two days after the individual is infected; and always within five days. This *incubation period* may, however, last only a few hours.

Cholera is a filth disease of warm weather. Its germs are very sensitive to high heat and to drying. Yet the infection can be carried overland through the dryest regions. It can also survive winters, and even attack people during cold weather. The remarks made on page 408, as to the desirability of cleanliness in typhoid fever and the necessity of using only cooked food and boiled water when such a disease is nigh, apply equally to cholera.

Cholera germs are, as has just been stated, very sensitive to heat. Shortly after they come into contact with a moist temperature exceeding 140° F., they perish. Hence the value of very hot or boiling water and steam for disinfecting clothing, rags, and other articles that possibly retain infection from having been in contact with a cholera case.

If steam be used for the holds of vessels, great care is needed to see that sufficient heat reaches every part. The bilge-water and ballast require to be disinfected. All portions of the interior of a cholera-infected vessel must be disinfected. Where very hot water or steam cannot be used, and in dwellings, hotels, lodging-houses, railway stations, railway cars and other conveyances, the disinfectants mentioned on and after page 439 suffice if used thoroughly.

Cholera bacilli perish very promptly upon being exposed to the action of acids. Even sour wine destroys them after a time when it is added in equal parts to water in which some of these are present. Yet it is preferable to have drinking-water invariably boiled. Nor should aërated waters always be relied upon by travellers. Beer, when good, is made of cooked water. Hence, proper beer does not contain any germs of cholera that may have been in the original water used for brewing. Yet water used for rinsing kegs and glasses may contain very many kinds of bacteria.

Crude hydrochloric and sulphuric acids are very valuable for disinfecting bowel discharges from cholera cases. They are to be used so as to equal at least one per cent. of the discharges. Carbolic acid solutions ought to be acid as explained on page 440. Fresh milk of lime is valuable, but should be in stronger proportions than the usual one per cent.

Copper sulphate is well recommended by some ; yet recent experiments discredit it when used in solutions of less than five per cent. Camphor is one of the agents that, in laboratory tests, have proved valuable in the strength of less than half of one per cent. Its use must be a limited one. Since cholera bacilli are, in experiments, sensitive to drying, it is probable that exposure of light, delicate tissues to sunlit, dry, open air destroys any stray germs that may by chance be on apparently clean clothing that has been upon a cholera ship. If discretion be well used, unnecessary and promiscuous steam (or other) disinfection of finery may be obviated. The fumigation of voyagers is worse than useless.

Yellow fever (sometimes called "*black vomit*" from the frequency of that symptom, due to changed blood from the stomach) is a very dangerous, rapidly fatal, infectious disease of tropical America, including much of the eastern coast of South America. Although most to be dreaded by our Gulf ports, it at times goes inland. It has never affected places in North America that had a high altitude, although in South America it has been a serious pestilence at a height of more than two miles above sea-level.

It does not get a foothold in places, like San Francisco, having a mean temperature under 60° F. Yet it has several times reached New York and Boston, and has occurred as far to the northward as Portland, Halifax and Quebec. The disease has been seen in Great Britain (at Swansea, in 1864) in a northern latitude of 51° 30'.

Yellow fever is a filth disease, being usually limited to crowded sections of hot, moist ports, on rivers or on the sea, where sanitation is very defective. White people from the north, who are not acclimatized and have never had the disease, should be very careful when in unclean tropical places. Sanarelli's study of the peculiar bacilli of this disease shows that they thrive in mouldy places. They live very long in ordinary water, but are destroyed as soon as it is heated to 160° Fahr.

It is well to drink only boiled water where the disease prevails or is suspected: all food also should then be freshly cooked by clean and healthy people. Mosquito-nets and the use of ointments on the hands prevent the danger of receiving the infection from the bites of flies or mosquitoes. In the day-time, a tube of fine netting can be worn drawn in above the brim of a stiff hat so as to hang over the edges and to go well down upon the shoulders. Thus it is kept away from the face, ears and neck. It is also better in this respect if a whalebone or split-rattan hoop be attached to the netting just at the top of the shoulders.

Typhus fever (*jail fever, ship fever*) is quite contagious; but is usually limited to filthy and degraded people who are ill-fed and crowded together in poorly ventilated and dirty places. Cold weather most favors the conditions that bring this disease to a place. Yet it also occurs in summer. When once it has entered a community, it may last for several years. Quarantine officials ought always to be on the lookout for it. The period of incubation appears to be very variable. In some cases, considerably more than two weeks may elapse between the time of infection and the outbreak of the disease. Its microörganic cause is as yet unknown. Possibly protozoa (see page 400) are causative of it.

It is imperatively necessary that *disinfection* be thoroughly carried out in the lodgings or other places where cases of typhus fever have been. The presence of such a disease indicates that better sanitary conditions are needed. This and other infectious diseases are best cared for in special hospitals however small. Isolated tents (afterward disinfected) answer very well for the purpose. It is desirable that the attendants upon such cases be selected from among people who themselves have had the disease, and that they be cleanly and careful not to carry the infection further.

Venereal diseases are disseminated and propagated almost entirely by impure sexual contact. Of these, *gonorrhea* is probably regarded, by the great majority of enlightened physicians, as much more serious than *syphilis* when the ultimate effects of these infections are considered. In view of the general, ophthalmic and especially uterine derangements that these entail upon the innocent, it is desirable that more rigorous restrictions be imposed upon the semi-criminals (of both sexes) who knowingly remain the dangerous sources of these infections.

Glanders (and *farcy*), *splenic fever* (anthrax), *puerperal fever* (or other fever), *actinomycosis* and other diseases that have rendered meat unfit for food,—all require that a **carcass** condemned for such reason be at once destroyed. Burning it is the best way.

If a carcass from splenic fever, for instance, be buried, there is a slight possibility that the very hardy and dangerous bacteria of that disease may be brought to the surface of the ground by earthworms and the infection may then survive, as explained by Pasteur. Suspected cases of animals having these diseases or *tuberculosis* are to be isolated for careful observation. The places where they have been kept, as well as food and all objects that such animals have contaminated, ought to be thoroughly disinfected.

Erysipelas is a rapid infectious fever. The skin is red and elevated over (usually) a small portion of the body. This raised, red area is sharply defined against the healthy skin. In the skin within this irregular, inflamed area, very many small, round bacteria that grow in chains (*streptococcus;* see Fig. 67) are found. They are in appearance much like some of the microörganisms that cause suppuration or other bad symptoms in infected wounds.

Erysipelas and all wound infections indicate that some kind of harmful bacteria has probably got into the wound or scratch or other injury. It may be that a knife, a razor, the surface of the injured part itself, the hands or unclean dressings had the infective bacteria present upon them, and were the means of introducing these germs into the skin and thus causing the disease. The clothing, hair and beard may carry infection from a previous case if they be left uncleaned after they have been in contact with such a case or even near it.

WOUND INFECTION, ETC.

Tetanus (*lockjaw*) and *childbed fever* are to be classed among the infections that may result from lack of cleanliness and care in regard to making or treating wounds, however slight. The hands (and *finger-nails*) of midwives, nurses, operators (surgeons, dentists and veterinarians) need to be especially clean. So also must all instruments or anything else that comes near a wound. The use of (1 to 2000) corrosive sublimate solutions (or of water boiled after the addition of half a per cent. of common salt) to rinse wounds is desirable in all cases. The skin to be cut requires to be cleaned before an operation. (See page 449.) The dressings and instruments should have been sterilized by heat. If heat will cause injury, instruments may be immersed for several minutes in a five per cent. carbolic acid solution. This suffices in an ordinary case.

TETANUS
× 1100.
FIG. 78.

When it is *tetanus* that we are guarding against, a 1 to 500 solution of corrosive sublimate in acidulated water is to be used for cleansing the skin. (The peculiar shape of the bacilli that cause tetanus is shown by Fig. 78.)

After *childbirth* (or after *miscarriage*), the parts affected are to be treated as wounds requiring rest and the extremest cleanliness. By the observation of thorough cleanliness in every detail of operating and after-care, all operative surgery is successful to-day to an extent that less than a quarter of a century ago seemed impossible.

As indicated in the chapter on Schools, granular lids (*trachoma*) and catarrhal diseases of the eye are infectious and liable to be communicated, especially from one child to another. So, too, are various common skin diseases.

Diphtheria is generally regarded as due to infection with bacteria called the bacilli of Klebs and Loeffler. These microörganisms are sporeless, of varying and irregular shape. Fig. 79 represents them fairly. They are often longer than shown there. As may

DIPHTHERIA
× 1400.
FIG. 79.

be seen from the figure, the ends are rounded. These bacilli can be stained by means of the usual aniline colors, especially by methylene blue. They are found in numbers in the dense, white false membrane which they cause upon the throat and other surfaces into which they become inoculated and grow. Yet they are not found diffused throughout the blood and other organs. The marked symptoms with and following diphtheria are to be considered as due to organic poison (*toxalbumin*) generated by these localized bacteria and absorbed into the system.

Diphtheria appears to have increased in amount and severity during the last forty years, and that especially in cities, while formerly it was more a disease of the country. Those who are most familiar with the disease, ascribe much of this increase to complex and very faulty house drainage. Fewer cases occur in summer than in those colder months of the year when children are most crowded in close, warm rooms.

The germs of this disease thrive best in damp and dark places, and are there most dangerous. Diphtheria may occur on ships. Almost any article, as well as the dust of the air, can be the means of conveying the infection. The bacilli of diphtheria have been found alive and virulent after months of drying. Shreds and small bits of membrane coughed out from the throat of a diphtheritic patient are therefore very dangerous, and should be looked after and promptly disinfected. The disease can be acquired from pet birds, cats and other animals. It can also come from the use of unboiled milk which has received the infection.

Diphtheria germs perish if exposed to a temperature above $140°$ F. Hence, if the soiled garments and all other washable articles, that have been near a patient having diphtheria, be kept for a very few minutes in water not far below the boiling point, we can be certain that the infection on these articles is destroyed. It is required, of course, that *every part* of the infected fabrics be exposed to the heat. If not otherwise treated with disinfectants, coughed-up matters should be caught, at once wrapped up in paper or cloth and burned without unnecessary delay.

For draperies and other furnishings, steam disinfection is to be advised if practicable. For the walls, floors, etc., of the sick-room, the standard (1 to 1000) solution of *corrosive sublimate* is to be freely used. This solution is very valuable against the germs of diphtheria. Loeffler found it of great potency even in the strength of 1 to 10000. In general, it is best to use a strong solution (1 to 1000) of this or a three or four per cent. solution of carbolic acid made with water to which half its weight of alcohol has been added. This is better than *lysol* or any of the proprietary disinfectants.

For rinsing out the throats of people who wish to prevent any possibility of the disease, Loeffler's authoritative experiments allow us to recommend the use of a 1 to 10,000 solution of *cyanide of mercury* as being efficacious against diphtheria germs and yet not unpleasant. Chloroform water answers the same purpose. [See *Antidiphtherin*, page 396].

If diphtheria is prevented from entering a place, no cases can occur there. When a case occurs, it ought to be isolated and careful disinfection insisted upon in order that the infection shall go no further. At times, *sore throat* that is not regarded as serious proves, by the subsequent paralysis and other signs, to be mild diphtheria which however can in its turn give rise to the most virulent infection. The term *croup* is often used for cases which should be called diphtheria. These facts must be remembered by school authorities, who ought to have the fullest power to exclude suspected cases of sore throat even without waiting for medical recognition of the exact nature of the ailment.

Whooping-cough (*pertussis*) is a very infectious disease of childhood, but can occasionally occur in adults who have not had it in early years. It is most serious in the very youngest children, and not only causes many deaths but, by its complications and consequences, may leave the young child very weak and burdened with lung disease. So, it is best that a child be guarded against the infection as long as possible. Thus the disease will be evaded altogether or will be milder if it comes. The general employment of isolation, disinfection and exclusion of cases from school for two months after the disease has begun needs to be insisted upon. The infection may linger in (and be carried by) the clothes of persons who have been in contact with a case of whooping-cough.

Mumps, although very much less serious, can also be classed among the infectious diseases to be prevented by the general means above indicated. It can be epidemic and attack many persons. The infectiousness of a case may persist for weeks after the peculiar swelling of the glands near the jaw has subsided. To prevent infection of other people (if not to lessen the liability of other glands of the body becoming inflamed) the patient ought to be kept in bed. After a person receives the infection of mumps, from two to three weeks may be required for the disease to manifest itself.

Exanthematous diseases comprise scarlet fever, measles and small-pox; also such less important infectious diseases as German measles (or *Rötheln*) and chicken-pox (or *varicella*). Like nearly all skin diseases, these call for the observance of cleanliness and care. Most important are the following three *eruptive fevers*.

Scarlet fever (or *scarlatina*) is very widely distributed throughout the world, especially in the temperate zones. It occurs at all times of the year and is associated with no particular soil or geological formation. Although occurring especially among young children, all ages may occasionally suffer from it. It is very rare that one has it a second time.

Some epidemics and isolated cases of it are much less fatal than the average. In an ordinary, mild epidemic, considerably less than a tenth of the cases end fatally. Sometimes, however, a third of the infected children die. Serious injury to the ears and kidneys often results among those who survive the disease.

Scarlet fever has at times been traced to the use of uncooked milk that had taken up the infection from a case in the family of the farm-people supplying the milk. This disease is probably not derived from animals. It is very contagious, and the infection can be carried by a careless person not having the disease, but who has not been properly disinfected after visiting or nursing a case of it. This applies to physicians as well as to others.

The *scales* cast off from the skin appear to be exceedingly dangerous as carriers of the infection. Hence salves or oil, used for relief to the skin, are to be recommended for the further purpose of keeping the cast-off scales from flying about.

To prevent the spread of scarlet fever, the patient and attendants ought to be isolated. In the very beginning of the disease, all matters that come from the mouth require to be disinfected. The same may be said of any disease attended with sore throat, sore mouth or cough. Not only the bed-clothing, but also all things that have come into contact with the patient, need to be disinfected. It is safest when the room and furniture are faithfully disinfected as explained on page 445. If the other children of the family where the case occurs are allowed to come into the sickroom, they ought not to be permitted to attend school.

The patient should be kept out of school for at least seven weeks; and before readmission, it is well that the child receive a physician's certificate of health and noninfectiveness. It must be borne in mind that, after recovery, the child is delicate for months. Accordingly, physical health then needs consideration more than progress in school. If schools are closed because of the presence of this or another infectious disease, the buildings must be thoroughly disinfected in every part, including the ventilating shafts and flues.

Measles (called also *morbilli* or *rubeola*) may be said to be usually much less fatal than scarlet fever, although more common. Only a small percentage of the average children (in cities at least) escape an attack of measles. It is very rare to have the disease a second time. Like whooping-cough, it is common for measles to leave the lungs or bronchial tubes in an inflamed or delicate condition and liable to take in the infection of tubercular consumption. In warm weather, inflammation of the bowels is to be guarded against after an attack of measles.

Schools are a very common source of infection, and therefrom the disease may become epidemic; for it is exceedingly contagious. What has just been said regarding precautions for disinfecting and restricting cases of scarlet fever applies also to measles, although the latter disease runs its course more rapidly than the former. If a very malignant epidemic is prevailing, it is desirable to remove and completely isolate children, especially if they be delicate.

Small-pox (*variola*) was formerly a terrible scourge. Nowadays, it causes comparatively few deaths; yet numerous cases occur now and then in districts where sanitary precautions are disregarded. It is most common in winter and spring. The colored races are most liable to it. It rarely attacks those who have been vaccinated within a dozen years, and the cases that occur among the vaccinated are quite mild (*varioloid*).

From one-seventh to two-thirds of the unvaccinated, who are attacked by small-pox, die. This disease is not always easy to recognize in the beginning. Accordingly, suspicious cases of fever accompanied by a pustular eruption and back-ache ought to be very carefully watched, especially if known to have been exposed to the infection. Vaccination should be urgently recommended, particularly when an epidemic is present or apprehended. Some statistics—those of India, for instance—appear to show that vaccination slightly lessens the tendency to other diseases.

Vaccination is an invaluable preventive of small-pox. The clean and carefully obtained virus from the calf is best for general use. (See page 394.) The operation is harmless if the operator be cleanly and careful. The knife or needle used needs to be well wiped and held in boiling water for a minute (and allowed to cool) before using. The portion of skin selected should have no sign of disease. The part to be vaccinated needs to be washed clean and then rinsed with water that has been boiled. The first vaccination should take place in early infancy. The second one ought not as a rule to come later than the thirteenth year. Not more than two vaccinations are needed.

Rags for paper-making sometimes cause small-pox, and domestic rags seem as dangerous as those that are imported. Rag-handlers especially require vaccination. Steam is a valuable disinfectant for rags. For small-pox cases and the places where they have been, the most complete isolation, cleanliness and disinfection are necessary.

Influenza (called also *grippe* and *epidemic catarrhal fever*) has prevailed epidemically at least eleven or twelve times during the last century. The epidemic that began in 1889 proved exceedingly severe. Unlike the infectious diseases that have been so far considered, this often attacks the same person a second time. It is probably due to bacteria (Pfeiffer's); very little is known of these to aid one in preventing or treating the disease. There is no sufficient evidence to support the belief that influenza is caused by some great cosmic or climatic *influence*.

It is important to note that the infection of this disease does not travel any faster than the human beings who carry it can travel. Furthermore, it has not been known to occur in places wholly shut off from contact with those who had themselves received the infection or carried it in their clothing or in some object. Not all admit, however, that it is communicated by human intercourse. A few consider that it is connected in some way with a similar disease of the horse.

Influenza is usually severest during the six or ten weeks of mid-winter. It may prevail in warmer weather. People who have lung disease (or heart defects) and also the aged or weakly have most to fear from the influenza infection. It is most fatal when lung complications exist or arise in the course of the disease. It is usually much more serious than an ordinary cold, and may leave behind it a nervous or other weakness which lasts for a varying time. Infants and young children show very little fatality from this disease.

Influenza cannot apparently be prevented with any degree of certainty unless absolute isolation be possible. For those who greatly desire to escape the infection, it is advisable for the time being to avoid all entertainments and social intercourse. Since schools afford a means of diffusing the disease, they may at times need to be closed.

Pneumonia (*croupous pneumonia*) has for more than three centuries and a half been ranked among the communicable diseases. Of the various longish and round forms which numerous competent investigators have identified with the causation of this disease, a double coccus enclosed in a mucous capsule (see Fig. 70) is most common. The same form occurs also in many cases of endocarditis and cerebro-spinal meningitis. From various careful experiments, we know that the matters coughed out, or which otherwise come from the mouths of patients with this and other diseases, can become dried to dust with full exposure to light and air for days and yet remain very infectious.

Such half-solid matters and saliva can retain their virulence even after many hours of exposure to direct sunlight. Hence it is proper to enjoin caution upon attendants lest they fail to have these disease products always enter suitable moist receptacles for speedy disinfection by burning or by the use of a five per cent. *acid* solution of carbolic acid.

It is advisable to disinfect the room, bed-clothing and garments after such a disease. Especially in hotels and lodging-houses is it necessary to attend carefully to the disinfection and isolation of infective cases.

Tuberculosis (commonly called *consumption* or *phthisis*) oftenest attacks the lungs. Hence the term, when not otherwise qualified, indicates the chronic, destructive disease of the lungs. In young children, it is quite liable to occur in the meningeal layers of the brain. The abdominal and other glands are frequently invaded by this disease. Glandular tuberculosis is often called *scrofula*. Recent careful autopsies made, by Pizzoni and others, upon the bodies of people apparently free from the disease have showed that, in more than two-fifths of these cases, the glands or other organs had regularly present, in a *latent* state, the peculiar bacteria that cause tuberculosis.

These microörganisms (discovered by Koch) are called the *bacilli of tuberculosis*. Their length is usually from one-fourth to one-half the diameter of a red blood corpuscle (or from 2 to 5 *mikrons*). They are very often slightly curved and are even more slender than is indicated by Fig. 80. They may contain several spores, appearing as glistening, colorless dots in these slender rods when staining has been employed upon them. They are slow to take up the aniline colors used in laboratory work; yet, when once colored, they resist (more than do other bacteria) the decolorizing action of dilute mineral acids.

TUBERCLE
× 1100.
FIG. 80.

These bacilli cause "consumption" and are parasites,

thriving well only in the tissues of human beings, cattle and some other animals. Poultry have the same disease. Goats hardly ever acquire the disease, and sheep are much less liable to it than are swine or cattle. Steam-heat, or even a lower temperature than that, quickly destroys the germs of tuberculosis. *Mercury* solutions, usually very potent against bacteria, are less valuable than strong *carbolic acid* solutions for disinfecting the expectorations of consumptives. *Creosote* and the chemical products allied to it are also valuable against these bacteria. In expectorated matters, tuberculosis bacilli may remain dangerously alive for months after they have become dried. They can also live very long amid vigorous decomposition bacteria.

Exposure to abundant daylight (especially *sunlight*), with a liberal supply of *fresh air*, appears to destroy the bacilli of tuberculosis within a few hours or days. This natural process of destroying these dangerous germs of consumption is much more active in open streets and free air-spaces than in closed apartments. Indeed, the infection ordinarily comes from the dust of crowded, ill-ventilated rooms, that are frequented by consumptives who are careless about their expectorations.

Since the greatest element of danger lies in the innumerable harmful germs that are coughed out of the lungs of those who have the disease, it is important to see that such matters are received in proper receptacles and at once disinfected. *Spittoons* ought to be easily cleanable, smooth and simple in construction. They always require strong disinfectant solutions in the bottom so that the expectorations received in them will remain moist and not dry up to become harmful dust that will carry infection. Five per cent. carbolic acid solutions answer the purpose.

For the *portable spittoons*, that all consumptives ought to be required to carry about and invariably use, a little "excelsior" or oakum may be used in the bottom to prevent splashing of the disinfectant solution. These receptacles may be of varnished pasteboard (and therefore inexpensive) so that they can be burned with their contents and not used a second time. It is wrong to use handkerchiefs or dry cloths for receiving expectorations unless to be at once disinfected (by boiling or by the use of chemicals) or burned. The sawdust-filled spittoons, common in manufactories and taverns, are similarly objectionable, apart from the danger of fire that accompanies their use.

All expectorations should, as above said, be received in a disinfectant solution, if not to be immediately sterilized by steam or burned. Not only do such precautions lessen very greatly the danger of infection to others, but also the sufferer from the disease is thereby somewhat less liable to receive further infection. The bowel discharges from those who have tuberculosis of the intestine contain the infective bacilli in abundance; yet they are a very much less serious element of danger than are coughed-up matters. Whatever is coughed up ought not to be swallowed; for secondary tuberculosis of the intestines may therefrom be produced.

The infection of tuberculosis enters the body most frequently through weaknesses in the lung surfaces after bronchial catarrhs and other diseases. Very reliable observers have found that the bacilli can apparently enter the system through healthy mucous membranes (as of the lung surface or stomach); yet such is not the rule. When these bacteria enter the stomach, they are not always destroyed, but occasionally cause infection. Hence the importance of not using, in an *uncooked* state, any meat or milk that come from diseased animals.

If a few harmful germs enter the system, they may be destroyed by the chemical and vital activity of the body tissues. If not thus destroyed, they may remain "latent" in the system for an indefinite time, to multiply and enter more or less extensively upon their destructive activity whenever the system is weakened by disease, privation, excesses or other influences. Even then, the disease manifestations produced by these microörganisms, if not very extensive, may wholly cease under proper hygienic surroundings. An open-air life in a high, dry and sunny region or in a suitable ocean climate tends to restrict or cure the disease. (See page 35.)

Hereditary and acquired weaknesses render a person, who is exposed to the infection, more liable to become consumptive or to develop "scrofula," joint disease or other forms of tuberculosis. The bacilli are only one of the factors in the causation of the disease, although exceedingly important. Consumption is probably not very often inherited in the way in which it was thought to be prior to and even long after the demonstration by Villemin (in 1865) that tuberculosis was a communicable disease.

Recent studies by Gärtner and others appear, however, to show that a small percentage of cases are probably transmitted to the offspring before birth. The infection in such cases seems to be inherited from the mother rather than from the father. In the great majority of cases, the infection may fairly be considered to be acquired after birth. Some people are born with apparent susceptibility to the disease. Their lungs and other organs seem unable to resist the infection unless under exceptionally good hygienic conditions.

Most of us are to a varying extent exposed to this as to other infections by reason of the prevalence of unclean dust and other unhealthful influences. Hence the importance of removing the harmful conditions that we can control. The general health ought always to be cared for. Inoculations with the culture "lymph" which Koch introduced have, unfortunately, after the most thorough trial, proved unsatisfactory. Yet they seem of value as a means of recognizing tuberculosis in cattle.

From what has here been outlined, the measures to be employed toward insuring prevention of tuberculosis ought to be obvious. Cleanliness in work-places, public rooms, conveyances and elsewhere; with careful disinfection of whatever comes from a victim of the disease, and scientific cleanliness wherever such a person is,—all these measures are needed in order to destroy the infection. On a dry site and at a high altitude, it flourishes least. The importance of thorough cooking of milk or meat of suspicious origin is explained elsewhere. All slaughter-houses should be under the supervision of public officials. The value of gentle chest gymnastics as a preventive is unquestioned. For climatic indications, see pages 33 to 37.

Leprosy is a very rare disease with us. Yet it deserves mention for the reason that it is on the increase and cases are occasionally brought here. It is due to a bacillus exceedingly like that of tuberculosis; but it is at any rate a much less infectious disease than that. Many of the ablest observers question whether it be communicable at all. The (1893) report of the Leprosy Commission in India states that the risk of contagion is very small, and that *fish* and *salt* food do not cause the disease. Special predisposition to the disease is regarded as a quite important factor. The observance of strict cleanliness, the use of cooked food and all avoidance of immediate contact with lepers or objects that they have used insures immunity from the disease.

Cerebro-spinal meningitis is to be classed with the above-mentioned diseases, as one that calls for the adoption of precautions to prevent its spread whenever it is present. Cases ought to be isolated as well as is possible. Disinfection is needed.

DISINFECTION. RESTRICTION OF COMMUNICABLE DISEASES

To restrict infectious diseases, the most important measure is an insistance upon rigorous *cleanliness*. Not merely is visible and obnoxious filth to be kept away, but of much greater consequence is the exclusion and annihilation of the subtler and more dangerous kinds of uncleanliness that result from and produce disease. The pages just preceding are intended to aid the comprehension of these causes of infection. The present chapter considers the practical means for annihilating such infection as is present, and of preventing any further disease invasion.

Besides localizing, isolating and then stamping out any immediate source and cause of infection, the entrance of any disease from without and the possibility of its further extension when it has reached us must be guarded against. The practice of measures to effect the exclusion of disease is spoken of, in a general way, as *quarantine*.

General and special measures are required, wherever indicated, in order to lessen the liability of individuals and communities, as well as of localities, to receive and foster infection. In addition to the general recommendations given elsewhere in this book, a special consideration of practical disinfection is required.

Disinfection means in any case the *total* destruction of life in the low organisms which can perpetuate and communicate an infectious disease. *Sterilization*, as we have seen in speaking of the "Pasteurization" of milk (see page 385), may be incomplete and yet satisfactory to the hygienist; for the infection, that the milk may possibly have contained, has been destroyed by the heating, even though some harmless bacteria may have remained alive. Disinfection, however, must always be complete. That is, the sterilizing process must have been carried far enough to insure the destruction of *all* germs of disease. The use of disinfecting solutions that are too weak is worse than using none at all; for it gives a false reliance. Sprinkling people with carbolic acid does not remove infection from them.

Deodorizers are not to be recommended as effective against an infectious disease unless at the same time they are potent disinfectants. An agent which simply lessens or overpowers an odor without *destroying the cause*, if that cause be harmful, is as a rule an unsafe reliance. Of this class are most of the proprietary articles that are lavishly recommended by those who sell them, and which even appear to be endorsed by some physicians. Simpler, safer and less expensive means answer the same purpose. *Chloride of lime* has the merit of both removing odors very efficiently and at the same time serving as a disinfectant when fresh and strong enough.

If, for instance, charcoal or dried and powdered loam be freely sprinkled over the matters that have passed from the bowels of a patient having typhoid fever or cholera, the odor is lessened or it wholly ceases. The matters are then said to be *deodorized*. The bacteria of disease are not thereby destroyed, but may live for a time in a dangerous form. Being dried, they do not then increase or give off odor. After days or months, the natural disinfectant power of fresh air and light will have destroyed the harmful germs. The natural process is more or less certain, although too slow to be considered safe.

If, on the other hand, a sufficient amount of fresh milk of lime (or of any other suitable disinfectant solution) be added to the dangerous disease discharges, this soon kills all the harmful bacteria that make these matters a possible source of further disease. Disinfectants must always be strong enough to effect the desired sterilization of the disease germs against which they are used. Rapidity of action is also important.

Sunlight and fresh air are disinfectant forces of considerable efficacy. Yet they are not to be relied upon when the object is to annihilate speedily the infectious element in any case. We cannot be assured that these valuable natural means have acted upon the disease germs under entirely suitable conditions in every instance. Thus, if they be in masses and surrounded by various matters, certain germs of disease can resist the action of air and light for many weeks or months.

Cholera germs, however, seem very sensitive to these influences combined with drying. Much more certain in their working are heat and chemicals. With these means, we can be absolutely sure that our disinfection is complete. Yet sunlight and fresh air are always to be employed as accessories whenever possible.

Water, freely flowing over a surface, will have removed very many of the bacteria that may chance to have been there. We know, by experiment, that if a clean bottle be rinsed out with water having many bacteria in it and then emptied, very few of the bacteria cling to the sides of the bottle. However unclean they may be, the hands, when washed in the ordinary manner with soap and a brush and then rinsed, have remaining upon them very few of the bacteria that were upon the skin and under the nails in their unclean condition. Yet when extreme cleanliness is demanded, as for a serious surgical operation, several further rinsings in suitable disinfectants (as in a 1 to 1000 corrosive sublimate solution) are needed so that no germs that can cause wound infection shall remain alive upon the hands.

Mechanical removal by such means as beating, shaking, brushing and wiping carpets and other articles of furniture and clothing, disposes of many of the germs that may be upon and in these objects. Yet many of these germs may remain within the fabric. In any case, a liberal exposure to sunlight and fresh air should follow the mechanical attempts at removal of the infectious elements. It must further be borne in mind that such means are liable to diffuse the danger by scattering the shaken-out germs upon various people and places. Since we lack scientific evidence of the value of immersion in *naphtha* (which is sometimes used) for such infected articles as carpets and furniture, heat or suitable chemicals ought always to be preferred if permissible for the disinfection of these things.

Burning readily and effectively disposes of objects that are infected. For small, valueless articles and worthless clothing, this means is especially serviceable. In order that no infective germs be shaken off while articles are being removed to the destroying fire, it is well that they be wrapped in moist cloth (or paper). *Heat* has already been spoken of (on page 385). It is the *best* of all disinfectants wherever practicable. When used to treat ordinary clothing and utensils, heat is an excellent destroyer of all infectious germs. Yet articles of leather, fur, whalebone or rubber shrink when exposed to such warmth and are therefore usually treated with corrosive sublimate (1 to 2000) solution.

Woollen goods suffer somewhat with high heat; but when seriously infected, they are generally best treated by that means. In such a case the temperature of the hot water used must not at any time be below 175° F., and the goods ought to be kept in that for half an hour. Steam, acting for nearly the same time, is preferable. Before the garments are heated, any spots that have recently been produced upon cloth by medicines, blood, discharges, etc., ought to be moistened with a very weak solution of permanganate of potash (one-fourth of a grain to the ounce of water). Thus the spots are rendered less liable to become fixed in the fabric.

Moist heat is more effective than dry heat, both being of the same high temperature. Hence *superheated steam* is made use of for disinfecting-stations where rapid but thorough work is to be done. In such places, a tightly closing, strongly constructed chamber (represented by *E* in

FIG. 81.

Fig. 83) is used to hold the clothing, bedding, etc., during the process.

Such a steam-chamber with the accompanying boiler can also be made portable. (See Fig. 81.) This can be hauled to a camp or to an infected tenement or lodging-house or elsewhere. It can be used for disinfecting bedding and clothing or anything else that can be put in it and is considered proper for steam disinfection. When the door at the rear is opened, a rack or other arrangement similar to that shown in Fig. 83 is run out for receiving the articles to be steamed.

The value of such appliances has frequently been demonstrated in France and Germany during the last few years. They have recently been introduced into the United States. The cost of the complete portable apparatus delivered in America exceeds a thousand dollars.

The disinfecting chambers shown in Figs. 81 and 83 are constructed by Geneste, Herscher & Co., of Paris. Similar ones are made in Chemnitz and elsewhere in Germany. The Parisian firm gives figures showing the average cost of steam disinfection. From these, we learn that the use of the *portable* disinfector (shown in Fig. 81) makes the complete disinfection of each mattress cost less than 9 cents (43 centimes) in Paris. The apparatus is in this estimate supposed to be used for ten hours per day. In that time, from twenty to thirty mattresses could be disinfected.

The cost of disinfecting one ton (2,200 pounds) of bedclothes, clothing, etc., in the ten hours would be a little more than two dollars (10.70 francs). With a *fixed* apparatus, such as is shown in Fig. 83, the cost is less than half of that.

For laboratory purposes as also for sterilizing bandages, surgical instruments, etc., we use a strongly constructed steamer (*autoclave*), tightly closing like the larger ones and also having a safety-valve arrangement to prevent danger from an excess of pressure due to the superheated steam. (See Fig. 82.)

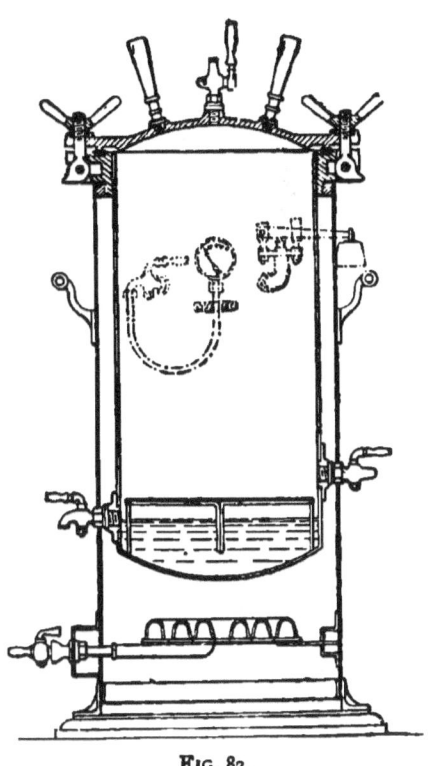

FIG. 82.

For domestic use, and for most ordinary purposes, a wash-boiler of hot water or any simple steamer, if large enough and manageable, serves nearly as well as the more elaborate apparatus would. A big kettle of boiling water answers for cotton goods and other articles that hot water will not injure. A closed, steam-jacket kettle works admirably for institutions.

It must be remembered that the higher the temperature, the less time is required in order to effect complete disinfection. The looser and more open articles are and the less they are packed together, the more readily does the sterilizing hot water or steam penetrate into all parts. When tightly bundled up or baled (like rags), more than half an hour of steaming should be allowed.

In less than ten minutes after the temperature of 212° has been reached in the interior of bundles, all infection must have been destroyed. Yet a full *half hour* ought to be allowed in order to be certain that the heat has penetrated sufficiently. Electric thermometers are best for testing steam disinfection. By these, a bell is made to sound automatically as soon as a desired temperature is reached.

An advantage of the more elaborate steam apparatus is that, if it be desired, the articles can there be heated with dry heat for a few minutes before the steam is introduced, as well as after the steaming has ceased. When the clothing and other articles are thus warmed in advance, the efficacy of the steam is increased and there is no moistening of the articles by condensation of the steam upon them.

This dry heat can be produced by means of a steam-jacket as a casing to the steam-chamber. Into this jacket, steam can be preliminarily introduced independently of that which goes into the interior where the infected articles are treated. Thus the inside can be made hot even without any steam being introduced, and whatever steam is in there can be superheated by means of the jacket-steam heat if desired. After superheated steam (having a temperature of 230° F.) has been used, the articles in the steam-chamber are found dry. In these disinfectors, the steam enters from above, and the cool air is driven out through an opening at the bottom. This opening is closed shortly after the steam begins to enter.

Disinfecting stations may be constructed upon the plan sketched in Fig. 84. That is based on the arrangements at the model establishment in Berlin. The boiler may be located nearer the steam-chamber, and may be in a cellar. The sterilizing steam-chamber (marked *E* in Fig. 83) is open

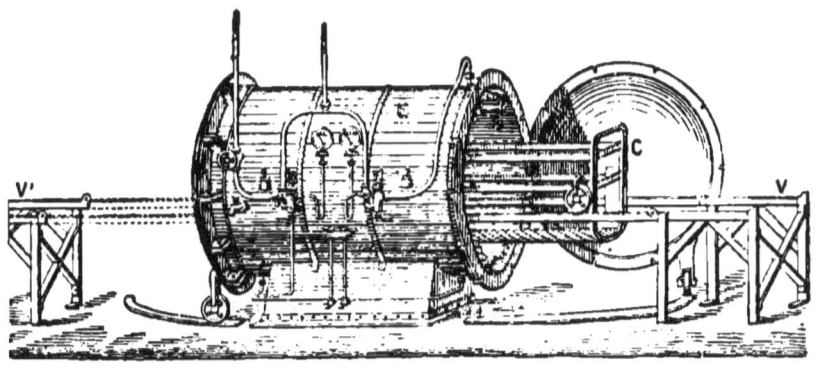

FIG. 83.

at both ends and is placed in the wall between the discharging room and the receiving room.

From the latter room, clothing, bedding and other articles to be disinfected are hung upon or laid on a cage or rack drawn out from the steam-chamber. The rack (to the left of the letter *C*, in Fig. 83) is then returned into the steam-chamber which thereupon has both doors tightly closed. Steam at a temperature of 230° F. or higher (that is to say, under a pressure exceeding twenty pounds) is then driven into it for half an hour *after* the thermometer shows that the interior, with its contents, has reached a temperature of at least 140° F.

After that, this thereby sterilized chamber is opened by unfastening and swinging back the door into the *discharging room*, the rack containing the clothing, etc., is drawn out and the disinfected articles are removed This rack is at once returned to the steam-chamber, the door of that is closed and other infected articles may then be put in from the receiving room to undergo in their turn the same process.

While their clothing is being sterilized, the people are being conducted in a roundabout way through bath-rooms where they are bathed and thoroughly cleansed. In Fig. 84, the longer dots show the route of the persons to be

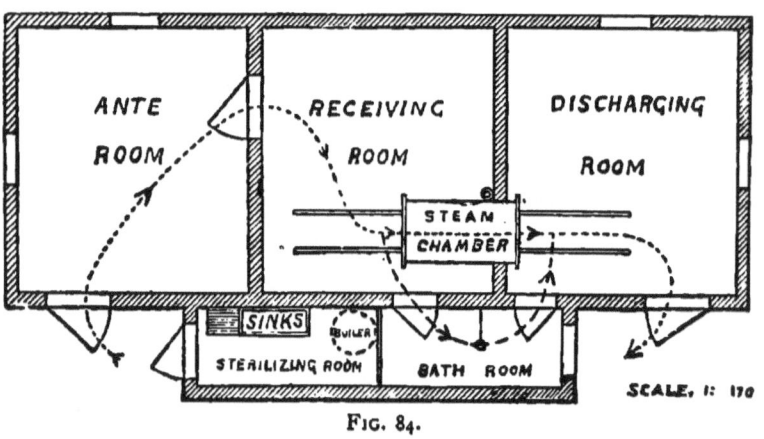

Fig. 84.

cleaned. The articles to be disinfected go through the steam-chamber as indicated by the shorter dots. The bath-room ought to be more commodious. Shower baths are the most convenient kind for such places.

For buildings, soil-pipes, and other places where it can be introduced and held sufficiently to maintain a prolonged high temperature, moist heat is exceedingly efficient as a disinfector. Yet it is not always practicable for such situations, since it causes damage to some materials by inducing expansion. Besides this, steam or other heat may cause paint to "blister up" and is apt to make the pitchy matters run out of resinous woods. For many purposes, accordingly, we have to employ chemical disinfectants.

Chemical disinfectants are spoken of on pages 386 to 388. Others, such as permanganate of potash, peroxide of hydrogen and numerous substances known to scientists, are not discussed there or here because they are either too expensive for general use, or they are demonstrably inferior or will probably be shown to be so when more fully tested. Only the disinfectants of actual superiority deserve to be considered here. Chloride of zinc will not be especially commended, since most competent observers discredit it. The same may be said of various proprietary disinfectants which certain interested experimenters praise highly.

It is proper that all chemical disinfectants bear the label POISON in order to lessen the liability to accidents which occasionally result from ignorance or carelessness in their use. Poisoning from ordinary disinfectants is not uncommon. The addition of harmless colors is of value for disinfectant solutions. The poison label must however always be insisted upon. The hands ought not to be kept in contact with these chemicals. Some of them injure the skin very much.

Corrosive sublimate (*bichloride of mercury*, $HgCl_2$) is our most valuable chemical disinfectant. It was spoken of on page 387. It is very potent and relatively inexpensive as compared with carbolic acid; yet it is more poisonous than most chemicals. Practically it is not very quickly soluble in water. So we add ammonic chloride or common salt to improve it in this respect. By the addition to it of five times its weight of common salt, a mercury salt is formed which is more effective against the germs of disease, chiefly because the compound does not so readily coagulate albuminous matters that may be about the germs and which, when coagulated, prevent somewhat the action of the chemical.

The standard disinfectant solution of this salt is of the strength of one part to one thousand of water. For this, we take a little more than one drachm (sixty grains) of corrosive sublimate (to which the same amount of ammonic chloride may be added for increasing the solubility and efficacy) and with this five drachms of common salt. These are dissolved by stirring well with one gallon of warm water in a wooden pail or a non-corrodible vessel. Corrosive sublimate attacks metallic surfaces.

This makes a solution slightly weaker than 1 to 1000. Yet it answers the purpose. On a large scale, one pound (avoirdupois) of corrosive sublimate suffices exactly for adding (preferably with salt) to one hundred (imperial) gallons of water, thus making the standard solution. Physicians (for their own use) find it convenient to carry a twenty per cent. solution of the salt in alcohol and to dilute this fifty or one hundred times when needed.

For ordinary purposes, a corrosive sublimate solution of 1 to 2000, that is to say, half as strong as the standard solution, is the weakest that should be used. For the disinfection of discharges, the standard solution is required, as this becomes diluted by being added to the infected fluids.

Carbolic acid was spoken of on page 386. It does not corrode metals to any extent. For disinfection, we use the best quality and in the strength of five per cent., which is practically all that water will dissolve. As with all other solutions, we prefer for this that the water be distilled or at least filtered clear. If not to be used for surgical instruments or other metallic surfaces, the carbolic solution is more effective when half of one per cent. of hydrochloric acid (or one per cent. of tartaric acid) is added to it.

Lysol and various proprietary coal-tar products show good results in some cases; but the better tested agents are preferable. Crude carbolic acid is of value because of the *cresol* in it, but is fit only for coarse uses. These products should have stood for one day with equal amounts of strong sulphuric acid before a solution of them is made. *Solutol* (alkaline cresol) is highly recommended by some observers.

Crude sulphuric acid or hydrochloric acid may be classed among the very strongest and most valuable disinfectants. (See page 386.) Being corrosive, they should not come into contact with metals, and are to be handled as dangerous poisons. They are to be used in the strength of at least one fluid ounce to the quart of the discharges to be disinfected. Thus, a large wineglassful is to be added for every two quarts of cholera discharges. It is to be well mixed into the discharges and preferably allowed to stand for several hours, if that can easily be managed.

Quicklime and chloride of lime, when very fresh, are most valuable disinfectants. One per cent. solutions of these will destroy many kinds of bacteria. Yet it is best to employ them in greater strength. To prepare *milk of lime*, fresh quicklime is put into about four times its bulk of water (a little over two pounds being allowed for a gallon). Milk of lime, recently prepared, may be added directly to the matters to be disinfected. It acts most speedily and thoroughly if well mixed in, as with a stick. One part is to be allowed for ten times its bulk of typhoid or other discharges, although somewhat weaker solutions are effective upon long standing. When poured into water-closets, care must be taken that abundant water be used some hours afterward, so that no obstruction be formed in the pipes.

Sulphur fumigations, though familiar and venerable, are less valuable than they are generally considered. We feel safer when other disinfectants are also used with the sulphur gas. Even for destroying vermin in old wooden houses, it is well that at the same time corrosive sublimate or some other agent be employed. Where sulphur-burning is relied upon, the floors, walls, furniture and other parts of the room to be fumigated should always have been previously moistened (as with corrosive sublimate solution or water). All crevices and outlets of the room must have been stopped up.

Three or more pounds of sulphur are required for every thousand cubic feet of room-space, whether cracked "brimstone" or the convenient prepared sulphur "tapers" be employed. Usually, roll sulphur is broken up and put on shallow metal surfaces, supported (by wire or otherwise) above tubs or other containers of water. Alcohol is then poured upon the sulphur and set fire to by matches. When the sulphur has begun to burn, every one must have left the room. The closed door should then be tightly stopped up from outside with rags or by pasting large sheets of paper over the entire door-opening. The room is to remain unopened for several days after this fumigation.

For cleaning papered walls of an infected room, v. Esmarch's method appears after many trials to be a very good one. This consists in using thick, freshly cut (but not very moist) slices of quite fresh bread to wipe systematically every part of the wall. Although expensive, this effects the removal of bacteria. The slices must be used lavishly and (with all crumbs and gathered dirt) *carefully collected* upon sheets of paper. No crumbs are to be left on the wall. Bread, paper and dirt are all to be speedily consumed by fire. Moist sponges and cloths appear nearly if not quite as effective for the purpose. They are more destructive of delicate wall coverings.

Walls and ceilings of public rooms, vessels, etc., can be very satisfactorily treated by the preliminary employment of disinfectant solutions propelled against the surface in the form of a fine spray or mist. If the room-air be not too dry, this spray will remain as a moist film upon the surface and thus act to destroy the infection. If such a spray be allowed to dry immediately upon being applied, and the wall or ceiling does not remain moist for any time, the infection may not be entirely destroyed. All germs of disease are not instantly killed upon being moistened with a disinfectant solution. The longer they are kept wet by it, the more certainly will they be destroyed. Moistening restricts bacteria from flying about.

For producing this spray of carbolic acid or other solution, an *atomizer* is used resembling the one shown in Fig. 85. The use of corrosive sublimate solutions, which are found very valuable against diphtheria and other infections, would corrode any metal parts. Therefore, non-corrodible tips ought always to be employed on such spray producers. The same principle (of disinfecting by the use of copious sprays) is applied on a much larger scale. Thus, large wagons are constructed (of the size of that shown in Fig. 81) which use steam power to drive disinfectant sprays against and into all parts of railway cars, markets, etc.

It is desirable that the tip of such a spray-producing tube when in use be, as is shown in the figure, within less than a yard of the ceiling. If more than two yards away, it is much less effective.

Fig. 85.

On paint, for instance that of walls and ceilings, cleansing is best done by washing down the surfaces with five per cent. solution of carbolic acid (or 1 to 1000 corrosive sublimate solution). Large amounts must be used and the sponges or mop-cloths frequently changed by being dropped moist into pails of the solution, and fresh cloths then used. The application of fresh paint has been shown to be an adequate means of destroying all germs of disease present upon surfaces or wherever the paint can reach. Whitewashed surfaces should receive abundant, strong whitewash as simply and freshly prepared from fresh quicklime as possible. For small rooms where formaldehyde gas can be satisfactorily used, the older liquid disinfectants may be sprayed into crevices and recesses as above indicated; for diphtheria bacilli, e. g., may have entered crevices or settled in a floor deeper than the gas penetrates.

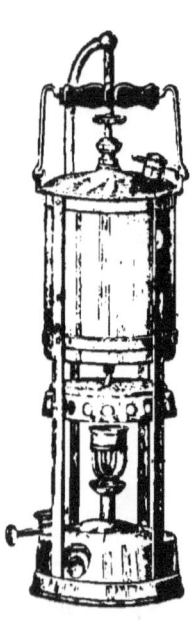

FIG. 86.

Formaldehyde is a harmless and valuable superficial disinfectant for walls, ceilings, the outside of furniture, hangings, clothing (if hung loosely with pockets turned out) delicate fabrics, leather goods and furs. It does not penetrate, in spite of statements to the contrary; hence it is useless for pillows, mattresses and deeply infected goods, and cannot supplant steam and chemical disinfectants. It is better than naphtha or benzine. Unlike sulphur, it works best when objects are dry. Of the several ways of generating the gas the commercial pastilles and lamp are most expensive. The apparatus of Trillat or that of the Sanitary Construction Co. is efficient. For the sickroom, the F. C. Robinson lamp, made extra large, burning 20 to 30 ounces of wood alcohol for each thousand cubic feet of space, is reliable and cheap. The room is to remain tightly closed for at least ten hours. Precautions are needed to prevent fire.

Floors and mopboards need to be mopped liberally with five per cent. carbolic solution, even though formaldehyde or sulphur have been used. If a floor have been well laid, smooth and prepared as indicated on page 149, a single thorough application of the strong carbolic solution will suffice. In a bad case, and especially for our ordinary floors upon which filth has fallen, fresh milk of lime may also be freely applied with great advantage. Ventilating flues are to have their surfaces thoroughly treated like walls and floors.

Bed-clothing and wearing apparel when infected should, if washable, be put into a five per cent. carbolic acid solution and left there for one day. Or they can be enclosed in a moistened sheet and carried to the place where they are to be boiled in water or steamed for more than thirty minutes. For these, and especially for articles which will not bear washing, the use of a steam disinfecting apparatus having an inner temperature of over $220°$ F. (see Fig. 83) is to be preferred. This latter means is also best for hangings, draperies, carpets and other fabrics or articles liable to hold infection from having been in a sick-room.

Such things are to be removed before any other cleaning is done in the room. They should be wrapped in damp cloths, then carefully carried away and promptly disinfected. When put into the steam-chamber they are to be only loosely rolled. Bundles are to be loosely disposed and well separated so that the steam shall penetrate freely. Feather-beds, for instance, need to be in some way kept from packing solid. Window-shades and rollers should have been burned or treated as above indicated, according to their material, quality and exposure to infection. Steaming is usually the best means of disinfection for these.

Disinfection can best be carried out by conscientious people who make a business of that work. They should be under the control of experts who are familiar with all scientific progress, but yet are not liable to make the mistake of adopting a mere novelty for an essential advance. Such employees ought to use rubber or other suitable material for their outer clothing. They require rubber boots for use while doing their work. The blouse shown in Fig. 85 is long enough if rubber boots be worn. It is important to guard against the possible event of the disinfecting people themselves becoming the carriers of infection by careless disposal of their outer clothing.

These articles, as also the hands and other exposed surfaces, should be rinsed with a standard solution of corrosive sublimate (1 to 1000) when the work is completed. The articles are then to be rolled up and carried away. The room is left with closed windows and doors for two or more hours in order that the bacteria may settle and that the solutions on the floor and other surfaces may not dry too rapidly. Then the windows are to be opened at top and bottom. The fresh air ought to be allowed to circulate freely over the infected objects and surfaces.

Hotel-keepers or others who lease rooms ought always to be legally required to have any infected room promptly disinfected to the full satisfaction of experts. A severe penalty should be enforced upon any one who leases or offers to lease a room or rooms without truthfully informing the possible tenant in case any infectious disease has occurred there within two months.

Hotels are at times very remiss in this respect. The author is informed of four fatal cases of diphtheria where the disease attacked successive occupants of a "very desirable" room in a prominent New York hotel. The infection would not have survived the first of these cases if proper measures of disinfection and isolation had at once been instituted as soon as the nature of the disease was recognized. A hotel-room is, at the best, an unsuitable place for the treatment of any infectious disease. This comprehends tuberculosis as well as the more acute communicable diseases.

During the course of an infectious disease, all discharges from the bowels and all that is coughed up or that comes from the mouth ought to be immediately subjected to careful disinfection. The same rule applies to any wound discharges, dressings or cloths, etc. The nurse and all other people that have been in contact with the disease need to be thoroughly cleansed. Clothing, books, papers, food and other articles that have been near a contagious case must be prevented from carrying the infection to other people. Burning effectually destroys the infection that may be in or upon such articles. Carriages or wagons, used to convey patients having such diseases, should be swabbed well (inside, at least) with five per cent. carbolic acid solution. Cloth cushions ought to be steamed. Atomizers (see Fig. 85) cause the disinfecting solution to penetrate very effectually into fissures and cavities.

Wound dressings, cloths and other things that have been applied to diseased surfaces, should be caught in paper, rolled up and promptly burned. The (1 to 2000) corrosive sublimate or other solution used to wash diseased parts in cases of puerperal fever or wounds must be received in special vessels. Such receptacles for discharges ought always to contain at least a small amount of a strong disinfectant solution. Excellent for this purpose is fresh milk of lime having one part of lime to ten parts of water. A weaker solution suffices, but is slower of action. The standard (1 to 1000) solution of corrosive sublimate is nearly as good.

After the discharges have entered the vessel, some of the disinfectant solution that is selected can be poured on satisfactorily by using an enamelled-ware ladle. This, being of known measurement, allows a fairly accurate estimate of the amount used of the solution. If, for instance, the milk of lime be made by adding one pound (avoirdupois) of fresh lime to one imperial gallon of water and if the ladle have the capacity of an ordinary goblet (eight ounces), one ladleful suffices to disinfect one quart of the matters with which it is mingled and allowed to stand. Of the 1 to 1000 corrosive sublimate solution or of the other solutions recommended in this book, an amount should be used which at least is equal to the total volume of the discharges requiring disinfection.

Instruments for ~~serious~~ operations must invariably be sterilized just before they are used, even if there be no suspicion that they are possibly infected. They also need to be carefully cleansed and disinfected after any operation. The hands and person of the surgeon, and also of all who aid or who come into contact with the instruments or dressings, must be scrupulously clean. The use of an instrument without carefully sterilizing it, after it has been upon the floor or upon an unclean table, is very wrong. It is in place here to remark that the lips are not clean enough for holding instruments.

It is a very careless operator (whether surgeon or dentist) who does not take thorough measures to destroy all germs that may be on instruments and anything else that is used near wounds. Mechanical removal by the usual cleaning takes away most germs that may be on polished surfaces. Knives, and articles that are not injured by a temperature under 300° F., should be kept in metal cases. Superheated steam, as produced by the apparatus shown in Fig. 82, is excellent for disinfecting these. With care, rusting need not occur. Baking in an oven heated just below the point that slightly browns cotton-wool is a very effective means of sterilizing instruments, needles, etc. Yet moist heat, as has been said, is more quickly effective.

Whenever a knife or other object has been in contact with *malignant carbuncle* or any virulent and resistant infection, it should be disinfected by being exposed for forty minutes to the continuous action of superheated steam (see Fig. 82) or of dry heat (not much below 300° F.), if this heating be practicable. If heat cannot be used, careful cleaning and prolonged immersion in a strong carbolic solution is imperative.

Ordinary wound-infection bacteria (as also the infective element of syphilis) are very sensitive to the sterilizing action of heat and disinfectant solutions. In most cases, the immersion of a clean knife or hypodermic needle for a minute in boiling water suffices to destroy infection. It is always well to have at hand a five per cent. carbolic acid solution to put instruments into. This solution proves at times too strong for the skin. Accordingly, the instrument (after having lain in this strong solution) may be dipped into boiling water, or into that which has just been boiled, in order to remove any remnant of the strong, irritating solution. This is not necessary in ordinary cases.

Less efficacious, but usually sufficiently strong, is a two per cent. carbolic solution or a three per cent. (saturated) solution of boric acid, to be employed with perfectly clean instruments used for cutting delicate surfaces. Manicure instruments need to be disinfected; for we sometimes see very bad infection arise from careless use of such things. Before cutting "corns," the feet and knives ought to be cleansed. The neglect of such precautions is occasionally followed by considerable inflammations.

For all operations, whether upon human beings or animals, the skin (to be cut) must be carefully cleansed after soaping and shaving it. It is then to be rinsed with alcohol and water and, after this, with a 1 to 2000 solution of corrosive sublimate. The hands of the operator must also be bathed in a similar solution. All water used for rinsing should have been boiled. If the hands and all else that comes near the wound have been thoroughly cleaned, the dressings disinfected (by heat) beforehand, and if these protective dressings be thick enough to keep out disease germs, there need be feared no erysipelas, tetanus or other complication coming from uncleanliness.

Spittoons and other receptacles for the expectorations from consumptives and other lung cases as well as from diphtheria and other diseases of the mouth and throat ought in every case to contain enough of the standard disinfectant solutions to moisten any matters that may enter. It is well that they be suitably covered. To disinfect any enamelled or porcelain articles used for such a purpose, steaming for half an hour is sufficient. The covers require the same disinfection, as a rule.

For consumptives in general and for railways and some other purposes, inexpensive, varnished pasteboard receptacles and spittoons are to be recommended. These remain water-tight for a while. They ought to be burned after using. Such things must not be thrown away until they have been sterilized by burning or other efficient process. Strong milk of lime quickly disinfects them. A little "excelsior," or other means of preventing splashing of the contained disinfectant solution and disease matters, may be in the bottom of spittoons.

For the disinfection of water-closets (including their traps), considerably more than a gallon of solution should be poured in and allowed to remain for some time in the bowl and the trap without any flushing from the tank. The seat and sides of the bowl should be well mopped with the same solution. The five per cent. carbolic acid solution is always valuable, especially because it does not attack metallic surfaces. Half a pound (avoirdupois) of this acid is needed for each five quarts of water used. Cheaper and more effective as a rule is the (1 to 1000) solution of corrosive sublimate. Two drachms (or a little more) of this *very poisonous* salt and an ounce of common salt are to be dissolved in two gallons of warm water. The above solutions suffice for the disinfection of sinks.

Of the various other chemicals, fresh lime is to be recommended as above explained. Sulphate of copper (*blue vit-*

riol), half a pound being dissolved in two gallons of water, is recommended by some observers. The latest experiments (1893) throw doubt over the claims made for this salt if it be used any weaker than above indicated.

The strong acids are very powerful, but act on iron and copper. Better are very strong, *hot* solutions of potash (or pearlash) or caustic soda, especially for sinks. They are disinfectants and also serve to remove grease. After the solutions have stood for a long time (*more than an hour if possible*) in the bowls, sinks and traps, these should be freely flushed out with water.

Privy vaults and cesspools, if their contents be unsterilized, must not be emptied at time of epidemics. The walls of out-houses at such times ought to be well coated with plain whitewash made of fresh lime. Privy seats should then be well swabbed with any of the standard solutions spoken of above. The 1 to 1000 corrosive sublimate solution is best for general use in such places. (For disinfection of privy vaults, see the following paragraph; also see page 362.)

The safest as well as most economical way is to disinfect all disease discharges before they enter a vault. If, in exceptional cases, it is necessary to disinfect an entire vault or cesspool, fresh quicklime mixed with a little water deserves to be regarded as the best means in most cases. One pound of the lime is to be introduced for every cubic foot of the vault contents. It is to be thoroughly mixed in and allowed to stand for hours at least. Chloride of lime is still stronger than this. Yet it is more costly as well as liable to change and thus become impaired. If copper sulphate be used, it should at least be in the strength above given for lime.

Quarantine

Quarantine embraces measures directed toward the prevention of the entrance of infection from without. The origin of the significance of this word lay in the barbarous mediæval notion that people and vessels coming from a locality having infectious diseases ought invariably to be detained for *forty* days before touching land or being allowed to enter a place.

The custom of herding many people together upon a disease-laden ship or in filthy enclosures near a frontier, so that the infected are liable to remain a constant source of further disease, is in every way harmful. Much less injury either to commerce or to health is caused when all the travellers are at once removed, the diseased and the suspected separated from the healthy, and each of these classes carefully kept by itself. Cleanly, ample and agreeable accommodations are necessary for those who are thus isolated and detained.

The ship, cargo and all personal effects that possibly can have been in any way exposed to infection are then to be detained as long as is necessary in order to insure that they have been thoroughly cleansed and disinfected. On pages 430 to 451, the practical details of disinfection are explained. A quarantine outfit calls for steam-disinfecting apparatus similar to that illustrated in Fig. 83.

Those who are especially interested in practical maritime quarantine are advised to read the booklet by Dr. Joseph Holt describing the excellent and tested Louisiana quarantine and disinfection methods employed at the mouth of the Mississippi river and which were introduced according to modern scientific principles.

For a large ship, not more than 8,000 gallons of (1 to 1000) corrosive sublimate solution and less than 1,000 pounds of roll sulphur for fumigating the hold are needed. Steam from a special steel boiler is also used; if properly employed, it is much more valuable than sulphur fumigations. If the bilge water is pumped out in port, it should have had corrosive sublimate dissolved in it one day beforehand so as to make a 1 to 1000 solution of the mercury salt in that water. Although this chemical acts upon iron or other metallic surfaces, any damage to the vessel should seem a minor consideration as compared with the necessity of destroying the infection.

The crew and passengers (if to be detained for a few days or possibly for more than a week, as in some cases is necessary and proper) may, after being cleansed and examined, be returned to the disinfected ship or to a thoroughly cleanly and commodious camp. *No suspected cases are to be allowed to mingle with those who are well.* The attendants upon one class of the detained are also to be restricted from contact with any others.

With zealous attention to cleanliness and the supplying of fresh, clean food and water, those who entered the quarantine in health can be allowed to go their way after the few days required for the period of incubation (of the suspected disease) to have passed. If, for instance, a ship brings cholera cases to a port, yet is promptly disinfected and the diseased and suspected cases are properly isolated, the passengers who are well can safely be discharged in four or five days. With yellow fever, a three days' longer detention may at times be called for.

In England, it is deemed better to allow voyagers considerable freedom. That country, pursuing a policy of detaining only the diseased and suspected, after carefully taking the prospective addresses of well people entering her numerous ports (which communicated frequently and intimately with cholera ports), was quite free from the disease in 1892. Yet, besides a number of suspected ones, eleven or more genuine cases of cholera occurred in September of that year in " widely separated parts of " New York City, these cases having entered from without through the quarantine despite the severe attempts there made to exclude the disease by the familiar methods.

In favor of an intelligent quarantine may be instanced the immunity of New Orleans from yellow fever during the few years that the present thorough system has been employed to guard the lower Mississippi valley. The certainty that all will be subjected to a faithful and searching examination makes vessel owners very careful to allow no persons from infected districts to embark.

Despite all this, an unprejudiced person who has undergone and observed quarantine inspection on all of our frontiers and coasts, as well as on various frontiers of Europe, at times of different epidemics, is likely to be convinced of the fact that no quarantine, however scientific or barbarous, is constantly able to exclude all cases of disease. Some infected people manage to evade even "shot-gun quarantines" and formidable cordons of soldiers.

For these reasons, it must be insisted that it is hygienically of the utmost importance not to place absolute reliance upon the exclusion of disease by merely quarantining it. The place that dreads disease and desires to remain free from infection must attend to general and special cleanliness. Dirt and infection must be kept away from streets, houses, railway stations and other places of assemblage and traffic. So, likewise, all food supplies and especially milk and water must be zealously guarded to prevent danger of epidemics.

People who are unclean are to be regarded as dangerous. Filth favors pestilence that has evaded a quarantine : a single case entering an unclean place can originate a serious epidemic. But when the best local hygienic conditions are maintained, even though numerous cases elude a vigilant quarantine and enter a perfectly cleanly community (supplied with pure water and clean food), the disease will extend no further if proper attention be paid to isolation and disinfection. At the same time, it is of great value to employ every enlightened and humane means to exclude the disease that threatens to enter.

Quarantines, even as ordinarily conducted, are of value in keeping out infectious diseases from American ports. Since broad ocean surfaces separate us from the regions whence our filthiest immigrants come, we have a valuable safeguard in that fact. The ocean passage usually takes time enough to have covered the period of incubation, between the reception of the infection by an individual and the time when the disease first manifests itself.

The period of incubation (see page 402) is less than a week with cholera and also with the plague. The same may be said of scarlet fever. In yellow fever and diphtheria, the period rarely exceeds a week. Measles, smallpox and typhus require twice as long a time to have passed before we can safely say that the person recently exposed to these has not received the infection. With typhus, the period may be a week longer.

The most rational general safeguard in the form of exclusion would be to require that every one who was about to emigrate hither should of necessity have already a certificate of health (and of presumable general fitness) secured from the United States consul of the region from which the emigrant came. Without this, no one should be allowed to land here. If, after the adoption of these precautions, no cases of infectious disease had arisen during the ocean passage, such people could be considered free from infection. International coöperation is of value in these matters. Desultory advices from foreign agents of municipalities or organizations here have proved to be an unsafe reliance.

When quarantine is attempted, it must be intelligent and consistent. Good executive ability and conscientiousness are needed in any case. It can be effectively carried out by a State, as is shown by the thoroughness with which the Louisiana quarantine method keeps out yellow fever and other diseases. Yet it seems preferable, for the sake of thoroughness and general security, that the national government should control this important bulwark against disease.

Cases of infectious disease that have entered a community in spite of a quarantine, must be isolated in special hospitals or dwellings. Notification to the authorities, whenever such cases arise or are even suspected, ought to be compulsory. By an equitable arrangement, those in close contact with the patients should be strictly controlled and kept from carrying the infection to others. The proper disinfection of the invaded apartments, and the other precautions already indicated must be observed in every case.

VITAL STATISTICS. LONGEVITY

To the actuary or statistician, the "probable duration of life" is a precise number of years in a given case readily determinable from "life tables" arranged by Farr and other experts in *vital statistics*. This mathematical aspect of the subject is interesting and important to life insurance companies, as it provides an average to guide them fairly well in their business. For an individual the question is very uncertain and complex. He has the same statistical data, but for him singly their applicability to the average person is only a very vague guide, and many subjective and objective incidents occur to modify the chance of survival to the traditional three score years and ten. From Farr's tables and Newsholme we learn, for instance, that there is one chance in seven that a person will die of phthisis, and seven times as much likelihood that some other disease will cause his end as that phthisis will. But in a particular case the probability may be much greater or much less than the average according as heredity, the usual surroundings, unusual circumstances, intelligent care and other factors influence the result.

Statistical records of the healthfulness and mortality of a locality and the prevalent diseases, especially if given for a number of years, are very instructive when reliable and accurately interpreted, with due allowances for immigrations, age- and sex-distribution and special conditions The *death rate* is usually estimated at so many deaths yearly per thousand of the entire population. This rate is reported by some of our cities as being less than 10. Under 17 is very good. Over 25 is high. Country districts have lower death rates than cities, and the denser the city population the greater the rate of mortality.

The very low death rate reported by certain of our western cities does not show that these are proportionately more healthful than eastern places having a higher mortality. The fact that the population of these budding cities is largely composed of vigorous young immigrants (under thirty years of age), and that in most of these young cities the birth rate is high, accounts in large part for the favorable figures. Somewhat the same may be said of residential suburbs and watering places, where also there are many young female servants.

A high death rate may be due to: (1) A high birth rate, if considered only for a brief period,* infant mortality being enormous. But if the birth rate remain high for a considerable number of years the increased proportion of young adults would cause the death rate to be lowered. (2) A low birth rate continuing for many years, although for a few years it would lower the general death rate. (3) City residence in unhealthful districts, crowding into unsanitary tenements, with consequent degeneracy and disease. (4) Alcoholic and other excess, causing poverty, misery, starvation, neglect. Bad food, patent medicines, soothing syrups to infants. (5) Crime, perilous occupations, and those directly and indirectly harmful. Epidemics. (6) Extremes of hot or of cold weather, especially if of long continuance.

Premature death, like suffering, disease and vague ill-health come, to a great extent, from causes which can be prevented, or at least mitigated in severity of incidence even if not wholly averted. With infectious diseases such is demonstrably the case. Thus, in Munich the pure water supply has made typhoid fever very rare, and compulsory vaccination has practically extinguished small-pox, a disease of which thousands of cases have occurred in a few localities

---

* Newsholme, *Vital Statistics*, pages 70, 84, 86.

in England recently because of a strong sentiment preventing vaccination. So, too, small-pox is exceedingly prevalent in Mexico,* although it might be quite possible to stamp out the disease.

We know that the causes of premature chronic diseases are to a certain extent preventable, and the tissue degenerations that they represent can be restricted like other manifestations of early old age. Yet the ideal civilized life, perfect and free from vice, intemperance and other manifestations of ignorance and indifference, seems incapable of realization. Ordinarily people tend, in part at least, to live so out of harmony with natural laws that there is a marked tendency to the early development of degenerative diseases of the vital organs. It is the brain and nervous system in general that most conspicuously show the effects of degenerative disorders, among civilized people as compared with savages. Healthy people who live simply and naturally with no great strain, worry or stagnation, are least likely to develop mental, nervous or other degenerative diseases.

Charcot's pupils have done much 'to show the intimate relationship between various phases of chronic disease and the protean and indirect way in which morbid heredity or degeneracy may be manifested. In one and the same class they accordingly include rheumatism, gout, asthma, neuralgias, neurasthenia, hysteria, epilepsy, criminality, paralyses and mental derangements. Defining degeneracy as a loss of the hereditary qualities that determine and fix the adaptations of the individual and the race, they find it manifested by physical, intellectual and moral deficiencies.

Such penalties being attached to an aberrant civilization and resulting from the complex and intense nature of the artificial struggle for existence and its developments, the cure and prevention of such things obviously lies in simple,

---

* *U. S. Public Health Reports;* March 4, 1898, page 211.

healthful ways of life and an avoidance of that which is unhygienic. Nature can then not only stop the process, but also seems capable in some instances of repairing somewhat the dissolution of heredity and favoring "regeneration." This calls for rest (including sleep), abundant food of wholesome quality, hygienically favorable surrounding conditions and entire absence of the factors that cause the degeneration. An illustration of the efficacy of intelligent efforts in this direction is found in the history of the Jews. That greatest of sanitarians, Moses, by judicious restrictions amid healthful surroundings, raised that people, in the brief space of forty years, from a condition of physical and moral debasement, disease and slavery to a degree of strength and vitality such as, maintained by temperance, has enabled them to survive many a civilization and to prosper despite all oppression. The ruling family of Russia may be mentioned as a prominent instance of successful resistance against beginning degeneracy.

Longevity results from conditions precisely the opposite of those causes of degeneracy, early disease and decrepitude. If we study many cases of sound and "ripe" old age, we find a good heredity figuring as the main factor, although some cases prove exceptions to this rule. But the advantage of descent from strong, sound ancestors is negatived and the strongest constitution undermined by excesses, the stress of unremitting struggle for wealth, influence and position, by yielding to the temptations and enervating influences that beset the luxurious rich. Like vice, destitution, misery, unceasing anxiety and worry, these tend to bring degeneration and insanity. Men confront these adverse influences in general, more than women do, and hence are more likely to "grow old before their time." Diversified hard work, either of brain or of muscles, does not appear to cause premature decay. Work or some occupation is quite indispensable to healthy life, while luxurious idleness is regarded as predisposing to bodily ailments, hysteria, and even insanity. The latter effect, especially in the form of religious delusions and fanatical outbreaks, comes also from mental stagnation and lack of healthy diversion.

In all walks of life, from Gladstone and Leo XIII. to toilers in the humblest social grades, examples abound to prove that a very advanced age may be reached without serious senility. Many a patient is virtually older at thirty-five than another at sixty-five. It is not the number of years alone that constitutes old age, but rather the condition of the arteries, the heart and other vital organs. These will probably long remain sound if so in the beginning and if the life have been lived with proper regard for the laws of health.

INDEX

A

Absorbability of food, 217-219.
Accidents, 115, 116.
Acclimatization, 10.
Acid drinks in fever, 272.
Acids bad for teeth, 63.
Actinomyces, 225.
Actinomycosis, 225, 416.
Adipocere, 373.
Adulteration of milk, 229.
    of wines and liquors, 245, 248.
Aërifying water, 287.
Aërobic bacteria, 383.
Ague, 404.
Air and bacteria, 142, 383.
Air-filter, 177.
Air, impurities in, 15.
Air inflow measurement, 207.
Alcohol, effects of, 246, 262.
Alcoholic liquors, 218, 244-249, 262.
Aleuronat in diabetes, 279.
Alkali for cleansing the skin, 57.
"Alkali water," to purify, 306.
Altitude, cooking at high, 257.
    and climate, 9, 29.
    for arresting consumption, 36.
    not causing lung hemorrhage, 37.
    of western routes, 39.
Albuminoid ammonia in water, 294.
Albuminous food, 214, 219.
    in chronic diseases, 272.
    in diabetic diet, 279.
Alum, clarifying water, 308.
    in bread, test for, 237.
American climates, 21, 34-41.

Ammonia in water, 292.
Amœbæ, 400.
Anaërobic bacteria, 383.
Anemometers, 33, 200.
Antitoxin, 395, 396.
Arsenic against malaria, 406.
    in cloth, etc., 51, 54.
    in wall-paper, etc., 153, 154.
    poisoning, 114.
    in kindergarten paper, etc., 109.
Artesian wells, 304.
Artificial feeding of babes, 264.
    lights, 128-139.
    comparison of, 135, 136.
    ventilation, 198-212.
Asphalt for floors, 150.
    pavement, 157.
Aspiration (exhaust ventilation), 202.
Assembly rooms, etc.,—quantity of fresh air needed, 196.
Athleticism, 72, 75.
Atomizer (disinfecting), 443.
Attenuation of bacteria, 392.
    of virus, 394-396.
Astigmatism, 69.
Autoclave, 435.

B

Bacilli, 380.
Back ventilation (plumbing), 338-344.
Bacteria and disease, 378-396, 400.
    and filters, 308.
    and floors, 147-149, 444.
    and health, 4.
    and meat, 226.
    and milk, 229, 230.

INDEX

Bacteria and sewage, 315.
    classification, 378, 380.
    held back by good filter, 286, 287.
    in air, 5.
    in corpses, 373, 376.
    in water, 288.
    nature and study of, 378–393.
    (of soil), 3, 4.
    universal prevalence of, 388.
Bacteriological test of water, 288, 293.
Baking bread, 235.
    meat, 253.
Baking-powder, 236, 237.
Baltimore heater, 169.
Bananas, 240.
Barley-water, 265.
Barometers, 28, 29, 30.
Bath-rooms, 61.
Baths and bathing, 41, 56–61, 65.
    and their effects, 59.
Bath-tubs, 61, 357.
Beard, 62.
Bed-clothing, 44, 54.
Beef extracts, 222.
Beer, 245, 247, 413.
Beet-roots, 238.
Berlin filter beds, 309.
    sewage fields, 331.
Beverages, proper temperature, 259.
Bicycling, 86, 87.
Bilge water, disinfection of, 452.
"Bitters," 262.
"Black vomit," 414.
Blockheads, 108.
Blood serum and infection, 393.
    (bacteria culture), 381, 382.
Blowers for ventilating, 203–206, 211.
Body-heat, its regulation, 42, 43.
Boiled water, 283.
Boiling improves hard water, 286.
Boiling meat, 255.
Boric acid (disinfectant), 387.
Bowl vents (plumbing), 353.
Boxing, 85.
Bread, 235.
    used for cleaning walls, 442.

Broiling, 254.
Building, 141, 142.
    material, 142, 144–148.
    material must be clean, 146–148.
Bulk of food required, 261.
Burial, changes after, 373.
Burying-grounds, 374.
Bushes and soil moisture, 140.
Butter, 232.

C

Caissons and diving-bells, 29.
California climate, 34, 37.
    wines, 244, 245.
Camping out, 40.
Canada, climate, 22–26, 30, 41.
Cancer, 395.
Candles, 128.
Canned vegetables, 239, 240.
    copper in, 239.
    lead in, 240.
Canoeing, 83.
Capillary attraction (in traps), 336.
Carbohydrates, 215, 265.
    in diabetes, 278.
Carbolic acid, 386, 413, 419, 426, 440.
Carbonic acid gas, 13–15.
    amount exhaled, 194.
    in bread-making, 235, 236.
    from muscles, 71.
    monoxide gas, 132, 164, 165.
Carcasses, disposal of, 371.
Carcinoma [see *Cancer*], 395.
Carlsbad, 280.
Carpets, 150.
Catch-basins (sewer), 322.
Cereal foods, 234.
Cerebro-spinal meningitis, 429.
Champagne, 244, 276.
Charcoal stoves, 171.
Cheese, 233.
Chemical analysis of water, 289–295.
    disinfectants, 386, 439–446.
    composition of foods, 220.
    standard of diet, 217, 267, 268.

Chicken-pox, 420.
Child labor, 118.
Children, age for school, 108.
  care of eyes, 66.
  food for, 266.
Chimneys allowing back-currents, 209.
  for ventilation, 199–201.
Chinook wind, 8.
Chlorine in water, 295.
  testing for, 291.
Chocolate, 244.
Cholera, 409.
  from unclean food, 236.
  infantum, 406.
  infection and flies, 402.
Cholerine, 392, 411.
Churches, ventilation of, 210.
Cider, 245.
Cisterns, 300, 303.
Cleaning the skin, 56.
Cleanliness of floors, 149, 150.
  taught to children, 89, 90, 121.
Climate (general), 1.
  choice of, 33.
Climatic factors, 8.
Clothing and warmth, 42, 43.
  disinfection of, 445.
  material, etc., 43–47.
Cloudiness, 24.
Coal, 163.
Coca wine, 248.
Cocci (round bacteria), 380, 387.
"Cocktails," 262.
Cocoa, 244.
Cod-liver oil, 273.
Coffee, 218, 242, 244, 259.
Cold and bacteria, 384.
  bathing, 281.
  feet, 48.
  food, 259.
  waves, 31.
"Colds," 46, 403.
Colony (of bacteria), 382.
Color-blindness, 67, 116, 117.
Color of clothing, 43.
Combustion, 161, 164.
"Comma bacilli," 380, 411.
Communicable diseases, 401.
  in schools, 88, 90.

Complexion, 61.
Complexity of plumbing, 345.
Compressed air for ventilating mines, 210.
Concrete floors, 150.
Condensed foods, 261.
  milk, 265.
Conservancy systems (excreta), 363–366.
Constipation, diet for, 274.
Consumption [see *Tuberculosis*].
"Consumption," climate for, 35–38.
Contagious diseases, 401.
Cooking, 217, 250, 257.
  required for cereals, 235.
  required for meat, 221, 223.
  required for milk, 227.
Cook-stove, 251.
Coöperative loan associations, 123.
Copper, action of fats on, 252.
  in preserved vegetables, 239.
  sulphate (disinfectant), 413.
  testing water for, 290.
Corned meat, 221.
Corns, 50, 449.
Corpses, after burial, 373.
Corpulency, diet for, 279.
Corrosive sublimate, 388, 426, 439, 440.
Corsets, 51.
Cosmetics, 61.
Cotton, holding back bacteria, 381, 388.
Cotton-seed oil, 233, 241.
Cotton underclothing, 46.
Country homes most healthful, 141.
Country life for workman, 122.
Court-rooms, fresh air needed, 196.
Cowls and caps for flues, 202.
Cow-pox, 394.
Cows and tuberculosis, 228.
  care of, 231.
  require fresh air, 212.
Creamometer, 229.
Cremation of corpses, 377.
Crematories, for garbage, 369.
Creosote (disinfectant), 387.
Cresol (disinfectant), 440.
Croup, 419.
Croupous pneumonia, 424.

474   INDEX

Culture medium (for bacteria), 381, 382.
Culture of bacteria. 381, 382.
"Cures" for reducing fat, 280.
Cyanide of mercury, 388, 419.
Cyclone, 31.
Cysticercus, 224.

D

Dampers, 165, 169, 170.
Dandruff, 62.
Darkness and bacteria, 124, 154, 383, 432.
Daylight and bacteria, 4, 142, 154, 384, 426, 432.
    and health, 4, 24, 125, 142, 154, 384, 426.
Death-rate, 467.
Decomposition due to bacteria, 3, 227, 315, 389.
    in corpses, 373.
Density of the atmosphere, 29.
Deodorization, 431.
Desert (American), 21, 35.
Desk, position of, 126.
Dew-point, 17.
Dextrine, 265.
Diabetes, diet, 278.
Diet, 267.
    for increasing fat, 281.
    in disease, 270.
Digestibility of food, 217, 255.
Digestive potency of bacteria, 390.
Diluting cow's milk, 264.
Diphtheria, 90, 417.
Diplococci, 380.
Direct-indirect steam-heating, 182.
Direct steam-heating, 182.
Discharges, disinfection of, 447.
Disease caused by tight clothing, 51.
Disease, diet in, 270.
Disease germs in clothing, 45, 52.
    in water, 296.
Diseased meat, 225.
Diseases of schools, 88, 90, 99, 101, 106, 109.
Disinfectants, 431-444.
Disinfection, 430-456.
    of beds, 54, 445.

Disinfection of pails, etc., 363.
Dismal Swamp water, 301.
Distilled water, 306.
Diversions necessary, 71.
Double windows, 93.
Drainage of house, 318.
Drain-pipes, 333.
Draperies, 154.
Draughts of air, 198.
Drinking water, 260, 282.
    with meals, 260.
"Dry-closets," 99, 180, 201, 359.
Dust and bacteria, 5.
    examination of, 6.
    of streets, 159.
    its dangers, 77.
    poisonous, 112, 113.
Dysentery, 406.
Dyspepsia, diet, 273.

E

Ears, care of, 64, 65.
Earth-closets, 364-366.
Eating, general considerations, 260.
Education, 107.
Effect of alcohol, 246, 262.
Eggs, 227, 256, 272.
Electric light, 136-139.
Electrolytic destruction of pipes, 313.
Embalming corpses, 374.
Endospores, 381.
Erysipelas, 62, 416, 449.
Exanthematous diseases, 420.
Exercise, effects of, 71-74.
    for invalids, 38.
Exhaust ventilation, 199-202.
Explosions, flour dust and coal dust, 113.
    inflammable liquids, 115.
    boilers, 115.
    gas, 134.
Eye-glasses, 68, 69.
Eyes, care of, 65.
Eyesight and occupation, 66.

F

Factory women and children, 118, 122.

INDEX

Fans for ventilating, 203.
Farcy, 225, 416.
Far-sightedness, glasses for, 69.
Fat, diet for reducing, 279.
Fats, 216.
    acting on copper, 252.
    in chronic disease, 273.
    in summer diet, 270.
    not for fever diet, 271.
Fencing, 85.
Fever diet, 270.
Filling teeth, 63, 64.
Filtering air, 205.
Filters, for water, 283, 287, 308–311.
Filtration of sewage, 328.
Fire-damp, 210.
Fire-escapes, 151, 152.
Fire-pot, 170, 175.
Fireproof cloth, 52.
Fireworks, protecting from, 69.
Fish, 219.
    and leprosy, 429.
Flatulency, 274, 389.
Flesh, to reduce, 279.
Flies, etc., carrying infection, 402, 405.
Floors, 95, 147–151.
Flour, 234.
Flues of chimneys, 165.
    ventilating, 199–204, 212.
Fluid food, 260.
Fogs, 23.
Foliage (warding off heat), 193.
Food, amount needed, 213, 214.
    dangerous, 222.
    fluid or solid ? 260.
    for babes, 260, 263.
    in disease, 270–281.
    preparation, 250.
    temperature of, 259.
Foot, shape of, 49.
Football, 75, 85.
Forests and climate, 7.
    and malaria, 405.
Forms of bacteria, 380.
Formalin, Formaldehyde, 444.
Free ammonia in water, 294.
Fresh-air inflow, velocity of, 204.
    inlet (ventilation), 204.
    inlet (plumbing), 334, 336.

Fresh air to furnace, 176–178.
Fruit, 270.
Fruits and berries, 240.
Frying, 254.
Fuel, 161–164.
Fumigation, 414, 442.
Funerals and infectious diseases, 372.
Fur garments, 45.
Furnace, 175, 176.
Furnace-heating, 174–180.
Furniture, disinfection of, 444.
Fusel oil, 246, 248.

G

Galvanized iron pipes (plumbing), 348.
    water-pipes, 313.
Gamy flavor of meat, 226.
Gang-wells, 304, 305.
Garbage, etc., 368–371.
    furnaces, 369, 370.
Gas, illuminating, 131–136.
    dangers of, 131–134.
    leakage of, 132, 133.
    ventilation for, 136.
    sewer, 15, 132, 324.
Gas-burners, 134, 135.
Gaseous poisons, 16, 111.
Gas-pipes, 133, 313.
Gas-stoves, 172.
Gelatine, as food, 256.
    for bacteria, 381, 382.
Germs, 378.
Glanders, 225, 416.
Glare, to shield eyes from, 125.
Glasses for defects of vision, 68, 69.
Gluten, 234.
    in diabetic diet, 278.
Gonorrhea, 415.
Gout, diet for, 273, 276.
Granular eyelids, 89.
Grass, influencing climate, **7**.
Grate fires, 166–169, 202.
Graves, danger from, 375.
Gravies and sauces, 254.
Green vegetables, 239.
Ground for cemeteries, 374.

476 INDEX

Ground-moisture, 3.
Ground, temperature of, 6.
Ground-water, 3, 298, 301, 304.
Guinea-pig as test for tuberculosis, 228.
Gymnasiums, 78.
Gymnastics in "consumption," 429.
    in school, 100.

H

Hamburg and cholera, 410.
    and impure water, 310.
Hands, to cleanse, 432, 449.
"Hanging drop" (bacteria), 379.
Hanging rings for exercising, 79.
Hard water, 285.
    to improve, 286.
    test for, 292.
Harmlessness of most bacteria, 389, 390.
Hats, 43.
Heart disease, 38, 72-74.
Heat and bacteria, 4, 178, 384-386, 402, 412, 418, 433.
    as disinfectant, 433-439.
    regulator (thermostat), 192.
Heating, comparative merits and cost of different systems, 191.
Height and size of school-rooms, 94.
Hemorrhoids; diet to be simple, 275.
Heredity and physical endurance, 74.
    and infection, 428.
Hotels not best for invalids, 34.
    to use disinfectants, 446.
Hot food, 259.
Hot-water heating (merits of), 189.
Hot weather, protection against, 43, 192, 193.
House drainage, 318, 333-358.
Humidity, definitions, etc., 17.
Hydatids, 224.
Hydrants, 311, 312.
Hydrochloric acid (disinfectant), 386, 413, 441.
Hydrophobia, 395.

Hygiene, advantages of, 397, 399.
Hygrometer, 17.

I

Ice, artificial, 314.
    for irritable stomach, 272.
    to be pure, 313, 314.
    water, 259.
Illuminating gas, 131.
    requires fresh-air supply, 197.
Impurities in the air, 194-197.
Incubation, 90, 91, 402, 455.
Indian corn, 238.
Indirect steam-heating, 183-185.
Infant feeding, 263.
Infection from neighbors, 141.
Infectious diseases, 397-429.
    and schools, 88, 90.
    and corpses, 372, 373, 376.
Influenza, 423.
Immunity from infection, 393-396.
Inland climate, 9.
Insects carriers of infection, 402, 412.
Insanity, 461.
Inspection of meat, 222-226.
Insurance for workmen, 122.
Instruments, cleanliness of, 448.
Intermittent fever, 404.
Invasion diseases, 400.
Iron in water, 291, 298.
Irrigation farms (sewage), 329.
Isolation of bacteria, 381, 382.

J

Jumping rope, 84.

K

Kerosene oil and lamps, 129.
Kidney disease, 38, 60, 277.
Kindergarten schools, 108, 109.
Kitchens, 153.
Koumiss, 232, 278.

L

Lactometer, 229.
Lake water, 289, 299.
Lavatories, 356.
Lead and color-blindness, 67.
    in beer, 245.
    in canned food, 222, 240.
    in porcelain glaze, 252.
    in water, 285, 290, 300.
    poisoning, 113, 309, 312.
Leanness, diet for lessening, 281.
Leather for shoes, 47.
Legislation for workers, 119.
Lemonade and malaria, 406.
Leprosy, 429.
Lettuce requires cleansing, 239, 332.
Leucomaïnes, 390.
Light and health, 4, 24, 125, 142, 154, 384, 426.
    for eyes at work, 67.
    for school-rooms, 92, 94, 125.
    measurement, 125, 126.
Lime, as disinfectant, 431, 441.
    in water, 286, 291, 295.
Liquors (distilled), 245, 262.
"Lithia waters," 284.
Lithium for testing, 298, 363.
Liver disease produced by alcohol, 262.
Local ventilation (plumbing), 353.
Location of ventilating openings, 206–210.
Longevity, 461.
"Lymph" (of Koch), 428.
Lysol (disinfectant), 440.

M

Madness (hydrophobia), 395.
Maize, 238.
Malaria, 403.
Malignant carbuncle; disinfection, 448.
Malt liquors, 245, 247.
Manholes (sewers), 322.
Marsh fever, 404.
Massachusetts sewage filtration experiments, 328.
Meal-time, 261.
Measles, 90, 422.
    of pork, 224.
Measurement of bacteria, 379.
Measuring fresh-air supply, 207.
Meat, 219, 250, 253.
    canned, 221.
    cooking required, 221, 223, 254.
    extracts, 222.
    in fat-reducing diet, 279.
    inspection of, 223.
    parasites, 222, 254.
    preserving, 221.
Mechanical ventilation, 197, 203–207.
Meningitis, 425, 429.
Mercury salts (disinfectant), 387, 439.
    poisoning, 114.
Mexico, climate of, 8, 22, 24, 26, 36, 40.
Miasm, 400, 401.
Microbes, 378.
Micrococci, 380.
Microörganisms [see *Bacteria*].
Microscope, for examining food, 223, 244.
    for study of bacteria, 378.
Mikron (measurement), 379.
Milk, 227, 229.
    for babes, 263, 264.
    for fever diet, 271.
    for kidney disease, 277.
    in other disease diet, 272.
    temperature of, 260.
Minerals in water, test for, 290.
Mines, ventilation of, 210.
Mixed diet, 215, 261, 267, 284.
"Moderate drinking," 248.
Moist clothing, 46.
Moisture and bacteria, 10, 384, 388.
    in air, 16.
    in walls, 154, 155.
    needed with stoves, radiators, etc., 172, 173.
Morbilli, 422.
Morphine, 249.

Mosquitoes, etc., carrying infection, 402, 405, 414.
Mosquito-nets, 414.
Mountain climbing, 82.
    fever, 408.
Mountains and climate, 8, 22, 30, 37.
Mumps, 420.
Muscularity not health, 70.
Muscular stiffness, 72.
Mushrooms, 240.
Myopia, 101.

N

Naphtha as disinfectant, 433, 444.
Natural ventilation, 198.
    waters, few bacteria in, 289.
"Natural wool" underwear, 45.
Nearsightedness, 101.
    glasses for, 68.
Negroes, susceptibility to infection, 393.
Neurin, 395.
New England, summer climate, 41.
Nipples of nursing woman, 62.
    to cleanse, 265.
Nitrogen in air, 12.
Non-siphoning traps, 342.
Norwegian saucepan, 257.
Nose-bleed in school, 100.
Number of meals needed, 261.
Nursing-bottle, 264.
Nutrient gelatine, 381, 382.

O

Obesity, diet for, 279.
Ocean and climate, 8.
    climates, 34.
    for garbage disposal, 368.
Odors produced by bacteria, 389.
Offices ill-ventilated, 120.
Old age, diet, 269.
    glasses for, 69.
Oleomargarine, 233.
Olive oil, 241.
Omaha sewers (small), 320.
One-eyed, occupation for, 67.

Open grate fires, 166–169, 202.
Opium-eating, 249.
Optional parasites (bacteria), 390.
Ore roasters, 15.
Organic matter in water, 289, 290, 294.
Outer garments, 45, 52.
Overstrain, 72–75.
Oxidation by bacteria, 3, 389.
Oxygen and bacteria, 383.
    in air, 11.
Oysters, 219.
Ozone, 12.

P

Painted surface (disinfection), 443.
Parasites causing disease, 222–228, 400.
    of meat, 222.
    destroyed by cooking, 254.
Parasitic bacteria, 390, 400.
Paris green and vegetables, 332.
Pasteurization, 230, 385.
Pastry, 238.
Patent fuels, 171.
Pavement, 155–158.
Peas and beans, 239, 241, 268.
    to cook, 258.
People's baths, 58.
Peptones, 272.
Pertussis, 419.
Phagocyte theory, 393.
Photometer, 125.
Phthisis [see *Tuberculosis*].
Physical exercise, 70.
Pillows, 54.
Pipes for sewers, 320.
    for water, 312, 313.
Plasmodium of malaria, 403.
Platinum wire, 381.
Plague, 409.
Pleasure travel, 39, 40.
Plumbing, 333.
Pneumonia, 424.
Poisonous disinfectants, 388, 439.
    colors, 51.
Poisons produced by bacteria, 390, 391.
Pork, examination of, 223, 224.

INDEX

Port wine, 245.
Potato (for bacteria culture), 381.
Potatoes, 238.
Porcelain filters, 308.
Poultry, 222.
Powder for sweaty feet, 47, 50.
    on the face, 61.
Power for ventilating fans, 206.
Pregnancy, diet, 268.
"Prepared foods," 222, 261.
Privies, privy vaults, 360-364.
Privy contamination of water, 295, 298.
    vaults, disinfection of, 451.
Printed matter, type for, 102, 103.
Proteids, 214
Protozoa, 400.
Psychrometer, 18.
Ptomaïnes, 226, 390.
Puerperal fever, 225, 416, 417.
Pure air, amount required, 194-197.
Pure water necessary, 283, 285.
Pure waters, 289.
Purgatives, harmfulness of, 275.
Putrefaction due to bacteria, 389.

Q

Quarantine, 452.
Quicklime, 441.

R

Rabies, 395.
Rags and small-pox, 111, 423.
Rag-pickers, 111.
Rails for street-car tracks, 158.
Railway accidents, 116.
Rainfall, 20, 22, 23.
    and water supply, 300, 302.
Rain-water, 299.
Rapid eating, 262.
Recreation needed, 71, 120.
Recurrent fever, 404.
Registers, 179.
Regularity of meals, 261.
Relative humidity, 19, 23, 172.
Relief against summer heat, 192.

Reservoirs, 305, 312.
Rice, 238.
Riding, 85.
Rheumatism, diet for, 276.
River water, 289, 299.
Roofs, 146.
    and rain-water, 299, 300.
Rooms, disinfection of, 444-446.
    minimum size, 197.
Room space required, 197.
Rötheln, 420.
Rowing, 82.
Rubber boots, etc., 47.
    rings, 240.
Rubeola, 422.

S

Saccharin for sweetening, 279.
"Safety fuel," 172.
Safety traps, 341.
Salicylic acid (disinfectant), 387.
    in milk, 230.
    in beverages, 245.
    test for, 230.
Salt, 218, 241.
Salted meat, 221.
Salts supplied by mixed diet, 283.
Sampling water for tests, 293.
Sand filters for water, 309.
Sanitation, advantages of, 397-399.
Saprophytic bacteria, 390.
Saprol, 363.
Sausages, 222, 226.
Scarlatina, 90, 420.
Scarlet fever, 90, 420.
Schizomycetes, 378.
School-buildings, 91.
School desks, 103-106.
School-rooms, fresh air for, 196.
    space for each pupil, 197.
School-room ventilation, 210.
Scrofula, 425.
Sea climates, 34.
Seasons and infectious disease, 402.
Seats for scholars, 104-106.
Self-purification of water, 296.
Serum treatment of diseases, 395.
Sewage, 315, 325.

INDEX

Sewer-air, 323.
Sewer contamination of water, 295.
Sewer-gas, 323, 324.
Sewers, 315, 317.
    superiority of, 364, 367.
Shaving, 62.
Sherry, 245.
Shoes, 48–50.
Siemens' gas-burner, 135.
Sinks, 357.
Siphonage (plumbing), **336**.
Sites (selection of), 2.
    to be dry, 140.
Skating, 83.
Skim milk, 229.
Skin, to be kept clean, 56.
    giving off warmth, 42.
    treatment of wound of, 111.
Slaughtering, 226.
Sleeping-rooms, size of, 153.
Slivers, to remove from eye, 67.
Slope of sewers, 321.
Slop-sinks, 355.
Small-pox, 394, 422, 423.
    from rags, 111.
Smoke prevention, 162, 163.
    test for house drainage, 212.
Smooth wall surfaces cleanest, 154.
Snow, removal of, 159.
Soaps, their purity, etc., 57.
Soft water for cooking peas, 258.
Soil and climate, 1, 2.
    and malaria, 404, 405.
    dry, as deodorizer, etc., 365, 431.
    purification of sewage, 328.
Soil-pipes, 334, 346–348.
Sore throat, 89, 91, 109, 419.
Soups, 256.
Soya bread in diabetes, 279.
Specific gravity of urine, 282.
Spices, 218, 241.
Spirilla, spirillum, 380.
Spittoons, 426, 450.
Splenic fever, 225.
Spores, 380, 381.
Sports and games, 76, 77.
Spring water, 259, 298, 303, 304.
Sprinkling streets, 158.
S-traps, 333.
Staircases, 151.

Standard disinfectant solutions, 440.
Standard of good water, 288, **294**, 300.
Stand-pipes, 312.
Staphylococci, 380.
Starch unfit for babes, **265**.
Starvation, 214.
Starvation diet and "water-cures," 280.
Steam for disinfection, 386, 434–439.
    for drainage pipes, 358.
    jets (for ventilating), 202.
Steam-heating, 180–183.
Steaming vegetables, 258.
Steamships, ventilation of, 211.
Steps, 151.
Sterilization of milk, 230, **231**.
    of water, 306–308.
Sterilized milk, 231.
Stills for water, 306.
Stoking, 115.
Stone pavement, 155.
Storms (in U. S.), 30, **31**.
Stoves, 162, 169–173, 251.
Strawberries, 240.
Streams and sewage, 296, **316**.
Street cleaning, 159.
Streptococci, 380.
Strife among bacteria, 316, **361**, 376, 383.
Sub-soil irrigation (sewage), 329.
Subways, 133, 158.
Suction, in waste-pipes, 337.
Sunlight and bacteria, 4, 159, 316, 384, 426, 432.
    and health, 124, 384, 426, 432.
Sugar, added to milk, 265.
    in diabetic diet, 278.
Sulphur (disinfection), 441.
Sulphuric acid (disinfectant), 386, 413, 441.
Summer, choice of location, 40, 41.
    diet, 215, 269.
    diseases (infectious), 402.
    heat, relief against, **192**.
    ventilation, 209.
Sun destroys bacteria, 4.
Sunshine recorder, 23.

INDEX

Sunstroke (and humidity), 19.
Superfluous hairs, 61.
Superheated steam, 181, 434.
Surface irrigation (sewage), 329.
Susceptibility to disease, 392, 394.
Sweetness of saccharin, 279.
Swimming, 82.
Syphilis, 415.

T

Tapeworm, 224.
Tea, 218, 242, 243, 259.
Teeth and mouth, care of, 62–64.
    decay of, 62, 389.
Temperature, 25, 26, 27.
    at which bacteria perish, 384.
    of food and drink, 259, 264.
    of ground, 6.
    of living-rooms, 160.
Tennis, 84.
Test for lead, copper, tin, 252, 253.
Tests of impure air, 14, 15, 195.
Testing house-drainage, etc., 212, 345, 358.
    privies, etc., 363.
    water, 288–298.
Tetanus, 159, 417.
Thermometers, 25.
Thermostat, 192.
Tight clothes, 45, 51.
Tippling, 248.
Toasting bread, 258.
Tobacco, 67, 218, 242.
    dust, 113.
Tomatoes, 239.
Tongue, to cleanse in fever, 272.
Total solids in water, 292, 294.
Toughness of meat, 219.
Toxalbumin, 418.
Toxines, 390, 396.
Trachoma, 89, 417.
Traps, 318, 333–344.
Treatment of sewage, 326.
Trees and forests, 2, 7.
    and malaria, 141.
    in city streets, 143.
Trichinæ, 221–224, 254.
Tripe, 256.
Tropical climate, 10.

Tuberculin, 428.
Tuberculosis, 224, 228, 393, 425, 446.
    and room-dust, 110.
    bacillus of, 224, 228, 383, 393, 450.
    climate for, 35–38.
    testing milk for, 228.
    diet in, 273.
    of meat, 224.
    destroyed by cooking, 254.
Turbid water, 308.
Turkish baths, 60.
Type, illustrative sizes, etc., 103.
Typewriters, 66.
Typhoid fever, 406.
    milk for diet in, 272.
Typhus fever, 415, 455.
Tyrotoxicon, 259.

U

Udder of tuberculous cow, 228.
Urinals, 356.
Urine should not become concentrated, 282.

V

Vacations, 40.
Vaccination, 394, 422, 423.
Vital statistics, 457.
Varicella, 420.
Variola, 422.
Variolization, 394.
Varioloid, 422.
Veal, 221.
Vegetables, 238, 241, 258.
    in diabetic diet, 278.
    need to be cooked, 332.
Venereal diseases, 415.
Ventilating-pipe (plumbing), 334, 338–340, 344, 352.
Ventilation, 194–212.
    for artificial light, 136.
    for cow stables, 212.
    of privies, 360.
    of sewers, 318.
    of water-closet, 354.
Vents (plumbing), 337, 343, 353.

W

Walking, 80, 81, 87.
Wall-paper containing arsenic, 153.
    to disinfect, 442.
Walls, disinfection of, 442.
    double, 145.
    water-tight, 145, 146.
Warming, 160, 166.
    school-rooms, 95–97.
Warmth, clothing for, 43–45.
    and bacteria, 4, 10, 226, 384, 402.
Wash-bowls, 356.
Waste-pipes, 333.
Water and malaria, 405.
    and typhoid fever, 407.
    and water supplies, 285.
    in dyspepsia, 274.
    in fever, 271.
    means for improving, 305.
    of cemeteries, 376.
    pipes, 357.
    supply, selection of, 300.
    to be boiled, 283.
    with meals, 260.
Water-closets, 349–355.
    disinfection of, 450.
"Water cures," 277, 279.
Waterproof clothing, 47.
Water-seal, loss of, 336, 337.
    (plumbing), 333, 335–344.
Water-works, 303.
Weather probabilities, 30.
Wells, 297–299, 304.
    precautions with, 297, 299.
Welsbach burner, 135.
Western routes, 35, 39.

Wet-nurse, food for, 269.
Whooping-cough, 419.
Wind and wind gauge, 33.
Windows, 152.
    high ones best, 126.
    of school-rooms, 93.
Window-shades and curtains, 93, 126, 127.
Winds, 32, 33.
Wine, 244, 245, 248, 262.
    and bacteria, 287, 413.
Winter diseases (infectious), 403.
    ventilation, 208.
Wolpert's test for CO_2, 15.
Wood pavement, 156.
Woollen clothing, 44, 53.
Work, regulating hours of in summer, 193.
Workshops, 121.
Wound dressings, disinfection of, 447.
Writing, light for, 126.
    taught in school, 102.

Y

Y-joint (drain-pipe), 321.
Yellow fever, 414.

Z

Zinc, testing water for, 290.
Zinc chloride (disinfectant), 439.
Zinc-coated water-pipes, 313.
Zoöglea, 380.
Zymotic diseases, 400.

www.ingramcontent.com/pod-product-compliance
Lightning Source LLC
Chambersburg PA
CBHW051238300426
44114CB00011B/791